The Next Port

Cover Design by Heyward H. Coleman Jr.

Drawing of *Skimmer* on Cover by Philippe Jacquemin

Photographs and Charts by Author

The Next Port

Heyward Coleman

Vermillion Press

2007

The Next Port

Contents

Acknowledgements

Special thanks to the loyal "Friends of *Skimmer*" who followed our voyage through the series of emails that I wrote during our travels. It was your enthusiastic interest and encouragement that propelled me into writing this book.

I am indebted to John Lang for his patience and hard work during the long editing process during which he provided invaluable assistance. Thanks to Nan Morrison for her meticulous third edit and her encouragement that led to the resurrection of portions of this work that would otherwise have remained as scrap paper on the editing room floor. And thanks to Emmanuel Guillot for his patient and expert help in the layout of the text and graphics of this book.

Without a supporting family *Skimmer* would never have left the dock and this story would never have unfolded. Thanks to all of you and especially to my mother, whose enthusiasm for our travels was our greatest inspiration, and to our children: Margot for letting us go during her final year of college, Alex for being a part of our crew for the first year, and Heyward Jr. for the design of the cover of this book.

For Charlotte—my first mate, my wife, my love.

A Dream of Skimmer

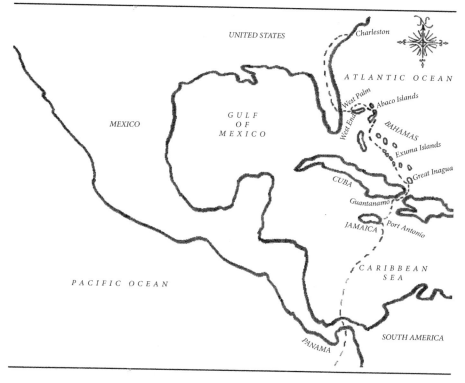

The subject was one of my favorites. The logic was impeccable and I thrilled to my theme. But it wasn't going to happen. It would only take a world map and an interested audience to get me going—"And after the Panama Canal we would head for the French Marquesas. Indonesia and then through the Straits of Malacca, the Indian Ocean and then the Red Sea." But they were names on a map and not really places we would visit.

Charlotte would listen with interest and often add specific comments on our wish list of destinations. "Once we get to France, we will go up the French Canals." But for her also, it was a dream. Wonderful in the telling, but vague in the future.

Was it my obses33333sion with my business and the happiness in the normality of our life in Charleston, South Carolina, that propelled me on? The security in knowing that the magnets of life would continue to draw and the dream would continue over the horizons of our daily cares? I could continue— enthusiasm rising, route becoming clearer, and destinations almost visible— but with the almost certain knowledge that we would never really do it.

***

"What is that loud noise?"

I had heard it also. Half dressed, half awake, I climbed through the hatch and could feel the coldness on my bare chest. One glance at the anemometer confirmed my fears and I shouted over the wind back to Charlotte: "Gusts up to fifty knots!" *Skimmer's* tranquil night at Black Sound was over. My son Alex was a sound sleeper, but the noise of the howling wind and the jerking motion of his berth in *Skimmer's* bow drew him out of his stupor and he came quickly on deck to help.

All three of us were thankful for some friendly advice we'd been given that afternoon as we dinghied ashore to begin our exploration of Green Turtle Key. "Wouldn't depend on an anchor if I was you. Nope, pretty bad holding here in Black Sound. Ought to pick up one of them mooring buoys. Just tell Elaine so's you can pay her. She works up at the telephone company."

How lonely it felt as we stood on *Skimmer's* bow deciding what to do. Hurricane Irene was not supposed to affect the Abaco Islands. She had veered into the Gulf of Mexico and the last report we had received had her making landfall somewhere on the Western coast of Florida. Clearly the Bahamas were out of danger and we had gone to bed with no further concerns. But there we were with fifty-knot winds and a wildly pitching *Skimmer*. Thank God we had picked up Elaine's mooring buoy. But what was its condition? How strong was its line, how large its anchor? Secure in the knowledge that Irene was no longer a concern, we had not bothered to dive and check. Now the wind was intent on hurling *Skimmer* over the fifty feet that separated her stern from the coral-studded shore. Would our tether hold? Or were three years of hard work about to be dashed to pieces on the rocks?

While Alex helped me with our anchor, Charlotte started *Skimmer's* engine and sat at the wheel, hoping her reflexes would be quick enough to make a recovery before the crunch if the mooring line parted. Down went our huge Bruce anchor and forty feet of slack chain. Would the anchor withstand the momentum of *Skimmer's* 15 tons if our Mooring Buoy failed? Or would *Skimmer* just jerk around as the enormous force of the suddenly tightened chain uprooted the anchor and allowed it to skip along the bottom as *Skimmer* met her fate?

As the sleepless night wore on, I found myself wondering how this new life compared with the dream that had so subtly turned itself into reality. Would we have done it if the sudden sale of Environmental Physics not removed financial constraints? Or was it really financial constraints that had held us back? The company had been my creation, livelihood and soul. It had occupied nearly every thought during the day and invaded my dreams at night. It was unthinkable that I could ever leave it. But after the sale there had really been no excuse left.

Our two oldest children had finished college and our youngest was just about to graduate. The ties to family, friends, and community that had seemed such an obstacle to "taking off" had receded with the knowledge that it was really possible. The trap of old age overcoming youthful dreams had not yet snapped shut. We were in our mid fifties. Lots of energy left. If we were ever going to do it, it was time.

Happily we never had the opportunity to see if the Bruce anchor would hold. The night passed and we reentered the comfort zone. Our trip down the Intracoastal Waterway and across to the Bahamas from West Palm Beach had taught us that the highs could be very high. Our bout with Hurricane Irene was the beginning of our education into the potential for the lows.

Leaving Home

***

After our walk down the beautiful beach on Stocking Island with our new friends, the inevitable question arose. But Jack's reaction to my reply came as a surprise and left us wondering. "Panama and then the Pacific? Why would you want to do that? It's so beautiful here and ..."

The shocked expression on Jack's face had been more eloquent than his words. His world of adventure consisted of winters in Stuart, Florida, and summers in the Bahamas. The route from southern Florida to the Exuma Islands was all the excitement he cared to face and the beaches and water surrounding Georgetown and its islands were enough beauty for a lifetime. Why would anyone want to cross the Pacific?

Georgetown's reputation as "Chicken Harbor" is well founded. It's the end of a hard sail south with a string of obstacles separating it from Nassau that include avoiding uncharted reefs in the expanse of Yellow Sound and negotiating high winds and shifting banks in its entry channel, the poorly marked Conch Cut passage. With wonderfully protected anchorages and excellent restaurants and facilities ashore, Georgetown is a yachtsman's Mecca. For many, it's like coming to the edge of a square world.

Further progress involves heading east and beating into trade winds. Bruce Van Sant's *The Thornless Path to Windward* outlines strategies to ride fronts to get to the eastern Caribbean Islands and is required reading for Georgetown's would-be blue water cruisers. It's a fascinating account of what might be, but probably won't. And at the end of a vicarious voyage most put the book back on the shelf, dinghy ashore, and enjoy another cold Kalik Beer at the Chill and Chat Restaurant. The next chapter of *The Thornless Path to Windward* quietly waits as anchor chains encrust with barnacles.

But *Skimmer* was on the move and we had not yet settled into a community of like-minded wanderers. There had been the welcoming group at West End when *Skimmer* had finished beating into force six winds to cross the Straits of Florida after leaving West Palm Beach—Kim and Sandy of *Chieftain Seaquel*, Jim and Suzi of *Sea Fever*, and Marti of *The Other Woman*—but they had been heading in the opposite direction. There had been amazement in their eyes as they watched us come into harbor having beat against the same wind and seas they had decided were too rough to ride on their passage back to the States. And there had been Sylvie and Fabrice of *Soleil Noir* at Allen's Cay in the Exumas. Fabrice taught us how to stalk grouper and then hold them above water still on the spear while we quickly made our way back to the dinghy before sharks could be attracted by the kill. And Sylvie had imparted culinary secrets for deep-fried Snapper Fingers and garlic laden Aioli to Alex. But *Soleil Noir* had been on a tight budget and their travels were stop and go as both of them found work at ports to fund their travels onward.

In fact, the only other boat we had met that had even mentioned the Pacific was *Nighthawk*. And that had been early in our trip. At the Golden Isles Marina in St. Simons, Georgia. We had been about to leave when an attractive young lady and her two daughters greeted us. Janet, her husband Randy, and their two young daughters were still in the midst of frantic preparations. They still had lots of work to do, but hoped to be in Panama in time to start across the Pacific in early 2000. We hoped so also. After exchanging boat cards and life histories a smiling Janet and her two little children had helped us with our lines as we all shouted our farewells.

***

Alex's blooding came in Georgetown. Our middle son, Alex, was twenty-three years old and a recent college graduate. Like many of his generation, he hadn't decided what he wanted to do and was taking a year off for pleasure and contemplation. Not exactly how Charlotte and I had approached life at that age, but we were delighted to have the company and had reluctantly given our approval to his lark. Familiar with the inner workings of *Skimmer* (Alex had helped me with our overhaul), an excellent cook (he had catered dinners as a side interest in college), and an enthusiastic boater, Alex was a good shipmate.

By all rights hurricanes should have been over by mid November. But somehow Lenny hadn't gotten the word. The waters surrounding Georgetown were glassy and *Skimmer* was gently swinging on her anchor in the wonderful protection of Stocking Island as Alex had dinghied Charlotte and me over to the town quay. We had received the emergency call from Charlotte's sister that morning via VHF radio and were heading home for her father's funeral. Alex had been elected to stay behind and care for *Skimmer*. Glued to CNN at our hotel during our evening stopover in Nassau we watched with a mixture of fear and relief. Lenny was developing into a major hurricane, but it was forecast to expend much of its energy raking the southern coast of Cuba before heading into the Gulf of Mexico. Far away from Georgetown, but still a nagging concern. We were glad we had anchored with such care.

Four o'clock in the morning two days later, Alex had been jerked into consciousness by the noise of grinding chain, howling wind, and a steady beep, beep, beep. Even before he was fully awake he knew what had happened and he knew the urgency. The beep, beep, beep, coming from *Skimmer's* Global Positioning System (GPS) pounded into his brain shouting to him that the anchor had dragged and *Skimmer* was in mortal danger. Instead of three to face the crisis, there was only one.

Alex horsed our second anchor, a fifty pound CQR, from its housing on the stern platform up over the stern rail and along the length of *Skimmer* to the bow as the boat yawed and pitched below him. Quickly, but oh so carefully—there was no room for the screw up of fouled lines if *Skimmer's* slide backwards was to be halted—he attached chain and line. And then the hard part.

Back to the cockpit to channel *Skimmer's* eighty two horses in the right direction. Darkness, disorientation, and confusion from wind and seas made it hard to tell if he had succeeded in pushing *Skimmer* forward and to the left of her currently deployed anchor. Finally, judging the time right, he ran forward from the cockpit and lowered the CQR. Fifty feet of line out. Cleated. Tension. It held! *Skimmer's* backwards slide had been arrested. Bone tired and bruised, but immensely pleased with himself, Alex went back below to continue his sleep.

∗∗∗

It was a good indication of how hard the wind had been blowing and how worried we had been that the front would catch us. We had researched potential penalties. Up to $200,000 in fines and up to three years in jail for entering Cuba. We had wanted to go, but it just hadn't seemed worth the risk so we had put up our cruising guides to Cuba and buried the charts on the bottom of the stack.

But ever since leaving Georgetown's "Chicken Harbor," there had been no respite from the elements. The planned overnight at Landrail Point on Long Cay receded into our wake as wind and waves made anchoring impossible. Great Inagua had been another missed opportunity. One of the largest of the Bahama Islands and the furthest south, its deep harbor had beckoned. Against my better judgment we had dropped the anchor and I had dinghied ashore to check *Skimmer* out of the country while Alex and Charlotte fixed dinner.

Six foot waves in Great Inagua's Matthew Town harbor threatened to worsen. We ate and ran. Cold, wet, exhausted. We had not been accustomed to extended passages with the rigors of overnight watches and this had been our second bitter disappointment.

Haiti on the left and Cuba on the right. Our plan had been to hug the Cuba side of the passage and head southwest for the two-day trip to Port Antonio on the northeastern tip of Jamaica. But a guy named Herb had changed our plans. Comfortably ensconced in his shore side office in Toronto, Herb dispensed weather advice from his giant radio antenna and Single Sideband Radios all over the Caribbean tuned in at nine o'clock every morning to devour his sage advice.

On the morning of December 1, 1999 Herb warned that conditions would worsen as the strong Caribbean winter winds strengthened and a front moved in from the East. When we had received Herb's report it was already blowing thirty knots and the seas were over twelve feet high.

The whiteness of Charlotte's face wasn't seasickness. It was fear. I had told her to quit watching the giant mountains of water that were approaching from our stern and looked like they would engulf us in white foam. My advice had no effect. The fact that the waves would pass gently under *Skimmer*, lifting her stern and providing steep water slides for exhilarating downward rides was irrelevant. She was focused on waves to come.

"I don't care what the penalties are! I don't want to be out here in a big storm." She sobbed, and stared longingly at the shore. Out came the charts and pilots for Cuba. I reasoned that the theoretical potential of three years in jail was probably better than the near certainty of a divorce and altered course. Baitiquiri was only twenty miles away. Its wonderfully protected lagoon harbor greeted us and up went our Cuban courtesy flag. The die was cast.

Not for the first time, we learned how quickly our environment could change. One moment violent motion, deafening noise, fear of the strength of the seas, and fear of hidden obstacles in entering an unfamiliar port. And then, the next moment, silence, tranquility, and a warm sense of well being.

We stared at the crew aboard the weathered, gray gunboat anchored across the bay from us and they stared back. The minutes turned into hours and still nothing. There had been no replies to my broken Spanish calls on the VHF radio. We knew that Baitiquiri was not an official port of entry but had hoped that they would have pity on poor waifs from the sea. We couldn't find the term for "force majeure" in our skimpy Spanish dictionary and settled down for the wait. Besides, this was a term that would probably be more useful in extricating us from the jaws of the US Coast Guard if they were to greet us upon our exit.

Finally they came. Two of them. The one in uniform rowing, the one dressed in civilian clothes sitting in the bow. "Buenos Dias" from the one in the bow. He then spoke his Spanish slow enough to make us understand that he was the interpreter.

"Quantos personnes?" He inquired.

"Tres" I replied.

He then paused to "translate" our reply to El Capitano.

"Donde venidos?"

"Los Estados Unidos"

Again a "translation" for El Capitano

It went on this way for an hour. We managed to convey that we wanted to come ashore. Would they please try to get us permission? With big smiles on their faces and promises to return "mañana", they rowed off and left us to enjoy the tranquility of Baitiquiri Bay. Mañana turned out to be *Grandma* Landing Day, a Cuban national holiday celebrating the landing of Castro and eighty-two rebels at Cabo Cruz on December 2, 1956. No rowboat appeared to invite the gringos ashore. During the morning of our third day of solitude, our friends reappeared, but with the unhappy news that we would not be able to come ashore at Baitiquiri. Santiago was the nearest official entry port and if we wanted to visit Cuba, we would have to go there first.

We suspected that the favorable weather forecast they gave to us was more designed to get us out of their hair than to paint an accurate picture of what we would see outside. But we were pretty tired of sitting around, so on the morning of the fourth day of our quarantine, we departed Baitiquiri, en route to Jamaica.

The relatively calm water of Baitiquiri's entrance gave way to conditions worse than those we encountered as we came in, so we headed for Santiago instead. All day, the sea mountains got higher and the wind blew harder. Suddenly a loud noise, a veering to the left, and uncontrollable flapping all about us! Charlotte took the helm off of the autopilot as Alex and I cautiously crawled forward to deal with the mad flailing of the jib. Our huge genoa had come loose from the mast and was now half in the water and banging against *Skimmer*'s topsides.

It was an hour of hard work, made more difficult by our rules of survival. One hand for the boat and one for the work. And always attached by a life line on our safety harnesses. A little of the genoa out of the water and into the boat, a pause to untangle and reposition our safety lines, then a little more retrieval. Finally, with the genoa out of the water and lashed to the deck, we managed to raise our storm jib and *Skimmer* was back under control.

During the crisis, Charlotte had been calm and efficient. But as we had regained control over *Skimmer*, the white face returned and I knew she was going to be very unhappy if we did not make port that evening. I went below to check the charts. We had lost time retrieving the genoa, and the reduced sail area of the storm jib had slowed us considerably. A daylight arrival in Santiago was no longer a possibility. There was no way we were going to violate rule number one—no nighttime entries. But I emerged with potential good news. Guantanamo was near. Why not give it a try?

We knew the heavily protected US Naval base at Guantanamo was a closed port and visiting yachtsmen were not welcome. But what about force majeure?

"Guantanamo Naval Base, this is sailing vessel *Skimmer*. We have lost one of our sails and request permission to enter port for repairs." A pleasant but firm voice acknowledged our request over the VHF radio and then proceeded with an exhaustive list of questions. Nationalities, social security numbers, dates of birth of all on board—and the list went on.

"*Skimmer*, Guantanamo Naval Base, please stand by while I go to base operations to see if I can get you permission to enter."

"Guantanamo Naval Base, *Skimmer*, it's pretty rough out here and I am afraid we may sustain more damage. Can we enter the outer bay for protection while we wait for your reply."

A pause and then: "*Skimmer*, Guantanamo Naval Base, you may enter the outer bay. I am sending an escort, please stay close to the escort and do not anchor."

Sleek, gray, and bristling with guns, our escort was at the sea buoy as we entered and we turned lazy circles in her company as we waited. After what seemed an eternity, the radio crackled. "*Skimmer*, Guantanamo Naval Base, do you have any casualties on board?"

Before replying, I looked at Charlotte. Was this the penultimate question before rejection? I shrugged my shoulders and picked up the microphone.

Guantanamo Naval Base, *Skimmer*, no actual casualties, but strong potential for a marital casualty if we are turned back out to sea." Our escort then led us through the bay and into the harbor to an empty spot on a long pier where a large group was assembling. We couldn't believe our good fortune. The executive officer of the base was the head of our welcoming committee and he was graciousness itself.

"Stay as long as you need for repairs and feel free to use any of the base facilities. It's pretty nasty out there, but the weather is supposed to improve in several days." This was too good to be true. The Exec's next question brought me back to reality.

Pulling out pen and clipboard he asked, "What was your last port?"

Time stopped, thoughts of prison at worst and ejection from port at best flashed through my brain as I carefully formulated my reply. "Our last port of call was Matthew Town at Great Inagua in the Bahamas."

The base received us with open arms. "Plucked from the dangers of a storm ..." went the account in the base newspaper and everyone knew us before we had a chance to introduce ourselves. Four days later, sail repairs complete, greatly refreshed by the wonderful entertainment lavished upon us, and fully stocked with provisions from the Naval PX, *Skimmer* was ready to depart. The Executive Officer

Provisioning

was there to see us off. After thanking him profusely for all the hospitality, I cautiously asked what I should say our last port of call was when I arrived in Jamaica. He thought for a few minutes, smiled, and then said: "Tell them your last port of call was Matthew Town at Great Inagua in the Bahamas."

As we sailed out of Guantanamo Bay I thought to myself "What a great way to not visit Cuba—two times!"

***

Peter Dodds, a close friend and the broker who had arranged our purchase of *Skimmer*, had put it succinctly: "I have had clients who have looked at many boats before making their decisions. But Heyward Coleman is the first client I have ever had who has looked over the entire country for a boat in the worst possible condition he could find before making his final choice."

The night Peter had called to confirm that my offer had been accepted, Charlotte reaffirmed his opinion. By the time I had returned to the dinner table, she was crying. "Its so ugly. Why couldn't we have bought a pretty one?"

For the tenth time I tried to explain my purchase philosophy to Charlotte. "We both have agreed that the Whitby 42 is the ideal cruising boat for us. We have also agreed that I am going to completely rebuild whatever boat we purchase. They quit making Whitby 42's in the mid 80's so any boat we get is going to need a major overhaul and there is no point in paying extra for things I am going to have to change anyway. It's really only the hull and spars I am buying, so why not go for the lowest price boat and build up a war chest for the refit?"

Although the rigging was bad, the exterior teak weathered and warped, the topside and deck paint faded and chipped, the interior decor sadly neglected, and the sails completely worn out, the price had been right and we would have lots of money left for repairs.

"Sails worn out? You mean eaten by rats!" She quivered as she began to heat up. I silently cursed Peter for having told Charlotte the story. When the owner had taken Charlotte and me for a test sail, he had raised only jib and mizzen, claiming that she handled much better that way. But when Peter had gone back down to Marathon to put *Skimmer* through her pre-purchase sea trials, he had insisted on seeing the main sail in action. His description of the expression on the owner's face as the rat had fallen onto the deck from the furled sail was hilarious, but now I was paying the price.

I tried a different tact. "At least we are having her trucked up from Florida, so you won't have to ride on her until after she is all fixed up."

"Trucked up! Why don't you admit it? The only reason you won't sail her up is because the rigging and engine are in such bad shape that you can't get insurance. The rudder is leaking, the hull valves won't shut" she paused and her voice began to quiver again "and, and … she is just plain ugly!"

But the argument hadn't been that important. My business was going strong and the trip, if ever there would be one, had been somewhere way off in the future. Charlotte had been somewhat mollified by my promises of repairs to come and was even a cheerful participant at the celebration we held after the fifty ton crane had removed *Skimmer* from her truck and set her down into our back yard on Wadmalaw Island. The metamorphosis had taken three years. The proper nautical term is rebuild. Every piece of mechanical equipment, every electrical wire, every tube and hose, and every hull valve and thru hull fitting—all removed and replaced. New rigging, new sails, new cushions and upholstery, and the list went on. The only survivor was the engine. I had not been successful in finding a diesel school, so I had decided that the worn out hulk of steel in the bowels of *Skimmer* would be my classroom. Much to my surprise, underneath the corroded mass of what had been the marine cooling package, the Ford Lehman diesel had been in excellent shape.

Skimmer Arriving at Wadmalaw   *Heyward and Alex Removing Engine*

Each day an already ugly *Skimmer* became uglier. As layers came off, the job began to seem more and more hopeless. Friends would visit, take my tour, go away telling me what a great job I was doing—and thinking how happy they were it was me and not them who faced this task. By the end of the first year, I had reached bare hull and the un-build was finished. I was finally ready to take the "before" pictures and declare a beginning to the rebuild. The real milestone came at the end of the second year. Suddenly Environmental Physics was no longer mine and my part-time efforts in fixing up *Skimmer*, for a trip that might or might not happen, became a full-time job with a fixed objective. Little by little she took shape. Ugly duckling to just plain duckling and finally to almost pretty swan. And then fresh paint for the topsides and deck. Charlotte warmed to *Skimmer*'s new beauty, and enthusiasm began to build.

Launch, a big party on our dock on Adams Creek, champagne christening by Charlotte, a blessing and baptism with water from the Jordan River by the rector of our church—our excuses not to go had run out. September 26, 1999 was the big day. Hurricane Floyd had just reared its ugly head and we were in no mood to meet its successor on our maiden voyage. So it was down the intracoastal water way instead of out to sea as we began our voyage south.

***

Long white fingers of tropical paradise off the Caribbean coast of Panama, populated by small, handsome Indians with features more Asiatic than Latin. Here is a matriarchal society coexisting with male dominated Panama, home of the colorful mosaic cloth Molas. The San Blas Islands beckoned us to explore.

Our late afternoon entry into the isolated cove off the island of Banedup in the East Hollandes Cays had left us with just enough overhead sun to navigate through uncharted reefs. Excitement was in the air. We had picked up our daughter, Margot, in Panama and our oldest son, Heyward Junior, in the neighboring island of Porvenir. We were all excited about the prospect of having Christmas together in exotic surroundings.

It had taken us a long time to pick out just the right spot among the fifteen other sailboats that shared our anchorage and it was getting late. But that hadn't deterred Alex from his mission. Our new neighbors stared in puzzled curiosity. What kind of casualty had *Skimmer* sustained to merit climbing the mast in the dark? And why were so many tools being passed up and down?

Suddenly the riddle was solved and the whole community shouted their applause and approval. Charlotte had just turned the switch and *Skimmer's* mast, spreaders, and rigging had become a giant, sparkling Christmas tree. Our new home in Banedup was more than just another beautiful beach and anchorage. It was the beginning of friendships that were to last throughout our travels. An intrepid community was subtly beginning to take shape. The class of 2000. The day sailors had been left behind in Georgetown. Our new neighbors had all taken the giant leap from which there was no easy return. Most of us were biding our time in beautiful surroundings while we waited for the weather window west to open. Late February through early March was the ideal time33999 to begin the daunting voyage across the Pacific Ocean.

The slight chill of the evening air was cut by warmth from the large open fire. Steaks sizzled, beer cans cracked open, and we began to tell our stories. We had been delighted to find that *Nighthawk*, whose crew we'd met back on St. Simons, had arrived in Banedup several days ahead of us. We listened with great interest as Randy, the skipper, wove his tale.

"There were three of them. Dressed in fatigues, gun buts clearly silhouetted by the moonlit sky. The waves had been so large I didn't see how they could possibly board us without splintering *Nighthawk* or seriously damaging their cutter. But one by one they made the leap. The search had been thorough, but that hadn't been the worst of it. They then made us wait while they swiped surfaces and sent the swipes back to the mother ship for analysis."

I saw what it must have been like. The roughness of the Windward Passage, the fear of unwanted visitors from neighboring Haiti, the unwarranted violation of their space—and all during the unsettled and hostile night. I was outraged that it had happened and had to ask, "But by what right could they stop you. What had you done that made you suspicious? And once they saw that it was just a family with small children how could they believe it had been necessary to board and search?"

Randy gave a bitter laugh. "If you are the US Coast Guard and are driving a large warship, that's all the right you need." But then he softened a bit. "Actually the three young men were very polite and quite apologetic. They had explained that it was done randomly, and we had been unfortunate enough to be the unlucky number in their sequence of radar contacts that evening. The girls managed to get some sleep during the four hours it took them to shuttle the swipes back and analyze them. When the results finally came in, they declared us drug free and released us to go on our way. It was a terrible night!"

Even with our emergency "non stops" in Cuba, our passage seemed calm in comparison. Port Antonio had been lovely and we had thoroughly enjoyed our cab ride tour of Jamaica's Blue Mountains. Tour guide Elvis and driver Israel had not ripped us off too badly. The Jerk Pork at Boston's had been so good that we were almost willing to forgive them for not actually filling the propane bottle they had charged us so handsomely to handle.

Jamaica to Panama had been our first extended voyage and after five days at sea, watching the mountains rise out of the sea had been an awesome sight and our spirits had soared. But not as high as our adrenaline levels as we began to negotiate the chaotic activity of Colon Harbor. We couldn't decide which was more frightening—the giant ships jockeying for position for their transits through the Panama Canal or the mad dashes of tugs and pilot boats rushing to and from their charges.

The Panama Canal Yacht Club is a fancy name for dilapidated piers, a rustic restaurant, and crumbling support facilities, but it looked like paradise to us as we approached in heavy rain. Our repeated calls over the VHF had been returned with only static and silence. Darkness was setting in and we were bone tired. Refuge was so close, yet still so very far away! Shouting through the rain we finally got someone's attention. A figure in foul weather gear emerged from the strange looking craft tied along the outside of the second pier. He gestured towards a narrow opening between a sailboat and bare concrete pilings that had once supported a finger pier. I looked at the rusty rebar rods protruding from cracks in the concrete and wondered what they would do to the glossy white topsides we had worked so hard to achieve. But the decision had been easy to make. It took a lot of tugging from three helpers ashore and the entirety of *Skimmer*'s fender arsenal, but in the end I was satisfied that the network of lines and barriers would protect us from puncture and hold us safely at the dock. Firm ground never felt so good.

The next morning we began our trip south along the coast of Panama towards the San Blas Islands. An overnight stop in Portobelo to pick up Margot taught us how rain can actually fall in solid sheets, and another overnight in Porvenir to pick up Heyward Jr. taught us how buying one Mola can produce a fleet of canoes and Mola-laden women thicker than the sheets of rain in Portobelo.

Elvis's failure to fill the propane tank back in Jamaica did not surface until Christmas morning when Charlotte had started to preheat our oven for the leg of lamb. The in-service tank had just gone dry and I had replaced it with the fresh refill from Port Antonio. But no flame could be coaxed from our oven. Suddenly, fond memories of the wonderful Pork Jerk became less fond and we began to think of Elvis rather than the pork as being the chief jerk at Port Antonio. But running out of propane in the middle of nowhere on Christmas morning wasn't all bad. Alex's solution of dinghying ashore to roast the lamb over the previous night's coals had the happy effect of preventing the dispute that was brewing aboard *Skimmer* from blossoming into a full fledged family free for all. Margot's loud characterization of Heyward Jr. as an inconsiderate jerk had perhaps been a little severe, but the cacophonous sounds emerging from *Skimmer*'s bow as he diligently puffed along on his saxophone practice session were getting on all of our nerves. With Heyward Jr.'s agreement to accompany Alex ashore and the breadth of Banedup Cay separating Margot and the rest of us from lugubrious saxophone sounds, family harmony had been restored.

Good things often happen by accident. When it's a wonderful discovery in science, it's called serendipity. In the case of bringing the *Skimmers* into contact with the *Aragons* Charlotte and I thought of it as just plain good luck. Louis, *Aragon*'s Skipper, had been attracted to the smoldering pile of coconut husks by the ingenuity of Alex's adaptation of our spear gun into a rotisserie for our Christmas lamb. But why weren't we cooking on board like everyone else? Alex's explanation of the Elvis-induced propane fiasco earned Louis' sympathy and prompted his immediate action.

Back off to *Aragon* in his dinghy where he retrieved his wife Pat and his precious spare bottle of propane, and then over to *Skimmer* to wish us a Merry Christmas. It was the beginning of a friendship that was to grow strong and rich as we began to leap frog each other across oceans.

The Panama Canal

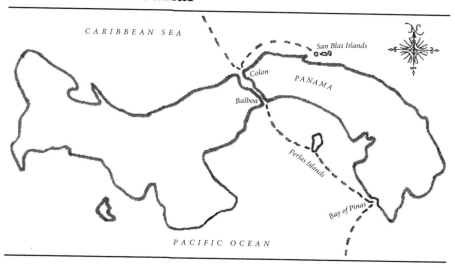

Tension grew. Four thousand miles of tension. That was the distance separating us from the Marquesas Islands—the closest point to Panama in French Polynesia. The tension would reach a peak and then suddenly recede, just like the giant waves we'd encountered off the coast of Cuba. But always it was there. I had begun to feel it as the day approached for our transit of the Panama Canal. Self-doubts, spouse doubts, children doubts, and even boat doubts. Were we really up to it? Although I knew we had already crossed both physical and emotional points of no return, somehow the Panama Canal began to take on a special significance. Was it to become my personal Rubicon?

Our reentry into Colon had been through driving rain that soaked us and robbed our vision. It was the first real test of *Skimmer's* radar and another challenge to our nerves. But the real test of our emotional stamina was to come after we had become securely moored at the Panama Canal Yacht Club.

Panama is famous for her jungles, lush, thick, and impenetrable. Colon is also famous for jungles. But there the jungles are of a different kind. Buildings as overcrowded as they are dilapidated. Abject poverty interlaced with abusive opulence. Filthy streets crowded with demented faces. Colon is a city out of control.

Despite its state of disrepair and the overcrowding of its docks, the Panama Canal Yacht Club was our salvation. A haven of normality. The staff were polite, honest, and friendly, but above all they were protective. Before we had even finished our check-in, the club manager had indelibly stamped

15

rule number one into our heads: "Do not, under any circumstances, even think about going out of the gate of the Yacht Club on foot. Always, always use a cab and make sure it stays with you wherever you go!"

Always using a cab was counter cultural for *Skimmer*, but it had taken only one look at the expression on the manager's face to convince us of the wisdom of rule number one. The sturdiest, best-maintained amenity of the Panama Canal Yacht Club is the twelve-foot high fence topped with razor-studded barbed wire separating its grounds from the madness on the other side. The most reliably staffed facility was the guardhouse at its gate.

But the most memorable feature of the Panama Canal Yacht Club had been the boisterous crowd of friendly faces at the club entrance. It was among this jovial crowd that the most important event of our stay in Panama occurred. The courtship had been brief but the results became binding. "Dracula" adopted us as his special charges and all our visits into Colon would be viewed through the windows of his beat-up cab. Dracula's nature was as gentle as his face was intimidating. It really was unnecessary for Charlotte to ask him how he had gotten his nickname—yet behind his protruding incisors there was warmth and caring. Dracula kept us away from the area of town known as the Vatican, where he explained the only question was whether you would be stabbed and beaten when you were robbed. I couldn't believe he was serious. But he was. The Vatican is separated from the main shopping district of downtown by only one street. On one side the one thing you had to guard was your wallet. On the other side, it was your life that was at stake.

Colon did have attractions. The world's largest and most comprehensive free trade zone is one of them. Once past the lines of armed guards and into the heavily barricaded area, we had the feeling of being in a giant shopping mall populated by Sam's Club clones. Not many people have a need for twenty identical Sony Walkmen, but our purchasing power was increased by the coordinating efforts of the substantial cruising community at the Yacht Club. Every few days a group would set out in an armada of cabs to scour the shelves and arrange their pooled purchases. Anchors to antifouling paint to anchovies—it was all there—and at prices we would never see again.

Back in Guantanamo we had met Maureen at the PX, and she had introduced us to the Panamanian community living there. When we arrived in Panama we had lists after lists of their friends and families. Our first contact was Dillon, Maureen's ex-husband. His entire career had been with the Panama Canal Commission and he was part of the transition team that was turning ownership over from the US to Panama.

At the end of the year, the rumor mill at the Panama Canal Yacht Club had gone into a frenzy and horror tales spread about how badly yachtsmen were going to be ripped off by the new regime. Dillon assured me that a thousand-dollar deposit fee that was going to go into effect on January 1, 2000 would definitely be returned after the transit. This helped allay some of the fears, but there were still undercurrents of mistrust. Why did they need the deposit? The basic transit fee was already much too high. Why did it have to be in hard greenbacks? When and how was the money going to be returned? Nothing any of us had seen in Panama inspired confidence that money once put in the hands of any Panamanian agency or bureaucrat had any possibility of being returned to its donor.

Those were the rules and unless we were willing to go twelve thousand miles out of our way through some of the most treacherous weather in the world, we would have to pay. I had ridden in Dracula's cab with both pockets crammed full of twenty dollar bills to cement our reservations.

Dracula's ancestors had come to Panama from Jamaica several generations earlier. They were part of a substantial immigration of Jamaicans bought in to help construct the canal. His insights into the current situation in Panama coincided with many of the opinions I was beginning to formulate for myself. He was very pessimistic about the forthcoming transfer of the canal. "Panama had it very good under the Americans. People get paid four dollars an hour. But now people who work for the canal will get only one dollar an hour. Where do you think the extra money goes? Into politicians' pockets. In Panama it's always the same. But now they are going to ruin the canal."

Dillon had explained that upon transfer of ownership of the canal he would have to move out of the house that had formerly been given to him at very low rent, unless he were willing to purchase it at an exorbitantly high price. "Who would purchase it if the price was so high?" I had asked, but he had only smiled at my question. As we drove through a particularly plush neighborhood he explained that these houses had not sold at the astronomically high asking prices and therefore had been turned over to high-placed government officials instead. For Dillon and thousands like him, the old way of life was coming to a screeching halt. Dillon's father and his grandfather had all devoted their careers to the canal. It was the same for Maureen's parents. The Panama Canal Commission had been a caring employer, and loyalty and hard work had been returned in kind. The result had been one of the smoothest and most efficiently run enterprises in the world.

What was going to happen next? Would the new ownership devote the enormous sums of money necessary to maintain this giant wonder of the world? Would they complete the ambitious construction projects that were being so proudly touted in all the canal literature? Dillon shook his head in pessimism as he pointed out the enormous level of construction activity in the neighborhood we were driving through. Already spacious homes were being transformed into palaces. Where was this money coming from?

Maureen, who had come back to Panama for Christmas and the gala millennium celebration, had given me her outraged description of the ceremony on new years day. "They puffed themselves up so big! It was like the Panamanians had built the canal all by themselves. And do they give any credit to the US? They say more about the French! And here Dillon and all the others working for the canal have been breaking their necks for the last two years—working long hours into the night—all to make sure that every thing is finished and running well for the new owners! It breaks my heart."

Transiting the Panama Canal

***

Going through the Panama Canal has to be one of life's great experiences. Concerns Charlotte had about our forthcoming Pacific crossing were forgotten in the excitement. All requirements were in place. Four heavy, 100-foot-long lines. Four people, each tending one of the four lines, and one person at the wheel. Margot, who was still on board, handled one of the lines, Alex another, Charlotte the third, and Dracula the forth. I took the wheel and with the required Panama Canal pilot sitting behind me and advising, we were off. It was January 8, 2000 and *Skimmer* was about to become one of the first sailboats to transit the canal under its new Panamanian ownership.

Each of the four line handlers would take up slack and keep their lines taut as *Skimmer* rose up between 80-foot-high steel walls. The trick was to keep in the middle and away from the sides. At the top, we were spit out of giant doors, and would then coast through mile after mile of tropical jungle—all the while being treated to close-up views of the monster tankers we so dreaded encountering at sea. Three locks up and we were in the enormous man-made Lake Gatun. How could the French have ever convinced themselves that a sea level canal would have been possible?

We made the long transit of Lake Gatun, then we began the three-lock descent back to the Ocean. Pedro Miguel was our first descending lock. Identical to each of the three ascending locks, Pedro Miguel took us down the first 80 feet to sea level. As the doors swung open and we disengaged ourselves from the ocean-going tug that had been our neighbor, we got our first glimpse at our home-to-be for the next several weeks.

Charming rustic or just plain ugly? It didn't really matter and besides all our effort was focused on following Commodore Clause's shouted instructions:

"Hard forward, hard forward! Give it full throttle!"

But I was giving it full throttle and still we weren't moving. When I was finally able to communicate this to Clause, he sent his assistant out in a rowboat with two heavy lines. They heaved from the shore and we winched from the boat, all the while with the motor racing and mud churning. After almost an hour of hard work it was finally accomplished. *Skimmer* had been dragged over the 50-foot long mud bank and was lying close enough to the rickety dock for a long gangplank to be rigged.

The whole process had been against my better judgment, but there had been little time to argue. The next lock opening with its massive out-rush of water and churning wake from the huge ship emerging would have put us hopelessly out of position. If we wanted to leave *Skimmer* at the Pedro Miguel Yacht Club while we took our planned plane trip to Peru, we had no choice but to follow the shouted demands of Clause and say goodbye to the fresh coat of bottom paint we had gone to such efforts to apply while we had been in Colon.

A relic of better days, the Pedro Miguel Yacht Club still maintained a certain charm. Showers, refrigerators, and electricity, and the huge second floor of the yacht club with its panoramic view of ship-laden locks was an ideal spot to grab a fifty-cent beer.

We had been ready to dust off our somewhat dormant French as we knocked on the pristine white hull of "*C'est Assez*" and were very surprised when an attractive red-headed lady popped out of the cockpit and addressed us in perfect English. It was the beginning of a lasting friendship. Glen and Julie gave us much good advice on the practicalities of the Pedro Miguel Yacht Club, how to get the bus into Panama City, what days the two-dollar lunch at the yacht club was almost palatable, and why the huge alligator that sunned itself in the grass between the docks never ate the flock of noisy geese that were always around.

French name, French boat, American owners? The explanation was actually rather simple. Glenn's fascination with the famous French shipbuilder, Amel, had led him to La Rochelle where he had been thoroughly indoctrinated as a Supermaramu owner and had purchased his beauty as she came off the ways.

Sighting the Pacific Ocean as we approached Miraflores, the sixth and final lock of the canal, was an emotional moment. How had Balboa felt so many years before when he had first sighted this endless body of water and given it such a beguiling name? And how long into our journey would it retain this sparkling and pacific appearance? As *Skimmer* headed under the giant Bridge of the Americas and approached the field of mooring buoys that has been given the elegant name of "Balboa Yacht Club," we knew we had entered another world.

* * *

With his right hand firmly grasping the bill, our guide Alexey used his left hand to stuff the guts back down the throat of the huge blue creature he was holding half in and half out of the water. He signaled me with a nod of his head and I eased *Skimmer* into forward. Alexey then lowered the beast and it began to move. Slowly at first. A gentle swishing of its tail from side to side. But as the boat picked up motion and more and more water was forced through its gills, the huge dorsal fin fanned out and the whole body began to move. Alexey then gently released his grip and *Skimmer's* first sailfish rolled away and began its slow descent.

There had been no way that we were going to take this outing. Our cruising guides were clear on the matter and those in the know at the Balboa Yacht Club had confirmed their admonitions. The Tropic Bay Resort in Pinas Bay was for high rollers only and sailing cruisers were definitely not welcome. But *Skimmer's* crew were fishermen. And one of Charleston's consummate anglers had just joined us. Just before we had left the Balboa Yacht Club, Andy Parker had flown in to join our crew. During *Skimmer's* refit period Andy had been my right hand man, and when he told me he was dying to cross the Pacific Ocean I had immediately issued an invitation.

Our initial plan had been to watch the fleet as they went out the following morning, hoping we could follow them into fertile fishing areas. We were all tired from our overnight sail from the Perlas Islands, but I could see through the binoculars that Happy Hour was still in progress and I managed to persuade everyone to put on spiffy clothes and come along with me for the invasion. I countered their initial pessimism by observing that I had seldom been turned away from a bar when I wanted to purchase a drink.

It was probably more Charlotte's graciousness than my insistence on the dress code that won the day. The puzzled looks of the staff of the Tropical Star Lodge as we had tied up our dinghy softened as we explained that we had just come for a beer and perhaps wanted to make dinner reservations for the next night. We were given a table on the veranda with a view of the manicured gardens and the fleet of Bertram Fishing Boats gently swinging at anchor in the glassy waters of Puerto Pinas.

The main attraction hadn't been the natural scenery. It was awards night at the lodge. At prices up to five thousand dollars a person per week, it wasn't surprising that the lodge would present exotic trophies over a champagne dinner. But the statistics the Lodge Manager was reeling off in his oration left us gasping. During the past week, nineteen guests had landed and released twenty-three marlin, and one hundred and eighteen sailfish.

Nathan, the club manager, had laughed and then sobered the group a little by telling them that for the week before, the count had been thirty-one marlin and two hundred and twenty six sailfish. After the speeches, Nathan came over to join us at our table. He and his wife were would-be cruisers and he couldn't hear enough about *Skimmer*'s adventures. At this point I dared to broach the subject.

Nathan did much more than just give us a little fishing advice. He arranged for one of his skippers in training, Alexey, to come out to our boat to act as our fishing guide for the day. Each morning he paddled his dugout canoe over to *Skimmer* and left it on our mooring buoy as we followed the fleet of Bertrams out to the rich fishing grounds of Pinas Bay. First we'd find a school of bonita and catch a dozen or so. Then, with needle and thread, Alexey taught us how to make trolling baits out of half-bodies of some, and how to pierce a line through head and eyes of others so that they could be used as live bait. After that it was strike after strike. Tuna and mahi mahi, and three long bouts with giant marlins that got away. The highlight had been the 70-pound sailfish that had made it to the boat and the ecstatic smile of a very tired Alex as he sat and admired Alexey's technique of resuscitating and releasing his quarry.

We put it off as long as we could but finally it was time to start. Although we had only been at Pinas for two days, both Nathan and his wife had become good friends and they agreed to sell us fuel and fresh vegetables so

Skimmer would be full for the long haul west. This was no small favor since Pinas was in the remote southern neck of Panama and all supplies had to be shipped in from Panama City, 115 miles away. The remoteness, however, made the emotional pangs of leaving easier. With jungles to the north and east and Columbia to the south, the guerillas here were not the kind that swung from trees. Other than the warm enclave of the Tropic Star Lodge, there was no place else to go.

Fishing off Bay of Pinas

The Long Crossing

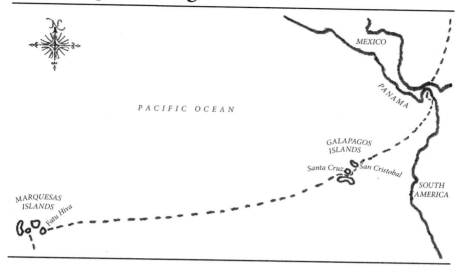

The Galapagos Islands. Almost a thousand miles off the coast of Ecuador. Their isolation in the middle of the Pacific Ocean had made them the ideal place for Darwin to develop his theories on evolution. That same isolation made them an ideal stop for *Skimmer* to cut a four thousand mile trip to the Marquesas Islands in French Polynesia into two legs.

There was a menacing aspect here that added tension to an already difficult passage. Ecuador has not always been happy to receive sailors into her tropical paradise islands. Rules varied from administration to administration. Sometimes entry was forbidden except in cases of emergency. Other times a three-day stay was allowed but only after paying a hefty entry fee. The only constant seemed to be that any visit there would be severely restricted and that moving among the islands would require the use of very expensive guides.

On February 27, 2000, we had left our mooring at Puerto Pinas and pointed *Skimmer's* bow to the southwest. Diverting to the south for a stop in the Galapagos added miles to the already long trip to the French Marquesas Islands. And sure, there was some chance we would not be able to stop once we arrived. But we agreed that a chance to anchor, no matter how slim, was worth it. Once in open waters the richness of the sea made itself felt. Giant sea turtles by the tens and twenties. Large patches of churning water where small fish tried desperately to escape the snapping bonita jaws. Even an occasional whale lazing to the surface for a gulp of air.

Still, there was the reality of nine hundred miles of separation between us and our destination. Once darkness had set in, we began three-hour watch rotations and I explained *Skimmer's* cardinal rule one more time: "Nobody falls overboard! On *Skimmer* it's absolutely forbidden. If you go over, you are dead ..." Alex groaned as I launched into the familiar speech. But he knew I was right. Falling over the side of *Skimmer* at sea could be as deadly as falling off the top of the Empire State Building. And he agreed with stringent precautions: safety harness and a tether attached to the boat during the night watches. Never leave the cockpit unless someone else was watching—and during the night the added requirement that I be awoken and consulted before anyone could go on deck. Man overboard pole, life buoy with its attached flashing light, man overboard button on the GPS—*Skimmer* had them all—but still the odds were against recovery, particularly at night or in high seas.

One sea story that had sobered us was the telling experience of one of our friends, who upon seeing his man overboard pole accidentally go over the side had taken immediate action to recover it. Despite daylight and good visibility, he was never able to find it again and after three hours of trying he had given up. A long pole with a weight at one end, a flag on the other end, and a float in the middle, its purpose is to greatly increase the visibility of the target. It is perhaps the most important aid to recovery in daylight hours, and getting it overboard and near to the victim immediately after his fall is of the utmost importance. But in this case even this essential aid itself had been impossible to retrieve.

✳✳✳

Willie of the "Panama Canal Breakfast Club Net" had said we would have winds of 20 to 25 knots from the northeast for the next few days and this would probably extend down as far as three degrees north. It hadn't taken long into our travels before I became convinced that the $3,000 I had lavished on a state of the art single side band radio (SSB) with its capabilities for very long-range communications was one of the best investments I ever made. At each critical gathering point, as if by magic, a net would form to give important reports to those participating.

The Panama Canal Breakfast Club Net was typical: at promptly eight o'clock each morning, first a call for emergency or priority traffic, then a role call with each respondent giving his position and weather conditions, then a weather forecast by a self-proclaimed meteorologist, and finally the opportunity for vessels to contact each other and switch to other frequencies for a chat.

Except after evenings of heavy drinking, which were not entirely unheard of aboard Willie's boat, *Malibou*, his weather forecasts were pretty accurate. Early each morning he would conduct his research on the internet and then, broadcasting from *Malibou*, moored at the Panama Canal Yacht Club, he would share his weather report with other Breakfast Club Net members as they began their treks across the Pacific. Charlotte was beginning to wonder if there had been a big party aboard *Malibou* the night before. Motoring all day through dead calm seas, *Skimmer* was beginning to eat into her precious reserves of diesel—and still no wind from the northeast. Charlotte had been on the point of going below to wake up her relief when suddenly it hit. Shrieking wind, flapping sails, and a loud alarm from our autopilot signaling that *Skimmer* was out of control.

Willie's wind had finally arrived. Alex, Andy, and I had been immediately aroused from our stupors, and after fifteen minutes of hard work *Skimmer* was riding comfortably on fully reefed sails. Thirty knots settled down to twenty and we kept fingers crossed it would last. We knew that as we neared the Galapagos, perched just south of the equator, we would begin to enter the doldrums and begin to lose our wind. During the previous two weeks we had monitored the progress of *Aragon* and several other boats on the Panama Canal Breakfast Club Net. They had left the Perlas Islands headed for the Galapagos a week before we had left for Pinas Bay and had been becalmed at about the half way point. Day after day their reports of no wind gave those of us behind a very sobering picture of what to expect. But Willie had promised wind as far south as three degrees north of the equator.

"Alone, alone, all all alone, alone on a wide wide sea" (Samuel Taylor Coleridge—*Rime of the Ancient Mariner*). But *Skimmer* wasn't completely alone. We had received the good news the evening of our first night out. Faint crackling from the SSB over the agreed-on frequency finally took on the sound of Julie's cheerful voice. *C'est Assez* and three other boats would leave the Perlas Islands for the Galapagos the following day. Although they were almost 200 miles away, it was nice to know that someone else would be out there.

And we had other company. Churning the water in our wake, darting from side to side, and transmitting streaks of sunlight from its mirror eyes, our teaser, the Big Kahouna, was doing its job. Two daisy chains of rubber squids snaked behind each side of *Skimmer's* stern and the giant teaser looked like it was chasing them. From a fish-eye perspective, it looked like a feeding frenzy was taking place just off *Skimmer's* stern and it was a clear invitation for others to come and participate in the fun.

Lurking just behind the Big Kahouna were *Skimmer's* powerful artillery. One to port, one to starboard. Carefully chosen, our lures with their freshly sharpened hooks were attached to stainless steel wires on the high-grade 50-pound-test nylon lines of our heavy-duty Penn Senator fishing rod and reels. If our skill could match our equipment, quarry of up to two hundred pounds was possible. Our preparations for fishing were beginning to pay off. Frank Middleton had won fame in an around-the-world rally for his success in trolling and had kindly shared his secrets with *Skimmer*. At sea, the fresh bait we had used in Pinas was out of the question. Lures alone would have to do and the techniques Frank had developed aboard the sailboat *Bon Ami* would be key to our success.

Alex with Tuna

Andy's efforts getting all our fishing gear deployed early in the morning of our second day at sea paid off around noon. A 30-pound yellowfin tuna. Just in time for a Sashimi lunch. There was so much meat left over there was hardly room for it in our freezer. The following day Andy and Alex each reeled in another yellowfin, so it was photos only and then release.

But catching tuna and other edibles wasn't our game. We were after billfish. Tension mounted and we wondered if we could do it on our own, or if it required special fishing grounds and professional help. Suddenly, less than two hours after the twin tuna toss, a loud whirring from the starboard side of the stern threw us into frantic activity. Andy grabbed the rod as Alex pointed and shouted. In a voice that was anything but calm, Andy admonished us to stay calm as he timed his final hard jerk. At this point we were all still pretty green, but after over an hour of hard work, the sailfish was finally up to *Skimmer's* stern. This was when things began to go wrong.

Back in Pinas, Alexey had made it look so easy. Was it that the fish wasn't completely worn out? Or was Alex's grip simply not firm enough? It was so fast we really couldn't see exactly what happened. We did hear Alex's loud scream and saw him leap over the rail from the stern platform holding his bleeding foot. The bill had gone in far enough to hit bone, and suddenly we were faced with a serious situation. Charlotte was *Skimmer's* chief medical officer and she had furnished the boat with supplies capable of meeting any emergency short of an appendectomy. Within moments, she had Alex's foot soaking in Betadine and his mouth crammed full of antibodies. We reread our medical books, searched our CD's, and picked each other's brains to make sure we were taking the appropriate measures. Infection was the enemy. We knew enough to be very concerned about a puncture wound from a bacteria-laden fish.

At this point the patient was looking stable and we didn't argue with his insistence that beer was helping more than the pills in easing his pain. We took the precaution of sending out an email to Andy's father Tee, the doctor and who had given Charlotte the antibiotics before we had left home, asking him if our treatment had been correct and if there was something else we should be doing. Although we knew that an answer would be at least 24 hours away, it was comforting to know that outside advice would be on the way. I was again grateful for our SSB radio and its ability to link our computer with a radio station in Florida.

An intermediate solution on which we had all been placing more and more reliance was an emergency call over the Panama Canal Breakfast Club Net. When 8:00 AM finally came I keyed the microphone: "This is *Skimmer* and we have a medical emergency aboard. My son received a deep puncture wound in the foot yesterday as we were releasing a sailfish. We are currently five days away from the Galapagos and are worried about infection. Are there any doctors or nurses listening to the net who can give us medical advice?" I then waited as the net coordinator relayed our message so that boats over a thousand-mile radius could hear our plea for help. After a long pause the net coordinator came back: "*Skimmer*, I have not been able to raise anyone with medical advice, but several boats have requested that you tell the net what lure you used to catch your sailfish."

By noon Alex was doing better and there were no signs of infection. Later that day we got an email from Tee confirming that our treatment had been correct and giving us signs to look for and treatment advice if infection set in.

✳✳✳

As we approached the equator we couldn't believe how our luck was holding. Way past the point where those before us lost wind, *Skimmer* kept skimming. Anything over 125 miles a day was good for this boat. Up to then we had logged two of our best days ever at 180 miles each.

A subtle change took place as we neared the imaginary line whose crossing separates the exalted Shellbacks from despicable Pollywogs. It was the sea life. As we neared the equator and the sacred zone of King Neptune's kingdom, the sea came alive. It was as if sea creatures were surrounding *Skimmer* and escorting her to the place of initiation.

Early afternoon, and I was in the cabin reading when I heard Charlotte's shouts. Andy and Alex were already up on deck pointing. A sheet of white foam was longer than *Skimmer* by half and only a few feet off her starboard side. Undulating up and down, veering slightly to the right and then slightly to the left, but always keeping exact pace with our progress, the huge creature had our undivided attention.

Sighting a whale up close is an experience many would envy, but in this case it was beginning to be too much of a good thing, and the initial air of excitement and enthusiasm was beginning to be cut by fear. Charlotte began to articulate what was foremost in our minds. "I hope he doesn't start to turn towards ..." and her words trailed off as suddenly the flash darted forward and to the left. I found myself wondering what it would feel like to have thirty tons of thrashing whale collide with fifteen tons of *Skimmer*. But the moment passed in silence as the last of the sheet of bubbles disappeared under our bow.

March 3rd was the big day and nature seemed to know it. Early that morning the sea began to boil with dolphins. Jumping five feet into the air, darting towards our boat, dancing in our wake. Alex, Andy, and Charlotte had spent the morning making a feast worthy of our crossing. They had been so busy that they hadn't noticed my preparations, and when a perfect replica of King Neptune donned in a bed sheet toga, crowned with a cardboard crown, and equipped with a boat hook trident appeared on *Skimmer's* bow they were truly surprised.

King Neptune

Fortunately for the Pollywog *Skimmers* it was a kind and tolerant Neptune who greeted us that day, and as *Skimmer's* latitude magically changed from zero degrees north to zero degrees south, the only task the ruler of the sea demanded was that they drink a few bottles of beer. Neptune had given his blessing. Sails down, swim ladder over, a long line with a float trailing behind—*Skimmer* sat motionless in the ghostly stillness of the sea. It was a strange feeling to be taking a celebratory swim in the middle of the ocean with the bottom over a mile below our feet.

Then, from nowhere, it appeared. Was it smiling its welcome to the Equator? Neptune's personal representative to verify our crossing? The face was friendly despite the barnacles above its eyes and around its mouth, but we became a little nervous when it tried to sidle up to us like a lonely dog. Charlotte made it back onto the boat hardly touching the ladder and Alex and I weren't far behind. But Andy had been cut off. The giant sea turtle had placed himself under the ladder and above his razor sharp teeth his large eyes seemed to be radiating a message of love as he riveted his attention on Andy.

Alex tried to push him away from the ladder with our extra long boat hook, but at the end of each shove, back he would come, eager to show his affection to *Skimmer* and continuing to shower his undivided attention on Andy. Despite the completeness of *Skimmer's* medical arsenal, we were not equipped for amputations and we all breathed a sigh of relief when our new pet finally swam off and let Andy mount the ladder.

Skimmer's Shellbacks settled down to an equator feast. Vodka and Caviar that a friend had bought in Moscow and ... well, we had debated long and hard about the appropriateness of dining on one of Neptune's loyal subjects on this special occasion ... but in the end the thought of fresh tuna steak with wasabi mustard was too hard to pass up.

***

Eight o'clock the next morning we sighted the island of San Cristobal. Our joy was tainted from a lingering sadness of news we had received over the Breakfast Club Net two days earlier. I asked myself for the twentieth time, "How could he have possibly fallen asleep? He must have known that land was close." But the sailor had, and his boat had been dashed on the same rocks I was looking at through binoculars. The man's father, who had come along for the crossing and was asleep below, had died. And one of the Ecuadorian pilots who came to their rescue was in critical condition. Both he and the pilot had been air evacuated to Quito and the story was still not in on whether they would survive.

As we rounded the northern tip of San Cristobal and entered the lee of the island, calm returned to the sea. What was so different about the creatures we'd been seeing since we had approached the equator? As a giant frigate bird gently spiraled down from the sky and began to flirt with the anemometer on the top of our mast, the answer suddenly occurred. These creatures were not afraid of us. The whale, the dolphins, the turtle, and now the frigate bird. They all seemed consumed with friendly curiosity. And suddenly from nowhere, as if to confirm the revelation, a giant welcoming party arrived.

At first we thought they were another huge school of dolphin. But as they got closer we began to wonder. Dolphin stay below the surface more than above, and dolphin don't have whiskers. An excited shout from Andy solved the riddle: "Sea Lions, thousands of them. It's unbelievable!" Alex was busy slamming the halyard against the mast to try to scare off the third frigate bird that had taken a fancy to our anemometer. There was no question in our minds about who would be the survivor if delicate anemometer met five-pound bird.

Excitement rose as the details of Wreck Bay began to take form. Was there another welcoming committee populating all the boats gently swinging at anchor? It looked like people standing and sitting on stern platforms while others were reclining in open boats and dinghies. Soaking up the sun? But there wasn't any sun and it was actually chilly. Why would so many people be out in the anchorage lounging around their boats?

As we drew nearer, the whiskers again gave them away. And it also answered the question of why the only empty boats we saw had barbed wire strewn around their gunnels. I looked at *Skimmer's* stern platform and wondered if it would be capable of supporting two three hundred pound sea lions. Maybe we should buy some barbed wire.

***

Shortly after our arrival, *C'est Assez* dropped anchor near us. We had been in touch with them every evening since they had gotten underway from the Perlas Islands and they were beginning to feel like family. Glenn and Julie dinghied over to *Skimmer* for beer and popcorn that evening and then we were all ready for the big crash.

It doesn't matter if it is one night, two nights, or seven nights at sea—when we finally get to port we are dead tired. We try to wait until dark if possible, but once it starts, it will last for at least twelve hours. Deep sleep. Our bodies craved it and minutes after Glenn and Julie left, the *Skimmers* were comatose.

What pulled me out of my deep slumber and up on deck still mystifies. What I saw electrified me into action and my shouts had *Skimmer's* crew on deck in moments. There, bobbing up and down on the gentle swells that continuously swept our anchorage, was *C'est Assez* with only three inches of thin air separating her massive stern from our starboard side. The Amel 53-foot-long Supermaramu is a beautiful boat, but *C'est Assez* would have been less beautiful with her stern smashed in—and *Skimmer* would not have come out of the encounter very well either. I held the two boats apart while Alex and Andy made a second anchor ready and Charlotte started the motor.

Once it was over, the reason was obvious. *Skimmer* had been using rope on her anchor because we had moved the heavy anchor chain aft to lighten the bow and improve performance for the long passage. But *C'est Assez* had still been using chain. When the wind that had been holding the two boats well apart had died late at night, *Skimmer* had drifted forward on her light rope while *C'est Assez's* heavy chain had held her in place.

***

We picked one of the only spots on the long beach unoccupied by lounging Sea Lions, timed the waves to avoid being caught in a breaker, then gunned the engine to beach the dinghy. Out, over the side, lifting and running, we made it to the high water mark before the next wave arrived. It doesn't always work this smoothly, however, and that's the reason cruisers are among the world's largest consumers of ziplock plastic bags.

Luck held as we began the long check-in procedure into the Galapagos Islands. We could stay as long as we liked and there were no restrictions on our movements from island to island. Isla Espanola, Isla Santa Maria, Isla Santa Cruz, and Isla Isabela—there was so much to see—and it looked like we could pick and choose as we wished.

Glenn and Julie finished with customs about the same time. Two scruffy cowboys in a beat up pick up truck approached us and before we knew it the six of us were in Fernando's truck listening to Henri's enthusiastic description of San Cristobal and its exotic wild life.

We descended to the rugged coast on the southern end of the island where waves broke onto large black volcanic rocks. There hundreds of families of seal lions were braving rocks and waves between long and luxurious naps on the beach. The rocks were crawling with seagoing Iguanas. While nature was treating us to this

Heyward with Sea Lions

show, Ecuadorian families were frolicking in calm waters of the adjacent quiet cove as if this were the most natural scene on earth.

Henri insisted we visit his farm, and after we had penetrated into the thick interior, we saw the reason why. A few hacks with his razor sharp machete and Henri presented us two large trees with enough green bananas to last both boats the whole way to the Marquesas. Fernando took us to his home where his wife and sister cooked us the best lobster any of us have ever tasted, the flat-head cigale variety deep fried with hot spices. It was the hilarious conversation on sea cucumbers—their harvest and their use—that stole the show. Fernando had explained to us the intrinsic value of the ugly, long round brown objects that littered the ocean floor. We had seen them before and couldn't imagine that they could have been of any conceivable use. We had not been thinking aphrodisiac. Japan was the biggest consumer, and the whole island had been getting very nervous about the true intentions of the large Japanese "research vessel" that had appeared three days ago and was slowly cruising around the island.

***

Technically we were not allowed to be there, but the immigration officer at Wreck Bay didn't say no when we radioed our destination. Forty miles south of San Cristobal and reputed to be one of the most beautiful places in the Galapagos, the uninhabited Isla Espanola had drawn us like a magnet.

We watched him flap his way up the beach like a frisky puppy. A tiny 20-pound baby sea lion. He stood out from the hundreds of other sea lions lounging along almost every square foot of beach because he seemed to have a mission. But why was he heading directly towards us? The look on his face as he inched up to Andy gave the answer. He was looking for mother. We moved our picnic further from the water and the colony of Sea Lions and watched the sad plight of our orphaned friend. His friendly approaches to might-be mothers were met with angry growls and flashing teeth. Shunned and lonely, the poor little creature made its way down the beach meeting rejection after rejection. We knew that there was only one way this story was going to end and were saddened by the harshness of nature's way.

From a distance it had looked like the large rocks studding the beach were in bloom. But up close we could see they were beautiful red crabs. Sally Lightfoots. Thousands of them slowly crawling their way along the rocks. We were fascinated with this display of the prolificacy of nature. Even the dry bushes at the edge of the beach were alive with small iguanas. And, unlike Charlotte who had run in the other direction when she stepped on a snake, these creatures were not afraid. Even pelicans and small birds would come within touching distance.

Early the next morning that perfect harmony was destroyed by the arrival of an angry face in a small speedboat. "Why do you do here? Es prohibito! No allow come without guide. I call autoridad and you in big trouble." We had noticed the large boat that had arrived late in the evening and watched them disgorge their boatload of tourist on the island. But when we saw their small speedboat heading towards us, we knew we were in trouble.

Miguel perceived that we were horning in on his legitimate tourist monopoly. The only legal way to visit Isla Espanola was with a licensed guide in a licensed vessel. *Skimmer* and *C'est Assez* had no right to be there and Miguel was going to have us arrested. He calmed down a little when we finally succeeded in explaining that we had received permission from the emigration officer at Wreck Bay. But he didn't really believe us and had sped back to his boat to make his report. We decided to pull up our anchors and leave while Miguel was sorting the details out with the authorities on Wreck Bay.

***

Abandoned or still inhabited? It was hard to tell. We pulled our dinghy on the beach and walked down a lonely road until we came to a house. No answer to our knocks, so we were about to walk away when Walter came up the drive and welcomed us to his home. He confirmed what Miguel had told us—that visiting Isla Floreana was legal—and then proudly explained that he was a qualified guide and would show us his island. Puerto Velasco Ibarra was the sole town on the island and home to most of the island's 80 inhabitants. Walter's family had lived there for generations and he was a walking encyclopedia of Isla Floreana's history, wildlife, and sights. On our dinghy Walter led the way through dozens of giant sea turtles and then to spectacular reefs where he showed us how to hunt grouper.

Back on *Skimmer* Alex was below preparing our catch—deep fried grouper fingers—when Walter called us all out on deck. We had read about their existence, but seeing was believing. So close to the equator, how could it be? But the cold Humbolt current does strange things when its path takes it through the Galapagos, and frolicking all about *Skimmer* were tiny heads bobbing up and down. The world's smallest penguins—and they were everywhere. Fresh bounty from the sea, nature entertaining us everywhere we looked, and cold Equatorian Beer—it was a perfect setting for our celebration and although he had never met her, Walter enthusiastically joined us in our in absentia toast to our daughter Margot on her 21st birthday.

That night we received an alarming email alerting us that my mother was seriously ill. What would have otherwise been impossible was made easy by the fact that *C'est Assez* had a satellite telephone. I accepted Glenn's generous offer and within less than an hour of receiving the email I was on the phone with my mother. I couldn't tell her exactly how I was going to do it, but promised that I would be on a plane home within the next two days. The following afternoon we arrived at Puerto Ayora on Isla Santa Cruz. Academy Bay was well protected and we moored *Skimmer* in the crowded anchorage with two large anchors. The immigration officer had been friendly and knew all about our incident at Isla Espanola. "Lucky you talked officer at Wreck Bay and tell him you go Isla Espanola. If no, you be in big trouble. Now officer at Wreck Bay, he in big trouble for tell you wrong."

Puerto Ayora is the largest city in the Galapagos and home of their international airport. After two hours of searching, arguing, and begging, I had a semi-confirmed seat on a Tame Air airplane that would get me to Quito, Ecuador the following afternoon. Charlotte, Alex, and Andy would care for *Skimmer* in my absence and get her ready for the big crossing to the Marquesas.

***

My trip to Charleston lasted a week. Happily my mother's situation turned out to be much less serious than I had feared and I had had a wonderful week showing her pictures and trying to satisfy her appetite for details on the adventures of *Skimmer*. She had been *Skimmer's* strongest advocate and the focal point for whom I had created a series of email newsletters. Both Charlotte and I agreed that her enthusiasm for our adventure was more important to us than to her. We weighed each new experience through her reflected interest and would not consider it complete until we had sent details to her and gotten her reaction.

Our final step in leaving Puerto Ayora was such a debacle that it had masked our nervousness at beginning our long voyage. In retrospect, I believe that the confusion surrounding the event was the only way the *C'est Assezs* and the other three *Skimmers* had been able to convince Charlotte that leaving on a Friday was okay.

Fueling with jerry jugs. It was a first for *Skimmer*, but we really had no choice. No marina, no fuel dock—transferring fuel in small containers was the only way we were going to get the hundred gallons of diesel fuel that *Skimmer* needed into her tanks. Among the clutter of jerry jugs piled high in the small boat that was approaching, we could make out three spray-soaked figures. Roberto shouted out his orders, his two companions passed us lines, and we tried to secure their wildly pitching boat to *Skimmer*. The wind picked up, which was good news for our imminent departure, but bad news for what was about to take place.

Four hands reaching from the boat to *Skimmer's* gunwales were unsuccessfully trying to arrest the motion while the last two held a Jerry Jug in approximately the correct position as diesel fuel sloshed everywhere. One after another, the empty jugs were tossed back into the boat and replaced with fresh ones. Less than an hour later *Skimmer* was following *C'est Assez* out of Admiralty Bay. The long voyage had begun.

Two things struck us during the early days. First was the slowness of our progress. Eighty, 100, or even 120 miles a day didn't seem to register against the 3,200 miles separating Puerto Ayora from Fatu Hiva, our tiny objective in the French Marquesas. The other was how utterly alone we were. Since sighting one small fishing trawler a few hours out of Academy Bay, there had been nothing. Only the wide ocean.

There are many strategies for crossing the Inter Tropical Convergence Zone. An area that varies with seasons, currents, and water temperatures, the ITCZ is an obstacle that sailors want behind them. Unsettled weather, sudden rain squalls with violent winds, but mostly the still nothingness of the doldrums. The strategy we had chosen was to head considerably south of our course to Fatu Hiva. Willie of the Panama Canal Breakfast Club Net predicted that after eight degrees south we should be in the trades, so that was our objective. The sea was a beautiful deep blue, the air warm and sweet. We were still in the process of taming *Skimmer* and learning more about her responses to the almost limitless number of sail configurations. Five to six knots of wind isn't much but we were amazed at the performance we could wring out of her. Alex and Andy loved trying out new combinations and a large part of our energies were expended in experimentation.

As always on passages, watch standing was a major activity, but with four on board we were able to divide the burden so that each of us had only two three-hour watches every 24-hour period. There was also repair activity and the only thing predictable about that was there would always be some. On boats things break continuously and there was no one to fix them but us. Time remaining was free time. Cooking, eating, reading—all were important—but the activity that dominated *Skimmer's* daylight hours was fishing. And we were now in the absolutely prime area.

Skimmer Underway

Our fishing mentor, Frank Middleton, had extolled the stretch of Pacific Ocean between the Galapagos and the French Marquesas as the finest he had encountered on his entire around-the-world trip. His claim that *Bon Ami* could almost set its clock by the regularity of marlin strikes at noon was indelibly stamped in the minds of our two young fishermen, and each morning at first light lines were deployed, not to be retrieved until dusk. The daily marlin strikes were right on schedule, but during those first few days out of the Galapagos, we somehow couldn't get one hooked. Mahi mahi and yellowfin tuna kept the adrenaline up and our freezer full, but marlin was our real objective. By this time in our travels *Skimmer* had become famous for its fishing prowess—there had even been a spot on the Panama Canal Breakfast Club Net devoted to *Skimmer's* fish count—so we had a reputation to uphold.

***

We had to take turns but it was a wonderful way to beat the heat and take a break from the reality of our situation. It had been Alex's brainstorm and I had felt foolish lugging it the whole way back from Charleston on the plane, but Alex's theory that it would be a wonderful way to replenish our water supply by catching rain had appealed. Actually there hadn't been enough steady rain to fill a tea kettle—only occasional squalls over before they began—but Alex discovered another use for the giant inflatable baby pool that more than made up for the original objective.

Alex at Skimmer Beach

We called it *Skimmer* Beach. There was just enough room on the flat part of the bow forward of the cabin to inflate the pool and fill it with the salt-water pump we used for showers and cleaning. What a wonderful sensation. Well oiled with sun block, head resting on the soft pool side, and a novel open as *Skimmer* glided over a waveless sea—it was a perfect diversion to make us forget where we were. When the cry of "look, a school of dolphin" or "flying fish off to starboard" arose the others to action, all the relaxed beach comber had to do was raise his head and give a brief glance in the direction of interest before going back to reading.

Our third day out, a loud whirring noise roused Andy from his pool lethargy. He hurried aft to reel in a beautiful 15-pound fish. This had led to a lengthy argument and with fish books out and filet knife in hand the debate began to get emotional. Charlotte's unyielding position was that it was more bonita than tuna and therefore should be pitched. Andy, Alex, and I, all starved for some good fresh Sashimi, had vehemently argued that it was tuna. I finally found a picture in one of our books that looked like our catch that was identified as a skipjack tuna. Thinking that the argument was about to be terminated I thrust my book under Charlotte's nose and began my announcement: "Look, Charlotte, it's a Skipjack ..."

"Yes," Charlotte interrupted, "It's a damn Skipjack and Skipjack is just like bonita! Don't you dare bring that smelly thing in *Skimmer*. Throw it away now. The argument was then cut short by an excited shout from Alex: "Marlin, it's a huge marlin!"

We all watched as the giant fish teased our teaser, approaching the Big Kahouna then dropping back. Then it was headed for one of the chains of squid and the lure just behind. The head with bill protruding would come up and pounce on the lure. And then there would be a momentary loud whirring as line paid out and then silence. Excitement was running high. Three strikes and then a long pause. A fourth and then as suddenly as he had appeared our marlin friend was gone from the scene. Skunked again. We didn't have long to mope about our fishing loss. Charlotte had spotted the large black splotches on the 24-mile range of our radar and had been very vocal about what she thought should be done. But it wasn't until vertical stacks of dark clouds appeared over the horizon that she really began to become upset. I vetoed Alex and Andy's skepticism and put into effect the rule I had learned from a very seasoned Dutch sailing couple: "If one of us wants to reef, we reef—immediately. If it turns out it wasn't necessary, we argue later."

The tangle of whisker pole and second headsail was hardly off the bow when Charlotte's squall finally materialized. From nowhere, thirty knots of howling wind accompanied by cold pelting rain. It was a harsh reminder of the unforgiving power of nature, but *Skimmer* rode it beautifully. And as suddenly as the squall had appeared, it was over and we returned to flat seas and sunny skies.

Well, almost flat seas. As darkness set in the wind died to nothing and the scene was set for a wretchedly uncomfortable night. Simultaneously with the appearance of squalls, the flatness of the sea had given way to slow, gentle swells. With five or six knots of wind, the swells were barely noticeable. But with no wind to steady us, they were a source of utter misery. Jerky exaggerated motion, flapping sails, and the unsettling feeling of getting nowhere when there was so very far to go. Motoring helped, but we had to be stingy with fuel. *Skimmer's* capacity of one hundred and thirty gallons was good for about four days and our trip could last up to thirty. Like it or not, sailing was the only way we could make it, and the discomfort of sails up in light wind was mandatory.

Frustration was interrupted by our radio contact with *C'est Assez* as we listened with envy to the excited description from *Augusta*. Several boats had set out after our departure and we had transformed our morning and evening radio calls into a net. *Augusta* was regaling us all with the story of how they had landed, fought to the death, and eaten a 6-foot sailfish. But our jealousy evaporated as their story unfolded into a graphic description of flailing fish, thrashing bill, and blood flying around everywhere as they had subdued the giant fish on *Augusta's* stern. With Alex's injury still fresh on our minds, we didn't want to touch a billfish again, much less bring one aboard.

As Day Five began, we became more and more convinced. The wind was holding. Ten to twelve knots from the southeast. It had begun the day before a little south of five degrees latitude. The doldrums were over; *Skimmer* was now in the trades. As if in celebration of our achievement, a herd of Pilot Wales began to churn around us. Fifteen of them—they were eyeing our squid teasers and coming so close to our fishing lures that we reeled them in. We watched with delight as one of them would come right up to our stern where we could clearly see him gliding along ten feet below the surface, recede back for his blow, and then return to continue following.

Sometimes bad has to come with the good and in this case the bad had the potential to become very bad. The sporadic overheating alarm we had experienced the day before became a steady overheat alarm and I had had to admit it to myself—we no longer had mechanical propulsion. In a power vessel this would have been a disaster, but *Skimmer* was now in the trades and our sails would get us there—eventually. But there were related problems that were quite serious. Electricity and refrigeration. We needed to run *Skimmer's* engine at least two hours a day to generate enough electricity to charge her giant batteries and to run the compressor that cooled her refrigerator and freezer. Without electricity we would lose our auto pilot and our lighting, and without refrigeration we would lose our food and our cold beer. The problem had my full attention.

I spent the rest of that day working on it and isolated the problem to the pump that forces seawater through the engine. The impeller was shot and needed to be replaced. Simple problem with a simple solution but to my horror the solution wasn't quite so simple. With all the hundreds of spare parts I had hoarded on board, how could I possibly have forgotten a spare impeller? But my third exhaustive search convinced me that that was the case. Tired, discouraged, and even a little frightened I slept on the problem.

The next morning, a solution was brewing in my mind that had been hatched during the long hours of my previous night watch. Why not use the salt water pump we used for cleaning and showers to force water through the engine and just let the engine's salt water pump remain out of service for the rest of the trip. But how could we rig it up?

The others watched with skepticism as I drilled a hole into one of the heavy rubber hoses on our engine and then forced in a brass nipple from our spare parts bin. A little epoxy, a little tape, and lots of hoping—it was ready for a try. We then rigged a garden hose from the shower outlet in the cockpit to the jury-rigged fitting and started the engine. It wasn't ideal, but it kept the refrigerator going and the batteries charged for over two thousand miles.

Life began to take on a very pleasant rhythm. Melville says in *Typee* when he was crossing the same stretch of water that a languor sets in that is like a narcotic—it was easy for us to see what he had meant. Clear blue skies, constant eighty degree temperature, and very small swells, while the trades firmly propelled us towards our destination—all was right with our world.

***

Andy to starboard, Alex to port. Two marlins in play. Hearts pounding, sweat flowing—they were in heaven. It had come to pass quietly. Andy had been reeling in our second mahi mahi of the day, but had decided to leave it in the water to attract a third. The third mahi mahi hit on the other line and while Alex was cranking him in the real excitement began.

Andy's eyes recorded it all while his excited shouts kept the rest of us informed. A huge head emerged from just behind Andy's mahi mahi and, with a rapid turn of head and bill, swatted the hapless creature into the air like a tennis ball. Magically the worn-out mahi mahi gained its second wind and began making evasive moves as the giant marlin pursued with his swatting tactics. Swat, bite, evasive jump. How could our brave little mahi mahi withstand such punishment? But our focus was not on sympathy for the mahi mahi. We were near the end of our first week out of the Galapagos and had not yet caught a billfish. In fact, our last billfish had been the sailfish that had skewered Alex's foot. This was serious business and we were out for blood.

The mahi mahi Alex had been playing got away, but he had continued to reel the line in so he could deploy our heaviest marlin artillery. Our first giant Islander lure had departed firmly fixed in the mouth of Alex's sailfish assailant, but I had purchased a replacement during my trip back to Charleston from the Galapagos.

It took almost fifteen minutes, but Andy's patience paid off. When he was relatively sure our sacrificial mahi mahi had finally made it to friend marlin's stomach, he gave a powerful tug on the line to set the hook. And then … the action was on. Rod bent double, Andy bent double. Sweating man against thrashing fish. Marlin near the boat signaling imminent success, then screaming of the reel signaling renewed energy from the deep as marlin erased all of Andy's previous progress.

Suddenly another loud whirring sound and an excited shout from Alex. The Islander lure had found its mark and we had our second marlin on the line. *Skimmer* was pandemonium. I was worn out from reducing sail to slow our speed and Charlotte was a bundle of nerves fearing a wrong move at the wheel would gain her the blame for losing the precious catch. But *Skimmer* had become a precision fishing machine and the day ended in success. The loss of Andy's marlin after about an hour of play was disappointing, but more than made up for by the success in the new catch and release technique we had developed and employed on Alex's fish.

After two hours of hard work, Alex's 100-pounder was lying still beside *Skimmer*. Holding the leader in his gloved left hand, Andy guided the long boat hook with his right hand. Down under the precious Islander lure, and then a very careful, very slow retrieval up the long leader. Finally, with the Islander lure safely in the left hand along with the leader, Andy put down the boat hook, took up wire clippers and then "snip, snip." The marlin, the hook with no lure, and a short section of leader were away.

Once released, the marlin regained life and we watched him slowly swim away. It would be only a matter of time before he would rid himself of the hook and life would return to normal. And, importantly for us, our precious Islander lure would live to fish another day.

Amazingly, there had been another party to the fishing frenzy of that day who had survived. Badly mauled but still alive, the sacrificial mahi mahi had still been on Andy's line when he had reeled it in after the loss of his marlin. Gently, while Alex had still been battling his quarry, Andy had lowered him over the side and watched him slowly limp away.

Our banquet after the fishing excitement was to celebrate the end of the first week of our voyage. It was then that Andy had made the statement that so befuddled Charlotte. "I can't believe we have been out here a whole week. Time has gone by so quickly." For Andy, reveling in the joy of fishing, basking in the warmth of the sun, absorbed by the intricate balances that make a sailing vessel perform, it was the adventure of a lifetime and days were fleeing by all too fast. For Charlotte, searching our radar for signs of squalls, measuring the height of waves as they swept under *Skimmer's* stern, and straining her eyes at night for the lurking tanker intent on running us down, time wasn't moving at all.

During that first week, *Skimmer* had carried us 850 miles toward our destination and we were beginning to log days of almost 150 miles. Things were going too smoothly.

***

A cramp in my back and my left hand going to sleep. I find myself staring at the faint red glow of a slowly rotating compass rose as *Skimmer* pitches, yaws, and rolls down eight-foot swells. Slapping myself and periodically flexing all my muscles to prevent the hypnotic motion of the gyrating compass from making me fall asleep, I push the indiglow button of my watch to determine how much more time I have left before I call Charlotte for her watch. How could our world have changed so suddenly and so completely?

At first I had not noticed them. Tiny red droplets on the engine room deck. But as they grew bigger I realized they were coming from the hydraulic pump that drives our autopilot. Mild anxiety turned to deep concern as daily I watched the drops grow in size. Finally I had forced myself to accept that failure may be imminent. My concerns turned to mild panic when I measured the leakage rate and found that it had risen to almost an ounce an hour. At that rate, even if the leak didn't continue to increase, we would run out of hydraulic fluid in a matter of days. If that should happen *Skimmer* would not only lose her autopilot, she would lose her steering as well.

I had had no choice. Out came the huge aluminum emergency steering tiller, and Alex and Andy took turns sitting on our stern, guiding us down following waves while I performed major surgery on *Skimmer's* hydraulic steering. Finally, with the offending autopilot pump removed from the system and tubes sealed with plugs I miraculously had on board, hydraulic steering was restored. We could go back to driving from the cockpit. But unless I could fix the autopilot pump, it would be manual steering for the next 2,000 miles!

It didn't take long to isolate the problem with the pump. Failed seals. A simple replacement job at the factory—it was an impossible repair job at sea. So, two-hour shifts with someone always at the helm, not a popular announcement. Andy was the least ruffled. He had spent a lot of time crewing on sailboat deliveries, and was enthusiastic about almost anything that had to do with boat handling. As far as he was concerned, this just gave us all an opportunity to develop our helmsmanship. Like Andy, Alex was optimistic. But he expressed it in a different manner, promptly vowing to build us an autopilot to replace our loss. Having seen many of Alex's previous ingenious contraptions, none of us were prepared to dismiss his promise out of hand—but none of us were ready to take his declaration as assurance that our problem was soon to go away.

The strongest reaction to our mishap came from Charlotte. "I told you there was something wrong with the steering," she said in a decidedly unhappy voice. This was the understatement of the trip. Charlotte's crusade against the steering capabilities of *Skimmer* had started slowly during sea trials and had steadily gained momentum as we had gained experience with our craft. I had replaced every single component of our hydraulic steering and had convinced myself that it worked fine. But I did have to agree with Charlotte: with its long keel and undersized rudder the Whitby 42 was a dog to steer!

But there had been a solution—a good autopilot. We had set out with one that had not performed well, so I had replaced it with a new and very much better unit. This had not only solved the steering problem but had also given us a back-up. But autopilots come in two components—the brain and the brawn—and I had only replaced the brain. The brain is highly sophisticated and uses various sensors to give signals telling the boat which direction should be steered. The brawn is a motor that takes the signals and transforms them into a mechanical force that actually turns the rudder. My reasoning in not going for more muscle had been that the motor was a pretty standard and reliable device and that there was no point in spending extra money to upgrade—a decision I came to regret.

Alex's intention was to get our autopilot working again by manufacturing new brawn that could take signals from our undamaged brain and turn them into rudder movements.

The numbers on the compass were blurring again! Hard flapping of the sails roused me and the figures focused in—210—not my outer limit of 240. Damn—hard turns to the right—overshoot—hard back to the left—some fine-tuning—and then relief. I was back on a relatively stable course. How were we going to do this for over two weeks? Thank God there were four of us!

Between momentary lapses in concentration and the associated wild changes in direction, I was able to use half my thoughts to process Alex's request for raw materials. The motor was key. There was no way I was going to jeopardize the future of an important piece of working equipment. But before the end of that watch, it came to me. The old bilge pump that had been in place when I had purchased and gutted *Skimmer*. Even if it weren't powerful enough, it would keep Alex off my back and give all of us a project to work on.

Daybreak bought renewed energy. I dug out the old bilge pump (we don't throw out anything on *Skimmer*), held my breath, and attached the wires to our battery. It worked, and, more importantly, it would reverse directions when the wires were reversed.

In a way, losing the autopilot had not been all bad—all the inventive genius aboard *Skimmer* was now focused on making a jury rig autopilot. With tools spread all over the cockpit Alex announced he was ready to give it a try. We felt like Alexander Graham Bell when he was testing his first phone.

The long PVC pipe we bought in the Galapagos to use for an awning pole was transformed into one-foot split segments that we lashed on spokes of the steering wheel to make a track for a drive belt. The old bilge pump mounted to a scrap piece of board and its new drive shaft, consisting of a scrap piece of aluminum tube that ran from the pump to a newly constructed plywood bearing, didn't inspire much confidence. The bungee cord drive belt certainly didn't look robust. Nonetheless the atmosphere was charged with excitement as we connected the contraption to the brain of our autopilot. A few tense moments, whir, whir, and ... it worked. We were actually on auto steering for about five minutes, and the new device was successfully giving correct nudges to the rudder. We were in the process of trying to think of something clever to say to commemorate this great event, such as "underway on nuclear power", or "damn the torpedoes," when the bungee cord started binding on the aluminum drive shaft and the rubber bands on the PVC spokes started breaking under pressure. Andy grabbed the wheel in time to avoid a jibe and we were back to the drawing boards.

During the next several days, we all became proficient at steering and whiled away hours helping Alex come up with solutions to seemingly impossible problems. Each morning the tools would come out and Alex would begin working while the rest of us hunted in the bowels of *Skimmer* for essential raw materials. Finally, exactly one week after the fiasco, we were ready to try the new and greatly improved model that now had a three stage reduction gear. We hooked it up, plugged it in and....

The English Major side of Alex's brain took over as he conjured up a scene from Shakespeare's *The Tempest*. To the wild applause from the rest of the crew he shouted: "'Freedom high day.' Caliban is in control!"

And indeed, Alex's new creation—the monster Caliban—worked. It was steering *Skimmer* across the Pacific. Handel's *Messiah* blared in the background and a strong wind off our stern pushed *Skimmer* through confused eight foot swells. Tiny spinning wheels and taut bungee cord turned the helm. Up, up, up, to the top of the swell, then down rapidly as Caliban slue *Skimmer* in the correct direction. Then violent rocking as the waves took over, a brief period of calm, and then back up on another wave. One, two, three waves—and Caliban prevailed. With about a thousand more miles to go, we were back on auto pilot steering. Alex was our hero.

Caliban was a miracle that somehow kept on working. Sometimes we would just sit and stare at the array of spinning wheels that magically transformed power from the small bilge pump to the long bungee cord driving the helm and marvel at how this strange contraption could keep *Skimmer* under control. We were about to have the third huge banquet of our crossing and this time in celebration of the birth of Caliban. The curry was ready and condiments were wedged in every cranny of the cockpit. I had just bought up the beer. Charlotte was serving and reminding us—"one hand for your curry and one hand for the beer—no messes please!"

Motor and Two Stage Reduction   *Third Stage Reduction with Bungy Drive Belt*

And then it hit!

Alex knocked over Andy's plate as he raced to the stern and grabbed the howling rod. We all looked at the huge object behind our boat—his giant head was out of the water with half his dorsal fin showing—sizing up his foe.

I took the rod from Alex. Charlotte disengaged the wire and bungee umbilical going to the wheel to take over steering. The boys rushed forward to reef down the sails. I couldn't believe how fast the line was going out. I saw bare spots appear on the spool and announced the game was almost over. Fifty-pound test was not going to come close to stopping this monster once all our line was out. But again he surprised us. Up, out of the water, corkscrewing himself to the sky—down again—mad splashing—then back up. Writhing, twisting, to shed himself of our hook. It was a magnificent display and it lost the fish his battle.

During these frantic maneuvers the drag held and no more line was lost. It gave Andy and Alex just enough time to get the genoa in and put the third reef in the main. Charlotte jibbed *Skimmer* around and started running down the fish as Alex raced back aft to reclaim his prize from me. And then new visitors. Hundreds of them. Vectoring straight for the boat.

Charlotte was mesmerized, enchanted. "Dolphin, look, aren't they pretty—oh, look, look—I can't believe how beautiful they are!" Alex's reaction was different: "Dam, they are going to cut my line! Get the hell away from our boat!" He shouted as the herd dove, jumped and swerved around, under, and over his taut line. They, jumped across our bow wake, flashed silver as they dove under our keel, and other herds approached.

It lasted an hour and a half and ended with an exhausted Alex pulling an exhausted black marlin up to our starboard quarter and Andy gleefully retrieving our lure and cutting our friend loose. One problem with our release method was that it didn't allow for an accurate measure of size. Will anyone ever believe he weighed over 300 pounds? But it was the thrill of the moment that counted.

***

I often called it one of our most important pieces of equipment—second only to the autopilot. I pampered it, admired it, and every day gave thanks it was so dependable. But with seven hundred miles to go, the unthinkable happened. The ice in our freezer was melting. *Skimmer's* refrigerator failed.

The bad news came in the morning just after the normal routine of running the engine for an hour to freeze the cold plates that were the heart of our refrigeration system. Again Murphy's Law ruled supreme. This was a system for which I had no spare parts nor repair knowledge. Fifty pounds of frozen food was about to rot. We were going to acquire a taste for warm beer.

There was a solution and we immediately put it into action. Eat and drink everything before it went bad. After steak and eggs for breakfast, Alex began working on an elaborate receipt that would use a large portion of the rack of lamb at the bottom of the freezer. He was trying to decide what should accompany this culinary delight when an event off our stern changed the whole menu.

This time we didn't bother to lower our sails. We were already three days behind *C'est Assez* and with the loss of refrigeration we were ready to make a beeline for Fatu Hiva. It was going deep and not pulling nearly as hard as the others. Experience told us tuna. Alex was ready with the gaff as Charlotte cut up the ginger.

A beautiful 25-pound Yellowfin—Sashimi and all the tuna steak we could even think about eating. Why did the freezer have to be broken at a time like this? The next day Alex finished preparing the rack of lamb and used warm beer cans to thaw the meat. *Skimmer's* first use of thermal recycling.

***

With only slightly over a hundred miles to go, landfall was sure to be the following day. We were ready to stop rocking and rolling, waking up for watches, and holding swaying plates of food on our laps. Cleaning dishes that morning, I had placed a small innocent cup of milk to the side while I finished rinsing a half dozen plates and glasses. But before I could finish, the cycle of small waves was capped off with the usual big two or three, and the milk went over and right into the bin with all our large pots and pans. My little rinsing task turned into a cleanup of the dish bin—all while the boat rocked from 25 degrees to port to 25 starboard.

That last full day at sea brought unexpected good news. The refrigeration gremlin decided to take a break and started cooling again. None of us could figure out what had happened, but we were delighted—*Skimmer* was back into cold beer and there was still some partially frozen food in the freezer that hadn't gone bad.

Arrival at Fatu Hiva

Finally the big day. On April 17, at 4:30 PM, *Skimmer* changed course 180 degrees to approach Baie des Vierges on the west coast of Fatu Hiva. Rugged high mountains, deep ravines, a halo of clouds, green coconut palms and rock formations that looked like sculptures. After 24 days of nothing but

46

ocean, it was the most beautiful sight we'd ever seen. Nearing our anchorage, we could see *C'est Assez* and two other boats. The wind was howling down off the mountains, churning up small white caps across almost flat seas. With sails down for the first time since leaving the Galapagos, we came in to wild applause. That evening we had a champagne dinner on *C'est Assez* then went back to *Skimmer* where we zonked for twelve hours as *Skimmer* gently swayed on her anchor. Our trip from the Galapagos had covered three thousand and seventy eight miles over twenty-four days. Our average speed had been 5.5 knots.

French Polynesia

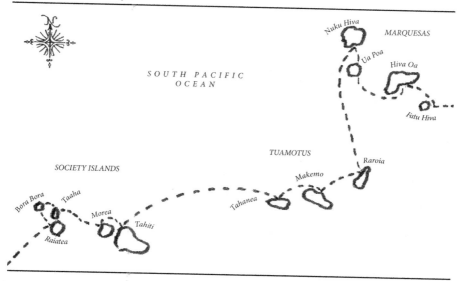

The tiny island of Fatu Hiva (population 200) is so pretty it is almost impossible to describe. Our first outing was a five-mile hike to waterfalls and a pool with torrents of warm water spilling down from cliffs above—like swimming in a huge warm tub with rainbows everywhere we looked.

Luc and Jeanne, owners of the sloop *Cigale* that was moored next to us, introduced us to their friends on the island and helped us make reservations for four loaves of bread to be baked and ready for us on our return. On our way up to the falls, we stopped to pick up a huge bag of limes (they grow wild everywhere), and on our way back we bartered for papaya and grapefruit (deferred payment plan—Charlotte promised to pick out old tee shirts or other small items from our boat to pay them back for the produce). The young girls loved Charlotte's hat and gave her flowers to wear in her hair.

The next day Luc arranged a truck and driver for a tour of the island. We bumped up steep roads I would have thought impassable to the town of Hanavave and from there hiked to a reservoir where Luc had helped construct a hydroelectric plant several years earlier. He had found the project especially rewarding and a challenge to finagle the necessary equipment that gave the island its sole source of electricity.

Luc was a fountain of information on the Marquesas and he led our armada of *Skimmer*, *C'est Assez*, and *Cigale* to the much larger island of Hiva Oa and then to the neighboring island of Tahuata where we spent Easter weekend. Festivities began with a picnic on shore featuring Poisson Tahitian

49

a la Luc—chunks of the groupers he and Alex speared that morning, marinated in lime juice and covered with coconut milk.

Alex's Improvised Grill

A crowd gathered around Alex's fire to admire his setup—a sheet of tin bent into a C shape and pierced with a fishing spear to serve as a heat reflector and rotisserie for a leg of lamb. A piece of wire mesh fencing supported his catch of the morning—a nice three-pound grouper that he stuffed with hot peppers Bahaman style. All of this on a beautiful white sandy beach surrounded by high lush green mountains.

Arriving in a port is a mixed blessing. Cruising is described by some as the privilege of repairing your boat in exotic parts of the world. To this I would add the corollary that these ports are almost always completely devoid of specialized assistance for yachtsmen and that any needed part is sure not to be available. But as we headed back to Atuona on Hiva Oa, one of the two largest ports in the Marquesas, I was hopeful. We had been extraordinarily lucky that *C'est Assez* had the same raw water pump as *Skimmer* and was able to lend us a spare impeller. I had sent an email weeks before to order a new hydraulic pump and had had it air freighted to Hiva Oa. I hoped *Skimmer* was about to be cured of all her problems.

The address we had given for receipt of our pump turned out to be the most beautiful hotel on the island, and the overnight stay I had promised Charlotte at the Hotel Hanakee Noa Noa as a birthday present was a great success. The bad news was not only the pump wasn't there, it had disappeared completely. In his infinite wisdom our shipper had chosen to use the US Post Office instead of Federal Express or DHL and our missing package was completely untraceable. The $400 pump and all hope of an immediate fix to our autopilot problems was lost in the mail.

Atuona surprised us with its combination of fine facilities and pristine beauty. The harbor was well protected by a jetty. There was an efficient fuel dock and showers and laundry. Everything was well laid out, clean, and well maintained. Construction was simple, serviceable, and in harmony with the panorama of colorful flowers, green hills, and rugged mountains jutting up to the sky. Most striking of all was the absence of poverty.

We had a hard time trying to understand the weird confusion that constituted the cost structure of French Polynesia. A can of beer costs over two dollars in the grocery stores—but the sight of Marquesans walking along with their cans of Hinano Beer was as common as the carpets of limes under trees alongside the roads. When we shopped for groceries we would ask the price of each items and would marvel at how they would fluctuate in such an arbitrary fashion. Beautiful New Zealand legs of lamb cost less than lamb in the US, but a medium sized watermelon could cost upwards of sixty dollars. Ask the price of grapefruit at a store and you could be told one or two dollars each—but mention that you like grapefruit after you have purchased your groceries and the owner would go outside and pick ten to fifteen of his huge ripe fruit and give them as a gift.

Luc had explained half the riddle—subsidies. Items in grocery stores with prices marked in red were subsidized and very low, while those with prices in black were free market and very high. Only a French bureaucrat could explain why pork and beans are subsidized and rice is not. Having children was still being encouraged, although the declining population problem had long since been solved. Luc referred to the payments as "zipper money". Agricultural use of land was encouraged by subsidies but, although much was paid, little was cultivated. Houses and automobiles were provided free of charge to "farmers" and to qualify as a farmer required as little as one acre and a naturally growing fruit tree. The busiest spots on the islands were the post offices where long lines queued up to receive monthly subsistence checks.

The other half of the riddle seemed to be related to the bounty of the islands. The Marquesans live in a land where enough food falls off trees to feed the entire population. With this supporting basic needs, they can pick and choose the luxury items they want and then do without the others. Tomatoes, lettuce, and cucumbers can thrive on the islands yet they are almost nonexistent. Why? The only answer that we could come up with was that picking a grapefruit or bread fruit off the ground was easier than cultivating a tomato. But wouldn't making money by growing tomatoes help put other luxury items on the table? Maybe, but they had enough money to get what they wanted so why bother?

***

We had heard stories about him even before we had arrived at Ua Pou, and his tour had cemented our feelings that this was the best of the Marquesas.

Tall, smiling, a boar's tooth in his necklace, a Hinano in his left hand while his right hand clung to the wheel of his shiny new four wheel drive—the description had been perfect—we had had no difficulty in identifying Claude as we tied our dinghy to the pier after mooring *Skimmer*. As agricultural inspector for the island, Claude knew everything about Ua Pou and our first priority had been to engage him for his famous tour of the island.

The following morning he was waiting in his truck and took us to the Agricultural nursery where he introduced us to his boss, Alf. The two spent the morning showing how they grafted grapefruit, lemon, and orange trees and then distributed them as part of an attempt to improve the island's agricultural production. Then they loaded our truck with fruit for us and drove to meet Alf's neighbor.

Rukka's Ukulele

Rukka makes ukuleles from big chunks of hardwood, using only hand tools. With a wide smile that revealed more open space than teeth, he played an island love song on one of his creations. We were so fascinated that we commissioned a uke as a gift for our oldest son, Heyward Jr. Rukka was an accomplished cook and after we feasted on fish, rice, and Poee-poee—a yellow concoction made from breadfruit that the Marquesans can somehow eat with their fingers without making a mess—Alf took us across the island to meet Rukka's wife, sons and granddaughter.

Piles of fresh fruit and a huge plate of french fried breadfruit awaited our arrival. What began as a brief tour of an island facility turned into an all day excursion. I've seldom seen Charlotte tire of speaking French—but between Claude, Alf, Rukka, and Rukka's family she had met her match.

The following day our plan was to go back to Rukka's house and pick up the ukulele. Marquesan hospitality jumped in to completely change our plans. A tall man had called out as we were walking by on the beach, so we went over to see what was going on. Tables of fish, fruit, wine, beer and juices. No, Ben would not accept our polite refusal, and we spent the entire afternoon sampling their dishes—white tuna cooked in banana leaves, raw fish with a ginger, soy and garlic sauce, fried fish, bread fruit prepared ten different ways, and many things we couldn't name. Charlotte impressed Ben by reciting all the details of the relationships of the Rukka family, and Ben reciprocated by giving us three generations of background information on his family. By the time we were ready to leave the island, we couldn't go down a street without meeting someone we knew.

**

While Ua Po was our favorite island in the Marquesas, Niku Hiva took a close second. This was the island that Melville had described so exquisitely in *Typee* and it wasn't difficult to see why he'd become so enchanted. Daniel's bay is a beautifully protected anchorage surrounded with lush green mountains. Alex and Andy had been primed by Luc's descriptions of the excitement so they had made their request at the outset. Our host Augustine's enthusiastic reply signaled that they had hit pay dirt. They had been reluctant to mention our shotgun because we had not declared it when we had entered the country. But that had only whetted Augustine's appetite. Their admission we had a dozen high-powered shells loaded with buckshot cemented the deal. Augustine would guide and Alex and Andy would provide the gun and shells.

The Marquesans are natural hunters and Augustine was among the best. Wild pigs were the quarry. Augustine's transformation began early the next morning as they started their hike up a rocky mountainside. His limp and his obvious difficulty in moving his giant frame melted away. Suddenly agile, he excitedly waved, pointed, and urged Alex and Andy to silence. There they were. Two perched on the rocks high above. But even Alex and Andy knew that pigs don't have horns, and they were disappointed to see that Augustine's objective had switched from pig to goat.

They had warned Augustine but apparently he had not believed them, and when his careful aim resulted in a direct hit, the hapless goat disintegrated as blood, bones, and fur flew over the side of the cliff. Augustine gained an immediate respect for the incredible force of our high-powered double-ought shotgun shells, and his next shot felled the second goat in a far less destructive manner.

Later that morning Alex and Andy returned with goat steaks instead of ham and bacon, but their excitement in describing Augustine's performance made up for their disappointment. The expedition was worth the cost of two shells and the goat meat went to the bottom of our freezer where it was to remain a long time.

The highlight of our visit to Daniel's Bay was a four-mile hike to Hakaui Waterfall. The ancient roadway was largely intact and made our sometimes near-vertical ascent considerably easier. Mares—huge stone platform foundations for their huts and pai pai—stone statues to their pagan gods—were in clusters where villages once had been along the four-mile road. Wild woods surrounded us and practically no one lived on this part of the island. It was hard to visualize how the road could have been built or maintained. We later learned that in Melville's time this part of the island had a population in the thousands and once a week one member of each family was obligated to devote a day of labor maintaining the common road. The top was magnificent. We swam in pools beneath the water cascading from a thousand feet higher. It didn't require much imagination to picture Melville bathing with his beautiful Fayaway in the stream that flowed from the falls.

***

I had felt like I was on fire. Every inch of my body screamed to be scratched but I knew better. During my watches it was more bearable because of distractions, but lying down and trying to sleep was misery. We had visited a pharmacy before leaving the Marquesas but they couldn't suggest anything better than the Calamine Lotion we already carried on board. With five hundred miles to go before we would arrive in the Tuamotus I had no choice but to bear it and wait.

It was a little late but I finally understood the wisdom of the burning coconut husks. Everywhere we went on Niku Hiva, the natives had clustered around their smoldering coconut husk fires to enjoy a No No free zone. I had made the mistake of removing my shirt during our climb up Hakaui Waterfall and the consequence had been hundreds of tiny red welts from the venomous No No's. "Don't scratch them! Rub lime juice over them! ALWAYS, always wear a shirt and long pants! Stay near coconut husk fires! ..." The advice had gone on and on, but now so did the itching and it went from annoying to bad to almost unbearable.

The Marquesas Islands were hauntingly beautiful, but after three weeks we were ready to continue our exploration. Sitting all by themselves in the far northeast corner, the Marquesas are one of the five groups of islands that make up French Polynesia. The Tuamotus were our next destination. Extending about a thousand miles from east to west, the Tuamotus consist of almost a hundred pancake-flat islands, in contrast to their mountainous neighbors to the north. Our destination, Makemo, was five hundred miles southwest.

I tried to downplay to Charlotte the fact our British Admiralty Pilot referred to the Tuamotus as "The Dangerous Archipelago" because I considered that information dated. GPS now made the low visibility of the islands much less of a problem and the traditional admonition against nighttime passages was probably overstated. But I was also aware of the importance of visual sightings before entering and based all our planning on a daytime approach. In fact it was a cardinal rule on *Skimmer* to never enter a port at night regardless of how visible or well marked. While GPS could give our position very accurately, and I carried two extras to make sure at least one was working, the charts were far less accurate. Running into an island that was supposed to be somewhere else posed a real threat. In the end there was simply no substitution for eyeballing position. I accepted the risk of navigating Tuamotu Islands at night but only after choosing a route to keep us many miles from any land or reef. Even so, I had instructed everyone to keep a close radar watch.

Except for ten seconds of sheer panic, the trip was uneventful. Our expectation of no shipping turned out to be correct and we were lulled into a false sense of security. I had just finished what I had thought was a thorough scan of the horizon and was settling back to eat the delicious lunch Charlotte and Alex had prepared. With plate balanced on my knees and beer wedged between by back and the cockpit combing, it was awkward to turn my head around to get a good view off our port side, so perhaps I wasn't looking as often as I should. But my glance just after having taken a large bite of chicken resulted in chicken gravy all over my shirt and pants.

From nowhere it was zooming down our port side with only a few feet to spare. A metal cylinder the size of an automobile. Fishing buoy! And in the middle of nowhere. Too deep for anchoring. What was it doing there? We watched dumbfounded as it merged into the sea off our stern. After that our watches were more rigorous

Five days at sea was long enough to cure my No No itch and I was excited about arriving in Makemo. I read that tides flow out of the atoll pass at up to twelve knots and carefully studied the pilot books for advice. All said to come in at slack water only, but none gave a precise formula for determining when slack water occurs. Some advice was based on moonrise and moonset. I spent hours with my nautical almanac and tide tables but the different approaches yielded entirely different answers. Seven hours out of Makemo a radio conversation with *C'est Assez* cinched the decision. They had successfully negotiated the pass the day before and had gathered more information. Two to three hours before high tide was the only time of slack water and dead low tide had the strongest flow. We would arrive at Makemo at one of the worst possible times.

We immediately turned to port, started the engine and headed for Raroia. A 30-mile beat into 30-knot winds. We knew the timing was still wrong (we would arrive at high tide, not two to three hours before) and that high wind made the outflow of water at the pass worse. We were beginning to appreciate more why the British Admiralty referred to the Tuamotus as the "Dangerous Archipelago" and why each of our pilots had their extensive sets of warnings and disclaimers. With Andy—our best eyes—half way up the mast, and Alex at the anchor winch ready to let go at any time, and Charlotte reading the speed over ground display of our GPS and relaying to me Andy's advice over the roar of the wind, I gripped the wheel. My attention was divided between watching whitecaps and standing waves in the narrow entrance (it looked more like rapids than an inlet) and monitoring the instrument panel that was registering 35 knots of wind and seven and a half knots of speed through the water.

Three hundred yards out Charlotte reported four and a half knots over ground. Three knots of current already and we weren't in the pass. The worst part would be after we had entered and had to turn 90 degrees to the right to avoid two large coral reefs just inside the entrance. Two hundred yards out and Charlotte called out: "three knots." There was still maneuvering room to abort, but once in and the turn made, we would be committed. In the entrance Charlotte sang out: "two and a half knots."

From Andy: "I can see the channel clearly—you have about one hundred yards more before the turn." Then we were in. From Charlotte: "three and a half knots over ground" Good news—the current was diminishing as we entered a wider portion of the funnel. I held my breath and turned *Skimmer* forty-five degrees starboard to crab her down her new course. From Alex: "I have the markers lined up and we are not slipping."

It seemed to last forever—near panic one moment—blissful peace and happiness the next.

***

Even on the tiny island of Raroia, French spending was lavish. The port that serviced the island's eighty inhabitants had a dock fit for a busy port of thousands, and the well-spaced navigation aids compared favorably with those of any major port in the US.

Tattooed from head to toe, barefoot, and bare-chested, Earnest and Felix seemed as unlikely as their surroundings. They had been imported from the Marquesas to work in Raroia's only industry—pearl farming. When we dinghied up to the huge dock, they immediately invited us across the bay to visit the pearl farm where they worked.

Their small, isolated house on stilts had just two rooms with thatched mats, but what immediately struck me was the presence of a refrigerator and overhead lights. How could this be on such a tiny island? I didn't hear generators or see any poles and lines. Then I looked at the roof—it was covered with glass panels. And a small shed in the rear was full of batteries.

Their electricity was solar generated. How could they possibly afford such an expensive system?

They explained that similar units were installed at government expense in all the houses, and the inhabitants paid for their electricity at the same rates they would have paid in France. But the payments lasted for only five years. After that, the government gave the units to the inhabitants and their electricity was free.

Earnest and Felix showed us how to make the lines that the oysters are grown on. Chinese grafters come to the island and put nuclei into each of thousands of oysters clinging to the hundreds of growing lines that make a labyrinth across the lagoon. Oysters are harvested three times a year. When the pearls are removed, the shells are cleaned and sold for mother of pearl and the oysters are eaten by the locals. About ten thousand pearls are produced each year on this little island.

Oyster Growers

Here, proximity lowers the price of pearls and remoteness boosts the price of CD's. Our crew departed with a match box full of black pearls while the two pearl farmers opened a fresh bottle of rum and listened to their newly bartered trio of reggae CD's.

∗∗∗

With Andy up the mast warning us of lethal dangers, we zigzagged around coral heads until we reached a large island—called a motu in Tuamotu—across the lagoon. The water was glass smooth and crystal clear. But on the outside of the atoll, we could see walls of water pounding on coral. Waves originating in South America deposited enormous energy accumulated during their long trip through open ocean. Just two miles north was the small motu where Kon-Tiki crashed ashore in 1947 at the end of its 4,300-mile drift from Peru.

Before arriving at Raroia, we had been confused about the nature of an atoll. Originating as a barrier reef ringing a volcanic mountain growing from the seabed, an atoll is the reef remaining after the mountain collapses back into the depths. Low-lying, with sparse vegetation, Raroia is a chain of small motus that circle a huge lake. Six miles wide and twenty miles long, Raroia is one of the 78 atolls that make up the Tuamotus.

The strong seas and winds on the east coast constantly push water into the lagoon. The stronger the wind, the greater the flow. On the west coast, the narrow, but relatively deep channel is where much of the water entering from the east funnels out. The combination of low tide and high winds from the east can create extraordinarily fierce currents in the inlet even though the tidal range is only a couple of feet. From our anchorage we could look down into the clear water and see six-foot sharks circling below. "Not to worry," we had been assured by the villagers, "as long as you are not spear fishing, they won't hurt you. Just hit the water with the palm of your hand when they approach and they will go away."

Alex and Andy fished for grouper with incredible success. As they drifted past coral heads in the dinghy, groupers would poke their heads out of the rocks to see what was up. The next thing the fish would see were the two trailing lures—and that was the end of the grouper. Unfortunately we couldn't eat them for fear of fish poisoning. The flesh of fish feeding on coral reefs can contain deadly toxins that cause a serious poisoning called ciguatera. But the few grouper that they did not release made great bait for their other form of recreation.

Ever present at our anchorage, sometimes circling close—the Black Tip sharks. Sometimes as many as twenty would be swarming around *Skimmer*. A grouper head on the end of a line was irresistible. With each pass sharks would become boulder until one would turn on its side, open its huge mouth and "whoosh"—gone with the grouper. A jerk on the line, a tug of war, churning, jumping and splashing, and then another Black Tip would have its turn. From that the boys went to hooks and lines—first heavy tackle, then spinning rods, and finally fly rods. Even Charlotte joined and reeled in a five-footer on Andy's fly rod.

***

I'd heard of Victor before our arrival at Makemo. Standing in the bow of his boat with a harpoon in one hand and a joystick in the other as he rocketed along at thirty knots stalking Mahi Mahi, Victor was a legend on our morning radio net. My first task ashore had been to ask if he would take us fishing.

After loading up with fresh French bread from the local bakery, we crossed the lagoon to join "C'est Assez" and dropped anchor among five other cruising sailboats while we waited for the right wind to fish with Victor.

The cook-out on shore that night was fun, but the chief attraction was the beached whale on the ocean-side of the reef. Alex, Andy, and I were up early the next morning and armed with gas masks, knives, and chisels, we began dental surgery. Five beautiful sperm whale teeth later, tired and feeling a little sick, we had returned for the cleaning job.

That night while we were again cooking on shore, a small motorboat arrived and we met Michael, a pearl farmer, and Becao, an engraver who one of the other boats had commissioned to engrave their whale teeth. Word was out about the beached whale, and they were the first wave of the salvage group.

The next morning we spotted another motor boat tearing off towards the whale and the race was on. During the next two days, the whale dissolved as bone and teeth filled the arriving boats for transportation back to the village.

***

We were set to go ashore to have Sunday lunch when a boat came speeding up to *Skimmer*. Standing in the bow, Victor shouted: "The wind is up. Hop on, we are going after Mahi Mahi." This was the invitation I had been waiting for. The boat was Victor's design, narrow, long, flat bottom aft, V bottom forward, with a fifty-five horse power outboard. We roared out of the pass with Victor pointing at hundreds of birds in a feeding frenzy while his other guest, Wolf, and I crouched behind the bow.

"Are they Mahi Mahi?" I asked. "No, Bonita." "How can you tell?" "Experience."

Over went his single lure at the end of 200-pound-test monofilament line. He was right. Bonita. Huge ones. Each time one struck he would shout "Bonita, sashimi, bon", and laugh, and take the line out of my hands. Six feet tall and muscled, Victor could pull in the line without even wrapping it around his hands—five feet at a time—then "wham wham" with a big stick of wood as the bloody fish fell to the deck. And we were off for the next one.

Constantly scanning the horizon and speeding from one

Victor's Mahi Mahi

group of Bonita to another, Victor suddenly turned the boat sharply to the right, speeded up to thirty knots and started shouting "Mahi Mahi." The clue was the group of small white birds circling much higher than the flock of larger black birds feeding with the Bonita. He picked out one bird and vectored in: the bird would go ninety degrees to the left and Victor would go ninety degrees to the left. It was all I could do to hold on. Right, left, slow, fast—we emulated the bird's every movement. And then I saw it. Streaking through the water, an iridescent blue and green—Victor had locked on.

Victor grabbed a huge harpoon in one hand while he manipulated his joy stick with the other. And then he was on top of the streak. Shouting "Ahee, Mahi Mahi" Victor left the controls to themselves, thrust the harpoon and drew into the boat a thrashing 40 pounds of blue green fish. Six hours after our departure we returned with 400 pounds of fish.

On the way back in, we passed Andy and Alex in *Skimmer*'s dinghy on their way out fishing and told them about the huge masses of fish and birds in the pass. Two hours later they had returned with another incredible story. This time the spectators had been the Tuamotuans. Armed with only spinning rods and fifteen pound test line they assaulted the huge school of fish just outside the pass. While a near-by native boat wrestled in large tuna and bonita with a hand-line similar to the one Victor employed, Andy and Alex cast their small lures into the midst of the frenzy.

The other boat watched with amusement as Andy latched onto a very large fish. Even though they knew he couldn't keep it long, they kindly pulled in their lines to keep out of his way and continued to watch. To their amazement, the fight lasted and lasted. At the end of an hour, Alex was able to grab the leader and gaff the huge fish. It was too big to pull up into the inflatable dinghy so the other boat came alongside to assist.

To their astonishment Andy had not only caught a fifty-pound fish, but it was their prized "Thon Blanc"—the best-eating fish in French Polynesia—a long finned white albacore. By the end of their expedition, Andy and Alex also caught two yellowfin tuna. They gave half the Thon Blanc to the other boat and a generous slice to Victor, who, despite his huge catch of the day, was delighted to get this treasured delicacy.

That night we dinghied over to Becao's house for our delayed Sunday lunch. Becao was in his open air workshop working on his whale teeth while his wife, Jacqueline, set the table for the magnificent meal she had prepared for us. We sat around the long table surrounded by a troop of dogs that outnumbered the people and enjoyed mahi mahi cevechi, grilled mahi mahi, and chicken curry made with coconut milk, while Becao told how he and Michael had gotten every one of the remaining whale's teeth before turning the carcass over to the other boat.

Andy gave Victor the lure that caught the Thon Blanc and Jacqueline was delighted with our gift of twenty pounds of frozen goat steak. Later we learned that some of the canine company we enjoyed that night will eventually make their way to the curry pot.

***

Even before we dropped anchor, we realized we'd found a very special spot. Tahanea was the first uninhabited atoll we had visited, and during a potluck dinner on the beach that night our neighbors from four other boats anchored there described the incredible beauty of the pristine reefs and beaches with an enthusiasm we had a hard time understanding. By this time in our travels we had seem some pretty spectacular islands. What was it about Tahanea that made it so special?

We saw on our snorkeling expedition across the lagoon at Paenoa Reef. Paenoa is in a class all by itself. It is not only the brilliant colors and immense variety of creatures and shells attached to coral heads, but the fish and their almost complete lack of concern at our presence. Huge Groupers would come out of hiding to look us over. Their isolation from the rest of the world made them fearless. We in turn learned to quieten our own fears and remain in the water exploring despite the presence of circling six-foot sharks.

Despite her fears, Charlotte was so enthralled with the beauty of our reef that she stayed with us for the entire expedition. Using a technique she has developed—I call it the ostrich—she minimizes trauma. When she spots a shark, she pulls her head out of water, shouts for me to accompany her, and without ever looking back quickly swims to the dinghy. Her quickness and agility in soaring out of the water and into the boat is impressive.

Tahanea was our last stop in the Tuamotus, and leaving it we got a reminder how treacherous these islands and reefs can be. I had checked our GPS several times and had even gotten out our backup battery-operated GPS to take a confirming fix as we entered the wide channel separating Tahanea from its neighboring Atoll, Faaite.

At first we thought it must be an isolated motu with coconut trees. But it didn't seem to be in the right spot—much further off the coast of Faaite than where the coral should extend. Finally I was able to steady my binoculars enough to figure it out. A huge ship sat atop the coral reef with almost the whole hull out of water. We watched in silence as *Skimmer* sailed by, imagining what it must be like to have one of these low lying Atolls to leeward during a big storm. We learned later that the ship was the victim of an out-of-season hurricane several years earlier.

***

Tahiti, Morea, and Bora Bora—the famed Society Islands, the playground of the South Pacific. We had returned to of civilization. Two hundred miles from our last island in the Tuamotus, Tahiti rose from the ocean and treated us to another dramatic change in topography. Mountainous, lush-green, bustling with activity, Papeete proved a perfect location to re-provision and arrange transportation home for the boys.

Everything imaginable was available, but, unfortunately, at unimaginably high prices. Three dollars for a head of lettuce. Two dollars for a beer, even at supermarkets. But cooking on board kept cost in check and we were happy to have fresh vegetables no matter what the price. It looked like restaurants would be out of the question, but during our first night a new alternative had presented itself.

The trucks that had been parked all day at the end of our quay suddenly became beehives of activity. The removal of side panels revealed well-stocked kitchens. Long benches were set around the vehicles. Now we understood what our guidebooks had been describing. "Le Truck." It was a wonderful innovation and suddenly well-prepared French food was within *Skimmer's* budget.

Tahiti was a significant milestone for us. Charlotte and I returned to Charleston for a two-week visit while Andy and Alex took care of *Skimmer*, and on our return in late June they flew home. It was hard to imagine what life was going to be like without the two most enthusiastic members of our crew.

Now We Are Two

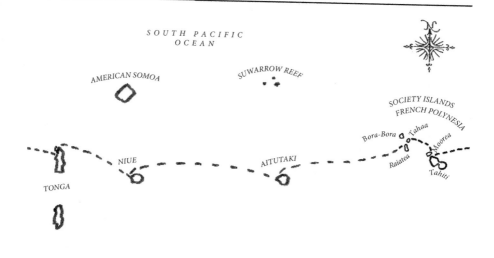

S eeds of discontent had been planted during our whirlwind visit to Charleston. It was wonderful to be home again—the party in our honor, seeing family and friends. But there was inevitable stress when so much needed to be done in such a short time. It wasn't so much that I had torn up our living room in constructing, weighing, and filling to the brim the four huge cardboard boxes. It was more my system of priorities that upset Charlotte.

I tried to explain why the new hydraulic helm unit, the new wind generator with 125 feet of heavy battery cable, the new heavy duty-inverter, and the giant cable cutters took priority over the 30 pounds of popcorn and 20 boxes of brownie mix she had purchased. I tried to stuff in a bag of popcorn, a box of brownie mix, a can of Crisco, and a roll of paper towels here and there before sealing the boxes. The evidence of my omissions, though, were strewn all over the living room floor. For family harmony I stuffed our carry-on bags so full we could hardly budge them.

***

Back on *Skimmer*—and alone. At first the projects were fun. Charlotte was enthusiastic about getting everything cleaned to her specifications and I enjoyed the prospect of beefing up all of *Skimmer*'s major systems to make handling the boat with only two easier.

The wind generator project had to wait for calm weather. By the time it came I had worked out logistics of how to get the 13-pound beast with its aluminum pole and heavy trailing battery cable mounted atop *Skimmer's* mizzenmast.

The day is dead calm, and I finally screw up courage to make the attempt. Securely tied, I'm able to overcome my instincts enough to let go the mast and practice the motions of placing the generator. Just when I am ready to hoist the generator and cables a jet ski's wake starts rocking the boat. The mathematics are simple—a five degree roll on deck translates to almost two feet of motion at the top of the mast. I think about shouting at the grinning joy rider as he streaks by, but know that it would just encourage him to make the next pass on his screaming machine even closer. My only choice is to hold with both hands until my tormentor decides to move on and share his noise with some other cruiser.

A little electronics eavesdropping helps Charlotte stay in good spirits as she cleans. Most of our neighbors monitor VHF Channel 72: *Rubicon* calls *Loafer*, and *Loafer* acknowledges telling *Rubicon* to go to Channel 68. Charlotte spins the dial and *Skimmer's* saloon reverberates with the plans for a potluck dinner. Charlotte even knows what wines they are planning to serve. But no potlucks for *Skimmer*. We are too busy with projects.

I think it is the oil on my pants as I sit down on freshly cleaned cockpit cushions that pushes Charlotte over the edge. I've just finished fixing the hydraulic leak in lines connecting the new autopilot pump and I'm late coming to lunch when the eruption comes: "I hate this boat, I hate projects, I hate cleaning, and I am beginning to hate you!" I look at Charlotte, look at my dirty hands, and it hits me like a ton of bricks. This is supposed to be fun. What have we turned our dream trip into?

* * *

It was the arrival of friends from Washington that got things back on track. Jimmy and Jayne had been planning their visit for months. We prepared gourmet meals, we played, and we laughed as we cruised the waters of Moorea, Taaha, and Bora Bora. Seeing the excitement in their eyes reflected in those of Charlotte I realized—joy had finally returned to *Skimmer*.

The peacefulness of Moorea's lovely Opunohu bay was shattered by a loud blast that jerked all of us out of deep sleep. From our anchorage we could see it all, and better yet follow it on our VHF radio. The sailing vessel anchored at the mouth of the bay, which so impressed us the night before with its beauty and size, looked like a gnat about to be squashed by the huge cruising ship that towered above it. The sound of *R4's* horns blasting the danger signal had roused us. On the VHF *R4's* master screamed abuse that overwhelmed the gentle voice coming from *Liberty*.

Liberty had inadvertently dropped anchor in *R4's* spot.

"I have a thousand tourists aboard and I must disembark them immediately! You must move! NOW!" And then the reply from a sweet feminine voice: "Yes, I am waking the engineer up now and we will warm the engines up." The angry answer: "You have to move NOW!" Followed by four blasts of *R4's* deafening horn.

This went on for almost an hour. *R4's* captain went from furious to the point of tantrum. We could hear a troop of boy scouts camped on the beach screaming their outrage at *R4* for spoiling the tranquility of our surroundings, and we could see the big smiles on neighboring cruisers' faces as they watched our heroine on *Liberty* humble *R4's* rude captain.

Jimmy and Jayne Taylor

Finally, in her own sweet time, *Liberty* moved on to make room for her giant neighbor, but not before one parting barb: "Captain, what proof do you have this anchor spot is really reserved for you?"

***

We had been told at the store just up the dirt road that Taaha's one restaurant was not to be missed. It was late afternoon when we hitched a ride in the back of a truck to head for the mountainous interior, and we wondered how we would get back. But the description of Chez Louise was so tempting we'd worry about return later. A half-hour later the truck let us out in town and we began searching. The first possibility turned out to be a schoolhouse, and we almost lost Charlotte to the crowd of children that gathered about her as she chatted and shared candy. We finally spotted what looked like a restaurant where a stout lady in work clothes covered with a fair portion of the island's soil inquired: "Vous venez chez moi? Alors, Je reste!" After giving us a tour of her vanilla bean farm, she led us to the porch of her restaurant where we sipped Hinano beer and watched the sun drop and turn the sky red. Our attention was riveted on the massive island mountain to the west. What a way to see Bora Bora for the first time!

The fact we were the only four clients in the restaurant didn't deter Louise and her husband—the twin of the French plantation owner in *South Pacific*. We all agreed the raw fish in coconut milk was the best. Marinated in fresh lime juice and mixed with diced peppers and onions, it would be indistinguishable from cevechi if it weren't for the coconut flavor that made it a completely different dish. Another treasured recipe was added to *Skimmer's* galley.

Bora Bora was the last island for Jimmy and Jayne and the prettiest place we'd seen, snow-white beaches and water so clear we could see the full length of our hundred and thirty feet of anchor chain.

***

Bora Bora to Raiatea was our first stretch handling *Skimmer* with just the two of us. Our marina lacked one important amenity—water—and it was imperative that we fill up before embarking on our long voyage to the Southern Cook Islands. So we had to shift to another marina. I thought it was going to be easy. The slot was directly up wind. All we had to do was to glide up to the quay, attach our bow line, and then grab the mooring line and attach it to the stern. Simple.

I was about to turn the helm over to Charlotte to go forward when I realized something was wrong. Forward gear, but no forward motion. I nudged the throttle forward but still no forward motion. Panic. I was unable to shift gears. We'd lost control!

Options rushed through my mind as the wind began to gently push us away. Go below and shift the gears manually. But how to communicate with Charlotte over the noise of the engine? Drop the anchor? Maybe. But the water was over eighty feet deep and an anchor wasn't likely to keep us off the rocks twenty feet on our right or off the line of neatly docked yachts to our left.

Waving frantically, I got the attention of a young man on a pier who ran to us and arrived just in time to miss the long line I tossed. By now we'd turned completely about and were headed for the pier he had just left. He ran back to his pier and got there in time to hold *Skimmer's* bow off the middle of the pretty blue aluminum sloop we were about to impale, while a Frenchman on the boat just aft caught our line and made us fast along the pier.

It was a two-beer lunch. But that didn't calm our nerves. Two screws that held the gear shift cable had worked loose—a minor problem with the potential for major damage. Should we have realized there was a problem earlier? For some time I'd been aware it was often hard to find neutral. But I was learning vibration was our biggest enemy and you can't check all mechanical fittings too many times.

After it was all over, the Frenchman who'd helped us made an interesting comment. "It is a sailboat you know. Don't count on your motor so much." At first I laughed it off. After thinking about it more, I realized that he'd been right. Let the Genoa out a little, turn around and get out of the marina—that should have been my solution.

We knew it before, but it sank in as we planned the post-Tahiti portion of our voyage. The South Pacific is enormous! One thousand miles from Panama to the Galapagos and over 3,000 miles from the Galapagos to the Marquesas. Once we had arrived in the Marquesas we felt like we had crossed the Pacific, but we were only about halfway to Australia.

We had decided to skip the last two groups of French Polynesia—the Gambier Islands 800 miles to the southeast and the Austral Islands 200 miles south of that. Our next destination would be the Southern Cook Islands.

French Polynesia is a major crossroad for boats sailing the South Pacific and Papeete is its hub. People come there from all over—many, like us, from Panama, others directly from the US West coast, some from Mexico, some from Hawaii, and even some from Alaska. Leaving Polynesia presented the first big fork in the road. Most of us were headed for Tonga, but almost all chose different routes to try to divide the 1,300 mile trip into bite-sized chunks. One thing we all found, however, was no matter which route is chosen, it's a very long trip with very few opportunities to stop.

Many American yachts elect a route that entails a fairly significant detour to the north. The first leg is about 700 miles non-stop to Suwarrow in the Northern Cook Islands. The next leg is 500 miles to American Samoa, and from there another 300 miles to the south to Tonga. The chief attraction for American cruisers is subsidized shopping in American Samoa, where you can stock up boats with US goods at very low cost—a particularly attractive benefit after the obscenely high prices in French Polynesia.

Charlotte and I thought taking this route with its very long legs was a little too much trouble to go shopping at Wal-Mart, so we had elected a route through the Southern Cook Islands and set course for Aitutaki. The only drawbacks were that the entrance to Aitutaki is narrow, the anchorage has limited space, and it is impossible to enter if the wind is blowing strongly from the west. We'd never had the experience of traveling five days to arrive at a place and then not be able go in—but if it happened, our plan was to sail on to Palmerston, 200 miles to the west. Niue, an island kingdom 250 miles west of Palmerston, was the third and final planned stop on our trip to Tonga.

We both had become more conservative and Charlotte seemed to be getting less nervous about things in general. The first two days of our trip to Aitutaki were smooth. We settled into watches of three hours on and three hours off, with Charlotte starting after dinner as soon as it became dark. Strangely, we almost looked forward to our watches. Days were more relaxed than nights and we both came and went as we pleased, but always with one awake and in charge.

My new hobby became weather forecasting. Charlotte had been so fretful for so long I thought I might be able to allay her fears if I could interpret the weather. We had recently acquired an incredible computer program that allowed me to get weather faxes through the same device I used for e-mail. I had two books and another computer program that told me how to interpret the faxes. Each morning at five I would get two weather faxes from MetService in New Zealand, one that gave current conditions and one that gave a 24 hour prediction. It was wonderful to behold, all those squiggly lines and numbers, with pointing triangles and half rounds that indicated fronts of various sorts. The jargon was great: occulted fronts, ridges, and troughs; and wonderful units: millibars, hectopascals, and even the Southern Oscillation Index to help forecast El Nino events.

Morning of our third day out, after studying my books and newly received faxes for almost two hours, I felt I was finally beginning to understand how it worked. Charlotte was skeptical as I talked her through the faxes and used my new vocabulary to explain why the wind and waves were going to be perfect for the next two days of our trip. We would get conformation, of course, when we tuned in the Pacific Island Net at 8:00 AM. on our SSB radio. Since our arrival in Tahiti we had been very pleased with the newly formed Pacific Island Net. The boats reporting in covered a very wide geographical area and we were particularly fortunate to have Steve as our weather guru. His reports were thorough, well organized, and, most importantly, always there.

I'd explained to Charlotte that the first boat reporting was heading to Rarotanga and south of our area, so his warning of 40-knot winds and rain squalls wasn't relevant. The next report, from a boat about to enter Aitutaki with 35 knots of wind and squalls was a little harder to explain. Subsequent reports all seemed to be in the same vein and I felt lucky as I announced to the net our 15-knot winds from the east and three foot seas. Steve's forecast pretty much bore out what the other boats had been reporting, so I decided to go back and review my weather books one more time before making any more predictions. Despite the fact wind and waves remained calm for *Skimmer*, we battened down hatches and reefed everything that was reefable to get ready for Charlotte's big blow.

That night it hit. Charlotte was just beginning her 23:00 to 02:00 watch when she called me on deck because of large areas of rain on radar. At her urging, we reefed further an already well-reefed boat. Mizzen down. Genoa reefed to a handkerchief. Main on the third reef. We were ready. I was glad I followed Charlotte's advice. Fifteen minutes later it was on us, heavy rain and wind gusting to twenty five knots. With it came cold and a switch of wind direction. That necessitated a jibe and the usual jibe argument was about to take place. I ignored Charlotte's steady stream of warnings and cautions and shouted to put the rudder over hard while I tended the sheet as our massive boom flew overhead. Once it was done, Charlotte was glad. By the time we were back in trim on our new course, the wind had picked up to a steady 40 knots with gusts up to fifty.

Pitch night, torrential rain, and the sound of relentless wind screaming through our rigging—Charlotte's nightmare was finally taking place. Periodically, as if to test our mettle, 50-knot gusts would angrily slap *Skimmer*, healing her over and causing the whole boat to quiver as we held our breath and waited for it to pass.

Slap, quiver. Slap, quiver. Suddenly a loud alarm from below rivets our attention. The sound is unmistakable. The engine low oil pressure alarm. Frightened and about to take the prescribed automatic action I suddenly realize—the engine isn't running so why should we get an alarm? Anger replaces fright as I realize that the ignition switch has suddenly failed. It has happened once before and I know—the switch has come on of its own accord and the maddening buzzing will not stop until the engine is actually running and there is enough oil pressure to deactivate the alarm.

Crouched in the engine room and braced with both feet and one hand, I use the other hand to feel for the fuse. Slowly and carefully—this is no time to make mistakes that could cause other problems—I remove the fuse and tuck it in a corner where I know I can find it if I need to replace it to start the engine. Back on deck where the slaps seem to be getting harder and the quivers more violent. I am about to get Charlotte to help me further reef the Genoa when I realize our mistake. The free Genoa sheet rope has come loose and the wind has spiraled it around the working sheet rope in such a way that further reefing or further trimming is impossible. I examine the tangled mess with a flash light and immediately determine the only way to free it is to go on deck for a half hour of very difficult work. Further reefing is out of the question. We are stuck with what's happened.

We don't have long to dwell on our new problem. Charlotte smells it and I act immediately. Smoke in the engine room. Where is it coming from? I make my way aft where it seems to be worse. Lifting the floorboard over the aft bilge gives me the answer. We have an electrical fire in our bilge pump. Back to the engine room, more groping around in the fuse panel, and then a final check to make sure I have the right one. Another problem solved and another problem created. I have a spare bilge pump but installation will have to wait.

Just after our jangled nerves are beginning to settle back down, we both hear it. At first I don't want to acknowledge it, so I look at Charlotte as she voices what I want to deny.

"Was that a horn?"

The radar is so cluttered with rain squalls that I can't make out anything. We tune the rain suppressor feature of our radar but can't find anything. And then we hear it again. After three days of not seeing a single vessel, it is hard to believe we would find one now in our storm. As we search through the rain and stare at the radar, our adrenaline levels begin to recede and we start thinking again.

A single honk. What does that mean? My numbed mind tries to cope, but can't come up with anything. Suddenly we hear the honk again. This time we both realize it is from *Skimmer*.

Our feared tanker was the normal lifting of a hydraulic relief valve in our steering system. When a larger than normal wave exerted extreme pressure on our rudder, the relief valve would lift, releasing pressure and thus protecting the system. An interesting thing happened in both of us during the first two hours of our ordeal. Fear had been replaced by determined energy. Was it the survival instinct taking over, or just that hard work didn't leave time for worry? I had seen it in Charlotte before and now it was so strong that she was transformed.

As the threat of troubled approached, Charlotte had a tendency to give way to a nervous chatter that masked the steel beneath. "I hate this! How did I ever let you talk me into coming? This is it. The Last time—and I mean THE LAST TIME!" But once trouble was upon us, the crying and machine-gun invectives would stop and be replaced with quiet competence.

Since we left home almost a year before I had watched it grow within her. Not just skills required by our new occupation. Her ability to control *Skimmer* under any circumstances, track tankers and storms with assurance, interpret charts and our array of electronic equipment had become very impressive. It was the growing confidence in herself that really stood out.

I wondered if in seeing these changes in Charlotte I was also seeing a reflection of what was taking place in myself. Part of her calm was because of increasing confidence in my abilities. From her point of view it was my knowledge and judgment that would get us through the many emergencies that were sure to occur. The fact that she was still with me pretty much stated her position. If it had not been clear before, it became very clear that night. Mutual trust was essential. Regardless of how trying the circumstances, we had to be willing to relinquish control to the other, and sleep was essential to our safety. Our survival depended on it. Once the alarms were over and

Skimmer's stability restored, Charlotte had offered to extend her watch to give me an hour of sleep.

I had no doubts of her ability to handle the situation and I went aft and collapsed. An hour later there was a smile on her face when she roused me to take over. When her words came out I was both stunned and amused. My reply had given her reassurance. "No, Charlotte, we are not going to die. *Skimmer* is handling beautifully and we aren't even close to being in trouble. As long as we stay calm and keep our confidence, everything is going to be all right." But my speech really hadn't been necessary. She knew as well as I that our challenges of the night had all been manageable. The biggest problem had been the wind and we had taken correct actions well before it even started. Morning bought renewed energy but not reduced wind. I was able to untangle the genoa sheets so we could finally furl in more of our Genoa to-fine tune *Skimmer's* trim.

I had never been more thankful for having insisted that our sailmaker include a third reefing point in *Skimmer's* main sail. He'd laughed and said "What's the point? With a ketch rig you already have a smaller main sail. The normal two reefing points should be plenty." But I was adamant and when the third reef was in our main sail was very small and very stable.

I'd let him talk me into our giant genoa, and with the miracle of roller furling we were able to reduce the size of it to anywhere between full and none by manipulating lines from the safety of our cockpit. Changing the size of the main sail, however, necessitated leaving the safety of the cockpit to go on deck and up to the mast. But once the third reef was in all further sail reductions could be accomplished from the cockpit by regulating the size of the Genoa. And that had been the configuration we had been in when the storm had hit.

The results of furling in more Genoa were immediate and dramatic. The slapping and quivering disappeared and *Skimmer* settled down—strained, but stable. The storm lasted three days but we adjusted and Charlotte seemed to hardly notice when giant walls of water slid past. Despite the wild motion of the boat, I was able to replace the bilge pump, install a new engine switch and get *Skimmer* back to normal.

Nothing has ever sounded as good as Louis of *Aragon* on the VHF radio, assuring us the island of Aitutaki would mask the wind and that we wouldn't have any problem with our approach. He confirmed what we already knew, that the channel was very narrow and was only six feet deep in spots and added the welcomed information that it was marked with metal stakes. "Keep the stakes to your port—stay very close to them. Once you are in, the first boat you will pass will be *Sparrow*, then us. Keep us to your starboard and we'll come help you anchor."

Without Louis' advice, I probably wouldn't have entered. Reefs and rocks everywhere and the only break a line of rusty iron poles—did they really mark a channel? The water color said yes. Or was it maybe? We circled twice and took the plunge. Charlotte on the bow searching for the middle of the channel, while I veered our rudder back and forth to compensate for the rushing tide. Once in there was no turning back. Bump, bump, bump, yes we had found the shallow part halfway down the channel, but *Skimmer* slid across the sandy bottom and we were in.

Aragon

John and Ann of *Sparrow* and Louis and Pat of *Aragon* were there in dinghies to lead us to our anchorage and help set two extra anchors. A van was to pick us up along with crews of three other boats and take us to a local restaurant on the other side of the island. Although we hadn't previously met any of the other boats except *Aragon*, they all knew about us from following our harrowing weather reports on the SSB. Over cold Lion Red beer, we got news of other boats who all weathered the same storm, although one boat had turned back to Bora Bora.

***

Aitutaki is one of fifteen islands spread over an enormous expanse of Pacific Ocean to form the Cook Islands. Technically the islands are an independent country with their own government, but there's a very close association with New Zealand that is vital to their economic survival.

The most striking aspects of Aitutaki are the people and their friendliness. Our arrival day had been on a Saturday, but the agricultural inspector and his young daughter came out to our boat on their own time to clear us into the country so we wouldn't have to spend the weekend in quarantine on board.

Church the next morning was a highlight. The huge white building was packed with islanders in bright shirts of varying patterns on the men and straw hats with wreaths of flowers on their women. There seemed to be groupings—the blue shirts with white floral patterns in the middle of the church, red shirts at the far end and yellow shirts at the near end. We couldn't understand a word, spoken or sung, but it didn't matter. The joy of the congregation as they sang out traditional hymns in Maori reverberated across the church—the red shirts singing one motif that was answered and amplified by another motif from the blue shirts and then another motif from the yellow shirts.

Our visit was dominated by the week of Constitution Day celebrations. The disco opposite the quay and dinghy landing ramp was the site—a tin shed with three permanent walls and one temporary wall composed of shipping containers. Sock hop decorations of gymnasiums are nothing compared to what the Cook Islanders did to their disco complex. Palm leaves were everywhere, woven around the poles supporting the tin roof, thatched into mats to hide the corrugated sides of containers, and strewn about everywhere to simulate the forests in the distance.

When we circumnavigated the island on bicycles, we stopped at the town halls of each of the 13 villages to listen to the drums and gawk at the young women and men gyrating to the rhythms in practice for the competition that evening.

The size of the crowd in the disco picked up considerably the second night. The unruliness of the audience was greater than the previous evening; children roamed everywhere and young girls and boys wandered on-stage during performances to show off their rhythmic abilities. Each night the performances became louder, more primitive, more interesting. These performances were not for tourists—in fact the villages had commandeered the entire fleet of tourist vans,

Aitutakian Welcomes Charlotte

trucks, and cars to transport the performing groups to and from their homes all around the island. The Aitutakians were kind to their interloping visitors from sailboats, but these performances were for their own enjoyment.

The third night was the climax. It was like something from a Conrad novel. Drums and dancing, followed by enactment of the Aitutaki founding legend. Half the population of the island turned out along with the Governor General of New Zealand and the Prime Minister of the Cook Islands.

It took several performances for us to understand the legend of the founding of Aitutaki. Ru, with twenty maidens aboard his small boat, had traveled far and wide when fate had finally landed their craft on Aitutaki. Ru loved the island and on the spot gave it its first name, Utataki, meaning "Ru turns his back on the sea." Given the seas we had seen coming into Aitutaki and the beauty we'd seen ashore, I thought it would have taken far less than twenty maidens to have made me want to stay. But I wasn't Ru and I only had one maiden aboard and it was time to leave.

* * *

Conditions weren't good for Palmerston, so we decided to continue on to Niue, an elevated coral outcropping that is the largest coral island in the world. By itself in the middle of a huge expanse of ocean, it is an ideal stop for boats on the way to Tonga. Like the Cooks, it is self-governing and under the protection of New Zealand, only in this case the entire kingdom consists of only one island.

This was our second long solo voyage—some 600 miles. The winds were robust but, happily, no storms. Charlotte was beginning not to worry about bad weather. I reveled in not having any projects that required my attention. After all, I'd promised Charlotte I wouldn't think about remounting the wind generator until after we had arrived in Australia. The promise was extracted under duress. Hanging by a thread and threatening to come crashing down on us at any moment, my wind generator had chosen the worst possible time to make trouble. We had been focusing all or our energy on fighting the storm on our way to Aitutaki and at my urging Charlotte had been willing to put it out of her mind—but only after my solemn promise.

Projects are a way of life for cruisers. Sometimes they scream out with urgency and other times they softly whisper seductive promises of a vastly improved lifestyle. There are, however, on rare occasions, those projects that somehow just don't work out and that serve only to cause frustration. Work had begun with daily trips up our mizzenmast while anchored in Tahiti. It's hard to describe my feeling of accomplishment when, after three days of labor, I could point to the whirling blades atop our aft mast and announce that *Skimmer* was now getting a major portion of her electricity from wind power. No more having to run the engine twice a day to generate electricity. No more feeling hostage to the danger of loosing all power if the engine failed.

It wasn't such a fine moment a week later during our passage to Taaha when Charlotte pointed to the mizzenmast. I couldn't believe it. There was my beautiful machine, still whirring, but the whirling blades and generator body were wildly gyrating around 35 feet over our heads. One of the bolts

I had threaded into the mizzenmast to hold the generator pole had come loose—and it wasn't going to be very long before the others would be torn loose also by the violent motion. Twelve pounds, aerodynamically streamline, my wind generator had become a bomb poised to drop right onto the middle of *Skimmer's* aft deck. I had two choices—wait for the bomb or climb the mast in rolling seas to secure it in place. The weather was fairly calm so I'd chosen the latter.

At this point, I'd not been about to call the project a failure. A slight setback sure, but after thinking about it several days both cause and cure became clear. I should have through bolted the aluminum pole to our mast instead of threading it into one side. After consultations with the boatyard in Raiatea and with other cruising boats that had wind generators, my new plan became firm and I had completed the project for the second time.

When we left Raiatea for Aitutaki I felt very good about my newly mounted generator. This time the pole was secured with two heavy-duty stainless steel bolts, tightened down with nylon lock nuts and doubly secured with two additional locking nuts. This baby wasn't going to come loose. Again, it was a wonderful feeling to have energy independence. It was fun to watch the amount of electricity we were generating as the wind picked up, almost 20 amps in 30-knot winds—more than enough to make us entirely electrically self-sufficient. But the fun didn't last.

When the storm hit us and all our attention was on reefing, jibing, and fixing other problems, one of the bolts snapped and again we had a gyrating bomb dangling on our mizzenmast. This time going up was impossible. We just had to sit and wait for it to fall. We watched it for three days. During our vigil we wondered what it would tear out as it came hurling down. The radar, the stays, even the mizzenmast itself, all were distinct possibilities.

The motions went from wild to crazy when the second bolt snapped. Still, the bomb didn't drop. A safety line I'd attached as an afterthought during construction and the heavy electric cables were all that were holding it up. I did manage to lasso the generator with a spare halyard and this tended to slow the motion somewhat, but after a day the halyard had worn through and come down. I tried to shoot a messenger line with a home-made sling shot over the top of the mast to put in place another tie down, but the rocking motion of the boat and high winds kept me from even getting close. We tried to shut it out of our minds. Dangling behind the stays, its position assured that when it did come down, it would come down aft, so it didn't pose a danger to us in the cockpit. We just settled down for the wait. Although I assured Charlotte that it couldn't possibly pierce the aft cabin roof, she seemed to favor sleeping in the amidships berths during the remainder of the storm.

Wind Generator During the Storm

The morning of our last day bought good news. The blades had become entangled in the mizzen stays and the motion had stopped—the wind generator was saved.

***

Where does the time go? What happens to the day?

Our third day en route to Niue is typical.

Charlotte drags me from sleep at 11:00 PM for my three-hour watch. I put on my foul weather jacket, strap on my safety harness, and we have a brief turnover— she points out rain clouds on radar, tells me there have been no contacts, shows me where the sweet rolls are and makes a bee line for the bed and her three hours of deep sleep. We used to call it snorkeling when I was in the Navy. The air is cool and my brain begins to function again. The moon is up so checking the trim of the well reefed sails is easy. Below to fix a cup of coffee and then back up on deck, this time to watch for shipping I know will not appear and to indulge in the contemplation I'd thought would occupy so much of my time. Charlotte's rain clouds approach, so I further reef the Genoa and wait for the heavy winds. This time they only come briefly, then it's completely still and no wind. I reef the Genoa the whole way in to stop the flapping, turn the motor on, and go below to make my midnight log entry.

The midnight entry has become an important part of my routine. I check and log everything—engine hours, oil level, barometer, bilge level, and various other items. It's an invaluable way to catch problems before they arise, and the one certainty in cruising is there will be problems. It is also a great way to break the routine of the watch with something definite to do— for by this time my mind has become foggy and even the slightest task takes enormous concentration and saps what energy I have left. I plot a position, calculate our progress over the past twenty four hours, calculate the amount of fuel remaining and return to the deck to fight off drowsiness for the last hour of the watch.

The magic hour of 2:00 a.m. comes and again Charlotte and I trade places. The wind is still dead, both main and mizzen are flapping, so before my turn at snorkeling, I take down the mizzen while there are two of us on deck—our very strict rule forbids that anyone leave the cockpit after dark without someone else being on deck.

Charlotte's watch routine is much like mine. She has gotten good at plotting positions, watching for shipping and storms, and keeping the sails trim. She is particularly adept reefing in the Genoa and there is an interesting interplay that occurs as we spell each other. When she relieves me, the Genoa is generally almost full. When I relieve her, it looks like a small handkerchief. But this evening we are motoring with only the main (under a second reef) to provide stability, so she has only the weather and shipping to worry about. At 5:00 a.m., the last watch of the evening, Charlotte wakes me and says the wind has come back up. After some brief negotiations we agree on a sail plan and she remains on deck to help.

My morning watch is my favorite one. It starts with tuning my SSB, booting up the computer and receiving two weather faxes from MetService out of New Zealand. One is a surface analysis map that gives conditions as of four hours earlier, and one is a prognosis map that gives predicted conditions for 24 hours later. By the time I've gotten the faxes, savored my coffee, and completed routine chores, sunrise is not far away. As soon as there's enough light on deck to read, I pull out my weather forecasting books, my new weather faxes, pencil, and paper and begin my lessons for the morning. I also take the opportunity to study sky, compass, sea, wind, and barometer to formulate the weather report for my position that I will give on the morning net.

Sunlight changes everything. Problems that bedeviled me during the night become clear and often disappear. I have to revise my weather report for the morning Pacific Island Net. The 100 percent cloud cover has now gone away and it's going to be a lovely clear day. At 8:00 a.m., half an hour before the net, I tune in *C'est Assez* and *Aragon* on the SSB to see how their evenings went and to compare notes on conditions. Charlotte wakes up to the chatting and comes to the navigation center where she preempts my role as radio operator so she can chat with Julie and Pat.

She's also up for another reason. Although she trusts me on most things, interpretation of the weather is something she absolutely must be involved in. I tune the SSB to receive the morning net and we listen as each of our fellow cruisers tells whatit'slike at their positions. Only high winds and squalls register with Charlotte, so even if there are ten successive good reports, the one bad report in Pago Pago (about 500 miles to the northwest of us and in a completely different weather pattern) puts her in on edge. She listens for the worst as our net forecaster gives us his predictions for the next few days. Today the forecast is good everywhere—and Charlotte's in a great mood.

A morning nap for me, a huge lunch with cocktails before if there is something to celebrate—and there almost always is. First day, mid trip, 100 miles to go, … and then an afternoon nap for Charlotte.

I find I'm spending all the spare time I have learning. There are so many things I want to know more about I often have a hard time choosing. I had intended to study more Pacific Island geography, but a failure of my computer (a problem with its BIOS) funneled my efforts elsewhere—but the problem was solvable and now I know a lot more about my computer. Charlotte is spending time learning also, but her pursuits are loftier than mine. Today (it's Sunday) she coordinates a church service with tapes and books she bought from St. Michaels, our church in Charleston. Rick Belzer's sermon on winning and Wade Logan's prayers for the state of the church boom out over the South Pacific. Charlotte's other principal pursuit is cooking. While I think about what needs to be changed or repaired during evening watches, she thinks about what we'll have for the upcoming meals. How she manages to do it with rolling seas and only two hands never ceased to amaze me, but the food is uniformly fantastic. Late in the afternoon is our contact with the outside world. Radio from Jupiter, Florida (our e-mail provider's base) is such that we can only access our e-mail in the early evenings. Email time is an exciting part of our day.

Then we participate in an evening SSB net with cruising friends. In addition to *C'est Assez* and *Aragon*, we have the pleasure of talking with *Osprey* (now almost in Vanuatu), *Horizon* (almost in the Torres Straights between Australia and New Guinea), and, tiny *Emily* who for the first time is actually in port while the rest of us are at sea. Before dark we argue a little over what the outlook for the weather will be during the night, reef the sails, batten down the hatches, and prepare for the worst—although, happily, it doesn't come.

***

After a very roly final night, *Skimmer* arrived in Niue early the morning of our fifth day. At about 3:00 a.m. we rounded the northern tip of Niue and suddenly found ourselves sailing very comfortably in the lee of the island as we waited for daylight and entry. People often ask, "What is the prettiest place you have ever seen?" In truth the answer often depends on when the question is asked, because "prettiest places" seem to leapfrog each other as we move along. Niue, with its rugged coral coast and myriad limestone caves, is an easy candidate for the title.

But I began to think about beauty in different terms. We had seen so many beaches, coral reefs, and snorkeling holes with crystal water that they tended to become indistinguishable. The beauty I came to appreciate more and more is the beauty of the people. We saw it in the Marquesas and Tuamotus, people genuinely interested in meeting us, in showing their homes, in learning about ours. Although it was present in Tahiti and the Society Islands, the large population and influx of tourism seemed to suppress it somewhat.

In Niue the constraints had disappeared. We were honored guests and they vied for our attention. It started before we had even arrived. Still wondering if we would be able to stop or if we would have to continue our voyage for 270 more miles to Tonga, we knew that the key would be the availability of a mooring buoy in the deep protected cove on Niue's western shore. Anchoring was impossible because of the depth and no free buoy meant no stopping, which would have caused acute unhappiness aboard *Skimmer*. My radio request to the Harbor Master for permission to land was answered by a friendly female voice with a heavy Kiwi accent at the Niue Yacht Club: "Good morning *Skimmer*. Welcome to Niue. There are plenty of free mooring buoys. Pick up any of them you like and when you are settled call back and I will give you instructions on entry procedures."

Once moored, we called back and Mary gave us step-by-step instructions on how to proceed through customs and the port police. More importantly, she gave us a complete description of the Yacht Club's facilities. Showers, lunches, guided tours, cold beer.

Once onshore and checked in, we went in search of what we had come to believe must be the focal point of the entire island—the Niue Yacht Club. The first place we were guided to served the lunch and cold beer Mary had promised—but upon closer interrogation of the owner we found that this wasn't really the yacht club—it was just where they held their gatherings. The next destination was the tourist bureau where we got the keys to the cold water showers—but again, not really the yacht club. We finally figured out the true location of the yacht club was at Alofi Rentals and Taxi Service, and it consisted of a VHF radio and Mary. Mary and her husband Wally had moved from their home in New Zealand to Niue five years earlier. As far as we could tell Mary, Wally, and the smiling lady at the tourist bureau ran the whole island. They recommended the Fia Fia, an island dinner and dance put on by the ladies of Niue, and the Nature Tour given by Misa.

A van picked us up at the dinghy landing and took us to the village of Hakupu. We got a guided tour of the village with explanations of what the forces of the modern world are doing to the Niuean culture. The declining population (many of the young now go to New Zealand to seek their fortunes) has resulted in abandoned houses that dot the island.

Wahoo wrapped in banana leaves, raw fish in coconut milk, taro, steamed ferns, pigeon, pig, the list went on. But the piece de resistance was coconut crab. We'd heard many stories about this giant land crab that can weigh up to ten pounds and tear coconuts apart with its powerful claws, but this was our first encounter. They steamed it almost exactly like we cook our blue claw crabs and it tastes like stone crab. We put it on our list as a must—to learn how to catch and cook coconut crabs. Our cooks were our musicians and they played their ukuleles, drums, and other instruments as we tore into our island feast. Then women led grass-skirted children and grandchildren into the room and arranged them in mid stage to perform for us.

Coconut Crab

Fia Fia

On Misas's Nature Tour we trekked three hours through the jungly interior of Niue and around coral mounds that jutted out of incredibly fertile soil. Misa taught us three ways to trap the coconut crab, showed us two ways to catch the Niuean chickens that nest high up in trees (one way if the chicken belongs to you and another way if you are stealing it from a neighbor), and taught us how to make rope from bamboo vine. Misa had turned his family lands into a nature preserve in his efforts to keep alive the knowledge of the jungle passed on to him by his ancestors.

Shortly after our arrival a huge humpback whale gave birth to a calf near where we were moored. For five days we watched as mother and baby frolicked around our boats. We would be below deck when suddenly from the VHF: "*Skimmer*, come up and look, they are right off your bow." At first the back of the mother would be visible—then as a prelude for a deep dive the giant tail soared 20 feet above the water and glided into the depths.

The drama was repeated day after day. Occasionally the baby would leap completely out of the water. One time the mother came completely out—and waves from her descent rocked our boats. Sometimes blowing streams of water into the air, sometimes diving, and sometimes just lazing on the surface; they mesmerized us.

We hated the thought of leaving. But Niue visits can last only as long as the weather cooperates. The only protection from the sea is the island itself. As long as the wind is from the east the westward facing bay is tranquil. But when a front comes and the wind switches to the west, the anchorage at Niue becomes untenable. A low was developing over New Zealand, so we decided to head for Tonga, 270 miles west.

***

The front brought nine-foot seas. The trip was bouncy but quick, and our third day out rewarded us with three big events. First, the day started with a two for one—we woke up at sea on Thursday August 17 and by 9:00 AM it was Friday August 18. Second, the rocking finally stopped and we were treated to a spectacular view of cliffs, caves, and jutting rock islands as we arrived in Vava'u Tonga. And we completed the 10,000th mile since leaving South Carolina.

How did we skip a day without crossing the International dateline? Easy—the Tongans have decided they want to be the country that sees the new day first. They simply declared their time to be 13 hours ahead of GMT instead of 11 hours behind. This results in no time change on the clock but a one-day change ahead on the calendar.

When we first stepped ashore in Neiafu harbor I couldn't quite put my finger on what was so different. The countryside was beautiful, the people friendly and the sun was warm. Then it came to me—for the first time since leaving the Galapagos we were back in a third world country. French Polynesia has the backing of France and the Cooks and Niue have New Zealand. Tonga is on its own. Dirty streets, poorly stocked stores, and high prices on everything. What a change from little Niue.

But there were other pleasures in Tonga. Vava'u consists of a group of stunningly beautiful islands that surround one of the most protected harbors in the world. Among the islands there are hundreds of coves, bends, and isolated anchorages where we could snorkel, fish or beachwalk. After the uncertainties of our anchorages in the Cooks and Niue it was luxury to know that no matter how hard the wind blew we would be snug and protected in Tonga.

Tonga is also a huge gathering point for boats crossing the Pacific. We saw a dozen that we had lost track of. The social life reminded us of Georgetown in the Bahamas but with one real difference—this was no "chicken harbor" where anchors develop roots. Almost everyone moves on before the end of September, some to Australia but most to New Zealand.

The anchorage off the northwestern shore of Kappa was the meeting spot. Only an hour away from the bustle of Neiafu, its deep blue water, white sandy beaches, and proximity to Swallow Cave made it a natural first, last, and intermediate stop. A short dinghy ride and there it was—a small opening in the shoreline of sheer cliff. We had found Swallow Cave. The tiny entrance expanded into a cavernous interior that looked more like a cathedral than a cave. Once inside, stillness replaced the cacophony of pounding surf and we found ourselves in a wonderland of refracted light. From our dinghy we could look 30 feet into the clear water, but the real view was from below. Snorkeling, we looked down on giant stalagmites that were just as impressive as the stalactites hanging form the vaulted ceiling above. And the fish. Millions of them, a kaleidoscope of slowly swirling silver. When I'd dive down and swim through them, they ignored me and moved only enough to prevent my touching them. Each time I passed through and looked back, the kaleidoscope image had changed into another intricate shape framed against the exotic floor and walls of the cave.

Our Tongan feast at Hinakauea Beach was fun and the presentation of the food was impressive, with individual servings in neat little woven leaf baskets and exotic clam shells. But the food itself fell a little short of the mark. Despite our many exposures, neither Charlotte nor I have become converts to taro, poi poi, breadfruit, or yams—and neither of us is able to appreciate the benefits of drinking coconut juice straight from the shell instead of beer from a can.

Last Stretch of the Pacific

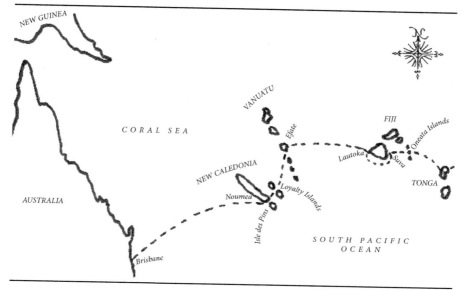

A fter months of traveling together, we had reached a fork in the trackless seas. *C'est Assez* had decided to remain in Tonga and then head south to New Zealand to wait out the hurricane season. *Skimmer* and *Aragon* had decided to continue west and spend the hurricane season in Australia.

Now Charlotte learned a new term to add to her weather watching vocabulary. We dinghied over to *C'est Assez* and *Aragon* to see if they could shed light on what "heavy convection" meant. Charlotte wanted no part of departing with the prospect of "heavy convection" lurking somewhere in our path and the heavy convection on her face and tears in her eyes broached no argument. Sympathizing with Charlotte's distress, Pat's pretty sunburned face beamed as she explained how it worked on *Aragon*. "Louis is the captain and when he makes a decision I do not question it. But if I am scared and really don't want to leave I just take off all my clothes and softly suggest, 'Let's don't leave today, baby!'"

No sooner than we had made the decision to stay than we saw a robust aluminum boat enter our anchorage. All eyes were focused on the giant fish that *Elan's* skipper was proudly holding on display. When Julie dinghied over from *C'est Assez* to get more info, no one was willing to take my bet that she would come back with dinner for all of us. When Julie returned, she not only had six of the most beautiful mackerel steaks I have ever seen, she also had the scoop on *Elan*. Scott Benerot has written a series of articles on fishing from sailboats and also a book—*The Cruiser's Handbook of Fishing*— that is the definitive work on the subject. He'd caught our dinner trolling around Tonga and I kicked myself for not having lines out during our island cruising. Over moist, grilled mackerel, red beans, and rice, we said our good-byes and early the next morning we were back riding the huge Pacific swells. Our destination was the island of Viti Levu in Fiji.

Despite articles we had read about the recent coup in Fiji we decided that it was safe to visit. More troublesome than political unrest was the geographical injustice of Fijian entry requirements. There they stood— beautiful and isolated—tempting beyond belief. The Lau Group of Islands. An oasis in the middle of the wide Pacific. But a forbidden oasis. The Fijian laws are absolutely clear on the point. Yachts must keep heading west to Suva on the island of Viti Levu—an additional two days at sea. Check-in at the Lau Group is strictly forbidden. Tempted to flaunt the laws, we watched the islands disappear beneath a red-streaked sky as we made our way west through the Oneata Passage.

Heavy rain hindered our early morning entry but this did not detract from the beauty of the enormous and well-protected harbor. Huge ships, large buildings, activity everywhere. We'd finally returned to civilization. Until we arrived in Suva, we did not realize how much we missed that. Tonga had been great, but after awhile even the most dedicated beachcombers finally get tired of sand, wild pigs and coral.

We'd read about the Royal Suva Yacht Club, but we were not prepared for what we found. Surprise number one—it was actually a yacht club. The pictures and letters along the walls in the reading room traced the process of the RSYC's obtaining royal status from Queen Elizabeth. Surprise number two had been the richness of services. The well-stocked bar served chilled Fiji Bitter on draft at fifty cents a glass. Showers actually had hot water. The dining room served excellent Chinese food. While it was evident the club had seen better days, it still maintained a graceful elegance.

Among customs that make up the culture of Fiji, none is more important or mystifying than the Kava ceremony. What looks like muddy water in a huge vat is actually ground up roots of a plant from the pepper family mixed with water. Relaxation, dizziness, and mild euphoria are symptoms that start after the second or third cup. We thought we understood how it worked and had bought several small bags of it to offer to chiefs in outlying islands, so that we could participate in their traditional hospitality. Our perspective quickly changed.

Being formally introduced by name to the congregation at the conclusion of the service at the Suva Anglican Church didn't come as a complete surprise, but what happened afterwards did. Joseph, our host, invited us to have a seat on the veranda at the rear end of the church to socialize with other members of the congregation. To our amazement, a huge Kava bowl was brought out. A layman squeezed the cheesecloth bag full of powdered Kava and the muddy substance oozed out and through his clenched fists, and we began to lose our appetites. Wishing for a coconut shell bowl only half full didn't work. An overflowing bowl of murky brown fluid was thrust towards me, and I made a loud clap of my hands, saying the ritualistic words "bula, bula"—and finally, bottoms up. Courtesy demands that it be taken in one swift gulp. Then it was my turn to watch Charlotte suffer.

Kava Ceremony

On hearing we wanted to visit the interior of the island, Father Tomasi gulped down his fifth bowl of Kava and told us about his friend Konisa who leads trips up the Navua river. We made reservations that night.

It was white water motoring and Konisa was heavy on the throttle of the 35 horsepower Yamaha. Our longboat skimmed over the rapids. But, unlike canoeing or rafting, we were going upstream. Giant boulders in the waves didn't deter Konisa—he delighted in the anxious look on Charlotte's face as he dodged rocks and we sped past a panorama of tropical jungle and crashing waterfalls to the village of Namuamua.

Stopping first at a state run school, we watched a crowd of small children running about brandishing toothbrushes and tubes of toothpaste. Our arrival coincided with hygienic hour, and the teachers took us from classroom to classroom to display their efforts working in humble surroundings with meager budgets.

***

Fiji's second largest city after Suva, Lautoka is located on the western end of Viti Levu. It was the port from which we would have to check out of the country. The ride there turned out to be more interesting than the city itself. Abdul Two appointed himself first in line and, as none of the other four Abduls or three Mohammeds objected, we got into his cab.

Abdul Two's chatter halted abruptly as we drew up to the first armed blockade. He was meekness itself, his nervous eyes darting from the husky Fijian soldier towering over his cab to the automatic weapon dangling from broad shoulders. Once the interrogation was over and the blockade was behind us, Abdul Two's boldness returned.

"Fijian mans always lazy. Never do work. You see policemen with their big guns. They always want be bigshot. I show you refuge camp where Indians live now. Fijians burn homes all up during coup. You think police they stop crazy Fijians? No, no, I am telling you, they just stand by and watch. Indians work hard, save money, able to buy house. Fijians, they just want house, they not save any money. When Fijian have money, he spend and give to friends. All Fijian want to do is drink Kava with his buddies. How many shops you see Fijian owner? I am asking you. How many? Yes, you see, no Fijian own shops. Only Indians. And this man Speights. He very bad man."

The name registered. George Speights, the Fijian Nationalist who had seized parliament at gunpoint and who had led the coup that had nearly prevented our visit. Abdul Two had our full attention as he continued. "Why Fijians no have trial? Each time supposed to have trial, judge say wait more time. You think Fijians going to do something? Maybe he in jail now, but I think nothing happen to this bad man."

Abdul Two's speech surprised us. Western Viti Levu is predominately Indian and it was our first time to get their point of view. In Suva and the predominately Fijian east, we were told that the trouble was over and it was just a question of working things out between the Fijians and Indians. The Fijian explanation was that the land originally belonged to them and they resented the enormous wealth and political clout that Indians have acquired over the past few generations. But Abdul Two's bitterness and sense of frustration painted a much deeper-rooted problem and one that will be very hard to resolve.

The two cultures are as different and as separate now as they were in the late 1880's when Indians were first bought into Fiji as indentured servants to work the sugar plantations. Since that time, through hard work and savings, the Indians have amassed power and wealth far disproportionate to their numbers. The contrast between the large, very friendly, and very relaxed Fijian and the small, very serious, and very industrious Indian is immediately apparent.

***

Corporal Samatha was large, handsome and cut a dashing figure in his fatigues and black beret. The Indian security guard and crowd of gawking taxi drivers were nervous and more than a little curious about why he had come to the marina to visit *Skimmer*. While I thought bringing a shotgun along in *Skimmer* was probably a good idea, we didn't anticipate the coup when we had made the decision. Customs at Suva was very accommodating when they received custody of the gun and assured us it would be a simple matter to reclaim it across the island at Lautoka when we were ready to depart Fiji.

It wasn't a simple matter and it took two days. Constable Arun in Lautoka explained that security was such that they could not possible ship a weapon on a bus. A trip to customs in Lautoka, a phone call to Customs in Suva, several more calls to police stations in both Lautoka and Suva and we finally had the problem worked out. Suva would send the weapon with an armed guard by taxi to the marina (at my expense of course). I would accompany the weapon and guard to the police station in Lautoka, and the police station would then hold the weapon until my departure the next day. The plan almost fell apart when Corporal Samantha and I arrived at the police station. An Indian clerk insisted he didn't want to take responsibility for the gun and it should be shipped to the armory instead. Fortunately for me, Corporal Samatha drew himself up to his full height and volubly explained to the Indian clerk in Fijian that the gun would be just fine at the police station. The scowl on his face left no maneuvering room for the deflated clerk and *Skimmer's* weapon had a new temporary home.

At 7:00 am the next morning after another cab ride into Lautoka I arrived at the police station. After 15 minutes of paperwork, the Assistant Customs Boarding Officer joined Constable Arun, the weapon and me in a cab and we then worked our way through the three police barricades to Vuda Point Marina. Each of these check points was like old home week for Constable Arun and the customs officer as they glad-handed with the soldiers on duty, but I could tell our Indian cabbie wasn't enjoying himself at all.

Fortunately the weather was beautiful the next morning and we didn't have to make the choice between a legal departure into churning seas or an illegal shelter stop in Fijian waters. Once out of Momi Bay, we began the 250-mile trip to Efate Island, Vanuatu. Twenty-five knots of powerful wind pushed us through gray skies dotted with black clouds. Our only company was an occasional seagull searching for dinner in the twelve-foot waves tipped with white foam. Our trip to Vanauatu was not only fast but another reminder that the Pacific is not pacific.

We switched over to the Kava Net that would take us the whole way to Australia. While the areas covered had changed, the format remained the same. Dedicated cruisers coordinate transmissions over the high frequency waves of their Single Side Band Radios at a set time each morning. Information exchanged includes positions and weather reports for boats under way, and location and gossip for boats at anchor.

But the Pacific Seafarers Net is something different and quite unique. Unlike the others, it's not free. The price of admission is the mental anguish caused by having to memorize long lists of frequencies and privileges; being forced to understand such erudite topics as ohms law, capacitance and inductive formulas, and various electronic circuitries and principals; and, worst of all, being required to learn the Morse Code. The latter was almost more than I was willing to pay—but somehow I struggled through the process and during one visit back home I'd obtained the coveted Ham radio operator's license. Among the brotherhood, I am now known as "Kilo Gulf 4, Echo Mike Quebec."

Unlike the other nets, the Pacific Seafarers Net is run by land-based Ham operators. From their powerful transmission stations on the West Coast of the US, they are able to reach almost anywhere in the Pacific. The operators are dedicated amateurs and scrupulous in the accuracy and timeliness of their reports. In addition to recording position and weather conditions, they record course, speed, names of those on board, and destinations. The Ham tradition has always been to assist in emergencies, and the Pacific Seafarers Net is dedicated to monitoring the progress of her chicks and making sure they arrive safely in port. Instead of vessels randomly calling in, the Net Operator conducts a roll call—and if a vessel fails to call in, the whole net begins a radio search. At the end of roll call each day, the Net Operator then puts all the information he has gathered on the internet so anyone with access can monitor the progress of vessels while underway.

There's another benefit to having a Ham license. Phone patches. The way it works is to call a Ham operator in the US with the necessary equipment and he connects the radio to his telephone and places a collect station-to-station call. The result is worldwide communications at US domestic rates. If one is lucky enough to get a Ham in the location he is calling, there's no charge at all. Charlotte has been so impressed with this arrangement that shortly after my initiation into the brotherhood, she announced her intentions to obtain a Ham license, too. I couldn't picture Charlotte attacking the necessary technical learning requirements, but she has constantly amazed me learning navigation and the mechanics of sailing. Maybe one day she will actually open up one of the three books I dug out for her when she made her startling announcement.

Our first night out we decided to try my new Ham benefit for the first time. Unfortunately, *Skimmer* can handle only one electronic marvel at a time. When my new Roberson autopilot pump is whirring and controlling the course, it emits a fairly quiet, almost pleasant, moaning noise. We love our new autopilot and call her Roberta. But when the SSB radio is on, Roberta's subtle moans become roaring hacking coughs that leap out of our radio speaker and drown any intelligible communications. As the only non-Ham operator aboard, it fell on Charlotte to don foul weather gear and step out in the howling wind to relieve Roberta of her duties while I made the phone patch.

Skimmer: "Contact"

Radio: "Go ahead contact"

Skimmer: "This is Kilo Gulf 4 Echo Mike Quebec marine mobile requesting a phone patch to Charleston, South Carolina. Over."

Radio: "This is Bob at (here he gave a call sign I don't remember). Yeah (a pause while Bob searched through the list of Pacific Seafarers Net participants to obtain my other handle) … Heyward … I have very good copy, give me the number and party you wish to call and I will put you through." I pictured Bob grinning behind his huge stack of radios and switch gear as he rotated dials and beamed his giant directional antenna towards a tiny spec in the middle of the Pacific Ocean.

I gave him my home number and waited with anticipation as I heard the numbers being dialed. Three rings and bingo—connection. I was ready to utter my greetings when the cabin of *Skimmer* was filled with the sound of a fax machine screeching its message in search of a mating machine. Rats. Our children had left the fax machine on.

***

At Vanuatu we decided to violate our most stringent rule. The only reason was that *Wild Goose*, whom we had just met over the Kava Radio Net that morning, had volunteered to vector us in by VHF when we approached. So, with fifty miles remaining to Port Vila we decided to go for broke—a night arrival in a strange port! The seas in the expanse of water between Fiji and Vanuatu continued to build and by mid-Sunday they were cresting ten feet high and Charlotte said she felt like she was in a washing machine. With the luxury of GPS, we were able to cut Pango Point fairly close, enabling us to sight the channel between the reefs off Iririki Island and Maiapoa Point in the distance during the last moments of daylight.

As darkness surrounded us, we made contact with *Wild Goose* and he helped us pick out entrance lights for the channel and distinguish them from the city lights in the background by counting cadence for each of them as they flashed. He also turned on his masthead strobe light to give us a reference point once we entered the crowded harbor. With a clear set of range lights ahead and the two lights marking the reefs, it was no problem. I turned the wheel over to Charlotte and went forward so that I could penetrate the pitch-black darkness without the interference of our instrument lights as we approached the mass of boats in the harbor. Meanwhile *Wild Goose* was telling us where various nearby boats were located so we could avoid them on our way in. He also pointed out that most of the boats at anchor did not have their anchor lights on.

While I could see ahead fairly clearly and could give Charlotte necessary helm orders to keep us away from other craft, I could not see her clearly at all. If I'd been able to, I could have told from the expression on her face that she had just gone into spin cycle. *Wild Goose* did a good job of talking us in before Charlotte had a chance to get really upset and we dropped our anchor in fifty feet of water next to our benefactor.

Vanuatu, originally named the Great Cyclades by de Bouganville, later called the New Hebrides by Captain Cook, is the modern name for the Y shaped chain of islands located some 600 miles west of Fiji and 300 miles north east of New Caledonia. The islands are steep, heavily forested and contain a number of active volcanoes. As we'd moved west, the population changed radically. Polynesian traits of tall statue, light skin, and straight hair were replaced by Melanesian traits of dark skin, curly hair and short frames. We had begun to see the mix in Tonga and Fiji. The original inhabitants of Vanuatu were all Melanesian, with the same origins as the people of New Guinea and the Solomon Islands. It was much later, beginning in the eleventh century, that the Polynesians arrived from the east in their giant oceangoing canoes.

Port Vila, the capital city, has many amenities with a wonderful mixture of French and English influences; at one time the city was jointly governed by the two countries. Port Vila seems to have inherited the best of both cultures—great French restaurants and French bread but English efficiency in government instead of chaotic French bureaucracy

But the civility of Port Vila is deceiving—in islands only a few miles away villagers live in the primitive manner their ancestors had for generations. Charlotte and I were amazed to learn that cannibalism existed in Vanuatu as recently as 1969.

On our visit to Ekasup village we were greeted by a stout warrior with a huge conch shell that he blew as he led us down a winding path through the jungle. Other warriors with fierce painted faces and sharp wooden spears leaped out of the woods, startling our group, and then posing for photographs. Once in the village we were formally greeted by the chief, and various villagers took turns demonstrating how they build their houses, how they clothe and feed themselves from what nature provides and by trapping animals. While our first impression was skepticism raised by our theatrical entry, the enthusiasm and knowledge of our hosts made it fascinating. Their objective was not only to make some money for the village but to help preserve the ways passed on by their ancestors

***

Too bad our ancestors didn't have GPS—Global Positioning System. A miracle in a tiny box. Now we have a system of navigation that mariners and astronomers even up to 50 years ago could not have dreamed of. When the network of satellites first began to beam their information in the early 1990's the world was changed. The tiny box—actually a computer and an antenna—searches the sky for the nearest five or six satellites and makes a calculation to determine its exact location. The process is analogous to a man using sextant, chronometer, and stars to calculate exact location. But here the analogy ends. GPS accuracy is measured in feet instead of miles and calculation time is measured in fractions of a second instead of hours. And the calculations are so rapid and positions are so accurate that GPS can also calculate speed and direction of travel. Our little box takes this information and plots it on a small screen map

Thus, technology has removed the largest uncertainty from vessels plying the oceans. More accurately, it has *almost* removed the uncertainty. There remains one small problem. The thousands of nautical charts that describe every detail of depth, land contour, banks, and navigational aids were created by vessels using the old sextant and chronometer. The accuracy of those positions is not nearly as precise as those calculated by the GPS. In some remote corners of the world the charts are based on surveys that date back as early as Captain Cook. So you can know you are in the right place, but you sometimes can't be sure that the reef you are trying to avoid is where the chart claims it is.it'salways a delicate balance.

On our way from Vanauatu to New Caledonia I was headed for one of those situations that I dread. We would pass through the Loyalty Islands in darkness. Was the five-mile separation between Vauvilliers Island and Oua Island within the accuracy of my charts? The fine print in the margins could be interpreted as yes or no. But I had two trump cards and the night was clear enough to allow me to use both. So with binoculars focused on the navigation lights marking the two islands and radar tuned in on a fine scale, I held my breath as we made our way through.

The real challenge was coming: two hundred and fifty miles long, stretching northwest to southeast and bristling with reefs—New Caledonia. Southeast of the mainland the Isle of Pines formed the southern jaw of a mouth so full of teeth it was hard to tell where the passage lay. I had studied and plotted, but Havana Pass still left me uncomfortable. Fierce currents, razor reefs, shifting channels. Conventional wisdom said negotiate the pass at slack tide and in full daylight.

About 3:30 in the afternoon, just as we arrived at our GPS waypoint where I should have been able to see the markers, rain started. In ten minutes our easy approach was history and we could wait outside and possibly miss a daylight approach, or enter and hope conditions improved. We choose the later. Again, GPS was our hero. Suddenly our radar was useless—rain registers just like land or ships—and for the time being we were blind. Blind or not, GPS let me track our positions so there was little danger of grounding.

It left only one real problem. And true to form Charlotte's greatest fear materialized in the form of a tanker appearing through the rain. We still argue about how close it came; Charlotte will not accept my opinion that the tanker had us in sight and could have made the avoiding maneuver if we hadn't chosen to make our 90-degree turn to port first.

For the first time since entering the South Pacific we experienced a complete change of scenery—pine trees and red hills. The island had reminded Captain Cook of Scotland and he had named it New Caledonia, the old Roman name for Scotland. The 35-mile passage that snakes from Port Boise to Noumea was stunningly beautiful.

Noumea is like a little piece of Provence dropped into the middle of the Pacific Ocean. Much as we loved French Polynesia and Tahiti, this was different. Here we were truly in a French country—the buildings, the roads, the vegetation, and the people (over a third of French origin) are almost exactly the same as in the countryside of southern France. The food is superb—a wonderful mixture of French, Vietnamese, Thai, Chinese, and Indonesian cuisines, and unlike Tahiti, the prices are almost reasonable.

Rich and Carolyn of *Sea Crane* had met a guide and arranged our tour of the island. John gave us a special price because we were able to fill his van to its capacity of eight. For the first hour of the tour, John never stopped talking. He warned us at the outset that there was so much to see and learn in the first part of the tour as we drove through Noumea and its surroundings, that it was really best to let him explain without interruptions or questions. I was so fascinated by the history, statistics, and anecdotes John was spouting out that I really didn't pay much heed to the other personalities aboard.

I had met H.J. over the VHF radio during our crossing from Vanuatu to New Caledonia and had classified him as another eccentric single-handed sailor with an Australian accent who obviously knew his way around in these waters. When John finally ran out of breath, H.J. began to satisfy the obvious curiosity of the rest of the passengers generated by his pirate garb—earrings and bandanna. He said he'd been sailing with a beautiful girl for over two years but one day she looked at his passport and discovered that he was 72 years old. "What happens to me if you die at sea" she wailed as she packed her belongings. H.J.'s rejoinder to us: "Hell, I'm only afraid of not dying at sea"—and he began recounting a story of a recent television interview of one of the oldest inhabitants of New Caledonia who in describing his most important memories told his interviewer how much he liked long pig. When the old man went on to describe how he particularly liked the wrist and fingers, realization finally dawned on the horrified interviewer of what long pig actually was and he'd abruptly terminated the interview.

When John began describing the racial mix of New Caledonia, H.J. seized the opportunity to break in with his view of political correctness in the United States. He complained of what he viewed to be a major inconsistency in permissive language: "What I can't understand is why it's perfectly okay to say 'motherfucker' at the dinner table, but try saying the N-word and everybody is shocked."

Everybody on the van was shocked and John quickly took over and somehow managed to keep H.J. under control until we finally arrived at the dinner table. It was after opening the third bottle of wine that John made his fatal mistake. The conversation had turned to sea cucumbers, and how many were shipped from Noumea to Japan where they are prized for aphrodisiac characteristics. John asked: "How about Viagra. Has anyone here tried that?" A good laugh by all and the conversation was about to take another turn when H.J. again claimed the limelight.

"Yes, I have tried it." Silence around the table as all eyes focused on H.J. "Never felt anything like that in all my life. It was like it wasn't my own. I have never worked so hard and then suddenly … you wouldn't have believed it! I'll tell you, I'll never try that again."

After choking on his glass of rose, John took control of the conversation again to refocus on the objective of our tour—New Caledonia, its sights and history.

***

Prony Bay is located on the southeastern coast of Grand Terre and is absolutely beautiful. It's four miles wide and five deep, with a coastline that twists and turns, creating little secluded coves that make it one of the best cruising areas we'd seen yet.

With the wind on our stern, we enjoyed an effortless sail past the site of an old penal colony and up to the Bay of Carenage, where we dropped our anchor in the mouth of a fresh water river. We felt like we were on the *African Queen* as we dinghied upriver past mango trees—hundreds of them standing on stilts of giant roots, looking like they were about to walk across the water. We were fascinated by thousands of tiny oysters clustered about the roots just below the waterline.

The river ended at a waterfall where we tied up to explore. The pine forests, the almost chilly air—it was a wonderfully refreshing change. With some skepticism we followed carved wooden signs pointing to thermal baths, but there they were. Just off the path on a ledge overlooking the river was a stone-lined basin with wooden seats and surrounded by pine trees. The pool was fed by a thermal well and we almost became waterlogged as we sat, read, and slept sitting on comfortable wooden seats.

Gathering Oysters *Heyward in Thermal Pool*

After two days the wind cooperated and we had a brisk passage through the reefs, arriving in the Bay of Kuto on the southern coast of the Isle of Pines. For maybe the hundredth time, we had arrived at the prettiest place in the world. It's the trees that set Isle of Pines apart. They are similar to giant Norfolk Pines, but actually are Arucarias Columnaris and only grow in the Southern Hemisphere. They look like giant arrows about to be catapulted into the heavens.

Our arrival back in Noumea coincided with the beginning of the cultural activities of the Festival des Art du Pacifique. In cultural terms, the city went nuts. Natives in costumes from everywhere—Tahiti, the Cooks, Guam, Hawaii, Tokelau and Tavalu, the Marshalls and Vanuatu, Fiji, Samoa and Niue, and the faraway Easter Islands. Aborigines from Australia, Maoris from New Zealand.

Confusion reigned. It was French disorganization at its best and islander enthusiasm at its most vocal. The opening highlight, a welcoming of the sailing canoes at Anse Vata Bay, involved two of them breaking down in the Havana Pass and three of the others deciding to make their landings somewhere else, leaving a single craft from the Cook Islands to steal the show.

Crowds were so thick that it was hard to move. Every fifty feet found a different group of drummers, singers, and dancers waiting for their turn to join the procession and march into a newly constructed grass hut village. Despite four years to prepare the show, French officials had waited until the bedlam of opening day to make programs and schedules available.

When we got to the stadium for the opening ceremony we found it had been cancelled. A cheerful policemen explained that there was no reason to worry—it would be rescheduled in a few days, probably.

Despite the chaos, the festival was fun. Each day we staked out a little space in the courtyard of the library where there was a continuous series of performances—painted faces and tattooed buttocks gyrating to the accompaniment of male voices shouting "Hukka Hukka", young girls in grass skirts with swaying hips, each group trying to outdo the other.

***

It was time to move on before the coming hurricane season. The Queen's Birthday Storm—sometimes known as the bomb—was on the minds of all. Several years ago this storm, born out of a squash zone in an offending isobar, resulted in the destruction or diversion of all the cruisers unfortunate enough to have departed for New Zealand. Thirty boats were sunk. The level of concern for those of us heading for Australia was less, but still there. The best weather window we could hope for would cover only the first half of the 750-mile trip. After that it would be a toss of the dice.

After several days of intense weather-watching, Charlotte finally agreed conditions were right. At first the Coral Sea was a piece of cake—sunny skies, low wind, and high morale. The morning of October 30 began normally and it looked like another perfect day with the trade winds on our port quarter. But two words over the Kava net changed our world: Gale Warnings! The morning weather bulletin from Brisbane announced a serious low off the north east coast of Australia. Then gale warnings were upgraded to storm warnings.

The sun was still shining, the air still warm, the seas still calm. But the sea was the only thing calm among the 20 boats strung out between Noumea and Brisbane. The projections were 60-knot winds with very rough seas. At this point, *Skimmer* was 300 miles out of Noumea. Prevailing winds made it impractical to return. We didn't know which way to turn to avoid the low, so we plowed on.

At midday, following the advise of Des on Russel Radio, we diverted north. We had come to respect Des and had been tuning into his service since we left Tonga. His deep, hoarse, Australian accented voice and ever-present good humor were always a comfort, and his predictions had been more right than wrong. So when he suggested north and then signed off with his customary "cheers and g'day" we took a 90 degree turn.

When evening came, 20 SSB's were tuned to 81180 kHz, waiting to hear where the storm would strike. *Salt Peter* drew the short straw—he was 300 miles out of Cape Moreton on the approach to Brisbane, and would be right where the eye was predicted to hit the next night. It looked like *Skimmer*'s turn to the north had been a good idea.

I was glad we had battened down the hatches. Wind came howling out of the west and we headed back south to avoid reefs to the north. We were about to congratulate ourselves with our avoidance strategy when the winds started climbing. For most of the night we were battered by 40-knot winds and 12-foot seas.

Next morning when we looked at the giant horseshoe on my chart and thought about the wind we had encountered, we wondered if the diversion had really been necessary. Then we heard what had happened to other boats over the Kava Net. *Salt Peter* had the roughest ride, but his strategy of trying to outrun the low to put himself southwest of the center had paid off. *Checkmate* fared less well with a blown sail and loss of autopilot right at the height of the storm. *Reflections* lost a sail and her forestay and limped into port with coast guard assistance.

After the storm the seas became flat and the wind so weak we were forced motor. Our biggest project became eating as much of the remaining food as possible before the strict Australian agricultural officials seized it. We elected to let the boat drift aimlessly when the motor cut out. Rack of lamb, rice, spinach, a wonderfully ripe Brie from France, accompanied by a fine Cabernet Sauvignon. This was too good to spoil—the engine could wait. Wine bottle empty, I dived back into the engine room for another bout with the gremlin.

It had been going on since we left Noumea. I thought it was contaminated fuel in the port tank and I cursed the marina in Vanuatu for selling us inferior product. After three days changing filters I decided it was an air leak, but the more I tightened suspect fittings the worse the problem became. It got to the point that the engine was shutting down every hour, and each time Charlotte would have to spring to the cockpit to trim the sails while I bled air and diesel from the engine and all over myself and into the inaccessible engine bilge. I decided that I would declare all-out war on the problem, tear the whole fuel filtration system out and rebuild it piece by piece. I began to remove the most inaccessible of the rubber hoses. On my back again and braced against the rocking of *Skimmer*, I traced the black tube as it snaked under the motor to the lift pump. About to loosen the hose clamp, I noticed that it rotated as I put pressure on the screwdriver. A light went on in my dulled mind—a fitting on the lift pump I could hardly see was loose. One quarter of a turn and it was done. Our giant Ford Lehman Diesel went back to its previous status as reliable shipmate.

During the six-hour trip through Moreton Bay, *Skimmer* left in her wake a thin line of pasta, couscous, long-conserved milk, and other forbidden products as Charlotte got us ready for customs. But, it was the meat and vegetables that were their true objective, and the inspector left *Skimmer* with a bag containing almost thirty pounds of goodies. It was a great way to clean our freezer, but we were surprised that even US and French-packaged meats had to go.

Skimmer Come out of the Wate

***

Australia was our third continent and represented 12,700 miles of travel. It was clean! Efficient! The shopping was unbelievable! Prices seemed equal to US goods except they were in Australian Dollars worth about $.50 US.

When we got *Skimmer* out of the water and onto her cradle to wait out the hurricane season, we returned home to be with family and friends for Thanksgiving and Christmas. It turned out an around-the-world ticket was actually less expensive than a back and forth ticket so we took the opportunity to visit New Zealand, to stay in Charleston until February and return to *Skimmer* via London, Moscow, Johannesburg, Cape Town, Perth and then Brisbane. Our long long crossing of the Pacific was over.

Australia's Queensland Coast

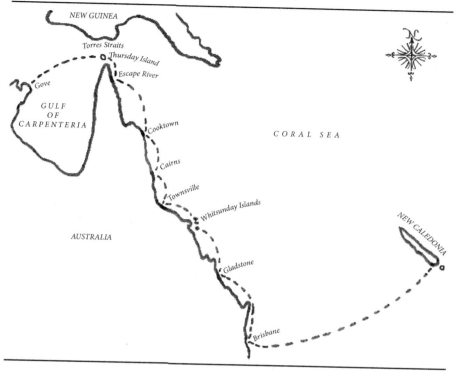

We arrived in Brisbane the next March after marathon travels through Moscow, London, Zimbabwe and South Africa—totally exhausted. After an anxious inspection of *Skimmer* in her cradle where she'd rested the past five months we sighed relief. Two weeks later and she was back in the water with fresh antifouling paint.

The reality of living on a sailboat is there is always something that can be done to make the boat better. By the time we'd returned, our wish list had become large. *Skimmer* now sported a new beefed-up bow pulpit to accommodate our new giant 65-pound CQR anchor (no more waking up in the night to anchor drag alarms), stainless steel railings on both sides of the mast, a sturdier seat for the wind generator on top of the Mizzenmast (any wind that could take it down would probably take the mast down too), and a roller furling for the cutter sail (we could now put up the storm jib without leaving the cockpit).

After impressing our neighbors with *Skimmer*'s enormous capacity for beer and wine—20 cases of Australia's finest lager and four cases of Australian Cabernets and Shirazes—we broke the weld joints that had held *Skimmer* in

Scarborough for six months and began our trek north. The plan was to hug the Queensland Coast inside the Great Barrier Reef, round the Northeastern Tip of Australia to Gove, a small town across the Gulf of Carpentaria, and join a rally of 30 boats for two weeks of exploring the wonders of the outback coast from Gove to Darwin.

***

Again, *Skimmer* had landed (for the 101st time) in the prettiest place in the world. Late one afternoon as we swung at anchor in Mourilyan Harbor, Charlotte was about to steam the two huge mud crabs we had caught in my newly acquired collapsible crab pot. Although assured by locals we met at the bait shop "sure mate, ya don't have to worry a bit—just take a hammer and look around the rocks close to where you are anchored"—I still had my doubts. I did take my hammer and the oysters were huge. I was having a great time climbing around the rocks trying to fill my bucket before the tide came in, when I remembered the rest of my newfound mate's advice: "Of course we have Crocs here, but you don't have to worry, as long as you are not in the water they won't bother you." Looking down at water rising above my ankles I decided we had enough oysters and dinghied back to *Skimmer*. We were amazed at the size. At home, oysters stuck to rocks or in clusters are so small they are not worth gathering. These looked like single selects someone had glued to the rocks—and they were everywhere—on rocks, on poles, on mangrove roots. There was the small matter of Australian law—oyster gathering without a license is permissible only when they are eaten on the spot. Charlotte prevailed and we returned the unopened oysters to nature.

***

Since leaving Brisbane we'd sailed almost a thousand miles of the Queensland coast. From Brisbane to Gladstone it's all open water unless you sail inside of Fraser, the world's largest sand island. Gladstone was an unexpected surprise. Industrial, difficult access, pollution—our cruising guide said nothing nice about it—but the guide wasn't written by Gladstonians and as far as they were concerned Gladstone was the finest place on earth. For them, being the largest industrial center north of Brisbane was a matter for boasting. We almost couldn't get out of the marina office because the manager was so insistent on what we must do and see while we visited his city.

North of Gladstone everything changed. The same treacherous reefs that had almost crushed Captain Cook during his first voyage of discovery now protected *Skimmer* from the huge waves. The Great Barrier Reef became our friend. As we headed north through the Percy and Cumberland Islands, the tropical vegetation became thicker as population thinned out.

Charlotte's sister, Jody, joined us for the stretch from Townsville to Cairns and we enjoyed introducing her to the wonders of our life afloat. The highlight of her visit was motoring through the Hitchcock Channel where we explored the mangrove swamps in our dinghy looking for crocodiles and birds.

Cairns was the last outpost of civilization and then we were in the outback

Jody and Heyward at Hitchcock

where small isolated towns stood like oases in the middle of a desert. *Skimmer's* arrival into Port Douglas on Thursday May 24 bought the population up to 3,002. The next day the population swelled to twice its size. We landed in time for the main event of the year at this outpost. Normally an Australian male needs no excuse to quaff his fair share of cold suds. But the Carnival is a different matter. For four days Port Douglas cuts loose to show the rest of Australia they've made a serious error concentrating so much growth and tourism to the south in Cairns.

By Sunday we couldn't take any more and *Skimmer* sailed on.

***

Two of our closest cruising friends were on the move. *Aragon* had just left Thursday Island for a thousand mile trip to Roti, Indonesia, and *C'est Assez* had finally dared to face the Southern Ocean to make a dash from New Zealand to Fiji. We had scheduled a radio net at 9:00 in the morning with *Aragon* so *Skimmer* could monitor her progress and record her positions. While we were unsuccessful in reaching *C'est Assez* by voice, we monitored their trip by email. When I was finally able to make contact with the Sailmail station in New South Wales, I could hardly believe what I was reading. The thing all of us dread had happened to *C'est Assez*—and naturally in the worst possible conditions. High wind on the nose, rough seas, and then they heard the dreaded radio call:

"Mayday Mayday!"

Eighteen miles off their stern, a couple and their two children wanted to abandon their sailboat. The shaft had broken and lodged itself into their rudder—no power and no steering—the crew of the damaged vessel were ready to call it quits. But for C'est Assez, approaching another sailboat in howling wind and pounding seas was almost as scary as the accident their unfortunate neighbor had just undergone. Glen and Julie were in the process of figuring out just how they were going to accomplish the impossible when help came. A small container ship had heard the distress call and responded— the family was safely hauled aboard and the boat left to founder. A happy ending for the four, but another nightmare waiting for any hapless vessel that came upon her.

As I read their e-mail, I was taken back to that inky night when we were half way through our 600-hundred-mile voyage between Fiji and Vanuatu. Out of nowhere a strobe pierced the blackness and startled me into action. How could it appear so suddenly and so bright? It must have been very low on the water. It took no more than a gentle nudge and whispered warning to bring Charlotte, clad in nightgown and safety harness, onto deck to help me. Our first actions were automatic—furl in the Genoa, start the motor, jibe around into the wind, but as the maneuver was unfolding, our dilemma became clearer.

Was it a person or vessel in distress that needed help or was it a net, long line, fishing buoy, or some other unknown object that presented a very real safety hazard? The wind and the sea were up, and there was no visibility, and as the light neared, our anxiety mounted. Since the sighting, I had been constantly signaling with a flashlight and transmitting on radio to evoke a return signal. But my efforts were rewarded with nothing but the unchanging pattern of strobe pulses. After two passes with no sign of life, we had abandoned the search, not just a little rattled. I could well sympathize with C'est Assez's concerns.

***

Our route from the Low Islands just outside of Port Douglas to Cooktown took us past Cape Tribulation and then the Hope Islands. This was where Captain Cook had met with disaster. Sighting the reefs around the Hope Islands, he decided to head for open water to the east as night was falling. His subsequent encounter with the reef that now bears the name of his ship was almost the end of what was to become one of the greatest voyages of discovery of all time. Fortunately the damage was reparable and during the seven weeks of intensive work, Joseph Banks and his team of scientists took advantage of the time to explore ashore. Who would have thought that Cook's grounding on the great barrier reef would have resulted in a new word for the English Language, but it did when the native word "gangaroo" became "kangaroo."

Even with our up-to-date charts, GPS, and electronic fathometers, we would never dare to do what *Endeavor*, under Captain Cook's guidance, routinely undertook—sailing at night in uncharted waters through reef infested areas. We got the best of it all. The locals said they had never seen better weather. Charlotte even had spells where she forgot to say her meteorological prayers. Everyday was the same—10 to 15 knots from the southeast with one to two-meter seas. This was paradise.

Sunset with the lighthouse on Low Isle shaded in rose-colored clouds gave me a wonderful view as I grilled a rack of lamb dinner on our newly renovated propane grill. The pleasure of seeing my repair job turn out successfully was almost more important than the tender Australian lamb. But, behind the serenity, there was the relentless wind! Trying to keep up with banging halyards served as a constant reminder of what was out there to greet us whenever we left port.

Cooktown marked the end of any semblance of civilization as we worked north. There the barrier reef rises in height, often permanently above water, and comes closer inshore. The mainland begins to narrow as it forms the Cape York Peninsula separating the Gulf of Carpentaria from the Coral Sea; and the vegetation changes from rainforests to arid scrub. But the main change we were experiencing was in the wind. Here conditions allow the southeast trades to develop to their full strength. Our two-day stay in Cooktown showed us why locals call it "Windtown" and quip that you can tell a native because he walks leaning at thirty degrees while the tourist is unmistakable as he rolls along like tumbleweed. If the wind is menacing in town, it can be disastrous in the harbor where it funnels down Grassy Hill to present a constant blast to anchored yachts.

One afternoon we were having popcorn in the shelter of our salon, trying not to listen to flapping lines and singing stays when we received the call: "*Skimmer, Skimmer,* this is *Kate Tee* … did you know that your dinghy has flipped?" We must have been developing a good sense of intuition because it was only a half hour earlier that we had taken the motor off and stowed it on the aft rail. *Kate Tee,* whom we had met earlier that morning while re-anchoring in howling wind, dinghied over to help us right and stow our capsized craft, and the emergency passed.

Having my new, killer 65-pound anchor, I'd felt secure that morning in leaving *Skimmer* for the day despite the buffeting winds. Our guide Justin was waiting for us at the head of the dock in front of the Kiosk Snack Bar and we boarded his shiny red four-wheel-drive vehicle for a trip to Lion's Den.

With a smile on his face and blond pony tail blowing in the wind, Justin stretched the city part of his tour out long enough to give us a history of its development and to explain its isolation. With no paved roads connecting to other towns, the only way to get there was by four-wheel drive, by air, or by boat. We then set out over hills and streams to Lion's Den, past black granite mountains, waterfalls, palm trees, and huge lakes full of water-lilies in bloom.

Outback beats redneck by miles. From the friendly signs—"You keep your dog out of my bar and I will keep my bullets out of your dog"—to the rusty beer can openers on display among old gold miners' tools. Lion's Den exuded pure outback hospitality.

Justin himself was almost more interesting than his tour. Not quite a Cooktown native—he was imported when he was one year old—he has nonetheless earned his place on the social register by excelling at various cultural activities. We were particularly interested in his description of pig hunting. "It's the dogs that do all the work. I have about seventeen. The first thing ya hear is the smellers yapping. This puts the big dogs on the scent. Once one of me big guys gets the pig in his jaws, you can hear the yelping and scuffle for a mile away—and that's when I starts running. Don't want to lose any of me dogs. Sure they have their leather collar shields, but still, I don't want to lose any of me precious warriors. So when I gets there, the first thing I do is dives onto the pig to roll him over..."

"Wait a minute," I interrupted, "what about your own leather collar? Aren't you scared of his tusks?"

"Aw no mate. I grabs his right front leg and his aft left leg and next thing ya know he's rolled. Can't do no damage with his tusks then. Neck's too short. Then out with me knife, a quick stab in his armpit and the pig's ready for eating."

In response to my question about what he does with the pig then—I was hoping to learn a new recipe—he quickly replied: "We sells them to the Germans. One dollar a kilo. Paid in cash by the truck that picks them up and sends them off to Germany. I then puts the hundred dollars in me pocket and goes home."

"But, don't you like to eat them?"

"No way, mate. Too bitter. And besides, we're scared that they carry diseases."

★

Lizard Island. A snowy white sandy beach wraps around Watson's Bay and from our very secure anchorage just off the beach we could see Captain Cook's Lookout on our left and Clam Reef on our right. Fortunately, there was much to do, because meteorological conditions in the Tasman Sea and on the Southeastern Australian coast had plotted to keep us there for several days.

Powerful wind that funneled between Cook's Lookout and a smaller peak to the west kept our anchor chain twanging as it howled over the fifty yards of absolutely flat turquoise water that separated us from land. The first day I didn't put the dinghy in the water because it was blowing so hard, but that didn't matter because Clam Reef was only a short swim away.

Although we were often tempted to say that "a reef is a reef" and "once you have seen one you have seen them all"—we know there are always fine shades of difference that makes snorkeling a unique experience each outing. Here it was giant clams that caused our gurgled "oohs" and "awhs" as we tried to communicate with tube in mouth. They were magnificent. The lips with their psychedelic colors were similar to those we had seen in the South Pacific, and it was fun to see them "clam up" when we came close—but it was their size that distinguished them. Some were as much as four feet long and weighed two to three hundred pounds. Enough clam chowder to feed a fleet!

An hour and a half of almost vertical climbing over slippery rocks and dusty hills in the hot noon sun might not at first seem appealing, but it was the highlight of our four days on the island. I was focused on how Captain Cook must have felt when he made this same climb. Trapped by the barrier reef and frantic to return to deep water, he used this high perch to pick out a narrow passage through the coral dangers. We took pictures, but they

Charlotte on Cooks Lookout

don't do the view justice. Dark brown patches with swirling foam at their edges and then a ring of light green surrounding each disturbance. These were what his ship *Endeavor* would have to avoid. Ironically, once Cook had successfully navigated his way out of the Barrier Reef, light wind and strong currents made the outside even more dangerous and he then had to get *Endeavor* back into the same waters from which he had longed to depart.

Close to Blue Lagoon, the Lizard Island Research Station was in the lee of the wind we had been experiencing since our arrival. Sponsored by the Australian Museum, the station has three laboratory buildings, a flow-through seawater aquarium system, and a fleet of boats to support reef exploration.

With facilities to house up to 28 visiting scientists and about 60 research projects a year, Lizard Island presents a real opportunity for oceanographers who like to combine business with pleasure. It was wonderful to enjoy the calm and grill steaks in the moonlight. We did some experimentation on the effect of Australian spirits on North American mariners and conclusively established that there is a relationship between physical dexterity and volumes consumed. By the time we began to grope in the darkness to determine whose dinghy was whose, Don of *Klondike* found himself to be the odd man out. With a dazed expression on his face and a dangling anchor chain in his hand, the reality simultaneously occurred to all of us. Sometime during our festive evening his dinghy's chain and anchor had parted company and his light inflatable, along with outboard motor, oars, and other essential equipment had begun a long ride straight out to sea.

With our recently purchased 10,000 candlepower spot light, Charlotte and I took Don out on our dinghy to search, but to no avail. With 35 to 40-knot winds blowing offshore, his dinghy had probably found Cook's passage before we had even begun hors d'oeuvres at the station.

After four days, we were ready to leave despite the continued strong wind warnings for the entire coastline. We almost aborted as short squalls and windblasts continued but the call of adventure won out.

We were quietly tending the sails and getting ready to jibe *Skimmer* as we began our approach to round Cape Melville when suddenly: "roar ROAR RRROOORRR ROAR roar." My mind went back to the demonstrations of the Doppler Effect in high school physics as I almost broke my neck trying to follow the rapid movement of the terrible noise machine that looked like it was going to get caught in our shrouds as it rocketed over at mast height—an Australian Coast Watch airplane. Crackling then followed a brief silence over the VHF and a cherry: "*Skimmer, Skimmer*, would ya mind please going to channel 14." As Boulder Rock and our imminent jibe came closer, "Crocodile Dundee" hotdogged his shiny red and white flying machine from cloud to cloud while he fired off a series of questions designed to see if *Skimmer* posed any real threat to the integrity of the Australian Coast Line.

Despite her shock, Charlotte was able to dig out our Australian cruising permit and with hands shaking tried to answer the questions. But try as she might she could not find an official number for our permit. It was my turn to laugh, however, when it took him three tries to finally understand and repeat back the spelling of our port of registry. I was hoping that the tongue twisting exercise he was going through trying to pronounce "Wadmalaw" would cause him as much trouble at the controls of his machine as his unexpected interruption and questions were causing me with mine. After 15 minutes of this and another buzz by (at my request for photos) the plane left us to harass some of the other yachts in our armada.

I suppose that husband and wife anchoring is always stressful, but in the case of *Skimmer* it often takes on heroic proportions. This time the cause of the argument was a wave from a fisherman aboard a prawn trawler anchored just to our starboard. Charlotte's adamant opinion was that he was signaling us not to drop our anchor and she summoned me from the bow to find out what he wanted to tell us. Our normal anchor stations are Charlotte at the helm and me forward at the anchor winch. Theoretically I am in charge and issue steering orders as we pick the safest and most tranquil resting spot for our evening in paradise.

Only grumbling a little as we started to drift away from the ideal spot I had chosen, I complied with my mate's order to call the trawler. As I had expected, there was no answer, but as I had not expected, a warm friendly voice from the ketch just behind us asked if we were having trouble. Seeing our boat careening around in circles and hearing our radio call to the trawler beside us, he wondered if something had gone wrong.

Not wanting to air marital spats over the radio, I explained that we thought we had been signaled by the trawler and were trying to reach him to find out what he wanted. Recognizing the Australian accent of our mentor and wanting to prove a point to my mistrusting mate, I decided to pose a question to him.

His reply was "Yes, he had been here before" and "Yes the spot where I had been about to drop my hook was a very nice spot." I tried not to gloat as he added that it was probably the best spot in the bay and that he would wait until after we had anchored before he would drop his hook. After we had both anchored, Alan and Patricia dinghied over and invited us to *Soleares* for coffee.

The only thing on *Skimmer* that we carry in greater quantity, spend more care in purchasing and cherish more than our supply of beer is our library of books. We devour books on explorers such as Captain Cook, accounts like *Mutiny on the Bounty* and *Men Against the Sea*, and almost feel we are personal friends of Aubrey and Maturin as we read and reread the Patrick O'Brian novels. But the most important friends in our library are our Pilots that tell us how to navigate our way safely through the waters we are sailing and through the streets we are walking.

Since reaching Australia, we felt particularly blessed with the superb Pilot by Lucas. With meticulously detailed chartlettes of anchorages, great information on places to see, and advice to mariners about routes and hazards, Lucas became a Bible to all of us as we threaded our way north among the myriad of reefs.

During our visit aboard *Soleares*, I was engrossed in Alan's account of how he had taken a design from Howard Chapell and modified it to make his Chesapeake Bay Skipjack, and was admiring his extraordinary handiwork when Charlotte, who had been in deep conversation with Patricia, felt compelled to interrupt me: "Do you know who this is?"

Soleares

"Yes, it's Alan, and he is telling me how he built this incredible boat in only just over a year", I replied, somewhat annoyed.

"No, you don't understand, it's Alan LUCAS, author of the book you spend almost all your time dissecting and studying with all your charts spread out at the nav station!"

Charlotte had done it again. While I was zeroing in on the details and technical items, she had gone to the marrow. Two of the nicest people we met in Australia were also the authors of the book we prized above all others in our library. The irony of my casual questions to Alan during our anchoring and his polite, studied responses touched both of us.

Alan had explained how to open oysters while they were still attached to the rocks, using a screwdriver and a hammer. Black Lips abound along the northern Queensland Coast, and I had just learned the only practical way to penetrate their shells—place the tip of my screwdriver on the left side of the shell just above the joint and drive the blade home with a hammer. A twisting motion and I had turned the shell, half still half stuck to the rock, into an oyster on the half shell.

We had looked up briefly and wondered who was in the eight-man inflatable with twin Mercury 90's that boarded *Soleares*, but the oysters were so good and we were having so much fun that we soon forgot about them. They didn't forget about us. Shortly after our return from oystering the giant rubber ducky nudged up to *Skimmer* and its uniformed chief made a point of not asking permission as he boarded our craft.

"How did you like the oysters?" He inquired as he took a clipboard and paperwork out of his waterproof backpack. "They were great" I responded, hoping that the fine wasn't going to be too large.

He surprised me by agreeing and stating that Black Lips were his favorite. Then, to our relief, he began to ask us the same set of questions his airborne associates had posed a few days before. It was all friendly, they declined our beer offer, and they were ready to shove off. I felt compelled to ask a final question. "Could you please show me where there is an official number on our cruising permit?" A puzzled look, a reexamination of our permit, and then: "There's no number, mate. Just the date of issue and the date of expiration."

Charlotte and I looked at each other and smiled—next time we'd be ready when Coast Watch buzzed the horizon.

Wahoo

Shortly after leaving the Flinders Islands I'd wiped cobwebs off our fishing gear. A five-foot Wahoo was irresistibly attracted by the chains of squid and the Big Kahouna teaser twisting and thrusting in our wake. With only two on board, landing a big one is challenging. With knife, gaff, bucket, and fish parts sliding back and forth across *Skimmer*'s fantail, I tried to keep my sandals partially out of the blood and guts sloshing everywhere and concentrate on cutting the fillets and not my fingers. By the time we were done, Charlotte was fed up with her job as gofer, and I was so fish-encrusted I could hardly move without spreading the contamination. That's when we heard the second whirring. Damn, I had forgotten to reel in the other line! It was a measure of how tired I'd become with my juggling act on the stern that

I decided to just leave it. With the rod screaming and the wind mounting, I decided that if nature was going to claim my prize Yousuri Lure and spool my reel, so be it.

Reefing the main got our speed down to just below seven knots, but was the wind still freshening? I rationalized that it wasn't and went aft to the rescue of my lure. Reeling in a fish when you're going seven knots isn't much fun. When my arms began to ache so much that I could hardly hold on to the rod, I put it back in its holder and again exposed my Yousuri to risk. By this time Charlotte had cleaned up the first mess and wasn't the least excited about the prospect of a second. My explanation that to save the lure I had to get the fish in fell on deaf ears.

Shipboard tension mounted as my Yousuri with giant fish attached came into sight. In order to avoid the usual "It's a beautiful tuna"—"No it's a trash Bonita" argument, I put my tuna on hold while I went below to dig out our fish identification guide. I returned to the cockpit with a big smile on my face and my finger pointing triumphantly at the photo of a beautiful Blue Fin Tuna. But I was too late. While I'd been making up my mind whether he merited our Sashimi plate, Charlie had yanked free and returned to the deep.

On our way to Shelby Bay, moderate wind pushed us over rolling seas past a site where one of history's great events occurred on May 29, 1789. It was the first time in twenty-six days that the eighteen nearly starved men of HMS Bounty's launch were able to leave the confines of their twenty-three foot open boat and walk on dry land. After naming Restoration Island in honor of the anniversary of the Restoration of King Charles the Second and in honor of their own salvation, Captain Bligh led his crew on to complete the 3,600-mile voyage from Tonga to Timor—one of the greatest feats of seamanship the world has ever seen.

As I was putting up the camera, I reminded Charlotte of how well we had it—a luxurious 42 feet with all the amenities of modern living—well, almost all. After her cold birdbath shower that morning, she seemed slightly less enthusiastic than me, but, I knew how much she had come to love our home afloat. After a tranquil night in Shelby Bay we headed for the Escape River. Fresh vegetables were gone, we were out of bread, our baker was on strike, and garbage was mounting.

***

Stark terror. I could hear it in Martha's shaky voice over the radio: "We've hiiit a rooock!"

Skimmer had been lead boat coming into the Escape River. The wind was gusting up to 30 knots, the seas were low but foamy, and it was two hours before low tide. We knew there was a bar at the mouth of the river but enough water in the channel as long as we kept in middle. We had way points set and tension was high as we approached, but the shallowest we saw was 15 feet and after what seemed an eternity we were inside the mouth of a very wide, desolate river.

Transit had followed our path almost exactly and was also safely in the river. Charlotte and I had turned our attention to figuring out just where the safe anchorage was up ahead when we received Martha's call. She was way over near the right bank of the river, near the rocks Charlotte had so studiously avoided, with red bottom paint showing and a cloud of diesel exhaust pouring from her stern.

We watched *Transit* rocking with the waves as she remained firmly in the grasp of the rocks. We had both heard vivid descriptions of similar situations where boats had slowly had their bottoms ripped out before finally becoming litter on the ocean floor. We circled back, offered comfort over the radio and tried to figure out how we could help.

While Richard tried to get his dinghy in the water so he could get a line to *Skimmer* for a yank off the rocks, we turned circles just off *Transit's* port side. It seemed like it was taking hours and the tide was still falling. When Richard announced that he was unable to get his motor on the dinghy and that the only way we could get a line to him was to come by and throw one, I faced one of those decisions we all hope we never have to make. If he was on a rock, then other rocks could easily extend out from his port side and it was sheer folly to attempt a pass close enough to throw a line. For half an hour this reasoning prevailed and we kept at a safe distance.

I am not sure what made me change my mind. I decided to act and Charlotte gave me her full support. The large diameter line was already flaked across our stern ready to tow, so all I had to do was get my 100 foot heaving line ready. I stood on our aft quarter as Charlotte began our approach. She followed my shouts as we neared—and for a moment it looked like it would work. I can still see the anxious expression on Richard's face and his outstretched arms as I heaved the line with all my strength.

It was the split second after I saw my throw was short that it happened. A deafening, sickening crunch. The looks of horror on Martha and Richard's faces as Martha cried out "Oh my God!" I thought I could actually feel our bow rising. My order to Charlotte to turn hard to port was unnecessary. She had all 82of *Skimmer's* horses straining to push her off and after two more crunches that squeeezed my soul, *Skimmer* was free.

Shortly afterwards two pearl farmers arrived in small boat, towed an anchor from Transit to deep water, and stood by as Richard winched her to freedom. I was shaking like a leaf. Our world had suddenly come crashing down. My worst nightmare had materialized and in a desolate corner of rural Australia. *Skimmer* had been violated. How bad was the damage? Was she in danger of sinking? Where could we possibly get it fixed? As we limped our way up the river to find a safe anchorage depression began to set in.

But once anchored and fortified by beer and popcorn, the reasoning side of my brain took over and I began to assess the damage. Although my initial check of the bilge after our grounding had indicated no major flooding, my more detailed inspection revealed that we were leaking—*Skimmer* had been holed!

The stream of water was as wide as a pencil. But how serious was the leak? The water level wasn't rising so it was obviously within the capacity of our bilge pump. Leaning over the side, I held a pot under the bilge discharge opening while Charlotte timed how long it took to fill it. We pumped the bilge dry, waited ten minutes, and timed how long it took to empty it again. Our leak rate was 10 gallons per hour. Serious, but not catastrophic.

We were up until midnight digging out piles of supplies as we tried to inspect the hull. We emptied the galley area—floor boards up, cans, bottles, and boxes came out and filled the middle part of the boat. When bare hull was finally exposed, we could see water coming from somewhere forward. Then we had to put everything back before we could get to the next area forward and repeat the same exercise. After three hours tearing the boat up in this manner, we found one area near the mast that accounted for about a third of our leak. Logic set in. Yes, we were leaking, but the rate was constant and was within the capacity of our bilge pump. On top of that we had two extra electric bilge pumps (each much larger than the one in operation) and one high capacity hand pump. Skimmer was in no immediate danger but we wouldn't be able to assess the damage until I went over the side to inspect. Even if I were crazy enough to suggest it, Charlotte would never have let me go into the murky crocodile-infested waters of the Escape River. Inspection had to wait until our arrival at Thursday Island.

The following morning, still pretty glum, we set off for Thursday Island with *Transit* and *Kamal* close behind ready to render assistance. I had reefed to the maximum to prevent any further stress in the 30-knot winds. It was an exhilarating ride through Alban Pass before sighting Cape York and rounding the northwest most point of Continental Australia.

By 4:00 p.m. we were anchored off Horn Island. The water was clear and I was tempted, but were there crocodiles? The wind was screaming through our anchorage, it was getting late, and I had no appetite to tempt the unknown. John of *Knockjohn* had tipped us off about the smorgasbord at the Gateway Motel and we got there in time for happy hour. Where was everybody? After several loud calls, a bartender finally appeared. With beer in hand, I began my inquiries. The Chinese bartender looked local

"We are in a sailboat anchored in the harbor and I wondered if there is a problem with crocodiles?"

A blank stare from the bartender and then his reply: "No, Clockodiles plotected." After rephrasing my question several times and getting the same reply, I explained that my concern was not in finding a Crocodile to eat, but rather was about not being eaten myself if I dove off my boat.

Mr. Lee finally became animated: "Ha, Ha, no. No wolly Clockodile! Here many fishies, Clockodile eat velly, velly good. No, no wolly clockodile. Wolly Saalk!"

I realized I would have to get my information elsewhere. That evening as the yachties starting pouring in for the big feed, I got a better picture of our situation. *Knockjohn* was the longest Horn Island resident present (almost four days) and they had seen crocs, but not near our boat. They suggested that I talk with the Thursday Island Ferry Captain in the morning, as he was the resident expert. This was the third time I had been given the ferry Captain's name in reply to questions about local

Thursday Island

knowledge—repair jobs, ideal tides for departure, places to get a boat hauled. Early Monday I was at the pier and wasn't disappointed at the enormous amount of knowledge Captain Greg had at his fingertips.

"No, mate, not where you are. Crocks are no problem there. Diving near boats is no problem. Crocs stay away from them, don't like the noise." After running the engine for half an hour, I went over with mask and snorkel. Charlotte beat on the hull with a hammer while I made my lightning-fast inspection.

A hole on the leading edge of the keel about three inches in diameter and about one inch deep. Localized with no cracks coming off it. Shiny lead visible. Our damage was minor. Nothing structural, just a puncture of the encapsulation surrounding our lead keel. A temporary patch would get us to Darwin where we could make a complete repair.

News of the dual groundings had spread like wildfire over the radio waves. We were touched by offers to help. *Southern Change* would divert their path from Adolphus Island to Thursday Island to meet us at Albany Pass with their high capacity portable gasoline pump. *Cinnabar* and *Capers* had underwater epoxy to throw in with the stock already offered by *Kamal*. I had all the supplies and expert advice I could hope for. With *Kamal* and *Transit* mixing dough balls of underwater epoxy, I donned scuba gear and began a series of dives to jam the gray goo into the hole.

I wished Captain Greg hadn't added the bit about how you can always see a Croc coming if it's swimming from the shore because it has to stay on the surface to breathe. But if it's lying on the bottom stalking, then it doesn't need oxygen and can stay like that for days. Despite the fact that Captain Greg didn't think there would be any stalkers around our anchorage, I worked fast and spent a good portion of my time looking down at the bottom.

Over the Top

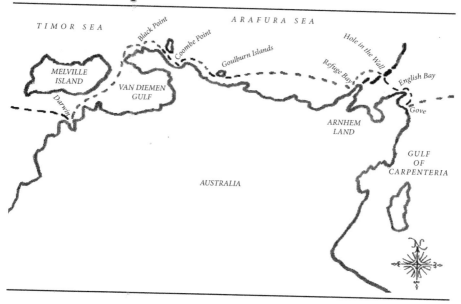

There is always a precipice ahead. A plunge of unknown proportions and the only certainty is that it will have to be faced. The one facing *Skimmer* for the past two months was the 340 miles between Thursday Island and Gove. We had read about the Torres Straits where the strongest and most prolonged trade winds in the world churn the 60-mile corridor between Australia and New Guinea. Our experiences of the last few days had borne out this statistic, and when we left our anchorage under heavily reefed sails it was in anticipation of rough going. Much to our delight, smooth seas and moderate winds greeted us. Maybe this was going to be a smooth one!

We felt we deserved it. In addition to the grounding there had been other problems. The Gremlin attacking our VHF had chosen the moment *Transit* had hit the rocks. It had left us the ability to receive but made transmission all but impossible. Backups are an important part of life afloat and two portable VHF's are permanent members of *Skimmer's* inventory. When these units are fully charged and somewhat laboriously set to the right channel and power level, they are great for short distances. But it's the permanently installed VHF with its antenna perched high above the sea that's the lifeblood of emergency communications at sea. So, setting out across the Gulf of Carpentaria we had very good ears but limited ability to squawk.

Our honeymoon in the Gulf of Carpentaria ended in about the middle of Charlotte's first night watch. Our practice was to go to the third reef on the main, second reef on the mizzen, and heavily reef the Genoa just before dark, no matter how calm the weather. Charlotte didn't panic when the wind started howling and seas began to toss us around. She was in fact so "together" that she went below to plot our position.

By this time she had the routine down cold and had already written out the coordinates—10 degrees 52 minutes South, 142 degrees 32 minutes East—when our VHF ears pierced the silence of our dimly lit cabin: "Vessel at 10 degrees 52 minutes South, 142 degrees 32 minutes East, this is Australian Warship—do you read me?"

Charlotte almost stabbed herself with the dividers as she leapt up from the nav station and seized one of our hand-held VHF's. After what seemed an eternity of trying various combinations with the unfamiliar buttons and knobs on the unit, she finally managed to transmit. She was sure she was transmitting because our stationary VHF, turned to max volume, not only picked up her message but added a screeching feedback that greatly assisted in rising the already high level of hysteria on board *Skimmer*. I was startled awake by Charlotte's, "Australian Warship, this is *Skimmer* and we are the vessel at 10 degrees 52 minutes South, 142 degrees 32 minutes East." I got out of bed thinking that Charlotte's voice had been so strong and her message delivered with such heartfelt sincerity that it could have probably gotten to the warship even without a radio. I was wrong.

Each time the Australian warship repeated its inquiry and failed to get our reply, the exact coordinates it was giving glowed so brightly on the screen of our GPS that they almost hurt my eyes. Three challenges with no perceived reply. Did this mean a shot over our bow? With our coordinates in his computer he certainly had a good fire control solution!

At this point *Southerly Change*, hearing our attempts to answer the Australian warship, entered into the fray on our behalf: "Australian Warship, this is *Southerly Change*, do you read me?

"*Southerly Change, Southerly Change*, this is Australian Warship. Are you the vessel at 10 degrees 52 minutes South, 142 degrees 32 minutes East?"

Charlotte and I exchanged relieved glances as we waited for *Southerly Change*'s reply and explanation. But it never came. Apparently the Gremlins didn't confine their work to only *Skimmer* and a very long silence followed the warship's transmission. The Australian warship had not heard!

Before panic could set in again, *Transit* picked up the ball: "Australian Warship, Australian Warship, this is sailing vessel *Transit*. I am not the vessel at 10 degrees 52 minutes South, 142 degrees 32 minutes East but I am sailing next to her. The vessel is *Skimmer* and she is having radio problems, but I would be happy to relay your questions." After the long series of routine questions, the Australian warship asked *Transit* if they had seen anything unusual since leaving Horn Island. Richard's reply: "no, nothing unusual ... except a warship in our midst!"

During the remainder of Charlotte's watch the red running light stayed clearly visible off our starboard quarter, and she hoped that Richard's wit had not angered the Aussies. Shortly after my watch began the red light faded and I put the incident out of my mind . But two hours later a white light appeared over the horizon and slowly a red light began to materialize just below and aft of it. This in itself would not have been a huge cause of concern except that the corresponding blip on my radar had been getting steadily closer with no change in bearing. Even the dullest midshipman learns early in his career that decreasing range and steady bearing leads to collision.

It was probably the warship back to stalk us again—and surely he saw us—but could I be certain? When the distance between the red light and *Skimmer* became less than a mile, my anxiety level rose. It hadn't been easy to get all my electronic instruments to talk to each other, but I had made it a major priority during the rebuilding of *Skimmer*. My GPS keeps my Radar informed of *Skimmer*'s exact location at all times, and since my Radar is very smart and keeps track of vessels around us, it can also tell me the exact coordinates of these vessels. With the cursor of my radar on the appropriate blip, I picked up the handheld VHF and inquired: "Vessel at 10 degrees 56 minutes South, 140 degrees 16 minutes East, this is the sailing vessel *Skimmer* on your port side. Do you read me?"

The silence over my radio after my repeated question was not matched by silence from our aft cabin where I thought Charlotte was quietly sleeping. She was up in a flash, and quickly came into the main cabin as she donned her safety harness and began to clear for action. My assurance to her that it was almost certainly the warship and that, as before, they couldn't hear our VHF, fell on deaf ears. My rapid surgery on our wounded VHF's mike resulted in my holding several pieces in one hand as screws and screwdriver rattled around a bowl in my other hand. A little tape here and there, some gentle pressure on the mike's keying switch and ... we were finally in contact with the Australian warship.

"Yes, *Skimmer*, we are the vessel at 10 degrees 56 minutes South, 140 degrees 16 minutes East on your port. How can we help you?" Instead of telling them that they were not only giving us a bad scare but also jeopardizing my marriage, and that they could be of most assistance by removing themselves to the other side of the Arafura Sea, I settled for: "You were getting very close and I just wanted to make sure that you saw us."

"Roger that *Skimmer*. We see you. Have a nice evening."

Even after all that, it wasn't over. The red light slowly drew astern, turned into a green light and then finally into a white light as it sank over the horizon. "At last," I thought and turned my attention to different matters. But an hour or so later, there it was again. A blip coming straight at me down a radial line on my radar. This time the light was green. And again the same dilemma. Fine if it was the Australian ship and he was watching me, but what if it were a fishing vessel with no one at the wheel? Same drill—except this time I had a working mike and struck pay dirt with my first inquiry. "*Skimmer, Skimmer,* this is Australian Warship on your port side and yes we see you. Do you require assistance?"

The question struck me as odd—why should they think I needed assistance? But I let it drop and told them that all was well aboard *Skimmer* and I just wanted to make sure they saw me. That was the last we saw of them.

The next morning during our radio net with *Transit, Kamal,* and *Southerly Change,* the ship was the chief topic of our conversations. All three boats had heard everything, and each boat had its own theory as to why. Charlotte and I chose to accept that put forth by *Transit.* Apparently someone on either Thursday Island or Horn Island (I had talked to every repair facility on both islands about my leak to obtain their suggestions for a repair job) had been concerned for our safety and had alerted the Australian Navy of our problem. The ship, standing by anyway, decided to shepherd us safely along our way. And who most likely to make the call than our friend Greg, the Ferry Captain?

***

They were like nothing we had seen before. Our introduction was during the All Pacific Cultural Festival in New Caledonia. There were entertainers from everywhere in the Pacific—from the pure Polynesian golden brown and giant physique that had become familiar to us in the Marquesas and in Tahiti, to the darker complexioned stocky Melanesians we'd seen in Vanuatu. Among them had been a continuity in dress—bright colored flower shirts for men and Mother Hubbard missionary dresses for the women.

Now we saw people utterly different from any we'd seen anywhere. They were the blackest black, with physical features light-years apart from their neighbors: Aborigines!

Since arriving in Australia our contact with Aborigines had been slight. It was only after we hit the remote northeastern coast that we began to learn about their culture. Until then most of our learning had come from signs we had seen in parks explaining far-fetched stories about how animals, birds, and fish interacted with geology and topography to create the world they saw around themselves. The stories were often so outlandish that we had a hard time concentrating enough to get to the end. Kipling's *Just So Stories* seem like absolute fact compared to these Aboriginal fantasies.

We'd tried to gain an understanding of Aborigines by talking with white Australians, but this had not been rewarding. Whites generally expressed guilt about the tragedy that western civilization had bought on these unfortunate people, but that didn't seem to be accompanied by much compassion or genuine interest in them. It was a delicate topic we'd learned not to pursue too diligently.

Although the Northern Territory comprises 17 percent of Australia, it doesn't merit the official status of a state because it's so sparsely populated. Gove is in a huge area on the northwestern edge of the territory known as Arnhem Land—an Aboriginal territory that can only be entered with a permit. It is remote, wild, and beautiful. Europeans probably wouldn't be there at all if nature hadn't deposited one of the largest reserves of bauxite in the world. Bauxite means aluminum and these deposits are at one of the best natural harbors in Northern Australia. After getting a long-term lease with the Aborigines, the giant company Nabalco transformed Wargarpunda Point into the world's largest alumina plant.

The compact, self-sufficient town of Nhulunbuy followed the plant and in the natural course of events a yacht club followed the town. We were guests of the Gove Yacht Club and did not have to seek the special permits that make land travel into this region so difficult. The reason that *Skimmer* and thirty other cruising yachts had converged on Gove was to participate in the famous Over the Top Cruise. Warwick, Helen, and "Monkey" Bill had been tasked

Monkey Bill

with organizing permits, social events, and cultural outings so that we would truly experience the many wonders of Arnhem Land and other Aboriginal territories as we enjoyed our twelve day slow pace sailing, fast pace social, cruise to Darwin.

Our first Aboriginal experience: the deep resonating sounds from a long cylindrical wooden instrument—a didgeridoo—seemed to put the dancers as well as the audience in a trance. Half-naked bodies, faces adorned with white powder, glided across the beach in jerky motions. After the performance, I went over to the portion of the bar that Aborigines had staked out for themselves and complimented their leader Merlin on her wonderful performance. Soon we were making gallant efforts to carry on a conversation. Merlin's state of inebriation didn't help, but the main obstacle was language. In that region there are over a hundred different languages. It's only recently their children have been taught English; the result is a generation that is culturally isolated

Our education deepened when we visited the Aboriginal Art Center in Gove. Will Stubs, the white curator, spoke in sentences that ran together as he gave us a very articulate, very confusing, and very long description of the wonderful collection or Aboriginal art at the center and of the Aboriginal way of life. It was a stream of consciousness articulated in his interpretation of Dreamtime—the Aboriginal spiritual realm. Will then began a diatribe against the evils of the Australians and how they have systematically despoiled the innocent Aborigines. He said the natives of Arnhem Land had been repeatedly robbed by the white man until the menace of a Japanese Army turned the tables. With invasion seemingly imminent, the Australians were happy to turn over ownership of the land to the Aborigines and then leave them to defend it with spears as they retreated to the south.

In the sixties when the alumina plant was built, Will said the Australians changed their mind and took back ownership of the land—and ever since they have been denuding the land and polluting the environment with their factory.

Two days later Lynne Walker, Public Relations Officer for Nabalco, described the harmony of man, beast, and nature Nabalco has bought about in their land reclamation program. She showed how giant earth levelers had smoothed the land—now 15 feet lower than it had been before the bauxite was removed and how other machines had planted trees and plants. She claimed all this was done under the guidance of Aborigines and told us how pleased they were with the program. She also said the Aborigines did not technically own the land, but Nabalco paid them very generous royalties anyway. Ten million a year on a two billion dollar plant didn't seem very generous to me. As we were leaving I told Lynn how much I had enjoyed seeing the Aborigine Art Center a few days before. She smiled and said, "So, you met Will Stubs. Did he tell you he was a litigation lawyer before he entered his Aborigine life?"

At this point, Charlotte and I both felt a profound sympathy for the Aborigines. Without work or purpose, but subsidized to a point where money is no problem, Aborigines seem swept into a downward spiral. We hoped to get a clearer view after we departed the unreal environment at Gove.

We'd participate in their natural state during our 30-boat cruise among the Wessel, Crocodile, and Goburn Islands. Our Fleet Admiral was "Monkey" Bill, whose white handlebar mustache quivered as he warned of the dangers we'd encounter. He told us of quick death from Blue Ring Octopuses, slow torture from Box Jelly Fish and almost certain fatality from stepping on a Stone Fish. It explained why he always wore thick white socks with his sandals.

Charlotte Reads About Dangers

***

"The Top" is a vast section of mainland and islands bordered by the Gulf of Carpentaria on the East and Van Diemen Gulf on the West. It is shaped like an anvil perched on top of the Australian Continent with its horn, the Cobourg Peninsula, pointing west towards Indonesia and its base trailed by fingers pointing east towards New Guinea.

Our initial cruising grounds were the islands that form the fingers jutting northeast into the Arafura Sea. Half the town of Gove was there to watch 30 boats sail out into large choppy waves coming in from the Arafura Sea.

Tides among these finger islands can be as much as nine or ten feet, making strong currents. Nowhere are they more pronounced than in Gugari Rip, more commonly known as the Hole in the Wall, a narrow, two-mile channel where currents can reach almost ten knots. Bill had admonished us to not even think about entering until the entire passage had opened up and we could see down its length—"looks like a bleed'n 'ole in the rocks!"

Negotiating the rip itself was plenty of excitement. But add 30 boats propelled by 25-knot winds on their sterns and the result is pandemonium. It was understood that we were to enter the narrow pass in single file and Charlotte was becoming very nervous as boat after boat streaked by our heavily reefed vessel as they jockeyed for position. Wind on the stern means wide swings and as the boats yawed and pitched their way forward we often found the bow of one pointed right at us, or our nose on a stern as we maneuvered.

Hole in the Wall

But, once in the channel, keeping from running down the boat in front turned out to be the real problem. Over beer that evening there were lots of theories on how to slow a boat down with the wind on the stern. Sheet in the main quickly (works well if it can be done very rapidly, but any delay can cause a loss of control), drop a sail (not easy in the middle of a narrow channel), start the motor and throw it in hard reverse, or jibe around and get out of the line as *Capers* did just before entering the rip—there are many methods, but none to our taste. During the heat of the passage both Charlotte and I vowed: "never again—this is the last rally!" But time heals all and by the time we were ashore exploring and looking for oysters we had put it behind and were ready for the next passage.

***

For dedicated stalkers of edible sea creatures, the Top is paradise. The boats in our fleet were hauling in mackerel, tuna, and wahoo in such quantities all freezers were full, and many cruisers were actually releasing. Oysters were so plentiful that all it took was a bucket, screwdriver, and hammer to provide dinner.

The rocky surfaces with thick prickly brush made the going tough. The oysters I had expected to see covering the huge boulders along the shore simply weren't there. Another Monkey Bill fish story? I started examining each rock in detail. And there they were. Mud brown, almost the same color as the rock, and so long and flat that they could easily be missed. Only one or two per rock, but there were lots of rocks and I was hard at it when Bill finally appeared.

"Them's only babies you got there mate—look UNDER the rocks and you'll find REAL oysters!" And I did. Several dozen under each of the rocks, and they were huge. The mother load! By this time I had learned to find just the right spot to place the blade of the screwdriver before giving it a sharp rap, and in less time than it took Bill to finish his last beer I had my bucket filled with beautiful huge black lips on the half shell. That night, to repay Bill for his guidance, I showed him how to make a REAL file' gumbo.

Monkey Bill was in his element as he led our expedition onto the flats hunting mud crabs. With long sticks with a large hook at the end of each, about 30 of us set out with buckets. "I just looks for a 'ole and 'e's in there for sure. I then puts me stick in, turns it gently so's to get me 'ook behind the crab, and then slowly I pulls 'im out." The trick was finding the right hole.

With 20-foot tides, extensive flats, and lurking crocodiles, logistics were not easy. But Bill had a plan. He first warned us to leave all dogs behind—unless the owners wanted to donate their pets to the local crocodile community. It took

Heyward and Charlotte after Mud Crabs

Bill much longer than I expected to find the first hole and then another 15 minutes to coach the crab out with his stick. I didn't see how we were going to fill the buckets. After the second crab I began to tire of the slow pace and Bill's explanations that the cyclone last year must have ruined the crabbing. "I tell ya mate, see where they's just sand and a few roots. Last year it warn't nothing but mangroves and they was all swarming with crabs." I decided to head out on my own to see if I could have better luck.

In just the sort of thick mangrove swamp that Bill lamented was destroyed by the cyclone I found a five-pounder. Under a clump of roots he was more the size of a small dog than any crab I'd seen. I was getting my stick ready when he lunged. Bill had shown me how to work the stick in the hole, but when I was down on my knees in the mud with my arm in the hole past my elbow and still not having any luck, I started thinking about the lurking crocs and decided to give it up.

It was a somewhat angry Monkey Bill who met me on my return to the beach. With two lonely crabs in his bucket, he was upset that his plans to extract his crabbing party form the beach had been foiled by stragglers like me. But his true wrath was aimed at the large group of crabbers stranded on a beach quite a distance apart from us.

The whole terrain had changed dramatically. The quarter-mile walk to the dinghies was now six feet under water. Bill's scolding was forgotten as he approached the group and perceived that their three buckets were full to the brim with large mud crabs. It turned out there was another crab expert, Ron of *Off Beat*. While Monkey Bill was out searching for holes, Ron had been waiting for the change of tides at a spot where he had anticipated that crabs would be coming from the mangroves. I can just hear Monkey Bill on next year's rally: "Ya just picks a spot outside of the mangroves and waits for the tide to start coming in. Then ya will see 'em swarming. All ya 'as to do is reach down and fill 'ya buckets. It's bloody marvelous!"

We had an exhilarating ride through Van Diemen's Gulf and into Darwin. Bill had planned our passage around Cape Don and entry into the Gulf to coincide with the beginning of the powerful flood tide. By the time we were in the middle, an equally powerful ebb tide spit us through Clarence Strait. Just as we entered Beagle Gulf, a third change in tides carried us all the way into Darwin. Our boost was as much as eight knots giving us a boat speed sometimes over 15 knots.

***

It was Australia at its finest. It was Cruising at its best. An act of selfless generosity and *Skimmer* was the beneficiary. Since our unfortunate episode at the Escape River, *Skimmer* had attracted a great deal of attention and sympathy. It had started with our arrival at Horne Island in the Torres Straits and continued to build as the fleet gathered in Gove for the rally.

Determined to get the hole in our keel fixed immediately in remote Horne Island, I had approached the huge unloading facility with cautious optimism. Saturday morning of the long weekend for the Queen's Birthday was not ideal timing, but Winnie, the manager, delayed locking the facility long enough to hear my plea.

I coldn't help noticing the intricate tattoos that began like argyle socks around his ankles and worked their way into snakes climbing up his legs. Winnie was all sympathy when I explained how we grounded *Skimmer* on a rock. He immediately picked up the phone and called the Plant Director at his home, distilling my long, pained explanation into: "Hi Bruce, got a bloke 'ere who's got a 'ole in 'is boat. Wants us to lift 'im out with the crane." Silence then, "Oh, no worries Bruce, we just puts a line on his bow and points 'er into the wind. Of course the masts gotta come down so we can get the cradle over 'er."

Visions of *Skimmer* suspended below the yellow crane in his plant made me realize that permanent repairs would have to wait, and swimming with the crocs to patch her wouldn't really be that bad. At Gove, with its large tides, there had been the option of careening *Skimmer*. But this would have given us only a few hours of dryness at a time, not enough to make the proper repair. The only real option was to be hauled out at the shipyard at Darwin and spend a week doing the job right. I'd simply have to live with the hole until then.

Each of the 31 boats in the rally gave their advice on exactly what we should do. Both Charlotte and I were beginning to get a little embarrassed about our notoriety and wanted to be left alone to solve our problem. That changed during the evening of our farewell dinner and awards presentation in Darwin at the conclusion of the Over the Top Rally.

Skimmer after Shipyard Repairs

Peter and Jan of *Penyllan* are retired schoolteachers from Melbourne. The VHF trivia quiz that buzzed over the radio at noon on every day of the rally had not really been a contest at all. They were determined to win the grand prize—a haul out, pressure wash, and free berthing for a week at the Sadgrove Quay Shipyard. They wanted to win—and give the prize to *Skimmer*. *Skimmer* had been wounded helping a boat in distress and they were going to help *Skimmer*. Three weeks of repairs in the shipyard left *Skimmer* in better shape than ever and us relaxed and ready for the next adventure.

The morning of July 23 *Skimmer* was just about to cast off—and suddenly we saw an Australian friend running down the dock waving a newspaper in his hand as he shouted the headlines: "Wahid removed from office, Megawati takes over, Martial Law Declared in Indonesia!"

A quick radio call to our new travel companions, George and Sara on *Kemo Sabay*, who had left an hour earlier and were cruising in lazy circles waiting for us, and an equally quick decision. We had already decided to avoid the trouble spots of Timor and Jakarta and concluded that the quiet island of Roti would be totally unconcerned with the current crisis. Moments later we cast off.

Indonesia

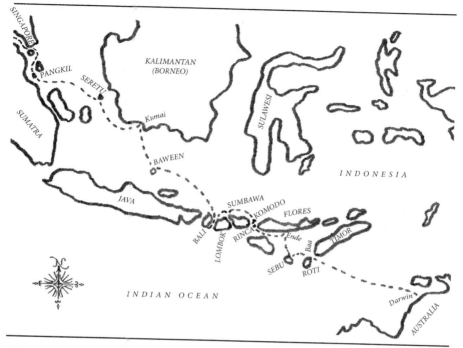

In the center three slender young women in long black skirts and white blouses and two young men in flowered short sleeve shirts. On the right, drums, electric keyboards, base guitar, speakers. We'd tried to sit in the back but had been led to the front as guests of honor. Voices and instruments became alive and the text of hymns in Bahasa Indonesian were projected against the white front wall of the church. The congregation joined in: "Yesus Alelulia" in increasing volume and mounting emotion.

When Schiller wrote his *Ode to Joy* and Beethoven set it to music, they must have had in mind the kind of joy that pervaded the Pentecostal church of Baa, Roti, that Sunday. Hymn after hymn, it was never going to end. The tempo couldn't possibly keep increasing, but it did. No one took notice of the dog as he chased the lizard up into the chancel and caught it next to the tapping foot of the drummer. The music didn't skip a beat when the power went out. The keyboard players switched to guitars and lack of electronic amplification was more than compensated for by increase in zeal.

Indonesia's political upheaval, its poverty, its problems—all were left behind as the people packed into Baa's Pentecostal Christian Church expressing their joy in their lives and in their religion. They prayed for the young doctor for whom they were raising money to send to Jakarta to continue his studies in special fields so that he could bring the knowledge back to Baa, and they prayed for their politicians in Java, and they prayed for their visitors from overseas.

***

From occident to orient, affluence to poverty, English to totally unfamiliar Bahasa Indonesian. From sophisticated government to political chaos. Only 470 miles from Darwin, *Skimmer* was in another world.

We kicked ourselves for not getting a better phrase book before we left Australia and had to accept the frustration of making new friends with so many questions unanswered.

After two days at our quiet little anchorage, we had set out with George and Sara of *Kemo Sabay* to explore the island. Our destination was Baa, the largest city on the island, located on the north central coast. Friends on another boat that had visited Baa a week earlier had alerted Cenda that we would be coming and had asked her to keep an eye out for us. We met her as she was coming home from school. About fifteen years old, very pretty and very friendly, she was the first person we had met in Roti who spoke English.

Cenda translated as we arranged our island tour at Ebenezer's restaurant. Three hundred thousand Rupiah seemed steep for a Bemo (minibus) for two days, but we did the arithmetic and decided that $15.00 US per day wasn't really that bad. We were happy to find that lunch and beer for the four of us had come to about $8.00 US.

George, Driver, Charlotte, Cenda, and Guides

The Bemo arrived after lunch. Its stenciled exterior was a bright purple shined to a blinding luster, with four maroon antennas jutting ten feet up from the rear bumper. The interior was equally elegant. A string of ten gold CD's were tastefully displayed among the miniature stuffed ducks; a dog doll with a swiveling head peered from the menagerie. In the rear two long benches provided seating for up to twelve passengers. Along the seaside, wooden houses with roofs of thatched Lontar Palm were interspersed with tin roofed concrete structures. Stretches

128

of horizontally laid palm-frond fences gave way to stacked coral walls as we headed for Batu Thermanu.

To say the music roared as it blasted out of four twelve-inch woofers under my bench would be an understatement. My lungs seemed to throb with the beat. Indonesian Pop, Heavy Metal, and other head-banging melodies turned our Bemo into a mobile boom box. The little dog's head wagged in beat with the music and lurching motion as we sped around bends and over potholes.

At Oeseli we saw inverted pyramid-shaped rocks as big as boxcars sitting on coral banks with surf swirling around their pointed bases. A small lagoon behind the rocks was home to a huge seaweed farming operation and I took photographs of gaily-clad elderly women harvesting piles of glowing green from lines on a grid of stakes crisscrossing the lagoon.

At Batu Thermanu, Charlotte and Sara, conforming to local customs, jumped into the thermal

Oeseli

baths fully clad in skirts and blouses, while George and I had the luxury of removing our shirts.

***

A gentle breeze against my face, morning coffee hot and tasty. From my perch in the companionway I watched the light, pink morning sky outline a long range of steep mountains rising from the sea. The sun's first rays broke through the clouds illuminating the mountains. We had arrived at Ende. A lone dugout came out of the haze and circled lazily in the distance.

Ende is gifted with a large, well protected bay and is one of the major ports of Flores. Our early morning entry was into a bustling harbor jammed with boats of almost every description except modern. Dugouts, junks, large, small, oars, paddles, sails. A rainbow of colors, a scene of intense activity.

We rigged the dinghy and picked up George and Sara of *Kemo Sabay* to begin exploring. We wanted to find a guide to take us to the volcanic lakes of Kelimutu and knew it wouldn't be easy, but a lone motorbike stopped and an nicely dressed man in a black helmet addressed us in flawless English. Had we seen the Maritime Museum and did we need any assistance?

We couldn't believe our luck. He led us to a Chinese restaurant that he claimed had the best food in Ende, and we learned over a delicious lunch at the restaurant that Gabriel was not only the curator and founder of the Ende Maritime Museum but also a Catholic priest. When Charlotte and Sara set off to visit the Maritime Museum, George and I set out on a search for diesel fuel. As the Bemo dropped us off at a large service station near the airport, I began to regret not getting Father Gabriel to write down exactly what we wanted. The attendants quickly understood we wanted fuel, but the part about wanting it delivered to the pier near our beached dinghy was beyond our infant vocabulary. But an old trick worked, and nods of understanding greeted my crude drawing of a sailboat.

George Filling Barrel

Two attendants rolled an empty 50 gallon barrel over to the pump and were just about to start filling when George and I frantically signaled them to stop. Sign language for "put the empty barrel into the Bemo before you put 400 pounds of fuel in it" was instantly understood. The bemo deposited the barrel, pump, and attendants at the pier while George and I went to retrieve our jerry jugs from our boats. A large surf had developed since our arrival and almost capsized the dinghy.

Our plan was for George to walk back to the pier and let them know we'd been delayed. Timing the breakers, I managed to get the dinghy back safely. The attendants were impatiently waiting at the end of the pier—but no George. By this time the surge was powerful and even if there had been ladders from the pier twenty feet over my head, there was no way to safely tie the dinghy and climb. I made signs for them to lower the jerry jugs by rope. With horror I saw that the group above had interpreted my circling around as a sign that unloading from the pier wouldn't work, and they began to roll the barrel down the long pier towards the beach.

Help came from a large lateen-rigged cargo ship that I had admired earlier. The crew motioned me over and pointed to their ladder. Once aboard there was another challenge! The fifteen feet between the rocking boat and stationary dock was spanned by a piece of timber held in place by ropes that rode up and down with the motion of the ship. The Indonesians looked amused as I was hesitating. Its only water below, I told myself, and made the dash. My next task was finding George. On his way back, bureaucracy had caught him, and he was at the gate being questioned by four officials. I pointed to my wet clothes and then pointed to the pier and made signs that I hoped looked urgent. That and a returning official carrying all of George's papers allowed us to escape.

Getting the jugs, like everything else surrounding this project, had had its problems, not the least of which was my dinghy getting entangled in a fishing net and my falling overboard as I tried to cut it off of my propeller. We were now three hours plus into the unloading. The Indonesians looked unhappy when they realized from my signaling that they needed to roll the barrel back up the beach, back up the embankment, and back down the pier. But it is amazing what $40,000 Rupia ($4.00 US) can do.

The fact that the hose from the rotary gear pump was too large to fit into the jerry jugs wasn't the main problem. It was the holes in the hose and loose fittings at the pump discharge that accounted for most of the spillage. But with three hands closed over the leaky parts, they managed to get a surprisingly large proportion of the diesel fuel into and all over our previously very clean jerry jugs. Neither George nor I could figure out why it didn't occur to them to stop pumping as they switched the hose from an overflowing jerry jug to an empty, but by that time the mess was so overwhelming we resigned ourselves to just watch and wait. What should have been an easy, quick operation had turned into an all-afternoon fiasco, with a clean up that would extend well into the evening. We did admire the Indonesians' determination to see their commitment through to the end.

Four-thirty came painfully early the next morning and we were tempted to cancel our trip to Kelimutu. But arrangements had been made, and we were committed. Now smooth water greeted our dinghy landing and we could see the headlights flashing through the pitch-black sky ashore, to signal the presence of Father Gabriel and our van.

At the end of a two-hour journey over terrain that was more potholes than road, we hiked through chilly mist to the peak, and there—giant volcanic craters with three lakes inside. As it became light enough to see, the first lake was a deep blue, not a sea blue—more like house paint than water. The second was a deep black, and the third a lighter black. Father Gabriel laughed and said the last time he was there they were green, red, and white.

Kelimutu is a place of deep spiritual significance to the people of Flores and legend says that when a person dies, be he young, old, evil or good, his soul or "Mae" is assigned to one of the three lakes and goes there to reside for eternity. Scientists can't give an exact explanation, but apparently the combination of dissolving minerals and the active volcanic life below results in a mystifying sight of ever-changing colors.

***

We were watching a waltz of death. It was beautiful, and frightening, and it was unfolding on the beach only a few hundred yards away from where we were anchored—off the home of Komodo dragons.

Sara saw the beginning: the head of a deer swimming along the beach. And there had been company. At first Sara had thought it was a rock on the beach. But rocks don't move so she got out the binoculars. Slowly, slowly the rock had been moving down the beach in the same direction as the deer. Focusing the binoculars, Sara was startled. Without having to leave the boat she was looking at the major attraction that draws people to Rinca and Komodo Islands from all over the world. She called *Skimmer* on the VHF and we all settled down to watch the Komodo Dragon stalk its prey.

The giant lizards exist only on the islands of Rinca and Komodo. With razor claws, they can reach up to nine feet and weigh two hundred pounds. They run at lightning speed, swim in the surf, and stun their opponents with blows from their huge tails. They feed on deer, wild pig, and water buffalo and have even been known to have a go at tourists who get too close. The horseshoe bay on the south coast of Rinca is dominated by a wall of mountains. The water had a blue glow and I could see the beautiful coral below. Our first onshore expedition had yielded two large nearly intact Nautilus shells. This was paradise and we had it to ourselves, except for the lizards.

From the moment Sara called us, Charlotte and I were mesmerized. We thought attack was imminent and pictured the gory scene about to take place, lizard darting in, stunning the deer with its tail, ripping it apart with teeth and claws, and then working it down its expanding throat like a snake swallowing a frog. Charlotte was rooting for the deer, but wanting to see some action, I was kind of hoping the lizard would strike.

The deer came out of the water and stood completely still. The dragon inched its way into a position directly inland from the deer. The deer would slowly move to the right. The dragon also moved to the right. The same game to the left. The deer would gaze almost directly at the dragon. Why didn't it bolt? Maybe it knew the dragon was too fast. The dance continued for almost an hour. Finally the dragon started moving in, head swaying from side to side.

Then for some reason we can only guess at, it was over. Did the dragon decide that its quarry was too large? From where we were looking he did look more like a hundred pounder than a two-hundred pounder. Or was he just too far away for a successful spring? But at the end the deer simply wandered off in one direction and the dragon withdrew back into the woods.

Two stops on Rinca and one on Komodo. We sighted ten dragons, scores of monkeys, deer, hawks, and bats. With the exception of two sailing dive boats, we saw no one else. It's hard to believe that such a populous country can have such a desolate coast.

In the 2,000 east-west miles of Indonesia there are very few passages north to south, and none of them easy. Linta is better than many, but it is still a formidable body of water. Whirlpools, overfalls, and currents in excess of six knots propelled us through and popped us out on the northeast coast of Komodo Island and then we were off to the neighboring Island of Sumbawa.

***

At 6:00 in the afternoon it had looked pretty straightforward. A simple ninety degree turn to the left after passing along the pier, follow the range lights, and then there would be nothing but the Sea of Flores before our overnight to Lombok. No night arrivals, never. Night departures? Not our preference, but if the exit isn't too complicated we'll do it. At Labuan we allowed sunset to come and go before finally pulling up the hook. It's amazing how quickly our world can change. From a red-and-pink sky accenting vessels lining the pier, the world became black, confusing, and hostile. Though my charts, compass, radar, and GPS assured there was only open sea in front, the sight that greeted us as we headed out started the adrenaline flowing. Lights in front, lights to the right, to the left. Hundreds of little white blips. I rechecked everything. Yes we were headed for deep water—the steadily rising digits on the fathometer gave confirmation. But the lights. Every fishing vessel in Sumbawa must have been out there, stringing nets, pulling lines—and for every lit vessel how many unlit were there? No moon, no visibility. With me on the bow and Charlotte at the helm, I shouted orders back to her.

This was our first encounter with the Indonesian fishing fleet. Our night passages before had been mostly across open water far from shore. But I had plotted a course four miles offshore and hoped that once we were out, our trip along the north coasts of Sumbawa and Lombok would be uneventful. A quick dinner and we started the night watches. We had passed most of the fleet and it looked like we were in for a pleasant evening. *Kimo Sabay* was astern on our port side and we were well off shore. Two or three radar contacts four to six miles away. All was calm when I went aft for my turn in the sack.

Charlotte was shaking me. Three hours couldn't have gone that quickly. It hadn't and Charlotte was genuinely concerned. Besides the vessels with lights she could track on radar, there were three on radar with no lights. And they appeared to be closing.

Darkness, fatigue, rumors, all play on our fears. We had read about pirates. Could this be them? It's a constant topic among cruisers, but our frequent radio communications and the supportive cooperation among fellow cruisers keep us well informed, and piracy has been unheard of in the waters we were cruising. But the contacts were there. Charlotte picked up the VHF to alert *Kimo Sabay* of our stealthy neighbors, but no response. Strange whistling over channel 16. A sudden flash of light only a few hundred yards away where before there had been only darkness. An answering flash from another quarter. Then the still and darkness again. Whistling on the radio all the time. Why wasn't *Kemo Sabay* answering? Were pirates jamming the radio? Should I get a flare? How about the gun? Reason told me to be calm and I managed to appear calm, but the same fears that were obviously driving Charlotte's actions were nagging at the back of my mind. I was sitting there flashing the powerful spotlight on our sails trying to decide what to do when George's cheerful voice boomed over the radio. He had had his engine running and hadn't heard our previous eight calls. Yes, he saw the radar contacts also and found them disturbing. We reassured each other that they were only fishermen, but closed the distance between our vessels and agreed to both keep better radio watches.

Did our radio conversation cause the three lightness vessels to head away or was it coincidence? I assured Charlotte there wasn't a problem and went back to sleep. But less than an hour later I was roused by the engine starting and Charlotte shouting for me to come up on deck. They were close enough to count the number on board. Charlotte thought three. The wind had died and *Skimmer* had lost almost all way. A shabby wooden vessel under power—the little stern cabin clearly visible. No lights. Its bow approaching our starboard side. High throttle, into gear, a sharp turn to the left and before I could even get on deck, Charlotte had solved the problem and the vessel drifted astern.

Had they been trying to warn us off of their nets or had they wanted to bum cigarettes or a soft drink? We alerted *Kemo Sabay* to watch out for them, but they passed without incident. It was only later when we talked with others who'd had the same experience that we got a reasonable explanation. Indonesian fishermen are extremely superstitious and believe that having evil spirits on board can ruin a whole night's fishing. As it is a well-known fact that evil spirits can only travel in straight lines, fishermen in the know simply speed towards another boat, preferably a well-heeled cruising yacht, and at the last possible moment turn away sharply, forcing the evil spirits off their boat and onto the other boat.

**

They do things differently in Gili Air—a small island with a wooden umbilical to the northwest corner of Lombok. Hundreds of beautifully crafted, gaily colored, outrigger canoes are Gili Air's sole link. The more modern versions feature twin Johnsons in their cutaway sterns and carry a stream of sun seekers from Bali to enjoy scuba, snorkeling, and beach walking. Their more traditional counterparts come in all sizes but are easily distinguishable from each other by the colorful patchwork on their lateen sails.

Lambok Outrigger

The Lambok version of the outrigger is a little different from what we had seen before. Wooden knees angle up and out, bend sharply down, then attach to the pontoons—grasshopper legs standing on water. Underway the crafts look like giant graceful insects skipping along the surface, with their bright wings fluttering in the breeze.

Everything comes and goes in the outriggers. Mr. Wong's coconut export operation was in full swing as we walked by. At a mountain of green coconuts, two men loaded up a cart and ferried them to the sloping beach and dumped. Two more men with long sticks channeled coconuts as they rolled down the beach and plunged into the surf. Finally two more men tossed coconuts from the floating pen made by the sticks and the bobbing outrigger canoe onto the ever mounting pile on board. Boat full, sail up, and then another took its place. Further down the beach bricks were arriving for another wing to the PADI Diving Complex. Heavily laden boats were unloaded by two men standing in waist-deep water. A line of men and women waited for loads of bricks on square pieces of wood that they balanced on their heads. Through the surf, up the beach, over to the construction site, seemingly without effort.

Tidy platforms with thatched roofs dotted the waterfront and offered shelter from the sun and a refuge from sand. Sitting on comfortable cushions, savoring spicy Mie Goering, and sipping cold Bintang Beer, we had, yet again, found the most beautiful spot in the world!

The most intriguing sight on Gili Air was the surf fishermen just outside the reef on the north shore. I snorkeled over for a close look. Surfacing outside the reef, I sat on a rock and watched an attractive lady with conical straw hat, long pants, and long sleeved shirt as she patiently baited her line.

Lone Sailor

A live minnow, hook, and small weight at one end of a long piece of monofilament line formed the tail of the mini kite she was about to launch. About six inches long, made of plastic from an old grocery bag, it looked just like a miniature version of the kites I had enjoyed so much as a young boy. Now the reason for her 15-foot-long pole became apparent. She swung it forward and back, released the line and got the same results as my youthful breakneck dashes down the beach against the wind. The tiny kite with its wiggling minnow suspended below soared out to sea. A spool of line in the left hand and the long bamboo pole in the right, the Indonesian fisherwoman placed her bait and retrieved her quarry in a symphony of quiet concentration and swaying motion.

***

Our early departure yielded an unexpected reward. The dots on the horizon of the morning sky became a swarm of brilliant butterflies, a cloud of color and excitement as they approached. A few at first, then they passed by in fives, tens, and dozens—each a lone helmsman with rainbow sail billowing out and propelling forward.

George and I had the same reaction as we watched in awe, embarrassment, even a little shame. Here we were in sophisticated yachts loaded with machinery and with every navigation aid known to man, while our tiny counterparts skimmed over the same body of water without care or device. Was there one compass in the entire fleet? I doubted it.

We passed the reef and neared our anchorage on Lembongan. We had crossed the two seas of South-Eastern Indonesia and had arrived—but where? What was that ahead? We strained and stared in disbelief. *Skimmer* had arrived at a giant amusement park, and it was open for business. Before us was a manmade island on pontoons, blaring rock music and sporting a giant spiraling water slide. Jet skis everywhere, long yellow banana floats making rooster-tail wakes as their riders shouted delight. Surfers gloried in the waves that swept by the floating carnival, and giant catamarans came and went, shuttling tourists from Bali.

The next morning the currents were right and we made the short crossing to Bali. *Skimmer* found a home at the Bali International Marina in Benoa where our son Heyward Jr. joined us from Japan for a tour of the island. Afterwards we took a plane to Ujung Padang so we could explore Sulawesi.

***

They had just sacrificed two spotted buffaloes. The six huge pigs we had gingerly walked around would be next. Trussed to stout long bamboo poles and dumped in the shade, they squirmed and squealed. An imposing figure in black sarong and fez motioned us into a long thatched pavilion teaming with activity. After we took our seats on a straw mat, he introduced us to his two children, told us he

Animals Awaiting Sacrifice

was honored that we had come to attend the funeral, and offered us coffee, tea, or palm tree wine. Mr. Nabu was the nephew of the deceased. Charlotte and I, George and Sarah, and our guide Lona were the only guests in this room and our hosts were almost as curious about our trips across oceans as we were about the extravaganza that we were about to witness. Tana Toraja is a mountainous area in northwest Sulawesi that has been isolated from its neighbors for centuries. The Torajans have a long history of doing things their way, and their way of saying goodbye to loved ones is something to behold.

If the ritual is not carried out properly, the spirit of the deceased will cause endless problems for the surviving family. But if done correctly, the Gods are impressed, the family gains face, and the spirit of the deceased has bargaining power with the Gods to do good for those he has left behind. Mr. Nabu's uncle's funeral was done properly. While his embalmed body lay in the large bamboo house at the head of the compound, hundreds of family, friends, and passersby participated in the celebration. His large wealth dictated the class of funeral, five days of celebrations with four buffaloes and ten pigs sacrificed daily, followed by an identical ceremony six months later. While feeding the guests, constructing the pavilions, and hiring the musicians and priests are very costly, they are nothing compared to the cost of the sacrifices. The spotted buffalo can cost up to $2,000 US each—an almost inconceivable expense in Indonesian where the price of a good meal in a restaurant including drinks is usually less than $5.00 US.

Anton, Mr. Nabu's oldest son, explained why he and many of his young friends were against the rituals. His objections were primarily monetary. A funeral like the one we were attending can literally wipe a family out. Despite taxes the Indonesian government has placed on the sacrifices to try to discourage the practice, it goes on. Anton lamented that often other Indonesians are so fearful of the obligations that they refuse to let their children marry into Toraja families.

Anton's explanations were cut short. Wild squealing rang through the air as the porters took up their pork burdens and proceeded to the sacrificing circle. Nabu took his place in the procession and Anton led us to the family viewing pavilion. A long line of black sarongs followed a gaily-clad priest who flailed a shepherd's crook and danced his way to the large bamboo house. Even if we had been able to understand Indonesian, it wouldn't have made any difference. The horrible shrieking from the doomed pigs drowned out all speech and we watched the gruesome sight of slashing knives as the priests hacked out parcels of buffalo and pork for the villagers.

**

Between burial sites where eyeless skulls stared at us from rock ledges in mountainsides or from recesses in dark wet caves, we drove through magnificent wet rice fields where workers threshed their harvest. Dominating the countryside were elaborately constructed Tongkonans. Facing north, with huge curved roofs assembled from many layers of split bamboo, they are a symbol of wealth and power, and only direct descendents of Torajan noblemen are allowed to build or own them. From a distance they look like ships with high bows and sterns sitting on top of highly decorated platforms.

The long jarring ride from to Bira on the southeastern tip of South Sulawesi took us to the site of the most renowned ship construction the world has ever known.

We had read about the Bugis and Makassarese and had been intrigued with accounts of their early exploration of Australia. We had also admired the endless variety of the wooden craft we had seen everywhere since our arrival in Indonesia. Here was the heart of Indonesian

Tongkonans

boat construction, where wooden boat building continues today much the same as it has since the early 1500's in the Makassar Kingdom of Gowa and the Bugis Kingdom of Bone. Each thatched shed housed a vessel under construction. Giant sailboats or pinisis over 200 feet long, modest vessels of 50 to 100 feet, and small fishing boats. Our initial wandering through the sheds left us with more questions than insights. They looked more like porcupines than boats—keels with varying numbers of strakes rising up the sides, ribs crisscrossing the bottoms and long pegs sticking out everywhere. It would have been a frustrating experience if Assam hadn't appeared. He and his father had quit for the day and were about to leave their partially constructed fishing boat, but when he understood that we were boaters and that our curiosity was genuine, he took an interest.

At first we thought we were getting a bad translation. No glue? No screws? No nails? But by doing Assam, showed the impossible was not only possible but actually a very effective construction technique.

He started with a warped, curved, unplaned piece of wet timber that I was sure was a throwaway. He and his father held it up against the growing side of the vessel, moved it around in several different positions, consulted back and forth, and then reached a decision. While the father held the board, Assam pulled out a chisel and traced a line around the board. In less than five minutes Assam's razor sharp hatchet transformed the piece of timber into a plank. The notched joint at one end matched exactly the notched joint on the plank it would soon join, and its notched joint at the other end would act as a template for the next timber.

He then spent a few minutes splitting wood with his hatchet and making long pegs that would go through the width of the plank to lock it in place. Holes bored, pegs ready, he began to assemble—no trial fitting. With supreme confidence that his initial scribing had been accurate, he placed shreds of a special bark in the gap between new plank and carcass, put the pegs in place, and then drove the plank home with a giant wooden mallet. I couldn't believe how perfectly the plank mated with the growing hull. No sooner was the plank driven home than the father started swinging his adz in rhythmic arcs. Chop, chop—chips flew—and suddenly the contour was there and the smooth lines of the fishing boat had grown ten more inches towards the gunwale.

Boat Construction at Bira

Assam explained that the bark would expand in water making the joint completely waterproof. The pegs were made of a different kind of wood than the planks, and they also would expand once the boat was in the water, making the joint as strong as the wood itself.

***

The magnet of Kalimantan—Indonesian Borneo—was drawing us in. The big attraction was Kumai and a trip up the Sekonyer River in search of wildlife—orangutans, black-faced monkeys, long-nosed monkeys, and gibbons.

The leaves were rustling, branches were swaying and the noise was becoming louder. The big ape named Cowboy was coming in fast. A tree suddenly bent double as the orangutan at its top rode it down. A mother with child at breast, two youngsters with their mouths full of bananas and sweet potatoes, and the teenager who had just pulled his head out of the milk pail all paused from their feast to look up and watch Cowboy's descent. But the most interested spectator was about six trees away.

Rambeau was angry. He didn't hesitate a second. Once Cowboy had completed his tree-riding descent and had latched with all fours onto two hanging vines, Rambeau made his move. Vine to vine in a descent of over 100 feet Rambeau attacked. Two seconds later, contact! With Rambeau's head driving right into Cowboys abdomen, the two hairy beasts fell another 50 feet to the ground and three anxious attendants with thermos bottles poised ran in to try to separate the combatants.

We had departed from Kumai early that morning aboard our guide Harry's longboat for our special tour of the Camp Leaky rehabilitation center and research site, a halfway house for problem primates. What would otherwise be the end of the road for delinquent orangutans, gibbons, and monkeys is the start of a rehabilitation that aims to restore them to the wild. At three separate camps dispersed throughout Tanjung Putting, a staff of about 40 meter out tough love to knock even the most desperate cases back into line. Upon arrival the inmates are given names, and a special relationship begins to develop between kept and keepers.

At Camp One signs warned not to feed, hold hands with or fraternize with the inmates, and the staff made a gallant effort to keep us apart from their charges. These were the real problem primates. Many were almost hopelessly tame and hadn't the least notion of keeping their distance from humans—cast off pets, refugees from slash and burn, or abandoned orphans.

Barry

Hunia and Baby

We had been off the boat for five minutes when a gibbon came barreling down the path. Little black hands in the air; arms outstretched, the furry ball of activity shot towards Charlotte like a well-aimed bowling ball and wrapped both its arms and legs around her right leg in an affectionate hug.

Charlotte is nervous about animals, so Barry's unsolicited affections were not welcome. But the faster she ran or the harder she shook, the tighter

Barry held. For Barry it was love at first site, but for Charlotte it wasn't. Fortunately, the staff were watching and aware of Barry's roving eye. A pretty young woman walked over, and in a flash the fickle ape shifted its amorous attentions to her left leg.

At Camp Two we met Hunia, an orangutan that was never going to graduate, and her baby. No matter how hard the counselors tried, they could never teach Hunia to act like a normal orangutan. She just couldn't understand that it was disconcerting to humans when she made her approaches. While the baby in her arms sucking on her breast was reassuring, her 150 pounds of sinewy muscle was not. The sweet smile on her face masked the mind of a mugger. A bag of peanuts placed in a pocket, a pair of glasses dangling around a neck, a wallet being placed in a back pocket, a camera being put back in its case—Hunia filed all this away. Then, when the tourist least expected it, her paw darted in the remembered pocket, and she was off at breakneck speed.

There were many stories. The American who glumly watched Hunia pick credit cards, licenses, and dollar bills one by one from his wallet and then casually throw them into the jungle air from her perch high above. The Japanese tourist who was almost strangled when Hunia decided to get into the photography business but failed to detach the camera from its strap around his neck before beginning her ascent up the tree.

At the elite third camp, we were introduced to inmates who had graduated to the status of fully wild animals. Here honor students like Cowboy and Rambeau were living examples of what determination on the part of teachers and students can achieve. The task remaining for the staff supervising students in this camp was to keep the orangutans from killing each other before they finally departed into the wild for good.

***

Kalimantan, the Indonesian portion of the island of Borneo, is a country known for its diversity of cultures, topography, and vegetation, and it was with a combination of awe and eager anticipation that we approached. There is shallow water for 40 miles offshore and then shifting banks bordering a constantly changing channel. The soot in the air from volcanic activity wasn't as bad as rumored so we didn't have any problem following the stream of junks, pinisis, and tramp steamers as they negotiated the 15-mile-long channel to Port Kumai. By late afternoon we had reached our anchorage opposite the port.

Behind the cargo craft lining the wharf, mosque domes loomed above stilt houses and run-down shops. Blue lateen sails propelled traditional white wooden pinisis back and forth, as cheesy little speedboats with outboards filled the same role in the harbor that their two-wheeled Honda cousins did in the crowded streets ashore. For the first time we felt we were really in Asia.

Before the anchor was down a rooster tail across the river turned into a pancake-flat speedboat with almost no freeboard rocketing towards us. Harry had found us. I had been so pleased with the Orangutan outing he had arranged for us that I decided to get him to take me into his hometown of Pangkalanbun to buy some ironwood and a blowgun. There, he introduced me to Victor, whose erect bearing, trimmed white beard, and neat sarong set him apart. He was obviously proud of his shop and particularly proud of the antique blowgun he was showing me. He had pulled the long black ironwood weapon from among an arsenal that adorned one of the walls of his well-stocked antique shop. I accepted his price, negotiated for extra darts, but declined his kind offer to also include poisoned darts. During his description of the significance of the red and yellow ribbons wrapped around the business end of the gun behind where the iron spear juts out, a long diatribe began.

While it was difficult to follow the facts, the emotional content was clear. The bloodbath that had engulfed the neighboring city of Sampit in February of 2000 had almost been repeated here in Pangkalanbun. Both Harry and Victor had friends who had been victims of machete-wielding Madurese, and they were prepared to take the same measures their Dayak brethren had finally resorted to in Sampit.

Originating from the island of Madura just north of Surabaya on Java, the Madurese had bought their desire to dominate and their machetes to Kalimantan. Harry went too fast for me to understand everything, and his description of the Dayaks as peace-loving and ready to forgive seemed to conflict with later events.

In his version it went like this: Finally pushed to the brink, the Dayaks of Sampit reverted to their historic nature—savage headhunters with supernatural powers. With bullets bouncing harmlessly from their chests and bombs detonating on top of their proud heads, these fierce warriors wielded their razor sharp Mandaus so fast that the severed heads of their opponents were attributed to flying swords. And there had been many severed heads. The final incident had been in a sealed-off building guarded by a regiment of policemen. Inside, seeking sanctuary from the fury of the Dayaks, over a hundred Madurese huddled in fear. Finally, when a policeman entered the building to check on the refugees, he saw that not a head was left attached. Shortly afterwards the Madurese left Kalimantan to harass citizens of other Indonesian Islands.

Red and yellow are the Dayak war colors, and the spear that I had just purchased was to have been part of the arsenal the Dayaks of Pangkalanbun were going to deploy if the Sampit uprising had not ended the Madura terror. I looked again at the dark stained tips of Victor's poison darts that I had refused—but this time with a new respect.

Victor's Poison Darts

Singapore and the Strait of Malacca

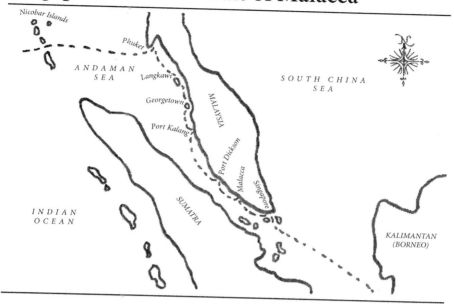

Isolated, shocked, frightened, but mostly sad. These were the emotions flowing through *Skimmer* as we caught key words over the radio from our barely readable morning net. Quietly anchored at Pangkil Island in the Strait of Riau with only one more day to go to complete our transit to the Strait of Singapore, we listened to the news. Garbled words from an outside world gone mad. We strained to understand: "planes ... two maybe three ... World Trade Center ... Thousands dead ... Pentagon..."

It was almost twelve hours after the fact and our informer was only partially informed himself. When he finally faded out, we tried desperately to tune in news from other channels, but the only news service we could find was Voice of America transmitting in Chinese. All we knew was that something terrible had happened. Details would have to wait until our arrival at the Nongsa Point Marina on the island of Batam just across from Singapore. Like Americans everywhere, we went into seclusion and grieved. Two days in our room at the fancy Nongsa Point Marina Hotel glued to CNN bought the reality of the situation and the enormity of the loss into focus.

Once the initial shock was over, we began to try to evaluate how the events in America affected our safety and our plans. Despite problems in Java, we had felt welcome and safe in Indonesia. Now the situation was changed, and we were happy that we were only 30 miles away from Singapore, one of the most secure places in the world.

Thinking about our experiences in Indonesia in a new light, both Charlotte and I remembered something. At the time, it hadn't seemed important, but now it did. Among the first to greet us when we had begun our exploration of the town of Seba on the island of Sawu in Indonesia were three young men from Afghanistan. We had become accustomed to shunning unwelcome advances and didn't think much about it once they were gone. But time and again we would see them sitting around on the waterfront or strolling through town. Charlotte couldn't understand what they were doing there. Why would three young men stay on a small isolated island for eight months? She asked our guide about them and received a pretty strong reaction: "Stay away from those men—they are up to no good—they should go back to their own country!"

Were they fleeing from a dismal existence at home, or were they seeds of a terrorist cell in tiny Seba? We'll never know, but Charlotte felt strongly enough about it to alert the US Embassy of our experience.

It was only 40 miles, but what a 40 miles! Giant crude-oil tankers, huge liquid natural gas and propane tankers, tramp steamers of every sort, a procession of highrise steel with barely enough room between for *Skimmer* to make its dash. I used five detailed charts and wished that I had more. Major shipping lanes seemed to come out of nowhere and as soon as we were clear from the ships clogging one, we would be intercepted by different ships moving up another. In planning it had looked simple. Cross the opposing traffic in the major Deep Water Fairway, then I could pretty much go along with the traffic. Wrong!

A 90-degree turn, high rpm, and then we were going in the right direction down the super highway. Now the steel giants were going with us and we just had to keep out of the way, or so I thought. But if I had been more careful in my planning I'd have noted that we would also have to cross the Southern Fairway before rounding Raffles Light. This time it was an opposing lane of medium sized giants I had to contend with, and they were so busy keeping clear of the monsters in the Deep Water Fairway that they were not about to take any notice of tiny *Skimmer* as she tried to bob and weave her way through.

Three times I yielded the right of way. Poised to go with the opposing ship to my port—just enough room to dash across—another look at the increasing height of the tanker sides—and then the chicken turn to port to go down the side of the tanker instead of across its bow.

By the time we got to Raffles light, we were so frazzled that we didn't panic when the huge oil tanker ahead appeared to be on a collision course. As we neared, my binoculars told me what a closer inspection of my chart might have revealed. She was on a mooring buoy disgorging her hundreds of thousands of gallons of crude oil through giant hoses and a submerged pipeline.

We made a hard turn to starboard around Raffles Light and then a cautious transit through Raffles Shoals, keeping a sharp lookout to find a gap in the intersecting traffic. We were just about to make our final approach up the Johor Strait to the Western end of Singapore and our refuge in Raffles Marina was getting close. If *Kemo Sabay* hadn't given us the warning, I think Charlotte would have gone into cardiac arrest.

Just past Sultan Shoal Light and there they were, hundreds, maybe a thousand! I have never seen so many ships in one place in my life. Big tankers, fishing boats, oil drilling ships, Pinisis, Junks, and more big tankers. It was a city of masts and smokestacks with barely a hundred yards between many of them. But *Kemo Sabay* had alerted us and we calmly motored ahead and wove our way through the anchored vessels, oohing and ahhing as we took photos.

While we had been worrying about the tankers crossing the straits, we had also been worried about our daughter, Margot, flying into Singapore that night. Hers was the first international flight to leave Los Angeles since September 11, and she arrived at Changi Airport late that night. We loved hearing about her experiences during her internship in film production and were very proud to hear about her success in landing her first job. Erhard and Coleen Joershal, our friends from Moscow, also joined us and

Charlotte, Erhard, Margot, and Coleen

we all visited the attractions of Singapore. Tiger Beer in frosted mugs, spicy crab, the beauty of Chinese lanterns blinking at us with modern skyscrapers in the background as our Junk took us along the Singapore River, and Charlotte's three hour visit to Singapore's exotic botanical gardens—it all went by too quickly.

***

The Strait of Malacca. Five years earlier when the purchase of *Skimmer* was fresh and I was explaining to people where I would take her, I often felt like I was talking about someone else. The Panama Canal, the Galapagos,

French Polynesia—it seemed unreal, and perhaps the most unreal was the part about going up through the Strait of Malacca to Thailand, the choke point were the Indian Ocean meets the South China Sea. This was the battleground where the Portuguese, Dutch, and British fought for dominance of world trade and the home of pirates for centuries.

While *Skimmer* was ready, was her crew? Late night discussions with *Kemo Sabay*, emails to *Kamal*, radio conversations with other cruisers—we were all forced to reevaluate what we were doing. What did the War on Terrorism mean to cruisers, was it time to stop? Was Malaysia more dangerous than Los Angeles or New York?

***

Charlotte doesn't like winds that have names. Hoping that with the end of the Southeast Monsoons in sight we might not encounter any, I had kept my research on Sumatras to myself. We had barely made it out of Raffles Marina and were just at the mouth of the Strait of Johor when I saw tell tale signs. Long black rolling clouds coming from the west.

The winds did not reach 60 knots—this was not a severe knock down Sumatra! But in the space of less than ten minutes *Skimmer* went from a clear view of the hundreds of ships swarming at the entrance to the Strait of Malacca into torrential downpours and near-zero visibility. And it wasn't a 20-minute storm. Heavy rain kept me dripping over the radar while Charlotte strained to see through the blinding curtain for almost six hours. The Strait of Malacca was living up to its reputation.

Our second day in the Strait was wonderful—calm seas with the beautiful scenery of the Malaysian coast flowing by—and for the night a nice protected anchorage. Things were looking up, until 1:00 AM and our second Sumatra. This time high winds came from the opposite direction of our protecting island. For the first time since I had purchased my giant 60-pound CQR anchor in Australia, *Skimmer* dragged! But we didn't drag far and the anchor dug back in.

Just north of the historic city of Malacca, a bonanza for cruisers and a disaster for investors waits for visiting yachts. So much money, so much concrete, such lovely furniture, such a nice swimming pool, and so few boats. The Admiral Marina at Port Dickson speaks of days gone by when it looked like construction would never end and investments would always turn into gold. A huge breakwater surrounds concrete floating docks capable of accommodating mega yachts. Facilities ashore include a marble lobby with fountain, a mahogany lined dining room, an empty hotel, and a huge model of the condominiums that never were. The Asian recession of the late 90's had hit Malaysia hard.

But for *Skimmer* and *Kemo Sabay*, it was paradise. Low rates, wonderful amenities, great service, and new friends. For the first time in our travels, we were beginning to meet cruisers traveling in the opposite direction, and those we met at Port Dickson were full of stories about even greater places ahead at Langkawi and Phuket. They were also full of advice on how to coexist with the Sumatras—advice we wished we had received a week earlier.

***

Port Klang pricked the bubble of the theory of ever-increasing beauty and luxury. We now approached the huge port that allows Kuala Lumpur to be what it is. Filthy water took on new meaning as we rode the four-knot currents up the Klang River. Nature has already endowed the water with thick mud, but what man has added in the way of oil, sewage, cardboard, and plastic sets the Klang River apart from anything I have ever seen. *Skimmer* ran an obstacle course through floating islands of trash and fish traps that became ever thicker and nastier until we reached the place that had been given such good write ups in our cruising guides.

My channel 72 radio call to the Royal Selangor Yacht Club didn't raise any reply, but it did raise Peter on *Tradewinds*, whom we had not seen since just before Borneo. Obviously his Dutch sensitivity to cleanliness had been aroused, and he sounded almost angry as he advised us not to even consider the yacht club. "I vas there this morning—they offer me a mooring—it stinks—I have never seen such a place—ve do not stay—ve are now at very nice anchor north of the whole mess." The plastic bags, sticks, and other garbage tangled in the waiting mooring line was so bad I didn't want to touch it, but the bumboat from the yacht club with two cheerful Malaysians arrived and untangled the mess just before I yielded to the temptation to follow Peter's advice.

There was an elegance about the Royal Selangor Yacht Club that we found very attractive and we were glad that we'd stayed. Ceiling fans, white linen cloths on tables that faced the river, a fleet of small wooden sailboats, and bulletin boards announcing races and youth activities. John, the Scottish yacht club manager, bought us a round of beer and we then sat on the porch discussing the many charms of Malaysia and Thailand with other cruisers heading east. Since talking to Malacca Strait veterans, we had adopted a strategy of staying close inshore to avoid the tanker traffic and anchoring at night to avoid invisible fishing boats and their ubiquitous nets and traps. Conventional wisdom was that even when there wasn't an island for protection, it was possible to go towards the shore and anchor when the depth dropped to about twenty feet.

So far we'd been impressed with Malaysia and had no trouble at all. Although we had't seen any signs of anti-Americanism, Charlotte followed the cautious advice from the yacht club and checked us in with the American Embassy in Kuala Lumpur.

***

We woke up at our quiet berth at the Lumut International Yacht Club, tuned in BBC, and listened with rapt attention. BBC had suspended all previously scheduled programs in order to give continuous coverage to events in Afghanistan. The bombings had started.

"Keep a low profile. Don't look like conspicuous Americans." This was the Embassy's advice and we were trying hard to adhere to it. But how do you make Charlotte look like a Muslim? I figured that no matter what we did, we were going to look pretty conspicuously like westerners. Maybe we could be mistaken for Dutch, French, Belgian, or Australian—but would that really help? What we did was smile, try to be pleasant, and keep a low profile. But neither the *Kemo Sabay*s nor the *Skimmers* were going to sacrifice beer at lunch after a two-day passage. Though there are many Muslims who's devotion does not include a dislike for alcoholic beverages, they weren't apparent in Lumut. We looked at menus in six restaurants, but all we saw was fried rice, fried noodles, and multicolored, syrupy looking beverages.

Persistence has its rewards and at last we found Hotel Indra. Wan, the Chinese owner, was all smiles as we entered the empty dining room, where CNN blared on the television in the corner.

Charlotte and Wan at Chinese Restaurant

"Can we have lunch here?"
"Yes, can, can!"
"Do you have cold beer?"
"Yes, have, have!"

We sat in our haven for the whole afternoon riveted to CNN, trying to understand what was happening to the world. Wan and his wife went out of their way to tell us how much they supported the US and how evil they thought the terrorists were. Up until that point, most of the Malaysian Muslims we had met had been very friendly and deplored the terrorist attacks on the US. But now the US was bombing Muslims. We knew that Malaysia was stable, has one of the most liberal forms of Islam in the world and is not in fact a true Muslim state.

We decided we felt pretty safe but that as a precaution we would always travel fully provisioned with fuel and water tanks topped off. Our back-up plan was simple. Any sign of trouble and we'd head for sea.

***

Langkawi yacht club was a well-known oasis, and no responsible yachtie would even think about bypassing it. We had heard criticisms about no breakwater and uncomfortable swells, but its location right in the principal town of Kuah and its proximity to duty-free shops sucked us in. The mooring lines were barely made fast when we realized the magnitude of our error. A noise like a jet plane zooming low claimed our immediate attention, and we watched a sleek ferry rocket by with its payload of tourists. Seconds later we watched with horror as the tidal wake began to do its thing to the Langkawi Yacht Club. The massive floating concrete docks began with slow oscillations that quickly picked up speed. Boats attached took up the motion, but with much greater force. Fenders groaned, pilings creaked, water splashed. If there'd been another sailboat on the other side of the pier, we'd have locked spreaders.

I thanked our dock attendant Hammud for his kindness in letting me dock at the epicenter of activity, but said that electricity really wasn't that important and that we preferred to move. Hammud explained why he had let the beautiful, blue 120-foot Dutch yacht moor on the outside of the offending dock, in a place even worse than where we'd moored. "Many important peoples on a big yacht like that. If yacht damage, Dr. Mahathir, he sure find out. Maybe he then make ferries go slow and go outside green buoy!"

Duty free liquor is not the only attraction that draws yachties into Langkawi like a magnet. The wailing Sirens of Rebak sing with soft lilting voices that penetrate even the most carefully placed wax ear plugs: "Come, come, stop your voyage here. Forget the mighty winds, leave the high seas, abandon your dreamed horizons. We have electricity, we have water, we have washing machines that work, we are protection. And all this for not many Ringets. Come, come … stay with us … and sleep."

Both Charlotte and I had thought we were going to lose Sara to the Sirens. On our exploratory trip by cab and ferry to the remote Langkawi island of Rebak they started calling. This is the location of the beautifully equipped Rebak Marina. With docks filled and acres of yachts on cradles, the skyline bristles with masts and the bars are filled with cruisers telling of splendors from Turkey to Tasmania. If you want to find someone, look in the bar, don't knock on the boat—the jury-rigged air-conditioning units suspended from forward hatches drown out all outside noise and promote hibernation within.

But somehow we got Sara out on the evening ferry and by the next morning she had recovered her senses. Before the Sirens could begin their seduction again, both *Skimmer* and *Kemo Sabay* bid farewell to the Langkawi Yacht Club, to Rebak Marina, and to Muslim Malaysia; and then set out for Thailand.

***

It could be another planet. Limestone cliffs jut out of the emerald green sea up into the sky. Riddled with caves, undercut at the bases by flowing water, covered with lush green vegetation on part of their surfaces, and striped with beautifully contrasting mineral colors on the bare spots—these monoliths are eerie, exotic, and breathtakingly beautiful.

Phang Nga Bay. Charlotte and I were still having a hard time pronouncing the name, but we loved every minute of cruising its miles and miles of islands, inlets, and mangrove lined shores. Gliding along under the overhang of the coastline of Koh Phanak we looked up at stalactites dripping down and caves going into the mountain at each turn. The trick was finding the right cave to take us into the Hong—a hidden lake.

Overhang at Koh Phanak   *Hong Entrance*

We had watched as day-trippers in banana yellow kayaks streamed in and out of a particular hole—so we thought we knew which was the right one. But when we tried that afternoon after the tourists had left, inky blackness past the second bend, disorientation, the smell of bat droppings, and fear of puncturing our dinghy on the oystershell encrusted rocks made us turn back. But the second try, this time with flashlights, our efforts were rewarded with a stunning entrance into the Hong. A lake enclosed by the mountain with the only entrance through the long winding cave—the Thais call them Hongs, or rooms. Blue sky and hot sunshine funneled down the chimney and we swam in the cool water under hanging vines and Pandanus trees.

We loved Thailand, but *Skimmer* had reached a critical point. November was upon us and it was time to make the Red Sea decision. The window for crossing the Red Sea opens in early January and closes in late March or early April. Steady winds that blow from the northeast, the winter monsoons, would propel *Skimmer* through the Andaman Islands to Sri Lanka. From there we would ride the same winds around the southern tip of India to Cochin and at this point the timing becomes more critical. Seven years before, our Australian friends Pat and John of *Rouseabout* made the mistake of leaving Cochin too late and got becalmed in the middle of the Indian Ocean. Like most of us, *Rouseabout* did not carry nearly enough fuel to motor for such a distance and it was only luck and a freak wind that carried them into Oman.

Back in spring we had huddled with *Voyager*, *Kemo Sabay*, *Ferric Star*, *Kamal*, and others to work out a plan—but this had been prior to September 11 and the War in Afghanistan. Late night discussions on board *Skimmer* and *Kemo Sabay*, long radio conversations and emails with cruising companions slowly converging on Phuket, chance meetings with other cruisers. The topic was always the same. George was adamant. He had worked all his life to make this trip and all that stood between *Kemo Sabay* and their dream cruise in the Mediterranean was the Red Sea. He was confident the political situation in January would be such that we could form our armada and move on in safety. George's assurances irritated normally mild Sara: "I'm not going to sacrifice my life to get *Kemo Sabay* to the Med." Eric of *Escapade* reasoned that winter bombing was impractical and wouldn't resume until spring. He wanted to hop on his fast boat and gallop on. And by the way *Skimmer*, how fast do you and *Kemo Sabay* go?

Charlotte was reluctant to report her conversation with Eric to George and me, but finally did so making sure she gave it the right shades of color to prevent any remote possibility of encouragement on our parts: "And he is also talking about hiring an armed escort to go with his group! Even he realizes how dangerous it would be. I just can't understand what he is thinking about. You would have to be crazy to …"

We had met Phil while he was sending email from a marina office and he had told us about a recent group of cruisers who shared the expense of hiring a boat of mercenaries to escort them up the Red Sea. "Five boats paid $5,000 US each. But half way up, the mercenary boat broke down and the five cruisers had to take turns towing them the rest of the way. This of course brings up the question of whom to fear the most? Theoretical terrorists along the many remote uninhabited islands in their path, or the gunslingers they bought along for their own protection?"

As December approached, we pulled *Skimmer* out of the water to paint the bottom, put our Red Sea fears in abeyance, and headed home for Christmas. But there was a major detour. Japan. Our oldest son Heyward Jr. was teaching English as a second language in Shingu, a small coastal town about 50 miles south east of Osaka. He had been preparing for our visit for a month, but Charlotte and I weren't at all prepared for what we were about to experience.

A land of enigmas, of haunting beauty, of mysterious and moving hospitality. We were enchanted from the beginning and each new adventure seemed to suck us further and further into their culture. We learned quickly not to be fooled by first impressions. Ultramodern trains with barbaric Turkish toilets. Japanese writing that is wholly unintelligible to us, with no English or even European translations anywhere and people bowing and scraping in what could be misinterpreted for subservience. It would be easy to think "third world." But nothing could be further from the truth. High technology pokes it head out from every corner. Behind the frequent and friendly head bows is a well-educated, highly motivated person who seems driven to better himself and his surroundings. Frequently between two modern nondescript buildings was an exquisitely manicured garden with every plant and rock placed with care, love, and good taste.

Charlotte and Heyward Jr. in Japan

We ate seafood until we thought we would grow gills and saw the country through our son's eyes as he led us on adventures that ranged from a visit to the Waterase Hot Spa Lodge to a high-speed boat trip up the Kumano River to Dorokyou Gorge. By the end of the week our knees were aching and our minds were exhausted from kneeling in on his various English classes and trying to keep up with him.

154

The Indian Ocean

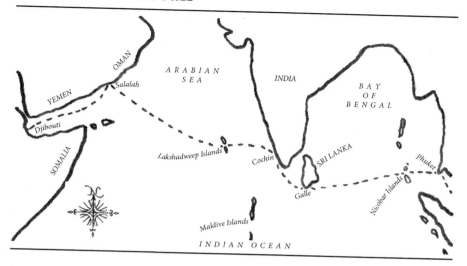

Returning from our Christmas break in Charleston, we found the fleet of would-be Red Sea Warriors had gained a new level of confidence. Oman to Bab-el-Mandeb was the key. With Somalia to the south and Yemen on the north, the passage from Oman to the entrance of the Red Sea was the riskiest part of the trip. But risks can be reduced by traveling in groups, and everyone had decided to meet in Oman and form groups of three to ten boats to make the eight hundred mile passage from there to Bab- el- Mandab—the entrance to the Red Sea—or, literally, "The Gates of Sorrow."

By the time we had arrived back in Phuket, some boats had already left and a large fleet was planning to leave on about January 10. We undertook an accelerated refit plan that left us gasping and got underway on the morning of January 16 to begin the 1,100 mile trip to Sri Lanka.

* * *

Hundreds of dolphins raced towards us, like torpedoes that veered off inches before impact. Flying fish skimmed the water all about them.

Just north of Little Nicobar Island the Sombrero Channel exits the shallow turbulence of the Andaman Sea and leads into the deep water and tranquility of the Indian Ocean. In a matter of hours we were feeling the effects of the steady, gentle, northeast winds generated by the Winter Monsoon's Mongolian High, settling down to the kind of sailing conditions cruisers dream about.

* * *

Departure is sweat and worry—sweat in completing the "must do" items in time to meet the "weather window" and worry over getting it wrong and

155

destroying vital functions of the boat. During our pre-departure sea trials, with wind on the beam and shade in the cockpit, all was right with the world. Our 60-degree turn to starboard to begin rounding the tip of the Phuket Peninsula changed everything. As *Skimmer's* stern swung into the wind and we slackened the main sheet to let the boom out, horrible realization set in. Our shiny new Bimini stood right in the path of the sheet rope! Seven inches isn't much, but in this case it was enough to put the aft Bimini support poles squarely in the path of the stout line that attaches the end of our massive boom to a pulley on *Skimmer's* deck.

We both had the same vision at the same time—pitch-black sky, howling wind, an uncontrolled jibe, and the wreck of *Skimmer's* cockpit with mangled canvass and twisted stainless steel tubes jutting out everywhere. The risk was unacceptable.

But the real low came as we limped back to Phuket Boat Lagoon to see what could be done about the Bimini fiasco. Moving it seven inches forward would solve the problem, but how? Short of a complete rebuild, it seemed an impossible task. Then I found another high price I had paid for another "improvement."

The outboard motor mechanic had seemed knowledgeable when I showed him the frayed throttle cable on the most reliable piece of equipment *Skimmer* possesses. Our Yamaha eight-horse power dinghy motor had never even hiccupped, but I was taking no chances. A frayed cable might part and I wanted absolute reliability. His cable replacement repair had also included a carburetor cleaning.

Cough, cough, cough—and the dinghy's motor quit, not to be resurrected by any amount of pulling, choking, or tweaking. Another impossible repair in an impossible time frame. That night, spirits were on the decline aboard *Skimmer* as we waited to see what the morning would bring. But I had enough energy left to tackle one last problem, the new hydraulic valves I had installed on our autopilot for insurance. They leaked slightly at the connectors. So I climbed into the hot engine room to tighten them up a little. On my back, lying across the still-hot engine, my head poking between cooling hoses and hydraulic pipes, sweat pouring all over my body, a large wrench in each hand, I finally was in position to make the adjustment. Big wrench on one nut, little wrench on another—push and pull at impossible angles—it was almost done when suddenly there was smelly hydraulic oil in my face, on my hands, on the walls.

I had sheared one of the connectors completely off the autopilot pump! It wasn't just any connector—no, it had to be the specialized Robertson Autopilot connector available only through Simrad in the United States or in

Norway. Lying there in the engine room I wondered if our trip to the Red Sea really was not meant to be. But Charlotte had just fixed dinner so I degreased and went to the table.

It's amazing what two helpings of rare lamb, fresh asparagus and okra, two very cold beers, and an encouraging wife can do for the spirit. We discussed the problems as rationally as we could. We didn't have much slack if we wanted to be able to catch up with the others in Oman.

There we were, anchored off one of the loveliest islands we'd ever seen, and we were beating our brains out to go somewhere else. Had we somehow gotten things wrong? We relaxed in the warm fragrant air and plans formed. There was that set of extra Robertson Autopilot fittings shipped to me in error, and it was possible I could adapt one of them. And rebuilding a carburetor didn't seem that daunting a task.

By eight o'clock in the morning the autopilot was fixed, the Yamaha was purring with newly rebuilt carburetor, and I was dinghying into Boat Lagoon to try to arrange our last impossible repair. Miraculously, Mussa, the sailmaker, answered his mobile phone on the first ring and was horrified at the news. A New Zealand transplant, he was one of the finest canvass men in South East Asia, and he immediately took responsibility for the incorrect measurements.

I had spent a good portion of the last two days measuring angles, making calculations, and formulating solutions, but Mussa's associate, Nop, politely interrupted me before I could get into my dissertation: "Mister Heyward, no talk numbers, take too much time, we no have much time, must done be today, electricity finish tomorrow. I bring my engineer team. They very very expert. They cut and bend and weld and see how you like. It's ok, yes?"

The good news was Nop was going to put himself on a deadline I couldn't have conjured up. The bad news was I couldn't imagine how he was going to make a change that would work.

Nop's engineer team consisted of Moo, an assistant, and a wheelbarrow full of welding equipment. My big decision came when Moo, hack saw in hand, pointed at the bases of each of the stout stainless steel Bimini supports. Oh well, if they couldn't fix it I didn't want it anyway and I unenthusiastically nodded my OK. Once the amputation had been preformed, they moved the structure three inches forward—an improvement, but still not enough. Moo pointed to the tops of the poles and gestured with his hack saw. Not seeing much choice I again nodded assent. Same cutting and tack welding process, but this time at the top of the poles. More grunting and groaning, and there it was, the same Bimini top but now seven inches further forward and enough room for the main sheet rope to clear safely. After four hours they had transformed the ugly weld joints into beautifully polished steel. The finished job was so perfect I couldn't even tell the tubes had been cut.

Nop had become a great friend during our stay at Phuket, and we celebrated the rebirth of our Bimini with dinner at the restaurant he owned. Charlotte was shocked to learn that he was not really married to his wife of ten years and asked him to explain how this affected their five-year-old son. Nop laughed and explained that marriages in Thailand are very expensive, and when he and Koi started their life together they decided to use the money instead to start his welding business. "This often happens with Thai peoples—Koi and I very very close—and I know that if I ever want leave her, she kill me. That keep marriage together very very well."

***

John Henry Dick's painting of the Black Skimmer dominates the forward bulkhead of our salon. His creation is frozen motion—racing across the sands of Botany Island searching for prey. So also had our *Skimmer* become alive. Gently bobbing, rolling, and pitching about her steady course westward. She almost sailed herself. An occasional shift in wind and she would tell us with flapping sails or jerking boom: "Hey there crew, do your part, I'm doing mine! Set my wings so I can soar." And with her reminder, we would break out of our lethargy, make the adjustment and then settle back down to the tranquility of wind, sea, and sky. Our Indian Ocean crossing was the smoothest we had yet experienced. Seven days after leaving Thailand, the coast of Sri Lanka loomed on the horizon—an incredibly short time that included several 150-mile days.

It was the familiar dilemma—wait outside for morning or enter in the dark. There was good moonlight, the sea was calm, and we had been given information by *Kamal* and *Cinnebar* on tricks of entry. But there were still problems. The way points that *Kamal* had emailed appeared to take us over a bank and right across a jetty.

Two days before arrival I conferred with *Kemo Sabay* and *Reunion*, our at-sea companions. We all agreed that *Kamal* must have made an error and we would go by coordinates on our charts. *Reunion*, as usual, had the latest chart, 1998. All charts agreed and *Kamal's* way points seemed wrong. For a daytime arrival, there was no problem—visual sighting of only one buoy or land mark and we could make the necessary corrections. But night, that was something different.

"*Kemo Sabay, Kemo Sabay, Skimmer*, I think I see the entry lighthouse, do you see it? Bearing 240 degrees, but it's three flashes at ten second intervals, not two flashes at fifteen seconds. What do you make of it?" We had slowed *Skimmer* and were desperately trying to make sense out of the maze of lights ahead. The only one marked on our chart with characteristics was the lighthouse—but was this it? If not, we could find ourselves on the rocks in moments.

"*Skimmer, Kemo Sabay*—I have your light and concur that it appears to be in the right position, but also concur that it has the incorrect characteristics!"

And then: "*Skimmer, Skimmer*, this is *Cinnabar*, do you copy?"

It's hard to describe the feeling of joy and relief that swept through *Skimmer* and *Kemo Sabay* as we heard Ed's voice. "*Skimmer, Cinnabar*, the light you see is the light house. We can see you from the jetty and you seem to be in the correct position for entry. The way points *Kamal* gave you are correct—it's the charts that are off. Once you sight the sea buoy, head north towards the bright green light and that will take you right in between the buoys." Great! We turned north—but no green light. Sudden realization from Ed. "There was a blackout in the city tonight—the light is probably out. Wait one."

We slowed again and waited, and then Ed's next transmission: "Look north—do you see the light? I just gave the Navy operator two bottles of beer to shine his spotlight. Head for that." Anchor down, a warm reunion with friends, beer and popcorn, and then deep sleep.

***

A three-decker came slicing through the waves. It had been dusk and the precursor of the Sri Lanka nocturnal fishing fleet was feeling its way into prolific fishing grounds. At least a dozen swarthy Sinhalese standing on tiers of poles suspended between masts stared out searching for birds, wakes, or any other sign of fish activity. From a distance it looked like a circus act with tumblers standing on shoulders and forming a human pyramid. That the craft didn't capsize attested to the effectiveness of the huge pontoon outrigger on their starboard side.

We didn't know the purpose or intention of this formidable vessel as it roared between our two boats at full throttle. Peaceful fishermen or pursuing pirates? After seven days at sea, paranoia comes easily and we hadn't been surprised by *Kemo Sabay's* call on VHF to get closer to them and keep our eyes peeled. But the precaution was unnecessary. Sri Lanka came as much as a surprise to us as it must have to Marco Polo hundreds of years ago when he declared Ceylon "undoubtedly the finest island of its size in the world."

At the end of our first day ashore, tired, Charlotte and I were getting ready for the deep sleep we both so richly deserved. Simultaneously, our toothbrushes dropped from our mouths as we both heard a jolting explosion right under our bow. Kaboom! Were we exploding? Wrong direction for our aft propane locker. What could it be? As suddenly as the panic had flared up, understanding had set in and we nodded our realization.

The Galle harbor nightly depth charging had begun. The Navy was sealing off the harbor for the night with cables and buoys, and cruising around tossing depth charges into the water. Kaboom, Kaboom, Kaboom—a not-so-subtle message to discourage Tamil Tiger Frog Men from attaching mines to the rusty Sri Lankan fleet moored in our isolated harbor. Our guide Marlin had explained that all the terrorism was in the north—"Galle very nice place to be. No problem with Tamil Peoples. We all very happy here."

"Yes Marlin, but why is it necessary for your armed forces to bomb us out each night in the harbor?"

The Portuguese, Dutch, and British had all enjoyed Sri Lanka's amenities: natural beauty, a wide range of industrial goods, some of the finest gems in the world, a gentle friendly people. But its reputation for violence and inability to find peaceful cohabitation with the Tamil minority has all but destroyed tourism in the country.

It's similar to what we'd seen in Fiji. Since the native Fijians hadn't been predisposed to hard work on sugar plantations, the British had imported colonies of workers from India. In Ceylon, it had been the unwillingness of the Sinhalese to work the tea plantations that precipitated British encouragement of the mass immigrations of Tamils from India. Hindu versus Buddhist—high work ethic versus a laid-back approach to life. In the north and along the eastern coast of the country, the problem was severe. But, as Marlin explained, life goes on in the rest of the country as if the problem did not exist, with the one exception of the nightly Galle depth charges.

***

Marlin somehow didn't fit his role—tout extraordinaire, wheeler-dealer, provider of all services. We had met his counterparts in many ports. The good ones can considerably ease the life of the visiting yachtsmen with local knowledge and understanding of what cruisers need. The bad ones make a difficult proposition almost impossible. Marlin was definitely in the good category, but what set him apart was his genuine friendliness and honesty.

Lord of land tours, prince of procurement, Marlin quickly made himself indispensable. The fact that he was omnipresent kept this dependency from degenerating into resentment. Outside the high security gate to the harbor there would always be a swarm of waiting Tuc Tucs—motor powered tricycles with a bench in back for passengers—and by some magic, a short, stocky, crew cut Marlin would be in the middle of the crowd smiling and waving his greeting. How could he always be there?

In some ways Marlin typified the Sri Lankans we met. Hospitable, friendly, and interested in making visitors feel welcome, with obvious pride in his country. We were touched by Marlin's invitation to come for dinner at his home before our departure.

While we all looked forward to an interesting experience, we were overwhelmed by what greeted us as we walked through the gates into the yard of Marlin's house. The yard was full of Tuc Tucs, and the house full of drivers and guides Marlin had arranged for us during our visit. It was a mix of family reunion and corporate farewell party. Marlin's wife had been cooking for two days, and the table overflowed with curried Sri Lankan delicacies. I was glad I'd taken my job as cold beer procurer seriously. The noise of frequent toasts to eternal friendship, and boisterous laughing was supplemented by reverberations from the evening port depth charging. It was as if the Navy decided to contribute free fire works, and our feast continued well into the night.

About two light years away there was Rila. Why had we underestimated him at first? Was it the scraggly beard and white skullcap? Or was it his friendly but decidedly subservient bearing? But we shouldn't have underestimated him so much—it had only taken slightly over an hour of his salesmanship to cement the Red Sea crossing for our three yachts.

The first mates of *Skimmer*, *Kemo Sabay*, and *Reunion* had left Rila's South Ceylon Industrial Agency and Handicraft Industries with smiles on their faces and big shinny rocks on their fingers. It was heart warming to see the sparkle in Charlotte's eyes as she stared at the glitter of the blue sapphire and surrounding tiny white sapphires set in gold. My wallet was lighter—but the future

The Red Sea Bribe

was set—the Red Sea Bribe had been paid and there would be no more hysterical discussions on how we would get to the Mediterranean.

But the riddle of Rila had yet to be resolved. Two days before leaving Sri Lanka Charlotte and I had gone by his shop to pick up the certificate for her ring when we were again taken off guard. "Would we give him the honor of coming to his home for dinner?" That night we consulted with *Kemo Sabay* and *Reunion* and the answer—conveyed through Marlin—was "Yes we would be delighted." Again, scouring of our vessels for gifts for children and wife—but this time our efforts were simplified by the absence of a request for us to bring beer and wine.

Tile floors immaculately clean, a room with modest furnishings that featured two display cases, and Rila dressed in white robes with his ever-present skullcap. Hands clasped and smiling he thanked us for coming and, seeing our flowers and gifts, explained why we would not meet his wife and children. "Muslim custom is that in the home, the wife cannot be in the presence of men other than her immediate family. After dinner she can meet your wives, but she will be covered except for her hands and her face from the bottom of the forehead to the top of her mouth. My children are daughters and must also not be seen." His manner and smooth gentle voice were so sincere that what he had just described seemed like the most natural thing on earth.

Sara, Rila, George, and Charlotte

While Rila was entertaining us in his living room, his wife was silently covering their large dining room table in the adjoining room with the fruits of her labor. We couldn't believe our eyes when she finally receded into her realm in the kitchen and Rila proudly led us in to be seated. Plates of food covered every square centimeter of the table— beautifully fried fish (his wife lightly boils it first with fragrant spices to seal in the flavor), flowers made of variegated eggplant and cheese, an exotic chicken fried rice (along with a matching shrimp fried rice because he had somehow found out that the Reunions are vegetarians), and the list went on. It was one of the finest spreads we had seen since beginning our travels in Asia.

Rila declined to join us at the table and explained that his role was to serve his guest and make them feel at home. He hovered over all of us— stuffing our plates and filling our glasses. Our prediction about alcohol, alas, turned out to be true.

Rila was as generous with his insights into his family, work, and Sunni Muslim religion as he was with the elegant food his wife had spent all day preparing. We were spell bound as he gave us a step-by-step description of what his pilgrimage to Mecca had been like and what he had to do to achieve Hajj. His audience was starved for knowledge about his religion and customs and he was able to assuage our appetites with wonderfully clear explanations and vignettes of what it is like to endure the rigors of Ramadan, how the Mosque and call to prayer five times a day affected his life, and even how he was finally able to win the heart of his recalcitrant Buddhist neighbor after five years of trying.

We were all touched by the rigors to which he exposed himself to be a good Muslim. We couldn't help being impressed with the similarity of his values with those of our own Christianity. It was such a boost to all of us to see such concern for fellow man from a Muslim at a time when we were hearing so much negative about radicals who were so abusing his faith.

That was the first night that Rila had entertained Americans in his home. And for some of us, it was the first time we had let a Sunni Muslim into our hearts.

***

We had just returned from a four-day tour of Central Sri Lanka and were exhilarated, bone tired, and ready to just relax on our boats. The ride back in the van had been hair-raising. Sharp turns, potholes, opposing traffic trespassing on our lane as we negotiated blind bends—none of it had deterred our driver from racing ahead of anything else on wheels. Back at the harbor we were happy to be alive. But an unpleasant surprise greeted us as we approached the floating pontoons. A very unhappy Swedish cruiser met us as we dinghied up to the peer: "Just an hour ago—just before dark—the damn fool came in at over twenty knots! Past the breakwater and into the harbor. But the crazy navy captain never slowed the cutter down! My boat took a huge wave into the forward hatch and everything there is ruined! "Your boats," he said, pointing to *Skimmer* and *Kemo Sabay*, "slammed into the pontoon and I think there was damage."

Apparently the language he had used in explaining the situation to George and me was mild compared to what he had said in the heat of his anger to the Sri Lankan Naval Base Commandant, and Lt. Dondallay's presence on *Kemo Sabay's* bow was a direct testimony of the Commandant's wrath. Lt. Dondallay hadn't driven the offending vessel, but he had been the unfortunate duty officer when the Commandant demanded immediate help be given to damaged yachts.

A large section of *Skimmer's* rub rail had been shattered as she pounded against her heavier and almost indestructible neighbor, *Kemo Sabay*. I was pessimistic that Lt. Dondallay could make this good, but the next day he was there with his engineer and carpenter. I disagreed with almost all of their suggestions and was about to tell them I would do it myself, when I realized how deeply sincere the group was in their efforts to make the situation right. Reluctantly I went along with their plan, and was absolutely amazed when two days later I was giving my profuse thanks for an almost perfect repair.

Repairs for Skimmer

Several days later we headed out across the Gulf of Mannar for the 350-mile trip to Cochin, India. This stretch proved to be an exception to the placid conditions in the Indian Ocean during the winter Monsoons, and we felt like we were viewing the world from the inside of a cement mixer. Suddenly over the VHF a loud voice boomed: "Sailing vessel off my starboard bow, this is *Kosmos*. Where are you headed?"

We had been watching the container vessel approach and were delighted to have the call. It was always reassuring to know that other ships could see us, especially when they were huge like *Kosmos*.

"*Kosmos*, this is the sailing vessel *Skimmer*. We are bound for Cochin, India."

"*Skimmer*, *Kosmos*, please to be careful about pirates. Where are you from?"

Before replying I tried to digest this piece of unsolicited advice. Why this warning? What was I supposed to do to be careful? Make myself invisible? And why was he asking me where I was from? Was he maybe one of the pirates I was supposed to be careful about and not the captain of *Kosmos* at all?

Before I could reply he came back with: *Skimmer*, *Kosmos*, you go to Cochin, yes? So also please to be careful about Naval Gun exercise there."

At that point we decided that he was legitimate and had a nice conversation with him about our Charleston, his Yugoslavia and the timing and location of the Cochin Naval exercise.

***

It was the motion of his head that intrigued us. Was it side to side, up and down, a combination of the two, or circular? Like a doll with grinning head pivoting on pin points, his seemed to be loosely attached to his body as it went through its ritualistic motions. What did it mean? Yes? Or yes maybe? Or thank you? Or I am happy?

Our arrival in Cochin began with a six-hour cultural experience checking into the country. We'd followed simple instructions: "Proceed into Cochin harbor and then anchor in front of the Taj Malabar Hotel. You will then please to wait for customs official coming." But the boat that met us as we were trying to decide where to drop anchor in the filthy, shallow waters was a tour boat, and the man on the bow signaling us that he wanted to board had not been in uniform.

"Are you from Customs?" was my suspicious reply as I signaled Charlotte to keep us far enough away to stop him from jumping on board. This was the first time I had seen the strange head motion. A smiling face, big almond brown eyes staring at me as the head swayed, and absolutely no answer to my question.

What then followed was a waltz of watercraft, the man signaling we shouldn't anchor in the spot we'd just chosen and *Skimmer*, halfway complying with his suggestion but keeping at least a boat length away. Finally I saw the papers in his right hand and decided this must be the first step in the elaborate Indian bureaucracy we'd heard so much about. Mustafa from port control came aboard and we began the paper chase.

Thirty minutes later he departed and we fended off a huge gray patrol boat as Krishna of customs jumped aboard with another huge fist full of forms. As we were filling out this set of forms, Ali's rowboat persistently nipped at our stern as he kept repeating a long list of services he wanted to perform for us.

We were almost two hours into the check-in procedure before, with Ali in tow, we headed in to the dinghy dock. It went without saying that Ali would watch our dinghy—he had officially been adopted—and we followed Krishna to his wonderful realm of paperwork.

Normally the ritual of checking into a country consists of going through port control, customs and immigration, and in most countries it can be done in one or two hours. But India has turned this into an exotically complex system that can consume a day and a half. The key to their success in this area is in sending a new arrival onto the next group but requiring him to come back afterwards to finish.

On our way into Krishna's office we thought we were about to finish with Customs. But no, with smile and bobbing head he directed us to the Port Control offices: "You see, the office under the stairs." I did see the office under the stairs and an office in front of the stairs and another office at the top of the stairs—all crammed with ledgers. But the one under the stairs had no people, so I went to a pleasant lady in the office in front. I asked my question and watched the friendly smile and prominent red dot on her forehead move in circles as her head motion signaled that she might or might not understand my question. She led me to a vacant desk piled high with papers and pointed to one on top. To my amazement it was one of the forms I had started to fill out on board *Skimmer*—but one item was missing, payment. Should I go back to customs to pay? Again the head bobbing. I interpreted this as yes and walked back across the street to Krishna where his head bobbing convinced me that her head bobbing had really meant no, and I then walked over to another corner of the triangle of bureaucracy. Here money was involved and there was a whole block of offices. On my third try it looked like I was about to score. But no, yachts were handled in the next office down.

Cautiously optimistic we entered, and as our eyes adjusted to the partial darkness we could see ledgers everywhere, floor to ceiling, shelf after shelf overflowing, covered with cobwebs, stacks wrapped in old newspapers and bound with brown string—and four desks. The occupant of the second desk motioned us over, but our attention was riveted on the first desk. The occupant had obviously succumbed to the excitement; he was sprawled over the top, his head resting on a pillow of unfinished paperwork, snoring.

While I was deciding whether I had the nerve to take a picture, the man at the second desk who had signaled us over made a quick decision. Polite to a fault, the Indian bureaucrats showed an almost maniacal desire to have both Charlotte and me seated before they felt it proper to begin their inquiries, but here there was no room. Sleeping beauty had commandeered the only other chair for his nap. With great dignity and politeness, the second functionary woke his office mate and led him outside so that Charlotte could have his seat.

Later we compared notes with other recent arrivals and no, our experience hadn't been unusual. They also agreed they had not resented the process and because the people had been so friendly they had almost enjoyed it.

***

Kerala is a country within a country. A narrow strip of incredibly fertile land near the bottom of the western coast of India with a vast and intricate system of waterways along its coast, a state that proclaims its superiority over its nation, a state where its inhabitants speak a different language, and a place where its residents refer to their land as "God's Country". It reminded us of South Carolina.

But it took our driver Peter to make us appreciate the finer points of this wonderful new land. During our forty-minute drive he captivated us with his enthusiasm for his native Kerala: a declining population in a country plagued with overpopulation, over ninety percent literacy versus less than fifty percent nationally, religious harmony among Christians, Hindus, and Muslims, a keen awareness of environmental problems and pioneering laws for recycling. At this point I had to interrupt him: "Wait a minute, Peter. Recycling? What about the piles of trash that are everywhere—even just outside the lawn of the Bolgatty Palace Hotel?"

He looked at me, thought a minute, gave me one of the better head rolls I had seen and explained it was older people who threw trash everywhere, but the young have been taught in school and as time goes on the pollution will diminish.

The conversation got interesting as we switched to September 11, Pakistan, and President Musharraf. Charlotte made a series of statements disguised as questions, praising the help the US had obtained from Musharraf, to get Peter's reaction. She interpreted Peter's head bobbing as agreement and enthusiasm for her views and got herself entrenched deeper and deeper.

Finally I felt I had to interrupt Charlotte's monologue: "Peter, do you like President Musharraf?"

"He was the head of intelligence before he was president. What do you think he does? Why do you think he let all the Taliban escape into Pakistan? He is a very bad man and America is fooled by him." From this relatively calm beginning Peter explained that in India people were not afraid of terror—they have lived with it for many years—ever since the British left. He said that he was sure India would never drop the first atomic bomb, but if Pakistan did so their response would be immediate and overwhelming— Pakistan would no longer exist as a country.

Less than thirty miles from the bustle and pollution of one of India's largest ports we stepped into an entirely different world. The wooden boat was about thirty feet long, six feet wide and capable of carrying up to 10,000 pounds of cargo. I was mesmerized by the boatman's graceful motion as his matchstick thin, sinuous arms and legs kept the long pole moving rhythmically and how effectively his efforts propelled us along the green countryside. Everything here moves by water and every family has a boat. Peter showed us how holes nine feet deep and nine feet in diameter are dug, filled with sand, and then fed by rainwater from roofs until the action of the fresh water flowing into the sand-filled holes begins to displace salt water in the surrounding soil and the ground becomes arable. He explained that even in these backwaters, education is universal and the children are transported by boat daily to schools.

Thailand and Sri Lanka had been dry holes as far as finding a Protestant service, and Charlotte wasn't going to miss the opportunity for us to attend

Sunday morning worship at India's oldest church. We did not realize that the "combined service" at Saint Francis would be entirely in Malayalam with only an occasional reference to the hymn number of the English version of a hymn—but it didn't matter. We just listened to the beautiful language, admired the rainbow of saris, and kept glancing at the impressive brass rails just to the right of our pew that surrounded what had been the grave of Vasco da Gamma before his remains had been returned to Portugal.

Charlotte at St. Francis Church

But the main attraction for us was the well-stocked bookstore we stumbled upon after our visit to the Cochin Synagogue. The proprietor spent half an hour with Charlotte helping her pick out a book on Indian horticulture, and I spent the time digging through the piles of books on Cochin, Kerala, the Malabar Coast, and India. Of the four books I purchased, my prize was a shortened version of *The Ramayana* compiled by R.K. Narayan.

Each time I've attempted to read about Hinduism and tried to understand the complex relationship among the deities, my efforts have ended with frustration and confusion. Vishnu the preserver, Shiva the destroyer, and Brahma the creator—it's just when I feel I have begun to gain a basis for understanding that the names and numbers of the gods begins to expand exponentially and I become hopelessly lost.

But in reading about the exploits of Rama, the hero of India's greatest epic, I had begun to understand how the pieces fit together. It began when Rama was young. Neither he nor his father knew that he was actually the incarnation of Vishnu. As he traveled through the land with his guide and mentor, the sage Viswamithra, he began to right the wrongs that jealous gods had wreaked among themselves and along the way, Viswamithra told him the various stories that explained the creation. It seemed like a mixture of Greek Mythology, Arthurian legend, and Don Quixote, all recounted with the realism and clarity of Alice in Wonderland.

Before coming to Cochin Charlotte had been quite vocal about her position. "I'm simply overwhelmed. I can't take any more tours; I don't want to meet 'the people.' I'm tired. I just want to lie down on a beach and relax.

Why couldn't we have gone to the Maldives like everyone else?" But she was just a little upset by the high winds off Cape Cormorin and a little scared of the possibility of pirates. I had known that once we got there, she would love Cochin and Kerala. When I asked her the morning of our departure if she wasn't glad we had chosen India instead of the Maldives, she stopped what she was doing, gave me a long stare, and then broke into a smile as she bobbed her head in non-answer to my question.

**

Forbidden islands. Why do they always have to be the most desirable, the most exotic? But we must leave them on the horizon of our dreams and sail on. We'd experienced this frustration many times: the Lau Group in the Fiji Islands, Tanna in Vanuatu, and the Nicobar Islands off the western coast of Thailand. The write-ups in our guide books are fantastic—and they are right in our path—nature begs us to come visit. But man has his politics. The end result is a sailor must watch through tired eyes as a paradise passes by.

The Lakshadweep Islands were about to be added to our list of forbidden islands. Our cruising guide had advised against stopping, and cautioned that travel on the islands was severely restricted and generally off bounds to foreigners. We'd have skipped them except they were the perfect location for a rendezvous with *Kemo Sabay*. Two hundred miles off the southwestern coast of India—a perfect place to lie in the sun. We knew the Indian bureaucracy was daunting but decided to give it a try. It was an afternoon well spent. The port police directed us to customs which said if it was okay with immigration it was okay with them. Immigration had given approval, and directed us to *MV Minicoy*, a ship that visits the islands regularly and could give us some information on navigation and anchorages.

On final checkout three days later, I asked immigration officials who had sanctioned our trip to give us something in writing. "Not to worry, Captain—you have India Visa—that is all required—have no immigration office at Bangaram—you not have trouble, that certain." I wasn't certain and decided to play my trump card. "It was very kind of you to refer me to *MV Minicoy* and they were very helpful. They go to Bangaram often and gave us very good information." While the two officials were beaming their acknowledgment of my thanks, I added: "But Captain Sivasan told me I must insist on written authority from you before I can go."

They exchanged looks, conferred in Malayalam, and then went into the back room to see the boss. I could hear the heated discussion, but the smile on their faces as they returned told me I had won. The paper contained our permission, a number of stamps in red and blue ink, and a clear statement that we were authorized to stop in Bangaram on our way to Oman.

The morning of our third day out of Cochin rose Bangaram. As the sun began to illuminate the sky I admired the beautiful sandy beaches and Charlotte planned her outfits and number of baths she would take at the island's luxury hotel. A sharp crackle on our VHF interrupted our reveries: "Sailing vessel, sailing vessel, this is Pappa III—please acknowledge."

"Good morning Pappa III, this is *Skimmer*. How can we help you?"

"*Skimmer*, please to tell us if you have peermiision to enter Bangaram."

Charlotte and I smiled at each other—here was where the special precautions would pay off. But special precautions didn't seem to have the magic effect we expected. Pappa III kept us on the radio for almost two hours with a series of questions, many of which we couldn't possibly answer.

"What is the phone number of peoples that gave you this peermiision?"

"I don't have a phone number but it was the Immigration Office at Cochin that gave us permission. I have a written document from them. If you would like to send a boat to our vessel, I can show it to them."

"Please to wait while we try to call Cochin. And please not to anchor. If you anchor this cause big problem."

We waited and waited and waited. And finally our answer came in the form of a boat full of uniformed policemen heading for our circling vessel. Their chief was the largest Indian I had seen since our arrival in India. The boat was huge and lethally bouncing in the waves that separated our two vessels. Charlotte had fenders rigged and the approaching boat was lined with tires—but to me their boat looked like a hole punching monster intent on doing harm to *Skimmer* and I wanted no part of it.

The sergeant was standing on the side rail ready to board, but the frown on his face told me all I needed to know. If there was any doubt left, it went away as he came within hailing distance.

"You have not peermiision to anchor here. Please to go away." As he said this three pairs of dark hands grasped our rub rails and made an effort to hold the heaving vessels apart.

Show our special "permission", receive the giant sergeant aboard, stay and argue while *Skimmer* was being pulverized by our neighbor? Or just let this paradise go the way of other forbidden islands and settle for cold showers on *Skimmer* instead of luxury on Bangaram? It was an easy decision, and we agreed that the best thing for *Skimmer* to do was immediately head for Oman.

It was a shame to miss these islands. The Lakshadweeps are a long string of atolls geologically and culturally very similar to their southern neighbor, the Maldives. They are predominantly Muslim and governed by India. We were not sure exactly why they were so restricted—*Lonely Planet's* explanation of overpopulation and environmental concerns seemed unlikely in view of the militant reception laid on for *Skimmer*. We both felt confident the answer was more likely territorial jealousy with Pakistan.

That was the end of our plan to sail along with *Kemo Sabay* for the longest leg of our trip to the Red Sea. She was four hundred miles behind, just nearing the coast of India, and we were just entering the vastness of the Arabian Sea with 1,100 miles separating us from Oman.

"Alone, alone, all all alone,"—but that was the irony—we were not alone. There were small groups everywhere—coming from Sri Lanka, coming from the Maldives, coming from India—and all converging on the same spot—Salalah Oman. And each day at eight in the morning and six in the afternoon the SSB radio waves came alive with boats giving their positions, their weather conditions, and miscellaneous information. Just 50 miles ahead of us was a group of three Kiwi boats we had anchored with in Cochin, five hundred miles ahead was *Reunion* and at the rear *Kemo Sabay* was slogging her way across the Gulf of Mannar.

Oman was where we would form our convoys before braving the Gulf of Aden. So far over thirty cruisers had arrived there, many of whom had already formed their groups and left for the Red Sea.

***

The sunrise that greeted me at my morning watch was particularly stunning. A perfect orange ball rose above a purple mist and revealed a glassy ocean. We had been motoring all night, but I decided to see if I could keep steerage with only three knots of wind. The reward was instant. Heavy diesel throbbing and vibration gave way to absolute silence and a profound calm settled. And it was this quiet that revealed what darkness, noise, and sail flapping had masked before. The sea was alive. bonita or tuna or Mackerel? I couldn't tell, but they were everywhere. Not the mad churning and frenzy you see in schools that are feeding, but gentle swishing motions as they quietly skipped just above the surface. The real treat came after my watch when I was taking my morning nap.

Charlotte shook me out of my trance and made me come on deck immediately. Right next to *Skimmer*, like a child showing off but staying close to Mama, a beautiful combination of iridescent blue, green, and yellow streaked through the water. Almost on the surface, then down a few feet, but always only three to ten feet off our starboard side. Usually the radiant magnificence of a mahi mahi only lasts seconds. Once landed the colors leave before death comes. But our new friend stayed with us for hours allowing us to rejoice in its beauty for an entire morning.

So far it had been like a giant lake. Gentle wind interspersed with dead calm. Flat seas, glistening with reflected sun all day, alive with phosphorescence at night. It would have been nice to get rid of the dead calms so we could get there faster, but still, it was near to being perfect for a comfort-loving crew.

We didn't change course. We didn't change sails. We allowed ourselves to be carried on by the breezes and watched for shipping that was rarely there.

At night the watch schedule was rigorous enough to make us physically tired but allowed almost unlimited time for contemplation. That is what made night watches so wonderful. The body was lethargic but the mind was active. I theorized on how the ancients did their navigation and mentally designed instruments to help them with their labors. I invented new ways to keep our refrigerator cold without the use of electricity, designed wind vane autopilots, and made improvements on *Skimmer* from stem to stern. In my mind. Near the end of my watches these ideas would become so clear and so brilliantly thought out that I couldn't wait to put them on paper. When morning came, enthusiasm waned, the hidden flaws became apparent, and the ideas receded to wait for another beautiful night to present themselves for further contemplation and refinement.

* * *

Our smoothest passage yet was about to end in the smoothest possible manner. For the past twenty-four hours I had been counting the miles, watching the speed log, and continually updating my calculations. Even if we lost our favorable one-knot current, *Skimmer*'s diesel was going to push us through the glassy seas and breathless air into Salalah harbor with daylight to spare. In only three hours we'd be comfortably anchored.

Charlotte was getting her afternoon nap and I was watching the steady stream of shipping into and out of Salalah, thinking how lucky we had been. Unlike most of the boats ahead of us, we'd not seen the very bright lights to the east that indicated fishing fleets with nets that strung out over four miles. Unlike *Reunion* and *Otter,* we'd not had the harrowing experience of having a Somalian ship come to within hailing distance and ask questions about number of passengers on board and destination. And we hadn't heard the constant warnings over VHF from the special operations seismic ship that was towing a seven-mile-long floating cable somewhere across our path.

Suddenly my contentment was interrupted by a heavy French accent over our VHF. I could have pretended not to have heard it. After all, the call had not been to *Skimmer*. But the fact was, I had heard it and my conscience wouldn't let me pretend. Reluctantly I woke Charlotte from her nap. Her happy smile faded when I told her, but she agreed, so I went back to our VHF, picked up the microphone, stared at it for a moment in hesitation and pushed the transmit button. *"Liberdad, Liberdad,* this is *Skimmer*. We are twenty miles out of Salalah and I heard your call to Port Control."

Their call to Port Control had been a sad one. They had lost their motor and were almost motionless in the flat seas just ten miles out of Salalah. Their request to Port Control for assistance in getting into port had been met with the unhappy news that this assistance would have to be in the form of a tug and the cost would be $300 US per hour. I heard the disappointment in Fabienne's voice as she refused assistance. This meant drifting around another night and hoping for wind. What I didn't know was *Liberdad* had left Cochin more than a week before us. She had been at sea three weeks and they were exhausted and also almost out of food. Fabienne's ecstatic enthusiasm at my offer to tow them in was heartwarming, but suddenly *Skimmer*'s easy daytime approach had evaporated.

Our first time towing was going to be into an unknown port and at night. We tried to work out all the logistics. Fabienne was to have a 50-meter towing line ready on the bow, and *Skimmer* would pass close by and heave a messenger line. They said they would be ready.

The blob on the horizon took on the shape of a sailboat, idle flapping sails came into sight, and finally the white hull and three passengers of *Liberdad* became visible. As we approached, the rust and seaweed on the formidable looking steel hull told of years of neglect. Whatever had happened to their engine looked like it could happen to the rest of the vessel at any time. If I could have seen it before I had called on the radio, would I have made the offer? I chastised myself. Yes, of course I would have.

The 50-meter line gave us a nice safety margin and *Skimmer* seemed to be comfortable towing the 38-footer at about half our normal speed. Port control was very helpful. They were happy that *Skimmer* had taken *Liberdad* under tow (their problem was now solved) and they gave us clearance to enter port. Everything was going exactly according to plan until about one mile from the sea buoy.

"*Skimmer, Skimmer,* this is port control. A large container ship is leaving port now and you are please to delay your entry until they are out." Was I on the edge of the channel as I hoped, or right in the middle? From my chart and from what I was able to see, I couldn't tell. And what were those other flashing red and green lights that weren't on my chart marking? It would have been hard enough to stop *Skimmer* by itself, but now we were two. A sudden stop would bring 15 tons of unkind steel into my stern. A turn was doable, but would be wide and slow. I was acutely aware of my reduced maneuverability as I waited to see the giant bow appear from behind the breakwater. As the time dragged my disorientation increased. At moments I would believe myself completely lost and would go below to examine my chart to reassure myself that we were okay and well away from the breakwater.

Then came a silent silhouette. If it continued straight, I would be to its starboard and all would be well. But at the end of the breakwater, the long silhouette began to shorten. The two range lights were coming together and forming a smaller and smaller triangle with the green running light at the bottom. I tightened my grip on the binoculars and prayed that her turn to starboard would continue. The range lights came together and then I was looking at the terrible triangle—white on top, green on the bottom to the left, and red on the bottom to the right. She was heading strait towards us. Mercifully the triangle stayed only moments before the green disappeared and there was only red. She had completed her turn and would leave us well to her port.

Tension had returned to almost normal levels when a long fishing boat turned our way. We all saw it at the same time and started shouting. From *Liberdad* "Tow, Tow, Tow", from *Skimmer* "Tow, Tow, Tow." But none of the Americans, nor French in our group knew the Arabic word for "tow" and the heavy boat kept on coming. It wasn't her fault. We didn't have proper lights to indicate towing, and as far as the fishermen knew we were just two boats traveling, one behind the other. They saw no problem in cutting in between.

But they did hear us and could see us frantically signaling to them. Just before intersecting our tow line, they raised their outboard motor—but the line still caught on their bow and as the long slide towards *Liberdad* began, my thoughts alternated between splintered wood with fishermen in the water and the unhappy knowledge that the fault would all be mine. But we were going slowly, the crew of *Liberdad* helped the fishermen with a giant push and the fishing boat slid undamaged down *Liberdad's* port side.

Liberdad at Anchor at Salalah

The Gulf of Aden

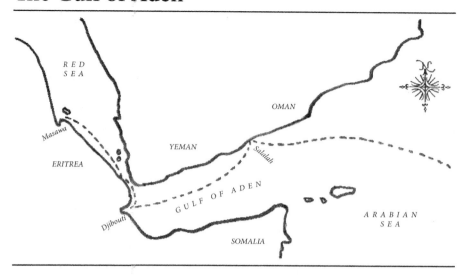

I f Mars were all white, it would look a lot like Oman. It couldn't look much stranger. Perched at the Southern end of the Arabian Peninsular, Oman shares the Arabian Sea coastline with Yemen. Our new home in Salalah was only about fifty miles from the Yemen boarder. The port is huge—giant container ships are constantly coming and going—the larger ones carrying a thousand containers. But the population is sparse, and Salalah is on the end of a single road that connects the desert to the east with the more thriving portion of Oman that borders the Persian Gulf. Where do the containers go? Who was going to use the contents of the hundreds of thousands of containers?

Our travel books said the region surrounding Salalah enjoyed the benefits of the monsoons from India and was the lushest part of the entire country. All we saw was dry white sand everywhere—high mountains of sand along the coast, sandy planes between the port and the city, and white sand broken only by whiter-than-white whitewashed buildings. In the city we were happy for the white because it deflected the almost unbearable heat as we dashed from the shadow of one large building to the shade of the next. It took just one visit to the city to understand why everything was closed from noon until four o'clock.

We were isolated at our anchorage in the port, and actually we were not officially visiting the country. The very pleasant and very polite port police took our passports into custody upon arrival and gave us a piece of paper we were required to have stamped each time we left or reentered the port. Stamping took place at the guard shack that marked the end of the long road to the port and the beginning of the desert. There were ten spaces for stamps, and we believed that when they were all full, we would be asked to leave the country. Each morning when we checked with the guards, they greeted us with smiles and firm hand shakes but also warned us to be back on our boats by ten o'clock at night.

The walk down the road from the port was long and hot, and from the guard shack to town was a twenty-minute cab ride even at the Omani's customary break-neck speeds. If you turned left at the shack and walked up a steep hill, you were rewarded with a deep blue bay and beach below, with white buildings surrounded by white walls and date palm groves. It was the establishment just over the top that won our hearts.

The Oasis Restaurant was the only place in Salalah that served alcohol. The main dining room featured a well stocked bar, tablecloths, uniformed waiters, and a menu that included Indian and European as well as Arab foods. It was one night at the Oasis that Andrew unlocked some of the mysteries of Salalah for us. Originally from the Channel Islands, he had been working in the television industry in Salalah for eight years. He explained the port had been enlarged and rebuilt three years ago, which is why I had such a problem reading my charts. It had been designed as a giant transshipment facility, and sophisticated computers and huge cranes redistributed the thousands of containers as they arrived in port and then sent them out to other destinations. Very little remained here.

And the lush greenery? He insisted that in fact the green in Salalah is magnificent—but it happens in another season.

Warships at Salalah

We had been on our way back from our nightly gathering at the Oasis Restaurant when I had noticed Charlotte was engaged in conversation with a blue man. He was a head shorter than her, and there was sufficient moonlight for me to see he wasn't completely blue—it was only the tattoos that covered most of his enthusiastically flailing arms. His name was Jimmy.

We accepted his invitation and followed him to the long pier separated from the rest of the port by yet another set of 12-foot-high-barbed wire walls. *HMS Port Rosalie* was docked in front of a British Aircraft Carrier and was almost as big. Jets, helicopters, missiles, and guns nestled on deck below a skyline of antennas and rotating radars.

A petite brunette in fatigues, with a machine gun draped over her lap, threw us a warm smile as Jimmy was checking us in on the quarterdeck. We passed huge crates of weapons and ammunition as he led us down two decks below. Already impressed with how different *Port Rosalie* was from anything I'd encountered in my five years service in the US Navy, I was surprised when we reached our final destination. The huge room was full, pulsating with activity—cute young girls to scruffy old lechers, tee shirts to dress whites, and a range of accents not to be believed. And five different beers on tap, plus scotch, gin, rum, vodka, liqueurs, cordials, wine, and sherry.

In white uniform with shoulder boards denoting lieutenant commander, David was one of the few officers in our group. He listened to our adventures and our concerns as we were on the eve of entering into the most dangerous part of our voyage.

"You don't have to worry. You are completely safe. Operation Coalition consists of five countries, and we are providing constant air surveillance from the Arabian Sea the whole way to South Africa. Every potential pirate knows we are out there. If you call us on channel 16 on VHF, tell us you are in trouble, and give us your coordinates, we will pick you up on our screens in less than a minute and have either a jet or a helicopter over your boat in less than fifteen minutes later. We have complete satellite coverage over the entire area and would even be able to see the individuals trying to board you."

What a feeling of relief! There we were, standing on firm British Steel, with this gentleman explaining that the might of the British, US, Australian, German, and French Navies was just a radio call away. It was the happiest I had seen Charlotte since we had begun our trek to the Red Sea.

Naturally we reciprocated and the all-afternoon party began on board *Nordhaven* the next day. *Nordhaven* was the first around-the-world trawler we had been with, and the configuration of freezers and iceboxes on board was truly impressive. It was an ideal setting to begin the oiling of our new British friends. The party had reached a high pitch when it came time to transfer festivities over to *Skimmer*. Jimmy was only normal-sailor-drunk when he reached *Skimmer*, and there must have been something particularly attractive about my rum punches that precipitated his downhill slide. Fortunately, his already difficult to understand Cockney degenerated at about the same rate as his vocabulary and the ladies couldn't really understand his descriptions of the actions he would like to take with them. His friend Will made valiant efforts to keep Jimmy on the strait and narrow, but these interruptions were only brief diversions before he went back to his favorite theme.

Will: "Jimmy, tell them about your wife and family."

Jimmy: "Aw mate, I ain't got no wife. I has me three Jap brats and me woman is waiting for me when I gets there. Ah yes, when I gets there. She is the sweetest thing you have ever seen and she is always ready to …" and off he would go again into what we all chose to consider incomprehensible.

But Jimmy and Will had become our new heroes and everyone was willing to make allowances. They were both enamored with our cruising life and despite Jimmy's lapses, they were nice young men. Both were able-bodied seamen aboard the supply ship *Port Rosalie* and both members of the British Merchant Marine. Before alcohol had assumed complete control, Jimmy explained to Charlotte that although the *Port Rosalie* was a merchant marine ship, her captain and officers were Royal Navy. He also explained with bitterness his hatred for all those in the Royal Navy: "They just ain't got no respect for us blokes in the merchant marine." Had he been born in an earlier epoch, Jimmy could become the prototype for one of Patrick O'Brian's colorful characters, maybe somewhere between Killick and Boden.

* * *

Nassar Ali   *Goat and Gun Market*

Nassar Ali was the best guide we'd yet had. Dressed in a tan *dishdash* with his head covered by an elegant red turban, he was waiting with his van in front of the British Bank. We started with a visit to the combination Goat and Gun Market. Squatting around the square were little groups of bearded, turbaned figures with their stacks of guns, bullets, and knives carefully arranged about them as goats wandered everywhere. It looked more like a CNN news clip of efforts to smoke out Bin Laden than a peaceful city market.

Any goat, knife, or gun was there to buy. About the only thing that wasn't available was an AK47, and we were told that these could also be purchased if special arrangements were made.

On our way out of town and up into the mountains, Nassar Ali pointed to the vast stretches of white arid desert and explained that during June, July, and August all would be green, and the density of visitors from the other regions of the Arabian Peninsula would be so high that it would be hard to stake out even a small picnic site. Annually over a million rain-starved Arabs made their way to this unique location where the Indian Ocean Monsoons deposit their last drops of water before dissipating into the endless sands of Arabia.

We saw camels by the hundreds. Nassar Ali pointed out the danger. Their huge mass on stilt legs is exactly the wrong configuration for an automobile traveling at near 100 miles per hour. Unlike deer, dogs, or cows, the camel's center of gravity is such that there is no deflection, and all the energy of the collision goes directly from hump to windshield to passengers. The many signs warning of camels are no joke. The previous year

The Camel Hazard

a seminar on camel safety had been aborted at the last minute because the seminar leader was killed in a camel collision on his way to the conference.

We visited Job's tomb but what impressed us the most was the recent excavation of Khor Rouri. There wasn't much left of what was once had been one of the principal ports for the export of frankincense, but our imagination could fill the gaps: ships coming and going from all over the world, converging here where 2,000 years ago was one of the wealthiest cities on earth. All of the frankincense in the world had come from southern Oman. An aromatic gum resin extracted from trees of the Boswellia family, it had been crucial in religious rites and medicine in almost all countries. It is speculated that the frankincense presented in Bethlehem by the Magi was worth more than all the other gifts of gold and jewels combined.

***

One doesn't visit the Sultan's Palace in Salalah. Visitors are not allowed. And there isn't just one palace; there are three—blocks of beautifully tiled,

179

domed roofs surrounded by high white walls. Nassar Ali drove us around the perimeters as he explained that the Sultan seldom visits his properties or his thousands of thoroughbred horses. But if we were not to have the pleasure of visiting the Sultan or his palace, we were to have the pleasure of the Sultan visiting us. Or maybe pleasure isn't the appropriate word to describe the event.

While the Omanis had been friendliness itself, the ugly face of autocracy was never very far below the surface. We weren't entirely surprised when they informed us all yachts would have to leave the port within 24 hours and re-anchor outside the breakwater. The reason they gave just didn't make sense. Even with over 20 ships in the harbor it still looked almost empty. How could the arrival of a few more ships possibly make enough difference to kick us out of our secure anchorage nestled in a small corner of the port?

Our answer came after the third beer during our visit aboard *Port Rosalie*. The ship had been talking about nothing else for two days. The Sultan and his private yacht were coming, and they would moor in the exact spot where we had all been coming ashore and tying up our dinghies. George and I watched from the pier. It was more a warship than a yacht, with a huge helicopter pad on the stern and modern guns on the bow. As we dinghied off, the ultramodern LST-like platform/bow was lowering to make a ramp for the exiting entourage. We were tempted to wait long enough to see if a long black stretch limo was going to roll off, but our boats were ready and it was time to depart for the Red Sea. At noon on March 2, 2002, *Kemo Sabay*, *Reunion*, and *Skimmer*, a tight formation of three, departed Oman on the 760-mile trip to Djibouti.

* * *

The Gulf of Aden turned out to be much like the Arabian Sea. Flat seas interspersed with gentle winds. The gulf laid claim to yet another unique phenomenon. The sand hills were receding over the horizon and we were just beginning to think about settling *Skimmer* down for the evening, when we saw huge patches of churning water. The sea was boiling with fish. Charlotte and I were both laughing, pointing, and thoroughly enjoying ourselves when it first happened.

Charlotte saw it first and made me focus my attention at a spot in one of the patches. Nothing there, but suddenly I saw another in a patch that was even closer to us. Fish jumping are always fun to watch, but this was something entirely different. They were huge and the jumps were impossibly high. Sometimes fifteen to twenty feet. How could a fish jump five times its length straight up into the air? And it wasn't just the height that captivated us. The silver streak went up, hung stationary at the top of its arc, then gracefully dove back into the sea. After seeing about a dozen spectacular dives, we were convinced that they were spinner dolphins.

As pleasant as our passage was turning out to be, we feared unwanted visitors. My exhaustive internet research had kept coming back to the Imray Publishing Company's Pirate Report that appeared on their home page. In the past three years there had been 15 reported incidents involving Cruisers in the Gulf of Aden and of those 15 only five were verified as actual acts of piracy. Imray calculated that with the number of boats passing through during that period the rate of incidents had been less than one half of one percent.

It's funny how differently people can interpret the same data. Instead of taking comfort from the report, Charlotte's repeated response to me had been: "If there is no danger of pirates, why do they have a Pirate Report?" I had to admit Charlotte's views reflected the majority opinion among fellow cruisers. During our stay in Oman we'd held frequent conferences at the Oasis Restaurant to determine the best strategy. We agreed the best route through the Gulf of Aden would be on a path about one-third the distance from the Yemen coast and two-thirds from the Somalian coast. We all knew Yemen was dangerous and Somalia disastrous. A forced landing in Somalia would almost certainly have led to the seizure of boats and quite possibly the loss of lives.

Groups of three to five boats had been departing daily and most had adopted the same precautions as our group of three. Minimize conversations on the VHF and when talking use only Channel 22A (a channel reserved for the Coast Guard in the US and generally not in use in other countries); use hand-held radios and transmit on low power (signal carries only a short distance so others can't hear we are out there); never give positions over the radio, only distances to pre-arranged way points with coded names; use deck level running lights instead of the long range masthead lights (some boats opted for no lights at all); stay within half a mile of other boats in the group so that if one is attacked, others can immediately close in; have high powered lights, loud alarms, and flares ready to try to scare off a potential attacker if he starts to close; and finally maintain a minimum speed (even it means motoring) to get through the dangerous parts as quickly as possible.

We left Oman on high alert despite the assurances we had received from Her Majesty's Royal Navy. Tension was high but nothing happened—not for the first two nights. Well away from shore, no other boats sighted since leaving Salalah except for occasional large ships, and constant radio traffic from warships that seemed to be everywhere, challenging any ships that came into their paths—I was sure my night watch on the third evening was going to be a calm one.

Coffee in one hand, a fresh blueberry muffin in the other, I was set to relax and contemplate the stars. At first I thought the light might be a star rising—but it didn't rise. It was very bright and just off the starboard bow. I called *Kemo Sabay* and *Reunion* and they were monitoring also. No running lights—only the single bright white light and no bearing drift. I didn't like what I was seeing at all. Willing the light to starboard didn't work, and then a terse radio communication from Sara on *Kemo Sabay* who was slightly ahead and to my right: "*Skimmer*, *Kemo Sabay*, I think he is going to come between our two boats."

Conventional wisdom said night attacks were rare. Danger was much greater in daylight and the Imray Report had advised to travel past the worst spots in the dark. There was enough moonlight to make out the shape of the boat beneath the bright light. Long, sleek, sinister, it was an open boat and very fast. The crucial moment arrived when it came abreast *Skimmer* and only about two hundred yards away. I tensed while gripping the VHF in my right hand: "*Kemo Sabay*, *Skimmer*, he is very, very close—I can't tell yet whether he is going to turn towards" and then I waited. Time stood still as I watched to see if I needed to have *Kemo Sabay* and *Reunion* converge. Did he slow and look us over? Almost as quickly as it had begun, it ended. The cigar shape turned away, accelerated, and receded into the night.

Two days later we had a repeat performance and this time in Daylight. We had allowed *Skimmer* to fall almost two miles astern of *Reunion* and *Kemo Sabay*. The boat looked the same vintage we'd seen two nights before and it was definitely turning in. Adrenaline was high when I made my emergency call to the others to head towards *Skimmer*. The boat rounded our stern and looked like it was about to come in strong. Did they see me holding the radio and hear me frantically calling for help? I switched to channel 16 so they would hear my calls to *Kemo Sabay* and *Reunion*. Or did they decide *Skimmer* was slim pickings and not worth the trouble? Or were they innocent fishermen curious to see what kind of animal lived aboard the fancy yachts? Whatever, before we could take any further action, they turned away.

Our last night at sea was amid a stream of warships, all part of "Operation Coalition." Early in the morning we were comforted when a large frigate silently glided by us and we could see through binoculars that guns were fully manned. And then beautiful brown cliffs came into sight as *Skimmer* approached her fourth continent. Our entry into Africa was into her smallest country. But size and might did not necessarily coincide and we watched with awe as helicopters hovered, jets roared, and warships threw huge wakes throughout our entire approach into Djibouti's harbor.

***

Djibouti probably would not exist as a country if not for its very strategic location on the west side of the mouth of the Red Sea. As a counter to the British presence in Yemen on the east side of the mouth, the French built and maintained a magnificent port here. For many years it was maintained as part of the French Empire, but in 1977 it was granted independence. Despite a continued French presence, Djibouti has gone downhill since its heydays. Its once proud buildings are in wretched disrepair and the stench of poverty is everywhere.

At the Djibouti Yacht Club a pretty, dark woman who acted as receptionist, waitress, and business manager greeted us and explained the protocol in beautiful French. Visitors pay a $100 deposit and then everything is paid for by signing chits. The exchange rate was 170 Djibouti Francs per US dollar which made figuring costs almost impossible. Had we calculated that the beer was costing over five dollars a bottle, we might have had fewer, but no matter, we were sailors in from the sea and we splurged on a wonderful dinner of green salad and grilled shrimp. When I asked Decca about tours into the interior, she arranged for a van and guide to pick us up in the morning. Promptly at 9:00 a.m. Decca took us to a twenty passenger bus that looked like it might still have some life left in it and introduced us to the guide and to the driver, who was her brother-in-law. Neither of them spoke English or French. But Decca produced an interpreter named Barracuda, and waved us goodbye.

The bus was halfway across the causeway when we found that Barracuda's French was almost as bad as our guide's. But Barracuda had been hired as a translator and translator he would be. While it was very difficult to discourse with the guide directly, it was almost impossible with Barracuda in the middle. Barracuda's teeth were more horizontal than vertical and I had a hard time concentrating on what he was trying so energetically to

Goats and Rubbish in Djibouti

explain as I wondered if his unfortunate denture had somehow given rise to his name. But he was persistent, and I finally understood that he was letting me know that he had a passport and would be willing to accompany us on our boat in our trip up the Red Sea. He was also offering his services for anything from diving our boats to doing our laundry.

As we traveled through the outskirts of the city we were appalled by the filth. Rubbish was everywhere and in some spots mounds of it were three feet high. For every rubbish pile there were two or three goats, forsaking the shade to forage in the filth. And for every goat in the rubbish piles, there were half a dozen more dozing under cars, beside buildings, under trees. I saw one goat basking in the shade provided by three people seated on a bench.

Gaily clad Bedouin women contrasted with the dirt and grime of their surroundings. Then there was just desert and rocks—but something funny about the rocks. In many places there were patterns. According to my *Lonely Planet* guide, pyramids of rocks marked spots where Bedouins had met with unnatural death, or rock walls marked shelters Bedouins had constructed to protect themselves and their animals, and piles of pebbles marked with little red flags denoted graves of Muslim Holy Men. But what about the miles and miles of rocks laid out in neat rows? Who put them there? Why?

Sara and Charlotte at Lake Assal

The countryside went from stark to surreal as we approached Lac Assal. At 500 feet below sea level, this is the lowest point in Africa and is located in a volcanically active area. The lake is salt water and through evaporation has become encrusted with acres of salt flats. It is unbearably hot. The geothermal springs spew water into the lake that is hot enough to cook an egg. Surrounding the blinding whiteness of Lake Assal, black volcanic rock stands in isolated mounds and stretches for miles. We were able to bear the heat just long enough to take pictures of what must be the closest thing to the moon that exists on earth.

***

It looked like getting duty free fuel delivered to our boats was going to be a breeze. And at a price less than a third of the price at the pump. But we had to give an estimate of what we needed and then pay based on that estimate. If we guessed too much, too bad—they kept the residual. *Reunion* was first in the relay of boats to go to our designated spot along the busy port pier. The fact the fuel truck didn't have a meter was the least of Joe's problems. Instead of a normal hose and nozzle, there was a four-inch diameter hose with a pipe at the end. Two men held it while a third kept his hand cupped over the pipe to try keeping diesel fuel from spewing all over *Reunion*. There was no pump and no throttle valve on the truck—both had been stolen along with the fuel meter. Fuel was transferred by gravity feed through the giant hose and the operator had little control over the flow rate. It was a fiasco. Not only did *Reunion's* decks, cockpit, and cushions get soaked, but also the dinghy that was trailing alongside got a thorough dousing.

And then Joe got his first lesson in Baksheesh. Not at all pleased about his dousing experience, Joe still decided to try to keep the operators happy by handing five dollars to the their chief. But this exchange elicited four more eager hands.

When *Skimmer's* turn came, I had already concluded that I didn't need help with the hose. The three unhelpful helpers laughed and waited to see the impending disaster as I sealed off the pipe with a heavy piece of plastic sheeting and rubber bands. In fact there would have been a disaster if I'd used their services, because the pipe would not fit into my deck fill. Charlotte brought out my large stainless steel Baja Filter with its built-in funnel. But even this wouldn't handle the flow and I had to stuff rags around the top to minimize the spillage. Help or no help, the hands were out after the job was completed, but this time their negotiating position had been severely weakened and after much discussion a total of five dollars finally produced somewhat satisfied smiles.

Nordhaven refueled without much spillage. Not wanting to offend anyone, Jim had generously doled out 15 dollars to the outstretched hands, despite the fact that they had done nothing at all. Unfortunately, a port official who had advised us earlier against baksheesh had been watching and informed Jim he had broken the rules by giving the helpers a tip and that he was in trouble. A carton of cigarettes for the port official made the problem disappear and

Jim thought he had finished. Then another official, who claimed to be from their environmental protection agency, started complaining about the fuel that had been spilled into the water. At this point Jim had had enough and, ignoring the "environmental official," he took *Nordhaven* back to anchor with a tale to tell: having to pay baksheesh for having paid baksheesh and then being reproached by an "environmental official" in what is one of the world's most polluted cities.

The supermarket was wonderfully stocked with cheese, wine, and other goodies we hadn't seen since Australia. But when we went outside to get a cab, we were surrounded by people with outstretched hands. When the cab arrived back at the port, the driver wanted twice the negotiated price and then had the nerve to ask for baksheesh on top of that. Our laundry came back clean and neatly folded but the bill that was over twice the price agreed upon—amounting to over a hundred dollars for about two machine loads. In the end we had to pay considerably more than the original price to terminate an increasingly unpleasant argument. Then Barracuda reappeared. By some logic clear only to a Djiboutian mind, he felt he was entitled to a parting gift. Djibouti—land of the outstretched hand—it was the first place we were happy to leave.

The Red Sea

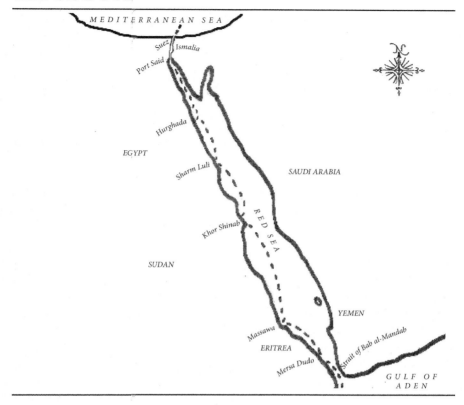

Transiting the Red Sea is one of those emotional issues that seem to divide the sailing community down the middle. Some look forward to it as the most rewarding part of their circumnavigation. Some see it as an obstacle to be overcome as quickly as possible. But there are many who wish to avoid the Red Sea at all cost. There are a few cruisers who like being at sea so much that they consider the 4,500-mile trip from Sri Lanka to South Africa, the 200-mile terror trip around the Cape of Good Hope, and then the 3,500-miles of open water from Cape Town to Brazil pure joy. But these maverick mariners are in the minority. For most who go south, the primary motivation is to avoid the Red Sea.

What about this 1800-mile shortcut to the Mediterranean merits so much concern from the sailing community? Basically, the wind. It begins at Bab al-Mandab with too much in the right direction and phases into too much in the wrong direction about a third of the way up. Relatively shallow water gives rise to short, high, turbulent waves that bring the boat to a stop when they are on the nose and turn the boat into a wild bucking bronco when on the stern. With the wind comes sand. The result is discomfort—sometimes intense discomfort.

***

We had left Djibouti at 4:00 a.m. to have daylight for passage through the narrowest part of the straits that marked the entrance to the Red Sea. When dark set in, we had been past the worst of the shipping, and had expected the wind to abate. Pitch-black coincided with true Bab al-Mandab winds. Shrieks in the darkness signified gusts to over forty knots, churning the waters. The scene was set for a long night of tanker tag. The strategy of hugging the Eritrean coast just inshore of the shipping lanes works for most, but with a group of us sailing in tandem, avoidance maneuvers were difficult. Joe of *Reunion* was out in front and spotted the first container ship to pass inshore of us. But after passing on *Reunion's* port side, the ship changed her course and went down the starboard side of *Skimmer* and *Kemo Sabay*. How close is too close? When you look up to see lights at the top of a giant wall of steel—that's too close.

Early morning brought refuge at Mersa Dudo. As we approached the black cliffs and white beach the wind went from the mid thirties to mid forties. But there was good protection from the seas and we dropped our anchors to wait for calm. It was a long wait. We were ready for some beach exploration by noon. But who wants to go on a beach with a gale blowing and go through the precarious procedure of launching a dinghy that would take off like a kite? But going to the beach wasn't really necessary. The beach came to us instead, in tiny almost invisible grains sandblasting us all and finding its way inside. And what pretty sand. It was a reddish brown color and at the end of only a day *Skimmer* looked like the crew had been engaging in a mud fight that went from deck to cabin and then back to deck.

It was indicative of how much we craved escape from our environment that for the first time in our two and a half year voyage, we showed a movie on board—*Lion of the Desert* was a wonderful escape and we went to sleep that night almost forgetting where we were.

We didn't sleep long. Suddenly there was an alarm, a loud, screeching that cut through the wind howling outside. Charlotte thought maybe we were sinking. Then I realized that it was our new VHF radio. We were tuned to channel 16 and hearing a May Day from some poor soul out there somewhere in the fierce wind of that terrible night. Finally the alarm stopped and we were able to make out a voice in English with a heavy Chinese accent. The distressed vessel was a German sailboat on the other side of the Red Sea near the Yemen shore. The Chinese voice repeated the coordinates and told the vessel his ship was on the way to help, but it would be at least two hours before they arrived.

Charlotte and I said a prayer for our fellow cruisers. Two days later we learned the sailboat was a catamaran de-masted by the same Bab al-Mandab winds we had been experiencing at our anchorage. They were lifted off their stricken craft by a helicopter from a warship in Djibouti less than an hour after we heard their alarm. The Chinese vessel had tried to take the sailboat under tow, but they had failed and the hope of recovering it was dim. Charlotte and I had actually talked with the boat's skipper about a month earlier when we had been on passage between India and Oman.

Two days of waiting for the wind to abate was enough. On the morning of the third day we finally heeded the advice of those who had gone before: "If the wind is behind you, go for it. If it's on the nose, wait it out." It turned out to be the right decision—35 knots turned into 25 knots—and a pleasant day and night afterwards we finally arrived at Charlotte's dream beach.

Port Smyth with its defunct guns, crumbling lighthouse, crystal water, and white beach invited us for a two-day escape. With no signs and no write-up in our guidebooks, we could only guess at its history as we walked the trails and examined the ruins of an island uninhabited except for camels and herons and giant skates that prowled the reefs in our beautiful lagoon.

George, Sarah, and Charlotte at Port Smyth

This marked the end of the easy part of the trip. As we approached Port Sudan, the following winds would disappear and be replaced by headwinds. The only variable would be the strength. Typically the day begins with the wind blowing from the northeast and as the day goes on it clocks around to the northwest—the direction of our route. This dictated the strategy. Get up early and check the wind. If it is blowing hard from the north, forget it and go back to sleep. If it's moderate and from the northeast, get underway and ride it until it clocks to an impossible angle to sail. If it's blowing light or calm, get moving and don't stop until it starts blowing hard in the wrong direction again.

Fortunately the coasts of Eritrea, Sudan, and Egypt are all blessed with hundreds of islands and sheltered anchorages. Beautiful beaches, crystal clear water, exotic coral, and an abundance of sea life—it's a beachcombing and snorkeling paradise and the weather stops can be great fun. The key is not being in a hurry. As long as you can take your time, it can be a wonderful passage.

***

We fell in love with Eritrea even before Asmara. Our expectations had been high when *Skimmer* had entered Massawa Harbor. From a distance, the large, well-protected port appeared to be thriving. Huge quays lined with warehouses and cranes greeted us close to the entrance while exotic buildings beckoned in the distance. And ships were everywhere.

Massawa Harbor

As we entered the breakwater, the true picture unfolded. The large warehouses in neat rows had no roofs and the sides showed huge holes. The beautiful mosque at the head of the harbor was more shell than building. The palace could be recognized for navigation purposes, but bore no resemblance to the stately edifice that once had dominated the harbor. And the shipping? Most were hulks that would never move again. Twisted, rusted, beached, broached—they stretched from the outer harbor into the inner bays. Even the proud-looking ships across the causeway became rust colored shells as we drew nearer. Almost more amazing was the fact that, actually, Massawa was a thriving port. The derelicts had been dragged far enough out of the main channel to allow shipping, and despite the skeletons along the banks, there were operating vessels loading and unloading cargo along the quay. Fleets of big fishing boats crowded the inner harbor and a very efficient Port Control kept everything moving.

We had begun our immersion into Eritrea's history—intense suffering during thirty years of war, yet a resilience and will to thrive. Once the crown jewel of the Italian colonies, Eritrea flourished in the late eighteenth and early nineteenth centuries. During World War II, Britain took over for ten years and Massawa became the largest industrialized city in East Africa.

Then the sellout. Britain, the US, France, and Russia agreed that Eritrea was best served by becoming a state of Ethiopia. The seeds for thirty years of suffering were sown. As western civilization stood by and watched, Eritrea amazed the world by defeating the well-equipped Ethiopian war machine and winning her independence. Despite aid and sophisticated weapons from the US, Israel, and Russia that flowed into Ethiopia, the determination of the Eritrean people prevailed.

From the moment we first put foot ashore we were impressed by the friendliness, industriousness, and optimism of the people. Their city was bombed out, but they didn't seem to notice. Life went on. The city was obviously poor, but the most remarkable feature after our experience in Djibouti was the complete absence of outstretched hands.

***

Asmara is an impossible city, rising above the desert like a mirage. Only fifty miles from the hot dry Red Sea coast, Asmara is 7,000 feet above sea level, with lush green vegetation and cool climate, more like Southern Italy than Africa. Handsome buildings along shady well-manicured streets with cafes and restaurants were everywhere, with Catholic Churches and Orthodox Christian Churches alongside Mosques. Obviously, restoration of their prize city took a high priority in post-war Eritrea.

Nowhere is Eritrea's true grit manifested more than in the four-acre complex of Medeber. Imagine a vast scrap yard with piles of expired

Asmara

191

automobiles, washing machines, steel barrels, and scrap iron, and several hundred Eritreans in blue coveralls, each with a mallet and a length of automobile leaf spring shaped into a chopping tool.

Medeber is the peacetime manifestation of the industry and ingenuity that enabled a determined people to defeat a highly mechanized nation. Now, instead of guns and bombs, these people have channeled their know-how into making consumer products from items that would cost money to dispose of in other countries. Old oil drums are chopped into pieces and hammered on anvils to make dampers for wood stoves, perfectly shaped woks, conical tops for cookers, ladles with long handles. In one lane of the complex, we saw cookers that could compete with Webber grills. In another lane were lines of steel beds made from scrap metal, sandals and water bags made from tires and inner tubes, ladles and funnels from heavy duty tin cans. This was recycling of a kind we'd never seen.

Cooker Made from an Oil Drum

Manufacturing in Medeber

***

Charts of the coastline along Eritrea, Sudan, and Egypt have more warnings about the poor quality of the data than they have navigational information. The pilots also have their share of warnings and it's a case of sailor beware. We'd heard reports over the radio of a French Boat going up on a reef further north and being pounded to pieces, so we were all in a high state of alert as we searched for the channel of the narrow winding bay at Khor Shinab.

From my perch half way up the mast, I could clearly see the reefs, but what really caught my attention was the land, a painted desert. The black silhouette of Quoin Hill contrasted with the reddish sand and the brown hills that stretched to the north. The contrast in colors was unbelievable. In the shallows I could see the browns, reds, greens, and yellows that accented some of the prettiest coral reefs I had ever seen. Beautiful water full of life surrounded by Sudanese desert.

After three sharp bends in the deep narrow channel, we entered a large, wonderfully protected bay. Anchor down and dinghy over, we were ready to dive the reefs and explore the shore. Although we had not cleared into Sudan, we reasoned that flying our Sudanese courtesy flag gave us at least the appearance of legality, and besides, who was there to object other than the camels?

The land was intriguing. The crusty, brown terrain was too high to be covered by the sea even during unusually high tides, so how did the thousands of shells get there? Shelling in the desert. It didn't take Charlotte long to adapt and she began to fill her bag with exotic specimens, many of which were entirely new to us.

The camel tracks were understandable, but where did the deeply embedded tire tracks lead? A straight line into nowhere. And close to the shore, piles of exotic shells. Perfect except for one common flaw, a neat hole punched in the crown. What a shame to see dozens of large spider conch shells—beautiful specimens of Lambis with their long delicate spines and Murexes with their shorter and wonderfully textured spines—all ruined by the knives of hungry Bedouins.

High winds in the night made us appreciate the security of our anchorage and made it clear that we would have at least one more day in our newfound paradise. The high winds of the morning should have tipped me off that dinghying ashore might not be a good idea. But the dinghy was already in the water from the day before, and I still wanted to climb Quoin Hill so we loaded up and headed in.

Prudently, I decided to motor upwind of *Skimmer* in case we had engine problems, but imprudently I let go of *Skimmer* before giving the engine a prolonged test. Our Yamaha patiently waited until we were one boat length away from *Skimmer* before it sputtered out. Confident that I could restart it, I used the precious seconds remaining to regain *Skimmer* to pull twice on the starter chord. It was interesting to see how far a 30-knot gust could push our dinghy—in this case it was far enough to make our decision easy and we grabbed the oars to help thread us through the reef that was downwind of *Skimmer*.

Other than being on the wrong side of the bay for Quoin Hill, the shore that was downwind of *Skimmer* was a good one to explore. I knew getting the motor started was going to be hard but decided to put the job off until after we had had our expedition. Besides, maybe the wind would abate and we would be able to row back if the motor wouldn't start.

It was Lawrence of Arabia country and we thoroughly enjoyed our hike. This time we were further inland and our views of the mountains and Quoin Hill were spectacular. Along the shore of the bay we saw more shells. Clamshells meant live clams must be near, and I diligently searched for keyholes. But it was high tide and my search wasn't fruitful. Then more piles of conch shells. If I could get my motor fixed, I was determined to explore the shoreline and get some of this prolific sea life into *Skimmer's* galley.

After a couple of hours of wandering and noting that the wind had not abated, we began to get nervous and returned to the dinghy. With twenty five to thirty knots blowing us straight onto the beach, we needed to develop a strategy for working on the motor. The solution was simple. We walked the dingy out to waist deep water and I forced our light anchor between some large rocks upwind. This allowed me to put the motor back in the water and pull on the chord to my hearts content with Charlotte holding the dingy steady. But pull as I might, she was dead.

Stranded on the Beach at Kor Shinab

Standing there on the shore with wind howling and sand blowing, we felt very lonely as we watched *Skimmer* jerking around on her anchor three hundred yards away. How long would the wind blow? *Kemo Sabay* was anchored too far away to see our predicament, but would they become alarmed when they couldn't raise us on the radio?

Staying ashore for the evening wasn't even remotely appealing, so we began to explore alternatives. Could we row? Inflatables don't row well, and our Zodiac was worse than most. But we decided to give it a try anyway.

In order to ensure success, we walked the dingy to the edge of the reef and thereby cut off almost a third of the distance. We practiced rowing at anchor to make certain we could make headway, and then set out.

My strength was almost gone but we had less than a boat length to go when it happened. A powerful gust spun us around and suddenly we were two boat lengths away and receding fast. I managed to get the anchor over, but by this time we were almost a hundred yards downwind. Rowing wasn't going to work.

Generally, the simpler the solution, the better the chance of success. Fortunately I had my mask, snorkel, and flippers in the dingy. It was an easy swim and I gathered all my small diameter line on *Skimmer's* stern. I could tell by the way the wind was blowing that my float would be well to the left of Charlotte and the anchored dingy, so it was important to have light enough line for me to swim with. It was a little crude, but it worked. Charlotte and I gently pulled in on the line to avoid parting it—kind of like playing a large fish—and slowly our bouncing dingy made its way back to the safety of *Skimmer*.

By day three the surroundings began to seem less romantic and exotic. The wind continued to howl at 20 to 30 knots and we were tired of admiring the swirling sand clouds over the desert and seeing *Skimmer's* coat of sand and dirt get thicker and thicker. It had been a good opportunity to catch up on maintenance and we had managed to watch a few more movies, but sitting and waiting was beginning to get old. Misery enjoys company and we certainly had both. *Kemo Sabay* was just around the corner of the bay from us, *Reunion* was at shelter about a hundred miles ahead of us, and there were a dozen other boats scattered to the south at various anchorages. Each morning over the radio we would compare our notes, say our weather prayers, and then decide to wait another day for moderation in the weather.

Looking for beautiful waterfront property at affordable prices? How about Sudan! North of Port Sudan an endless coastline of magnificent, sandy, coral studded beaches would appeal to sun worshipers anywhere. There are some drawbacks. Aside from the obvious problems of proper title, security of property, and personal safety, there is the almost insurmountable problem of remoteness. Other than a few conch-eating Bedouins, there was nothing behind the beaches other than the vast Nubian Desert. Sudan's population mainly clings to the banks of the Nile, leaving this corner of the world and its wonderfully unspoiled shoreline with no roads and no infrastructure of any kind. This lack of infrastructure poses a real problem for cruisers trying to make their way north to the Mediterranean.

The fourth day of our forced rest at Khor Shinab finally brought action. Dew on the deck in the morning, a very slowly falling barometer and good reports from boats ahead—it was time to make another run. *Reunion* was about 150 miles ahead of us and reported wind from the south. By Red Sea weather patterns and by the rule of equitable wind distribution to all cruisers, we could expect *Reunion's* southerly wind within twenty-four hours.

The gods of bad wind began to play their tricks on our small fleet. From dead calm as we were departing, the wind began to build. By noon it was 15 to 20 knots and then by evening it was gusting to 35. And by some perverse coincidence it managed to blow right on the nose even as we made changes in course. With the wind came the seas—short and steep—and our speed dropped to less than two knots. It wasn't just the discomfort of the jarring motion as the bow mounted high on a wave and then slammed down in the trough—it was the problem of fuel. And this was when the problem of the lack of infrastructure of the Sudanese coast really hit home. We should have had enough. Before leaving Massawa, we had filled our tanks to overflowing and also the dozens of jerry jugs that lined our decks. At normal fuel usage we had enough to motor the whole way to Abu Tig, the haven at the mouth of the Gulf of Suez. But hour after hour of motoring at two knots wasn't normal fuel usage.

Safely beyond the disputed boarder area between Sudan and Egypt, Marsa Alam was our logical refueling port. But by the end of day two of our bashing, it began to become clear that we wouldn't be able to make it.

The closest alternative was Abu Al Ghosen. But was there fuel there? One source said yes, one said no. We were going to chance it until we learned from our pilot that the anchorage was exposed to winds from the north and should be used only in settled weather. A little further north was Sharm Luli. The pilot description told of the military installation there and said that it might be possible to arrange for fuel but long delays were possible. It also cautioned that while the area was occupied by Egypt, it was also claimed by Sudan and was a potential trouble spot. But we had no other options.

A tongue of deep blue through turquoise shallows showed the safe path, and we found haven in a beautiful cove surrounded with sand dunes and mountains. This was our initial entry into Egypt and we were going to do it by the book. We went to shore carrying ships papers, passports and all other documents that could conceivably be requested.

Dressed in fatigues, the soldiers had been watching us through binoculars. Both George and I beamed our best smiles and started waving. A pause, the binoculars lowered, and then friendly waving in return. The one not in uniform addressed us in passable English: "My name is Mustafa and I will act as your interpreter." My reply, "Mustafa—like the famous Mustafa Kamal" bought surprised looks and then broad smiles from Mustafa and from the three soldiers. The ice had been thawed and we spent half an hour having tea with them and exchanging life stories.

Mustafa was a native of Cairo but was in Sharm Luli helping his father run his fishing boat. The three soldiers, Mohammed, Ahmed, and Ali were young men doing their military service in this outpost of Egyptian civilization. Once the pleasantries were over we got down to business. Mustafa helped with the translation and Ahmed managed to fill three pages of a notebook with information he extracted from us and our papers. All was going well until I took out my camera to get a group photo. Mohammed was adamant: "No photos—this military base."

Not realizing that the white garage-sized hut along with its two small sheds constituted an Egyptian military installation had been careless on my part, and I quickly put my camera away. Security was very important to them, and I'm sure they didn't want it leaked out that the hut contained three cots and a radio that predated color television. When I asked if it would be okay if I took a photo of the two camels out in back of the hut, Mohammed's emphatically shaking head made it clear they were classified camels.

One of the first things we had noticed coming into Sharm Luli was the coastal highway and the occasional truck. Where trucks come, diesel can't be far behind—maybe we were going to accomplish our primary mission!

The sobering call from *Reunion* that morning over the SSB served to put the fuel issue into focus. We had heard that a French boat had grounded on a reef, but hadn't been able to get the details. Joe reported that *Chamoise*, a spotless 45-foot ketch we had admired in Oman, had been running low on fuel and had decided to make a night entry into Marsa Mubarak to fill up. Joe saw what was left sitting up on a reef in the entrance.

The sparse surroundings at Sharm Luli didn't inspire much hope, but at least we had an interpreter and a guide.

"Mustafa, is it possible to get diesel here?"

"No here diesel. Diesel in Marsa Alam."

"Can you get us a truck to go to Marsa Alam?"

Mustafa's emphatic yes sent us back to our boats to retrieve all our empty jerry jugs. There were so many plastic containers in my dinghy that we could hardly see out, otherwise we might have noticed the dejected look on Mustafa's face before we had gotten back to shore. "Mohammed say you no able go Marsa Alam. Okay you walk here, beach and mountains, but no able to leave to go other cities. So sorry."

I tried a different tactic. "Mustafa, can you go to Marsa Alam and get the fuel for us and bring it back?" Mustafa disappeared for another conference with the security conscious base commander. Fifteen minutes later he returned with a broad smile on his face. Apparently Mohammed was willing to take the risk that we would not engage Mustafa to smuggle items into the base other than our desperately needed fuel.

Mustafa, our 21 jerry jugs, and 230 of our dwindling supply of US dollars headed north in a large truck for the 50-mile trek to Marsa Alam. He promised to be back in two hours with the fuel.

Bone tired from our three days of bashing into wind and waves, Charlotte and I finished our Pomidori Spaghetti dinner, sipped on our cold Beck's Beer and waited for the honking from Mustafa's truck. It was well past the two hours and my doubts were beginning to turn into fears. Loosing the money would be bad enough—but loosing all our jerry jugs while we were in the middle of a desert—that was my worst fear.

An hour past the expected arrival time and I was about to give *Kemo Sabay* a call on the VHF to see if they were also having a panic attack— but in a way I was past caring. By that time I was so tired that the idea of fetching the jerry jugs, and carrying them back to our boats by dinghy in the pitch-black night, was so unappealing that I found myself almost not caring whether Mustafa showed.

Mustafa

Charlotte's sharp ears heard it first. I poked my head out into the cockpit and there on the shore in the direction of loud honking were blinking headlights and a shouting Mustafa. Fifteen minutes later nine full jerry jugs were on *Skimmer's* bow and 12 on *Kemo Sabay's* bow. Our tickets to Abu Tig had just been punched.

The next morning we accepted Mohammed's invitation to explore the shore where sandy beaches ended in overhanging cliffs from the desert. But as I was about to leave I stumbled onto my real surprise. Right in front of me but I hadn't been looking. Oysters, hundreds of beautiful, plump, succulent oysters and firmly attached to the reef. If only I had bought a screw driver and hammer with me. I tried bashing them loose with rocks, prying with shells and pushing hard with the heel of my hand, but to no avail.

It was amazing how much excitement could be generated over a two-month-old issue of *Time Magazine*, a year-old issue of *Cruising World*, and a very old copy of *Angler Magazine*. The guard shack became very festive as everyone examined the booty fromm *Skimmer* and *Kemo Sabay*. Mohammed was pleased with the bandaids and medicine Charlotte had bought him for the festering boil on his eyelid, and Ali and Ahmed were delighted with the cans of beef stew, corned beef hash, and clams. Mustafa and his father were digging into the large bag of peanuts and everyone was in a great mood. With so much good will, I was sure Mohammed was going to relent and finally let me photograph the camels. But with Mohammed, pleasure was pleasure and duty was duty, and the party ended with absolutely no photographic evidence that two aged camels were part of the Sharm Luli garrison.

***

For once, our trip north had been wonderful. Light wind turned to no wind during the night after our departure from Sharem Luli and we motored at almost seven knots on a glassy sea. Cruisers behind us were still being bashed by heavy headwinds, but here the law of equitable wind distribution was working in our favor. Our progress had been so good that we had been able to make it the whole way to Hurghada, an official port of entry into Egypt and close to the Abu Tig Marina.

If not warned, I would have panicked. Suddenly a white sandy bottom was clearly visible and then giant coral heads jutting towards the surface. I re-checked the fathometer—40 feet. The water was so clear my depth perception was distorted, and what looked like menacing boulders were actually more than thirty feet below our keel. I stood on the bow and watched the panorama of skates, colorful fish, and swaying coral ferns below as we made our way up the

Lauren and Greg of Kamal at Abu Tig Marina

Straight of Gubal. It was clear why this was considered one of the best diving areas in the world.

A shore lined with condominiums, shops, restaurants and a world-class marina full of glowing fiberglass luxury bristling with the latest in electronics. It was heart-warming to see the tasteful statement of American taxpayer dollars moored in the choice corner of the marina, and I could only hope the American Embassy personnel thoroughly enjoyed their 60-foot yacht with the little jet ski mounted on deck.

The story of Abu Tig was that a wealthy Egyptian businessman had wanted a place to park his luxury yacht, so he teamed with a group of like-minded countrymen and carved out one of the most elaborate complexes we had seen since leaving the US. Miles of condominiums wind around finger coves—a little Venice with high density living made to look like low density luxury. As a promotion, the Marina was letting visiting yachts stay one month free of charge. This was going to be a hard place to leave.

***

It wasn't the gaudiness of Egypt's answer to Disney Land that attracted our attention. Just beyond the Thousand and One Nights Complex there was an endless line of buses and cabs forming up along the highway—along with armored vehicles and dozens of men in black shirts with machine guns. Hundreds of tourists gathered at the crowded concession stand so they could pay five pounds for cold coffee and one pound for the privilege of the last Egyptian toilet before our trek across the desert to Luxor. In the meantime the black-shirted men scanned the buses with metal detectors. The sun rose and we began to move in unison into one of the most desolate stretches of white heat I've ever experienced.

Forming Convoy to Luxor

There was an armored guard at the point, roving jeeps bristling with machine guns interspersed and another armored guard at the rear. Our driver was just as aggressive as his fellow countrymen and he would reluctantly give way as larger vehicles forced him off the road and then take his revenge on the smaller cars and taxis that were part of our armada. Right-of-way was directly proportionate to weight, and it didn't make any difference that no one could pass the front guard or go faster than the convoy. No self-respecting driver could pass up the opportunity to embarrass a smaller vehicle and give its driver a chance to prove his skill in pulling over to the shoulder at 100 kilometers an hour and continuing to maintain control of his vehicle.

The 1997 massacre at the tomb of Queen Hatshepsut's Temple had left its mark. Tourism, the heart of the Egyptian economy, was hit so hard that armed convoys persist today as the only legal and safe way for tourists to go to the archeological wonderland of the Nile.

Luxor, Aswan, and Abu Simbal were fascinating with their temples, tombs, and history, but every bit as important as our study of the dead was our study of the living. And modern Egypt was certainly alive. It was even capable of being enjoyed—but only if one had strong stamina and infinite patience. The constant transition from the New Kingdom of the Pharaohs to the Late Kingdom of Baksheesh as one leaves the temples and then runs the gauntlet of shops and hawkers is manageable. But, as with the blistering sun, certain precautions had to be taken to keep from being burned.

The first principle of doing business in Egypt is that the deal is not the deal. Just because the price has been agreed upon in the beginning, and repeated assurances have been given that no baksheesh demands will be forthcoming, that in no way prevents the inevitable confrontation at the end of the transaction.

I was quite aware of this reality of life in Egypt and therefore took special pains to explain to Abdul that the negotiated price for the van ride from Aswan back to Abu Tig included everything and that I was not going to add any baksheesh—no matter what happened. On the way out of Aswan that morning I was prepared for his demand as we drove away from the hotel and immediately told him to stop the van. I then gave my speech for the fifth time. The 550 pounds was for the entire trip to Abu Tig, not just to Hurghada, and there would be absolutely no baksheesh. I showed him the 550 pound figure written out and showed him again the map with Abu Tig clearly marked twenty miles north of Hurghada. Despite frustration and anger just beneath the surface, I smiled and told Adul that if I had misunderstood the deal, I would be happy for him to take us back to the hotel and we would make other arrangements. After a moment of hesitation and confirmation that I wasn't going to budge, he smiled back at me and our non-deal was back on.

The last part is always the trickiest. Happy to be back on *Skimmer* and pleased with Abdul's driving I did what I had been planning all along. After counting out the 550 in crisp notes and handing them over to Abdul, I then pulled out another 50 and said that because he was my friend and because he had treated us well, I was going to give him baksheesh despite our agreement. Adul's smile faded as he pocketed the 550 and explained to me that this covered only the trip to Hurghada. His frown clearly indicated that 50 pounds extra was not enough to compensate him for the extra distance to Abu Tig.

It was then my play. A big smile accompanied my: "Abdul, the 550 in your pocket is full payment for the trip from Aswan to Abu Tig. The 50 pounds in my hand is extra baksheesh that I had told you I wasn't going to pay. If you are not happy about this, I will be glad to keep it." It only took Addul about ten seconds to decide that he was happy with my generous tip and his frown turned into a smile.

As with everything in Egypt we had mixed feelings about the people. Despite the aggressive "in your face" dealings, we found the people we met genuinely friendly. The soldiers were professional, polite and always willing to help with directions or advice. The man on the street would go out of his way to make us feel at home. It was only the last stages of transactions that caused strain, and eventually we learned how to handle this without too much discomfort.

One of the first questions we were always asked was "where are you from?" and they seemed genuinely pleased to have US visitors. Our guides told us we were practically the only Americans in Luxor and Aswan. While their international tourism was booming, the American component had been missing for some time.

Our return to Abu Tig and our comfortable environment on *Skimmer* highlighted the clash in amenities we often observed in our travels. These clashes vary in magnitude from item to item, but nowhere is the difference as great as that in the world of toiletry. It's truly an area where East is East and West is West and never the twain shall meet.

It really comes down to the concept of what an adequately equipped bathroom should contain. Time and again we saw Eastern attempts at elegance result in absurd failures. Malaysia's luxurious Port Dixon Marina had beautiful marble counters around the sinks, dressing rooms accented with carved wooden panels, and showers lined with such beautiful tile. At first I didn't notice the lack of knobs on the fixtures. But upon closer examination I saw they were lying on the floor—all that was needed was to pick them up and hold them in place while trying to make the frantic adjustments that separate goose bumps from first degree burns. Phuket's elegant Boat Lagoon Marina had knobs on all fixtures—but each fixture had only one knob—the bathroom planning geniuses of Thailand had neglected to make provisions for hot water.

But showers, hot water, and fancy marble are not the items that elicit the most attention from visitors from the West. Usually Charlotte will wait until after her second beer before venturing to the door of mysteries. She is always hopeful, but knows what she will probably find. She opens the door and there it is—pride and joy of the East and the bane of all American women— the four-inch hole in the floor flanked by two footstones. In more elegant establishments the footstones are marble.

It's hard to imagine how cultures can be so different in their approach to this essential of creature comforts. I like to think of it as the conflict of the bowl versus the hole. While it is true that Asia is slowly changing and the use of the bowl is on the rise, it's still very much of a hole culture. Although their ultra modern supersonic trains still sport the hole, the Japanese are leaps and bounds ahead of us in the technology of the bowl. White thrones on display in department stores everywhere not only have flashing lights and electronic switches, but are also equipped with hand held remote control units. It was one of the times I wanted to be able to speak Japanese the most—to learn just which essential features of the throne were enhanced being controlled remotely.

Of all the hole cultures, perhaps Indonesia was the most firmly rooted in their traditional approach. It was therefore very heartening to both Charlotte and me when we saw that not only had the new four-star hotel at the Nongsa Point Marina adopted the bowl technology, but had also embarked on an ambitious training program in its use. Wonderfully explicit stick diagrams on the underside of the toilet covers displayed

The Hole

posture guidance for women and correct stance and aim instructions for men.

***

We have crossed deserts on buses, cars, horses, donkeys, and camels, but this was the first time ever on a sailboat, an eight-hour voyage through nowhere.

It was one of those trips you have to earn before you can take and we thought that with the Gulf of Aden, Bab al-Mandab, and over a thousand miles of Red Sea coastline in our wake, we had paid our dues. But Mother Nature and man's ingenuity had one last hurdle for us before we would be allowed to experience the joy of the Suez Canal.

A convincing claim can be made that we had assembled the world's best team of northern Red Sea weather experts at the Abu Tig Marina, and it was the overwhelming opinion of the group that after over a week of waiting the promised window had finally come: "wind expected to die down, switch to the north east, and then switch to the south." The fleet was ready to move out. At 5:00 a.m. *Skimmer* was the first to leave the marina—just enough daylight to thread our way through the reefs of the Islands of Gubal and just enough time to make an arrival at Port Suez early enough the following day to make a transit. We were planning on making a land trip from Ismailia to Sharm el Sheik to join friends Erhard and Coleen Joerchel who were flying in from Moscow for travels in the Sinai Peninsula.

It didn't come as a complete surprise when the flat calm of the marina gave way to gentle, then moderate, then strong wind from the north as we made our way through the beautiful reefs and sparkling water of Gubal. But a new phenomenon was about to present itself to us and we got our first preview as we came through the Tawila Channel. A ship on stilts? No, impossible. I refocused the binoculars. But yes, it definitely was a ship. And it was definitely out of water. And yes, there were long poles holding it way up in the air. Suddenly my days in the oil and gas industry came back to me and I realized that I was looking at one of the marvels of oil extraction technology—the jack-up drilling rig. The ship was a complete drilling rig and it simply had motored into position and then jacked itself up on the four giant towers that were part of its huge mass.

This was only the beginning. As we crossed the busy shipping lanes of the Gulf of Suez and began our voyage up the east side, I began to feel like I was in a city of steel towers. There were city block clusters, and then loners scattered in random patterns. Some were ships on stilts, some were just towers. Others were massive structures with cranes extending over their sides like giant wings. Huge container ships passing on the left and hundreds of oil platforms lining our route to the right. And there were the flames—fires at sea? No, just thousands of cubic feet of natural gas being burned to enable the steel monsters to extract the treasured oil. At one point we thought the swirling black cloud on the horizon was a water spout—but closeness revealed that it was just a particularly dirty gas flare spewing pollution into the beautiful blue sky.

During the day it was fascinating, but as night approached we hoped we had figured out the patterns. Sure the operating rigs were lit, but how about the abandoned ones? Charts were of no assistance—ours predated most of the monsters and probably only contained a fraction of those that existed when they were published.

With a near full moon and the light from the burning gas, we had good visibility and all was well until what appeared to be an exceptionally well-lit buoy with a fixed red light on top came into view. But as we approached, the red started moving relative to the buoy. The direction of motion meant that it should have been green if it was a vessel, but the red was unmistakable. Then it reversed direction, but remained red. Was it coming towards us? I turned and then it turned. This was not the way the rules of the road were supposed to work and I spent a very uncomfortable half an hour until the buoy and its mobile red companion finally receded behind. It happened to me a second time and Charlotte had the same experience on her watch. Others cruising with us reported the same phenomenon and none of us could come up with an explanation—but we were all in agreement that that night had been one of the most stressful in our entire trip up the Red Sea.

Port Suez was just another dirty industrial city, and after a scalping at the hands of our agent we were not in a perfect frame of mind to enjoy our transit up the Suez Canal. I kept the agent from raising his handling fees, but hadn't noticed what he had done in calculating the transit fee for *Skimmer*. Fifty Tons! Even with a full load of beer on board *Skimmer* weighed in at less than 15 tons. There was no time to complain if we wanted to make a transit that day so I shelled out the three hundred and fifty dollars and stewed as I learned that boats twice our size had paid half as much.

My bad mood didn't last long. The sight that stretched out before us was so different we couldn't stop snapping photos. Urban sprawl to the left and desolate sand to the right. Camels on the banks, fishermen in their small craft, and occasional ferries carrying everything from chickens to cars. The wind that had bedeviled us on our trip up the Gulf of Suez continued to meet us head on, but this time instead of high seas it brought sand.

The Suez Canal

Swirling in the air all about us, the tiny particles refracted the afternoon sun, turning the sky into a reddish orange. The isolated mosque, the lone rider on donkey back, the row of majestic date palms—they took on a mystical beauty that kept us mesmerized.

We had heard that Ismailia had a nice marina and was a safe place to leave our boat for our inland travels. It's the halfway point of the Suez Canal and was founded during construction. Ismailia has impressive colonial architecture, elaborate Mosques, and a thriving economy not dependent on tourism. We felt like we were finally seeing a truly Egyptian city and thoroughly enjoyed walking down streets where friendly smiles replaced the ubiquitous sales pitches for unwanted merchandise and insistent requests for baksheesh that plague tourists in Egypt.

***

Sharm el Sheikh is like a little piece of Myrtle Beach on the tip end of the Sinai Peninsula. It was Erhard's research that had led us there. A recent article in The Economist pointed out that after years of being closed to the public, the Monastery of St. Catherine had finally been opened up to visitors. If Erhard was willing to make the pilgrimage the whole way from Moscow who were we to claim hardship in making the rendezvous? Sure Sinai bordered on Israel and even touched the dreaded Gaza Strip. But that was in the north and our destination was in the far south at the confluence of the Gulfs of Suez and Aqaba.

We had developed the habit of using the creep method for checking security. From a distance it often seemed that the objectives of our wanderlust might be fraught with dangers: Fiji between coups, Indonesia during martial law, Sri Lanka with Tamil terrorism, and the Red Sea with reputed pirates. But as we would draw closer and scout ahead, local knowledge assured us that our fears were ill founded, and we would then slowly creep ahead. Our favorite analogy was that after September 11 the Japanese had refused to come visit the US, but our friends at home had assured us that walking the streets of Charleston was still perfectly safe.

The most difficult part of our search for security was finding a safe place to leave *Skimmer*. Ismailia with its yacht club and marina offered just the refuge we needed. A little travel planning, two five dollar bus tickets, and we were off on our adventure. The Ahmed Hamdi Tunnel under the Suez Canal took us to the long straight road down the western shore of the Sinai Peninsula. White monotony on our left and swirling blue, green, and turquoise beauty on our right. Our land view of the same engineering monstrosities we had seen by sea revealed the ugliness of their required onshore support. But these were mere specks and couldn't destroy the majesty of this enormous expanse of jagged hills and rolling desert.

A knowledge of Italian and German would have been even more useful than a knowledge of Arabic in maneuvering ourselves through the oasis of extravaganza that Sharm el Sheikh has now become. Started by the Israelis during the 1967–1979 occupation, the Egyptians have brought this promise land of vacation paradise to its present state of perfection by the addition of such essentials as water slides, bumper cars, and Coney Island style amusement parks.

The 100-mile trip through the desert to Saint Catherine's Monastery and Mount Sinai was a profound experience. Set in the middle of a desert, this enclave of Christianity was so rich in history and tradition that it was almost impossible to take it all in.

The fortress and monastery, built by the Emperor Justinian in the 6th century AD, commemorate the martyrdom of Saint Catherine. Did she perish on the four rotating wheels with flashing knives, was she hanged, was her body cut into many pieces and scattered throughout the land? Did Emperor Maximanus order her death because of his anger at her futile attempts to convert him to Christianity and his fear of her brilliance in poetry, philosophy, and mathematics; or had it happened, as our guide so eagerly recounted, that the lovesick emperor had had her killed because she refused his advances? Was the chapel around the magnificent tree outside the monastery really the site of the Burning Bush? And was that beautiful mountain in the background the Mount Sinai that Moses had climbed to receive the Ten Commandments? Maybe, maybe not. But what an experience to wander through this wonderful intersection of legends and think about the past. Charlotte thought of it as a walk through the Bible and we both regretted that we didn't have the time to make the midnight hike up to the top of Mount Sinai.

Another attack of wanderlust set in. Taba was only 150 miles to the north and what a wonderful opportunity to see the coastline of the Gulf of Aqaba. Eilat and Israel? Well, that decision could wait until we were in Taba and had a chance to evaluate the data collected during our "creep "to the north.

No matter how many people we talked with, the answer was always the same. Egypt and Israel were at peace and there was absolutely no problem for tourists anywhere in Egypt, including the Sinai Peninsula. Zakaria at the Blue Sky travel agency in Ismailia had taken us one step further in our understanding of the situation. We had already been touched by his warm hospitality and

Saint Catherine's Monastery

genuine interest in us and our travels and we were spellbound as he tried to explain his feelings about Israel over a boiling hot glass of tea.

"We have been at peace with Israel since 1979. No one in Egypt wants war again. Since the fighting began in 1948 Egypt has lost over one hundred thousand boys. We do not like what the Israelis are doing now—we think it is wrong—but we will not go to war. We pray for peace and are very sad about what is happening now."

Over the haze of desert sands at the Taba tourist complex, a new kind of desert came into view. A desert of concrete. Some buildings had just foundations, some were shells with openings for windows and doorways staring out into the emptiness, some were fully functional mega hotels with no automobiles in their lots or bathers on their beaches. The Taba Hilton hotel towered over its surroundings and dominated the view from both sides of the border. It also had a lock on all the tourism of the area. Judging from what we saw, that was about ten guests—almost enough to occupy one room on each floor. Taba depended entirely on tourists from Israel for its business, and the Israelis just weren't coming anymore. "Meester Heyward, it's so bad they not come. We welcome them and they know Egypt very safe country. Why they no come? Eets so sad for them. They miss so much."

Ihab assured us that there was absolutely no problem crossing the border into Eilat. Not having an Israeli stamp on our passport was very important to us, and we held our breath as the attractive young Israeli lady with stamp in hand asked us why it mattered. She knew the answer but wanted to make us acknowledge that an Israeli stamp could keep us out of many Arab countries and that we were asking her to bend her country's rules. She beamed a knowing smile at our admission, passed our unstamped passports back to us, and suddenly we were in Israel.

Our cab driver into Eilat gave a different version for the death of Israeli tourism in Taba. "If we go there in boats, they put us in jail and take our boats. If we go to visit their hotels, they are rude and question us for nothing. We do not go because we are not welcome. But we do not do the same to Egyptians who come here. Here we treat them like anyone else." I refrained from asking the driver if this "same as everyone else" treatment also applied to the Palestinians and wondered if an Egyptian would have been charged the same number of shekels for the cab ride we were taking.

Eilat stands alone at the southern tip of the Negev Desert. It is Israel's straw into the Gulf of Aqaba and the Red Sea, and they have crammed so much building, shipping, tourism, and shopping into the city that it pulses with an energy we hadn't seen since India.

Our bus ride back to Eilat from an excursion to Masada gave us another insight into daily life in Israel. It was full of young men and women, some in uniform, some in beach attire. What drew our attention were their guns. Machine guns casually slung across the back of youths who didn't look old enough to make the high school football team. How incongruous to see a bare-footed figure in cut-off jeans, tightly fitting tee shirt, and wrap-around sun glasses with a machine gun hanging over his shoulder. We learned that the penalty for losing a gun is seven years in jail, and these eighteen year olds were taking no chances by leaving their pieces back at an insecure youth hostel. Where they went, the gun went also.

***

After twenty-four hours of travel and three separate examinations of our luggage, we were bone tired. But there *Skimmer* was, riding proudly on her anchor, after our three week trip back to the US to visit family. It was not until I went to turn on the lights that I became aware of the enormity of what had happened during our absence. Our boat had become unplugged. Three months worth of frozen meat provides more than the necessary critical mass for a rapid growth of bacteria, and *Skimmer*'s freezer had become the breeding ground of the largest maggot colony I have ever seen. Actually, I think it made the security watch for *Skimmer* easier. It would have been a thief with the world's worst head cold who could have gone aboard and withstood the stench of rotting lamb, beef, and chicken to pick through our valuables.

Fortunately I keep two gas masks on *Skimmer*. Otherwise I don't think we could have stood it after we opened the freezer to remove the festering mess our gourmet meals had turned into. But scrub as we might, the stench remained. It was a week after the fumigation that the smell seemed to start diminishing—but we weren't sure if that was actual physical reality or was just a reduced sensitivity in our olfactory glands.

You can't get there from here. That's the way I had come to feel about Egypt. Wonderfully friendly people that can make problems appear out of thin air. Our unique location in Lake Timsah at Ismailia Yacht Club was a contributing factor. Lake Timsah, the half way point in the Suez Canal, was a mandatory stop for yachts in transit. *Skimmer* was technically no longer in Egypt; she had checked out of the country at the beginning of the Canal at Port Suez. But Charlotte and I were still on our Egyptian Visas. This had left us in never-never land. The Yacht Club was in a tax-free zone and less than one hundred yards away, a check point equipped with five armed guards and an immigration officer made ingress and egress to *Skimmer* an interesting and sometimes difficult experience. Each time we presented our passports to the guards, the rules would be different. Sometimes a near strip search, other times no more than a friendly smile, a nod of the head, and a lowering of the machine gun.

The good news was that we were eligible for tax-free fuel in the tax free zone; but the bad news was there was no fuel available within the confines of the Ismailia Yacht Club. This meant going out with empty jerry jugs and back in with full ones. Ahmed gave his advice: "Okay Heyward, you take out your Jerry Jugs, is okay six."

"But Ahmed, I have eight and need to fill all of them."

"Yes, Heyward, is okay eight. Six, eight, it no matter. You take now, because in one hour whole city close down and not start again until eight tonight. Big football game—everybody watch big football game"

This seemed odd. Normally everything closed between noon and four o'clock, and then reopened until about eight, but I took Ahmed at his word and proceeded to the customs barrier with my eight empty jerry jugs hanging from my shoulders by ropes. The guard seemed to be uninterested in my jerry jugs, but motioned that I needed to go to the immigration officer. This was annoying, but not unusual. The drill was simple. With passport in hand I would go to the little office with Mr. Sellah sitting there reading a newspaper. He would look up, smile and ask me what I wanted. My usual answer was that I didn't want anything but that the man with the gun had said I needed to check with him. His usual answer was that it wasn't necessary since I had already checked in with him and that would be the end of it. But this time I decided to ask him a question. "Mr. Sellah, tomorrow we leave for Port Said. Do you need to stamp our passports out before we go?"

"Why you no ask me before? Now cannot check you out. Maybe tomorrow. Why you no stay here longer? I want to help you my friend, but now check out is impossible." I had long since learned not to argue with Mr. Sellah, so I let the matter drop and decided to wait until arriving at Port Said to begin worrying about having our passports stamped. But in the meantime, the guard in charge had developed an interest in my Jerry Jugs. "Please Captain, you take only four" and to emphasize the point he thrust four fingers in my face.":

"But I must have all eight, otherwise I won't have enough fuel for my trip."

The unwavering four fingers conveyed his determination not to budge. I asked why only four.

"It's the rule. The lieutenant he say four. I no change. You want change, you ask lieutenant."

Okay, where is the lieutenant? I was ready for a wild goose chase when his expression softened and he picked up the phone. Ten minutes later he nodded his okay for eight. But before I could get away in my cab, Mr. Sellah was on his way out, presumably to be able to see the football game, and began to question me all over again about the jerry jugs. By this time I had two allies, and after a five minute shouting match between my taxi driver and the guard on one side and Mr. Sellah on the other, I was off for fuel.

Ahmed had been right. At 4:00 p.m. Ismailia became a ghost town. It was as if humanity had evaporated, except sporadic cheers from unseen thousands huddled around televisions and thunderous applause from the stadium. Suddenly at 7:30 hordes of people funneled from their homes to flood the streets of Ismailia with jubilant shouting, dancing, and singing as they gloried in their victory. The Ismailia Yellows had just won the Egyptian National Soccer Championship. Huge yellow and blue banners streamed from windows, honking automobiles crowded the streets, and flagpoles with banners carried by huge crowds of ecstatic celebrants appeared everywhere. As if by magic, all the shops in the city were then opened, and the city became more alive than we had ever seen it.

Apparently, our trip up the Gulf of Suez was the last of the smooth ones. What had taken us only two days to cross took other boats as much as two weeks. At the beginning of May the wind strengthens and comes only from the north. Later arrivals to Ismailia reported ferocious conditions; one French boat told us that it was worse than the North Sea. During those days three more sailing yachts were lost on the reefs of the Red Sea. One English boat ended her days just days after we had made our transit. Forty knots of wind on the nose, a lost engine, and the treacherous shoals of Gubal did the trick. Fortunately the crew escaped without injury. Shortly after this fiasco, *Liberdad*, the French Boat we had towed into Oman two months earlier, was put out of her misery.

I couldn't believe that *Liberdad* had actually been able to get underway again during that season. But the French owner had been persistent. Despite the fact that she needed a new transmission and his crew was abandoning him, he somehow patched her up and persuaded another crew she was seaworthy. One of our friends said he saw her just after she lost her engine and then watched helplessly as *Liberdad's* anchor dragged and the reefs of Gubal did their ugly work. Again, however, the crew escaped without injury. We never learned the details of the third loss in May—but we knew that it bought the total of lost yachts in the Red Sea during that sailing season to five.

Our Red Sea experience was almost over, but I was still smarting from the unconscionable overcharge that *Skimmer* had suffered in Port Suez. Assessing *Skimmer* based on a calculated Suez tonnage of fifty tons—high by a factor of three—this had been beyond reason and I was determined to right the wrong before leaving Egypt. The anchorage at the Port Fouad Boat Center just across the canal from Port Said was less than ideal. Open water was all that separated us from the giant wakes of the never ending stream of transiting ships and the pilings of the Boat Center piers looked more like deadly javelins than safe mooring points. I was tempted to get our passports stamped and move on, but my fight with the shipping agent was a windmill that needed tilting and I was too angry to let it pass.

Sitting on the Boat Center pier with the Felix agent while *Skimmer* bounced around in high wind and large swells and Charlotte worried about the anchor dragging, I was about to give up, but when I got the Felix Agency President on the phone. I was amazed at the response. Before I could begin my rehearsed speech on the shoddy treatment I had received from his agent in Port Suez, a warm voice came through in perfect English: "Mr. Coleman, this is Nagib Latif. We are truly sorry you have been overcharged by the Suez Canal Authority. You are not the first and will probably not be the last, but we would like to try to help you. If you stay in the Port Fouad Boat Center tonight, I will pay your fees and then help you present your case to the Canal Authority tomorrow. If you like, I will send my driver to pick you up tonight at eight o'clock so that he can bring you to my office and then show you around the city."

This was too good a cultural experience to pass up so Charlotte and I did all we could to secure *Skimmer* and waited for the driver to show up at eight o'clock. Not only did the driver show up, he was actually on time. And he was delightful. Massen was part of the family and took great pride in explaining the intricacies of the shipping industry and the infrastructure of Port Said as we took the free ferry from Port Fouad to Port Said. Massen joked about our ferry ride from Asia to Africa, but I felt that since my conversation with Mr. Latif we had done much more than just cross from one continent to another. Charlotte and I reasoned that if we could understand the Felix Agency and what we saw that night, perhaps we would have the key to being able to understand more of Egypt.

When his driver took us into the high rise that housed Felix, we were startled. Had the building been bombed out or was it just the disorder of new construction? Random piles of hardened concrete lay on marble stairs and hallways and the elevator shafts were empty. By the time we climbed to the fifth floor I was too winded to ask any more questions. What I saw next so startled me that I lost my whole train of thought.

The rubble in the hall and the tiles hanging from the ceiling framed two exquisite mahogany doors. Inside we found well-furnished offices, a huge conference room, and pictures of giant ships and luxury yachts occupying all the available wall space. But the people in the office were as incongruous to the office as the mahogany doors were to the dilapidation outside. Well-groomed men, attractive women, and several small children—it looked more like a family reunion than a working office. Before we had a chance to find out what work was being conducted in our new environment, the summons came.

We discussed *Skimmer's* problem with the overcharge, Palestine's problem with Israel, and America's problem with its public image in Arab countries. Mr. Latif's explanation that while he was pleased with the huge amount of foreign aid to Egypt from the US, the effect was spoiled by the size of our aid to Israel. "You give more to one child than another and what happens? Jealousy and the gift is ruined!" Looking at the opulence of Mr. Latif's office and the dazzling beauty of his third wife, I had a hard time empathizing with his jealousy.

The next day, Mr. Latif was true to his word and one of his yachts picked me up to ferry me over to the Suez Canal Authority. My Felix escort held my hand through the intricate process of making an appeal and within two hours I was back aboard *Skimmer* and ready to depart and enter the Mediterranean. Although my chances of any monetary recovery were slim to none—money once paid in Egypt is as likely to be returned as water is to flow uphill—I felt quite satisfied that Mr. Rammadan of the Canal Authority had acknowledged that it did appear an error had been made and he would look in to it. Don Quixote is not my role model, but somehow I don't think my efforts had been totally in vain. At a minimum, I had alerted all the cruisers behind *Skimmer* to beware.

Cruising the Mediterranean

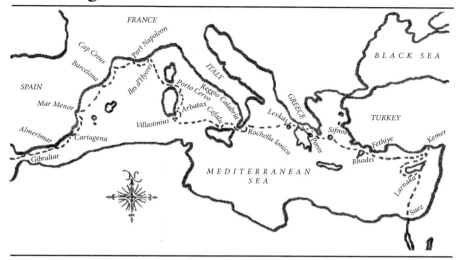

T he view was magnificent. Clear skies and bluer than blue water—modest houses in the foreground with waterfront high rises along the distant coast. It could have been a prosperous, luxury paradise. But it wasn't. We were standing on the roof of the closest Greek Cypriot dwelling to where the advance had stopped. Barbara, our hostess, provided us with binoculars and we stared at the ghost town across the barbed wire barrier just in front of us. The UN Complex was prominent in the foreground and the Turkish military presence was obvious in the background.

Close examination revealed that what appeared to be a normal village was nothing but a collection of abandoned homes. The houses, yards, and streets were empty and the only signs of humanity were the occasional Turkish flags denoting military installations. The high rises in the distance were empty monuments attesting to the fact that Cyprus's largest port had actually once been alive and well.

Once Varosha had been Famagusta's Riviera—luxury resorts along the most beautiful beaches in all of Cyprus. Then came the summer of 1974 when Turkey invaded. The Greek community fled in panic. They expected to return in a few days—but that was 28 years before, and now their once proud city was behind a barbed wire barricade.

Barbara showed us newspaper articles about British real estate agents illegally selling abandoned Cypriot Greek homes to British citizens. She told us about a friend of hers who saw her home advertised for sale on the Internet. The infuriated homeowners were trying to take legal action to stop the sales, but intricate international laws have made the process all but impossible.

The invasion resulted in Turkish occupation of the northern portion of the island comprising 37 percent of the land and almost 70 percent of the island's natural resources. Over 200,000 Greek Cypriots, one third of the population of the entire island, had been displaced from a region where they had formerly been an 80 percent majority. The Atilla line that separated North from South and divided Cyprus' largest city, Nicosia, Berlin style, into two separate cities had galvanized the Greek Cypriots into a campaign of hate that was apparent everywhere. Cell phones couldn't dial Turkey, passports stamped in Northern Cyprus precluded entry into the south, and even tourist literature exuded venom at the violence and deprivation Greek Cyprus has suffered at the hands of its northern neighbor.

A year earlier, our friends in Darwin had warned us to stock our boat well before leaving Australia because the next real civilization we would see would be in Cyprus. They'd been right. After our string of third world countries and sand blasting in the Red Sea, Larnaka was pure luxury. Out of the marina gate and to the right there was a beautiful boulevard with open air restaurants on one side and semi-nude beach goers on the other. We could have been in Nice. It was an incredible sight—women without veils and with very little to cover the rest of their bodies, clean sidewalks without huge potholes, a complete absence of donkey carts, and streets lined with buildings that had actually been completed. There were still hawkers trying to push us into their restaurants, but compared to the baksheesh-seeking characters that had breathed their garlic-scented demands into our faces from only six inches away, this was truly freedom from harassment. And there was another freedom—no more city-wide public address systems—no more wailing recitals of the Koran blasting from minarets. It was hard to believe it had only been two days since we had left Port Said.

For those of us up from the Red Sea, it was an opportunity to return to the real world, repair our boats, and reminisce about our experiences over the past six months with other cruisers. Here we learned of another boat lost in the Red Sea, *Cariade*. Her sad story involved entry into a port at night in high winds, a misplotted position, and an incorrect interpretation of a light. A reef ripped their boat to pieces. Badly shaken, but uninjured, the crew had been able to walk over the reef to shore as their yacht was being destroyed. *Skimmer* and *Theta* were the only remaining arrivals from the Red Sea, so we were the focus of many questions. But somehow our answers weren't completely acceptable.

"Yes, it had been difficult, but really not so bad. And despite the high winds, the places we visited were fascinating. No, we were never really bothered by pirates—in fact with the intense military presence we felt very safe . Well, we really don't know about the incidents that took place three years ago, but our experience was that piracy was not a problem."

As the questions continued, understanding dawned—our interrogators were looking for reasons not to take the plunge. Many of them had been in Larnaka for several years and they were very comfortable. Dreams of the Orient were giving way to contentment in Cyprus, and it would be only a matter of time before one more sailing yacht would be on the already crowded yacht market of Larnaka.

* * *

Tired from our two-day crossing from Cyprus to Turkey, we wondered if they were going to have space for us in the Marina at Kemer, or if they were just going to tell us to continue on our way. Charlotte went below to make the call on the VHF radio and came back on deck all smiles. A marina attendant in a new Boston Whaler guided us in. I was delighted to have the help. This was going to be *Skimmer*'s first stab at the dreaded Mediterranean Mooring.

In most parts of the world, Marinas have finger docks that come off of main docks, and mooring is accomplished by coming in between two adjacent fingers and then tying up to them. While this isn't always easy, especially if there are other finger docks that necessitate a very tight turn before entering the slip, it's a piece of cake compared to the Mediterranean Mooring.

In the Mediterranean to conserve space they do away with the finger docks, and boats moor at right angles to the main dock with nothing separating them except bumpers. The preferred method is to drop an anchor well out from the dock and then back in. This results in the boat being secured with its stern facing the dock and its bow pointed out. With its single screw, long keel, and small rudder *Skimmer* is very hard to maneuver. In reverse, it is almost impossible. The rudder is almost useless, the long keel makes her not want to turn at all, and the rotation of the single screw gives side thrusts. Add a little wind to the formula and all the ingredients are in place for a huge husband-wife fight. Poised on the stern with coiled mooring lines ready to throw and a bumper at her feet ready to fend off emergencies, Charlotte is the victim of any miscalculations I make as I fiddle with wheel and throttle to bring us in. She is generally more sensitive than I am to the potential of *Skimmer*'s ramming into another boat or dock and often feels compelled to deliver her constructive criticism at high volume. For my part, I like to think that I am in control of the boat and sometimes feel that the steady stream of advice is not all necessary. In order to get her attention, especially if she is facing away from me, I also have to raise my voice to levels that in other circumstances might not be appropriate. It is unfortunate when this happens, as it gives the false impression to the faces turned in amusement to watch our little drama that all is not blissful harmony in our wonderful home afloat. But at Kemer it went as smooth as glass. There wasn't a breath of wind, the turn hadn't been too tight, and *Skimmer* decided to go in the direction I wanted.

***

Despite the horror stories of Turkish cruelty we'd heard in Cyprus, we found that it was a delightful country and its people some of the friendliest and most considerate we had ever met. History has not reserved tragedy to the Greeks alone, and during the gut-wrenching forced migrations that took place in 1923 after the Treaty of Lausanne, ethnic Turks as well as ethnic Greeks unfortunate enough to be minorities in newly assigned regions suffered terribly as they made their forced migrations. But the Turks we met and the understanding we developed of their country indicated they had managed to put this suffering behind themselves and were eager to move on.

A ten-hour drive across the vast Anatolian Plains in a rented car brought us to Goreme where we met Salih. With an expressionless face and faraway look in his eyes, he silently nodded his assent to introduce us to the wonders of Cappadocia.

Home Carved in Tufa

Millions of years ago, violent volcanic activity in the middle of the Anatolian Planes created huge layers of calcareous tufa (porous rock) over a region that was to become known as Cappadocia. These tufa plains were unique in that they were composed of two layers—hard at the top, soft at the bottom. Over time, movement of the surface of the Earth caused these layers to crack, and then wind and water began their long erosion process. When the Hittites arrived on the scene around 2,000 BC they found cone-like structures with hard caps. The soft tufa underneath the hard caps was easy to work and the process of transforming the weird little mountains into shelters, homes, and fortresses began. The most architecturally ambitious of the many civilizations that left their mark on the tufa were the early Christians. During the Byzantine period, huge Christian communities carved elaborate churches complete with beautifully proportioned columns and arches and decorated with stunning murals of religious scenes. When the Arabs and Islam came to Anatolia in the seventh century, the Christians living in Cappadocia then used their cave churches and homes as hiding places.

We were not ready for the dramatic nature of the countryside as we began to follow Salih on our trek through this fantasyland. It was easy to understand why they were called fairy castles. There were thousands of them and each unique with its sides riddled with windows and doors that gave small hints of the intricacies that lay within.

Salih led us along a narrow path on the side of a mountain and then crawled into what seemed like a relatively small and insignificant hole. Once we were inside, Salih went over to an iron gate that had not been visible from the entrance, took a huge ring of keys from his pocket, and led us into the nave of a Byzantine church. There were carved columns beneath arches that separated the various chapels, and the walls and ceilings were covered with the vivid colors of beautifully executed religious paintings. And all of it had been carved out of the solid tufa of the mountain we had just climbed.

Charlotte and Salih in Byzantine Church

We visited at least ten other similar churches, climbed through the rooms and tunnels of a monastery, explored honeycombs of houses that filled Swiss cheese mountains and walked through valleys admiring the silhouettes of the fairy castles that surrounded us. It was unreal and magic.

And all the while Salih kept us entertained. We stopped for tea at his friend's cave home and stretched out on carpets as Salih and his friend told us that it would be years before they could make their Hajj. For Salih's friend the reason for the delay was purely monetary. But for Salih, the reasons were more complicated. Perhaps the biggest obstacle for him, he confided, was that before going he would have to give up beer.

***

Charlotte surprised me by agreeing to even consider a visit to the office of Cappadocia Balloons. Was it Lars' quiet competence or was it the wonderful album of wild flowers that Charlotte had been examining while Lars had been on the phone that pushed her over the edge? The end result was that Charlotte buried her fear and I managed to avoid cardiac arrest at the price, and we signed up for the trip early the next morning.

Hot Air Baloon in Cappadocia

The blast of heat cut the chill of the early morning air. Two more deafening blasts from the propane burner and then, ever so gently, we began to feel the motion. It was more like the earth was descending below us than that we were rising. Lars smiled as he watched the awed expressions of his ten passengers as they began to experience the pleasure of his passion. "You don't feel any wind because you are now part of the wind." And it was true. Between the occasional blasts of propane, the silence was almost deafening and we watched the beauty of Cappadocia glide by below us.

Lars took us up high and pointed out way stations along the oldest trading route in the world and then swooped down, brushing against treetops, and then skimmed along the tops of the fairy castles we had admired so much the day before. After two hours of floating we finally touched down in the middle of a field ablaze with wild flowers and said goodby to Lars over cold champagne that the ground crew had waiting for us in silver buckets.

***

After one last beautiful Turkish anchorage at Tersane Adasi, a small island tucked in the southwestern corner of Fethiye Bay, we set out for Rhodes, Greece. We had loved everything about the country during our wonderful visit twelve years ago except for one small problem. The Greeks themselves. But had they really been that difficult, or could it just be that our memories had distorted a few unfortunate encounters?

The sun was sparkling and the wind was howling as we approached Rhode's historic Mandraki Harbor. The familiar sight of the beautiful stone windmills on the eastern mole and the massive walls of the Knights of St.

Johns Castle in the background bought back nostalgic memories of our winter in the crowded yacht harbor back in 1991.

Our timing wasn't perfect. The tail end of the Sunday race from Lindos was winding up, and the raw aggression of the racing sailors frayed our nerves as they jockeyed to be the first to pass through the two pillars that once supported the legendary Colossus of Rhodes. We chalked it up to normal racing tactics, kept our distance, allowing them to pass unchallenged, and tried not to think bad thoughts about any ethnic group or nationality.

Not surprisingly, Mandraki was full. After circling twice, we decided to explore the two commercial harbors. The wind had reached 25 knots and even with harbor protection from waves, the enormous forces on *Skimmer* were making maneuvering delicate, and our futile search for a home in one of the other harbors succeeded only in bringing our anxiety level up to a higher pitch. It was either Mandraki or an unpleasant night of wind, foam, and spray.

When I found a space, the wind was blowing so hard I didn't even need my motor to back in. We were about to celebrate our arrival from Turkey when we had a visitor. One of those people who keep themselves so well quaffed that not even a thirty-knot gust of wind can produce a disheveled appearance, bearing himself like a Greek God on his chariot, Adonis circled his bright red motor scooter over to edge of the mole opposite us and shouted over the wind: "You not stay here. If your anchor drags, it's not safe."

Trying to be friendly, I replied, "Yes, if my anchor drags it is never safe. But it is a large anchor and it will not drag!" Adonis ignored my comment and continued his speech: "You see here no space. You go over to other harbor and stay in marina. There they have much space." And with that, adding cockiness to rudeness, he sped off on his motor scooter as if our immediate departure were a certainty.

Welcome to Greece! From our reconnaissance, Charlotte and I both knew that there was no other marina and that Adonis was simply trying to turn us out to fend for ourselves. I suppressed my anger and stepped off the boat to begin the check in process. Despite the warning from other cruisers about Greece's illegal cruising permit, I was optimistic. My optimism was ill founded. Immigration, customs, and then port police—each got their pound of flesh. Despite the fact that the ECC had eliminated barriers between ECC countries, Greece had continued to harass its cruisers with a transit log, hefty charges, and a check-in procedure for each port that would make the designer of King Minos' labyrinths proud of his descendants. Our authoritative cruising guide assured us that the charges were strictly illegal but somehow the Greek officials didn't see it that way. Before leaving the port police office I had asked one last question: "We are currently moored outside the first line of boats because there was no room along the mole—is that okay?" "Yes, if you stay only two maybe three days is okay."

Charlotte at Mandraki Horbor

Back aboard *Skimmer,* Charlotte and I were making preparations for a visit to the old city when Adonis pulled up again on his chariot. "When you leave? You here one hour already. You must now go." Trying to keep my voice calm and my temper down I replied: "Thank you very much but we are not going."

"What you mean you not go? You must go. Here no room."

"I mean that I am not going. I have talked with the Port Police and I am staying here for the next three or four days." What had been simply surly demands now became downright angry snarls. "What the Port Police they say to you?"

"The Port Police told me I can stay and I am going to stay" There was no room for Adonis to misinterpret my reply or underestimate my resolve, and with a string of Greek expletives that I was happy I didn't understand he revved up his chariot and stormed off. When we had been in Greece before, we fondly referred to it as the Greek 180-degree turn. It took Adonis about half an hour, but finally he came back. And this times all smiles. Mr. Hyde had become Dr. Jekyll and in a pleasant voice, as if our previous encounters had been nothing but friendly, he informed me that a space down the mole was going to open up in an hour and that he would come back to help us with our lines. Charlotte and I looked at each other and smiled. We had our confirmation. In spite of Charlotte's best wishes, nothing had really changed over the past twelve years. Greece was still Greece and the Greeks were still … well, lets just say … Greeks.

But if the cantankerousness of the Greeks hadn't changed, the beauty of Rhodes had. Our trip before had been during winter and the chill in the air had kept us in the Turkish Baths. Now it was summer and the city was transformed, crowded streets, wonderful smells from garden restaurants, and warm sunshine.

A large fertile island in the midst of relatively barren neighbors, strategically located along the major trading route into Asia Minor, Rhodes had flourished during its long and prosperous history. A wonderful exhibit in the Palace of the Grand Master traces its growth from the Dorians in 1100 BC through the defeat of the Knights of St Johns by Suleyman the Magnificent in 1522. Piles of stones lying about the castle walls are reputed to be projectiles hurled from the giant Helepolis siege machine when Demetrius Polioketes unsuccessfully tried to conquer the city after the demise of Alexander the Great's Empire. The moles on either side of the entrance to Mandraki Harbor are said to be the foundations upon which the giant colossus had been built in the image of Rhodes' patron deity, the sun god Helios, to celebrate the city's deliverance from Demetrius. And the castle itself lives on as a testimony to the bravery of the final defenders of Christendom in the Aegean Sea. Legend has it that a force of only 650 knights held out for five months against over 100,000 Turks.

***

A two day sail through tranquil seas and soft air bought us to an island that caused us to reformulate our whole attitude towards Greece. Could Sifnos really be in the same country as Rhodes? It is located at the western edge of a group of islands that form the middle Cyclades and is a vital part of the chain of islands that ancient mariners used as road signs and shelters as they navigated the treacherous route from mainland Greece to Asia Minor.

The sun was high enough as we entered Kamares Bay to perform its magic. Whiter than white, bluer than blue, the walls and shutters of the town leapt out of the dry brown background of jagged hills and steep gorges that supported the rising pyramid of houses. A sandy bottom for good holding and a deep bay for wonderful protection—we were in paradise. The surroundings were so beautiful that we opted for Pavarotti and pasta on board *Skimmer* rather than an evening in town. The setting sun and the delicious bottle of Doluca Antik 2000 were the perfect accompaniments for the panorama of beauty that unfolded before us as *Skimmer* swung on her anchor—small churches in impossible locations high up on the hills, an isolated house, a herd of goats. And all the while the sun was giving us its own show as it flung its differing hues of red and orange across the bay .

During a short bus ride over the mountains to Apollonia we tried to piece it together. If tourism hadn't arrived by mid July, when was it going to arrive? And the ferries. During the previous night we had watched the huge ferries come and go discharging and loading trucks, cars, and boxes of cargo. But where was their human cargo? Had we just been lucky, or were people in Sifnos always this friendly to their visitors? After a little thought, the answer had seemed clear. We had finally arrived in the real Greece. The ferries were their land bridge to civilization bringing in the essentials of life instead of flocks of sun worshipers to be fleeced.

Apollina, the ancient capital of Sifnos is a walled city—a vertical complex of white walls and houses perched on top of a cliff. In ancient times its thick walls and towering height protected it from the pirates that preyed upon the lucrative trading routes.

View from Apollonia

We had read that terracing was important to Sifnos as it gave the light rains of winter level ground to seep into and nourish the soil. But we were unprepared for the extent and the beauty of this terracing. In many cases it looked more like the steep sides of castles than simple agricultural walls to lessen the slope of hills. The extent was staggering. Whole mountains had been turned into concentric circles of level plains. The amount of work that it must have taken to accomplish what we saw was almost beyond our imagination. And the beauty! The small domed white chapels with their little bell towers outnumbered the vineyards.

***

Normally we would have been more observant, but we were still smarting from the rudeness of the German lady who had emphatically waved us away as we had been dropping our anchor. Thinking very unkind thoughts, I reeled in 150 feet of chain and repositioned us so that even if our assailant complained again, I wouldn't be able to hear her. Vidhi Bay was large and there were three boats. I hadn't paid much attention to our third neighbor other than to be sure not to anchor too close and Charlotte and I watched with interest as the little inflatable approached.

"What kind of boat are you?" from the friendly face with a strong Greek accent. Hoping I was addressing his question properly, I replied: "*Skimmer* is a Whitby 42." A broad smile spread across his face as he nodded his head "Yes, I thought so." I diverted my attention from the octopus painted on the seat of his dinghy to study his sailboat. I couldn't believe my eyes. Below the French flag, sun panels, aluminum poles, and huge sun awning lay *Skimmer's* twin. It was the first Whitby 42 we had seen since South East Asia.

Demy had retired from dentistry long ago, but not from gadgetry. Greek, raised in Egypt, educated in Scotland in one of Britain's finest boarding schools, and a lifelong sailor, Demy was so laden with knowledge that he had a hard time keeping it all in. The mere suggestion of a question and he was off and running. But more impressive than Demy's mind was his garrulous friendliness.

Charlotte and I were both charmed and mesmerized. A technical question from me led to a level of detail I had never approached, but before he could delve too deep, a name or place would remind him of a story and he would be off on a charming anecdote. We had both met our kindred spirit—but in entirely different realms. For me it was innovations, inventions, and gadgets. For Charlotte it was people and stories that shifted from person to person and theme to theme with no ends and continuous beginnings.

Aboard *Skimmer*, I regaled Demy with all my modifications and improvements while Charlotte lost herself in conversation with his wife Michele, who was French and every bit as charming as Demy. They were expecting their first grandchild at any moment and Michele was poised to leave *Samadhi* in Demy's hands to go to Athens to help her daughter when the baby arrived. Aboard *Samadhi*,

Samadhi

it was an inventor's paradise. Unfettered by aesthetic considerations, Demy had solutions for every convenience. Plastic porch chairs with their legs cut off littered the cockpit. Aluminum poles, hose clamps on stays, and an ingenious configuration for the space left between mainsail and mizzenmast were Demy's tour de force. The solar panels seemed to hang from the sky. He proudly explained how his series of lines and pulleys allowed him to control the angles of the panels from his cockpit while another set of lines could adjust the flaps of his giant sun awning so that it shaded only him and Michele while leaving the solar panels free to fuel the home-made refrigeration system he had designed and installed. I took copious notes and asked lots of questions. My "where to find" questions seemed to always have the same answer: "Oh, you find that at Mangelli's." I made a mental note to be sure to have Demy take me to Mangelli's when the picturesque little fishing boat came chugging up to our bay. Demy looked up and a delighted smile lit his face. "It's Mangelli—and I think he brings us oysters."

As the boat got closer, I noted that Mangelli wore the same uniform as Demy except that his skimpy bathing suit was bright red instead of faded black and the hair on his bare chest was thickly matted black instead of white.

From *Samadhi's* cockpit Michele explained why the quiet little bay we had happened upon was her favorite place in Greece. Far enough away not to hear, but close enough to take our breath away was the magnificent view of Poros. As the sun set, the lights lit up the island city like a crown of sparkling jewels. Just across a narrow channel from Poros and an easy dinghy ride from our anchorage was Galatas—and that's where Demy kept his car and Mangelli had his wonderful shop.

The next morning Demy parked his car well out of view of the town vegetable market—"I don't want them to think I am rich"—and then began to lead me through the stalls. I had been impressed with the vegetable markets in Greece, but none that I had seen before could compare with that of Galatas. A two-liter water bottle full of new wine, another two-liter water bottle full of local olive oil, and a third filled with small delicious olives. Tomatoes that tasted like sunshine, tiny zucchinis with the blossoms still attached, wonderful small, firm cucumbers. And with each purchase came a dissertation from Demy: "I wasn't even going to show you the—how do you call it—okra—But now that I know you like it, I tell you how to fix it. Never cut the end off—all the juice comes out—you make a conical cut around the stem—and then you put on salt and vinegar and leave it in the sun for two hours before cooking."

***

We had driven through Mangelli's orchards, passed by his parents' house, and stopped at his brother's filling station—but I was still eagerly waiting for the principal reason for my tour of Galatas. It wasn't exactly like West Marine and bore no resemblance to Sears Roebuck. In fact it bore no resemblance to any store I had ever seen. If it had not been for the large crowd milling around the stacks of barbed wire, fence poles, and tractor wheels outside, I wouldn't have known it was a shop at all. Demy quipped that I needed to be good at mountain climbing to enter. He wasn't too far off the mark, and I climbed over the piles of spilled nuts, bolts, and loose hardware.

Both Charlotte and I were acutely aware of my susceptibility to binge purchasing in hardware stores, but unfortunately Charlotte wasn't there to restrain. For reasons that I have never been able to explain, the fact that I don't need a mechanical item that I find particularly interesting has little bearing on the purchase decision. Particularly if it is very cheap. "Maybe one day I will need it," I rationalize, "and besides, it's such a good deal I can't afford to pass it up." Charlotte's main problem with my disorder is not so much the money as the space the new brazing torch, metric threaded stainless steel rod, or portable gas burner is going to take up aboard *Skimmer*. It was a wonderful visit and to help preserve harmony once I returned to *Skimmer*, I purchased several of the quaint little brass bells she had so admired on the necks of goats and sheep we would pass on our walks.

Our intended one-day stay at Vidhi Bay turned into one of the most delightful weeks we'd spent since leaving Charleston three years before. Each morning Charlotte and I would dinghy in to our rental car and drive along stunning coastline, get lost in beautiful surroundings, and explore ancient sites—the largest amphitheater in the ancient world at Epidavrous, a Venetian fort at Navplion, the ruins of one of Greece's oldest civilizations at Mycenae, and the beaches of Spetsai. We would return later than expected seeking only sleep. But Demy would intercept us before we reached *Skimmer* for the dinner he had spent the day cooking.

Demy had showered us with advice on avoiding high winds and finding safe and wonderfully interesting anchorages on our route west through Greece. He had been clear about his favorite: "Meganisi—it's not an island—it's paradise! Why do you think everyone from Europe comes to cruise in the Ionian? It's the most beautiful cruising place in the world!"

***

Demy and Heyward Sample Ouzo Aboard Samadhi

As we approached the Greek mainland, we had faced a fork. Go south around the Peloponnesus or head east through the shortcut. Started by the Romans during the reign of Nero and finished by the French near the end of the eighteenth century, the Corinth Canal deserves a place as one of the wonders of the world. What used to be an important isthmus across which Greeks and Romans dragged ships to fight battles is now a narrow, navigable canal that connects the Aegean to the Ionian Sea without the necessity of rounding the long treacherous fingers of the Peloponnesus. We opted for the short cut, because Charlotte wanted no part of the funnel winds and confused seas at the capes of the Peloponnesus.

Even though the Corinth Canal hasn't earned a place in Ripley's, the Greeks must feel that it ranks so high on the list of man's achievements that it justifies the astronomical price they unabashedly charge for their three-mile wonder. Per mile it's about ten times as expensive as the Suez canal and about five times more than the Panama Canal. The traffic is one way and we had had to wait our turn. After I had paid almost all my remaining Euros, I watched as the red flag dipped and the blue was raised in its place. They had just submerged the pontoon bridge across the entrance and our group was off.

The Corinth Canal

Tanker ahead, a power yacht second, and *Skimmer* bringing up the rear, we entered the gorge formed by the jaws of two giant cliffs. The height and steepness made the already narrow channel seem even narrower. Would the large tanker ahead really fit? From where we sat it looked like it wouldn't—but the tug pulling didn't suffer from the distortion that parallax gave from our vantage point, and pulling at a snails pace they threaded their tow through the needle's eye.

Slow speed meant reduced maneuverability for *Skimmer* so we had put our most reliable helmsperson on duty. I craned my neck, snapped pictures, and muttered a stream of superlatives as Charlotte's white knuckles grasped the wheel and held us as close to the middle as possible. No coves, no side creeks, nowhere to run, nowhere to hide! What happened if the motor failed? How much would they charge for closing the canal and towing us out? Far above, silent trucks and cars sped across spans that linked the two Greeces while *Skimmer* glided through to the Gulf of Corinth at the tail end of its convoy.

A warm afternoon sun had welcomed us into the Ionian. Was it an optical illusion or was the water really a deeper blue? Ionian Greece was so different from Aegean Greece that it was hard to believe they could be in the same country. Lush green replaced stark brown. Wonderful natural harbors abounded everywhere instead of the hazardous traps of the Cyclades and Dodecanese. Best of all, the powerful Meltemi wind that howled down from the north for days and sometimes weeks on end was no longer with us. Ithaca lay ahead and we could almost feel the excitement of Odysseus as he had returned after his twenty years of hardships. We would like to have visited, but Meganisi was calling so we headed north.

Meganisi is a small island snuggled up to its huge neighbor, Levkas. With its short bridge to the mainland, Levkas has been discovered by tourists and its major towns are swamped. But sandals won't propel sun seekers to Meganisi, and while it is true that a few intrepid travelers board the ferries, land tourists don't play a major role in the makeup of the island. There is, however, another path for those who wish to participate in this Ionian paradise.

Charterers. We'd never seen so many. In our small bay alone we counted over 20, but there was so much room that we were able to achieve isolation. In the main harbor of Vathi there must have been fifty. Watching the two coordinators in their hot afternoon task of keeping their flock off the rocks and properly positioned in the harbor, I thought of their less sophisticated countrymen who only had to keep their sheep from under the wheels of passing automobiles and trucks.

With radio in one hand and a waving flag in the other, our coordinator hero was talking them in, "Yes, now you drop anchor." Silence then a little more loudly into his handheld VHF, "I tell you again—drop the anchor" A shorter pause and then a more emphatic, "Drop you anchor now! Now! And please to slow down!" At this point the assistant came into play as they both put out hands and fenders to stop the momentum of the rapidly approaching stern of the charter boat.

While the coordinators seemed to be properly concerned with the safety of their charges and the safety of other boats around them, the charterers themselves seemed totally unconcerned. We watched in amazement as four charter crew members looked on with interest but without the least inclination to help, as their fifth member struggled at the wheel to keep his craft from crashing onto the dock and impaling the coordinator. A third member of the charter boat survival team became apparent as we saw a strapping young man in a dinghy grabbing misplaced anchors and then driving them out a hundred feet to reset them. Finally they were settled in a neat row that took up the entire waterfront.

Another of Demy's "must sees" was located on the island of Levkas. The huge bay that constituted Port Vlikho had a uniformly shallow depth that made anchoring possible anywhere and the shore was dotted with quaint little shops that had all the supplies we needed. We met Spiro and his family and filled liter water bottles with his delicious new wine at about $1.00 per bottle. Unfortunately, Jeff's Used Yachting Equipment Exchange was closed, but we couldn't suppress smiles of amusement as we looked at the incongruous array of equipment that littered his courtyard—so this was where Demy had gotten so many of his ideas!

It was Demy's friend Ellena who sealed our love affair with Greece and gave us wonderful memories of our last night in the country. Before our dingy had even slowed down, a beautiful young lady in a simple red skirt bent over to take our line. Ellena's smile was captivating and the beauty of her shoreside Taverna actually exceeded the list of superlatives Demy had reeled off as he had described his favorite restaurant in Greece. His description of "tying the dingy up to one of the legs of your table under a fig tree" proved to be literal and we said our farewells to Greece as we feasted on roasted peppers, stuffed eggplant, and grilled pork souvlaki.

***

At the end of a very smooth overnight sail, *Skimmer* arrived at the brand new marina of Rochella Ionica on the ball of the foot of Italy. Our late afternoon arrival left us with little remaining daylight, but Tom of *Voyager* had threaded us in through the unmarked reefs that had provided evening entertainment for boats in the marina over the past few days, and we managed to avoid the spectacle of being grounded and then towed off the reefs by the Italian navy.

After two days at Rochella Ionica I gave up on anyone coming to our boat to check us into the country and went to the Capitanerie in search of legitimacy. In contrast to Greece, I had to practically beg the young sailor in the office to issue us a Constituto, but judging from the lack of interest in any kind of documentation at any of the other ports we visited subsequently, perhaps our young sailor had been right and that pasta and prosciutto were much more important than ship's papers.

The long walk from the marina to town rewarded us with a beautiful view of the Italian Ionian coast. We wove our way through dozens of colorfully painted fishing boats that had been towed up onto the sand with ingenious little capstans deeply imbedded in the shore above. Lovers and picnickers used the boats as shelter from the wind and from penetrating eyes but their steady stream of "bon journos" convinced us that we weren't intruding and we continued our trek. Calabria is the southernmost state of Italy and also the poorest. But the Calabrians we met were some of the most gracious people we had yet visited. The butcher wrapped his paper-thin slices of salami with all the care of a florist preparing his best bouquet, and the vegetable man gave us three receipts and a bunch of his hidden stock of basil.

Our voyage from Rochella Ionica around the toe of Italy to Reggio Calabria was uneventful, but Reggio wasn't. Crowded, bustling, dirty—we had no great expectations, especially since our bicycle had been stolen there twelve years before, but our experience there was to show us again that Italians can be delightful people, even if they are Reggio Calabrians.

Getting to the fuel dock was an ordeal, but once there we were under Gino's wing.

Ionian Coast at Rochella Ionica

He was patient as I went through the tedious steps of getting every ounce that *Skimmer's* tanks could hold without adding to the already considerable pollution of the harbor. Once in the office Gino bagan to warm up.

"Italia—Calabria—no is very good. No workka. No money. Calabria isa very poor. Thirty years ago I move to America—to Trenton in New Jersey. I cutta the hair. But everybody he hasa long hair. No wantta the hair cutta. I no makka any money and have to come back to Calabria. Now I workka at the gas stazionne. I am too old to go back to America, but I likka very much!"

***

The early morning sky was a misty gray. Red bolts of sunlight pierced the clouds and accented the rugged beauty of the mountainous Italian coast. The air was calm but the sea was agitated. Overfalls signaled troubled water ahead and suddenly a loud "beep beep" signaled us that *Skimmer's* autopilot could no longer handle its job. *Skimmer* began to careen to the left and then to the right, and then we knew—the whirlpools of Skylla were real!

One and a half miles wide, five miles long, the Strait of Messina separates the northeastern tip of Sicily from the toe of Italy, and it's a body of water to be respected. The sorcerer Circe warned Odysseus of the dangers and the British Admiralty Pilot warns modern mariners of currents, whirlpools, and violent squalls that can "inconvenience vessels." Homer eloquently described Odysseus' "inconvenience" in *The Odyssey*: "Sobbing, gaining on the currents, we rowed into the strait—Skylla to port and on our starboard beam Kharibdis, dire gorge of the salt sea tide. By heaven! When she vomited, all the sea was like a cauldron seething over intense fire, when the mixture suddenly heaves and rises."

Charlotte wasn't sobbing and the cauldron wasn't seething when we approached the Strait of Messina. We had chosen our weather-window well. The wind was moderate and the waves low, but still there was an ominous feeling in the air. In the space of four boat lengths the current went from half a knot against to two knots in favor. And while the cauldron wasn't boiling, the sea was strangely unsettled. We had chosen the eastern shore and Skylla, not because we wanted to see the 12-footed, six-headed beast, but because the Strait is a high congestion area and has a traffic separation zone. We crept up on the far right side of the northbound lane along the steep mountain wall that led to the city of Skylla and the cave home of her legendary monster.

Theories abound on the authenticity of Homer's account. Differences in the times of tides in the Tyrrhenian sea to the North and the Ionian to the south account for strong currents; differences in the salinity of the two seas create a mixing effect at the interface that can cause eddies and whirlpools. Earthquakes have changed the ocean floor, rendering the whirlpools at Kharibdis and Skylla less potent than they were to the ancients, but the sight of the steep cliffs where winds can gather, funnel, and howl and the presence of spinning water in our relatively calm conditions gave us a good feel of what it would be like to negotiate the Strait of Messina in foul weather.

Our passage through the strait was brief and as suddenly as we had entered the turbulence it had disappeared and we found ourselves in a very tranquil Tyrrhenian Sea. While our friends on *Kemo Sabay* and *Voyager* chose to go north and explore the western coast of Italy, we decided to continue west and visit the northern coast of Sicily and its islands.

The Mediterranean has its own Bermuda Triangle. And like ours in the Atlantic, the triangle in the Mediterranean—the Aeolian Islands—is a place where winds can blow with incredible violence. It is fertile ground for marine archeologists interested in shipwrecks and a magnet for visitors wanting to see something truly different. Volcanic islands have pushed their way up just off the northeastern coast of Sicily and stand sentinel to the Strait of Messina. Stromboli with its active glowing volcano may be the world's oldest lighthouse with its illumination provided by geothermal energy.

* * *

Halfway across the northern coast of Sicily the Madonie Mountains dominate the landscape, and just behind the medieval city of Cefalu is the hundred thousand acre Parco Naturale Regionale Delle Madonie. Early in the morning we were off to the mountain village of Gratteri. The Sicilians are more Italian than the Italians and our bus driver was no exception. Charlotte and I had boarded early and taken the two front seats just behind the driver. Then a young boy deposited a bunch of packages in the front of the bus and departed. An elderly lady laden with overflowing shopping bags was next. In all, we were about fifteen, but no one went to the back. The bus filled from forward with each successive passenger taking the most forward vacant seat. Finally the driver took our money, and eased us out into the street, and then the reason for the seating arrangement became apparent.

How Luigi could carry on a conversation with everyone in the bus and at the same time navigate the suicidal traffic of Cefalu was hard to understand, especially since he drove with only his left hand. The eloquent right hand enabled Charlotte and me to follow portions of the conversations even though we didn't understand Italian at all. Fingers pinching, wrist gyrating, arm gesticulating and all at an ever increasing tempo as the conversations warmed up. It wasn't until we had left the city behind and started our ascent of the lusciously green mountains that his singing started and the arm movements went into another mode of expression. I watched as he began to negotiate the hairpin turns and hoped that the rhythm of his right hand wouldn't affect the accuracy of his left.

After our stop in Gibilmanna Charlotte and I were the only passengers left aboard. Luigi's silence seemed so unnatural that we both felt sorry for him and struck up a conversation. No matter our languages were different, Luigi was delighted to once again have an audience and told us all about Gratteri. Rustic, practically untouched by tourism, Gratteri was built on the side of a mountain with intricate stairways that led to streets on different levels, where old Romanesque churches, fountains surrounded by brilliant flowers, and pine forests in the background filtered the view of mountains above and the sea below.

Gratteri was a town of the elderly. No seats were empty in the outside cafes and we watched as cards were shuffled. By accident Charlotte found the principal activity in the town that day. Stepping into the post office, she found herself at the end of a long line. It was entitlements day in Gratteri and the eager citizens hobbled forward on canes to receive their stacks of Euros.

***

Our transit across the Tyrrhenian Sea from Sicily to Sardinia was rough. Charlotte complained of feeling like she was inside a washing machine, while I had reveled in being able to use wind power instead of diesel. We were both glad to arrive at Villasimius on the southeastern tip of Sardinia, which is as beautiful as it is inhospitable. Steep mountains come down to the sea and not only deny protection of any sort but also accelerate the winds. But halfway up the coast there is a shelter, Arbatax. According to our pilot and our guides, it is an industrial city without sights, without charm, but with a wonderfully protected harbor.

We knew we'd be subject to unconscionably high marina charges. The rope and boards tied around the box that was supposed to supply electricity didn't inspire confidence, but the dock, mooring rings, and mooring lines were all sound and I felt confident *Skimmer* was secure. The marina was full, mostly Italian flags, but I had a hard time concentrating on the other boats as I made my way to the marina office. Shapely, smiling—how could all that beauty fit into such skimpy bikinis? Each group on each boat seemed just a little bit more lovely than the one before, and I was in a mood to change my preconceived notions about Arbatax as I entered the marina office.

The manager gave *Skimmer* a special discount, assured me that the electricity would work, and then told me about the train that linked Arbatax with Cagliari. Things were looking up!

Il Trenino Verde della Sardegna

Il Trenino Verde della Sardegna. Through long tunnels, over high bridges, along steep mountain slopes, the route of our narrow gauge train was a miracle of engineering and a kaleidoscope of beauty. Six hours, 130 miles—past quaint mountain villages and thick pine forests.

Sardinia's capital city, Cagliari, is a perfect place to get a feel for history. Sardinia has never been wholly assimilated by any of the long succession of conquerors: the Carthaginians, Romans, Genoese, Pisans, Aragonese and Austrians each had had a go at it, but somehow the island managed to maintain much of its independence. Even in its present incorporation into Italy, it is categorized as an autonomous region and as such has considerably more independence than most of the rest of the country.

***

The wind starts in the Alps, screams down the Rhone Valley, and then spills out into the Gulf of Lyon transforming the sea into a foaming fury. When it blows, the skies of Provence are strangely clear, trees bend and snap, and mariners take refuge. It can last days or even weeks and in its relentless strength it annoys and infuriates. In times past it is said that under its maddening effects it was legal for husbands to murder their wives.

We met our first Mistral in a secure anchorage in northeastern Sardinia. We had known it was coming. It dominates the weather in the Western Mediterranean and is tracked and reported with the same care as hurricanes in the Atlantic and typhoons in the Pacific, and we had chosen our protected bay carefully. Golfo di Marinella indents deeply into Sardinia's Costa Smeralda and provides good protection against winds from all directions except the north.

The local advice was that with the Mistral we needed protection from the west and that Marinella was as good as they came. Judging from the presence of twenty other boats waiting at anchor, we believed that the advice had been sound and settled down to wait for the blow.

Slowly at first, the wind came. The twenty miles of Sardinia between us and the waters to the west filtered and veered the wind, but did not stop it. Short gentle gusts became longer and stronger. With the enormous force of 40 knots of wind on our beam, I could feel the anchor chain vibrating as it jerked taut. Yes, I had checked that the lock wire that keeps the shackle pin from loosening was firmly in place, but still, the dread of somehow having the anchor separate from its chain was never far from my thoughts.

After three days of captivity, the Mistral passed and we were ready to move on. Our destination was Porto Cervo, site of environmentally correct architecture surrounding a large protected bay on the northeastern tip of Sardinia. Positioned so that it cannot be seen from the sea and built to conform to the topography and blend in with the natural colors and vegetation, Porto Cervo was the model for the subsequent flood of developments that now cover the Costa Smeralda.

In Porto Cervo we didn't need a Mistral to make us fear for our safety. The kamikaze anchoring as more and more vessels crowded into the already full harbor kept adrenaline flowing. We were familiar with the aggressive "what me worry" attitude of Italians when it comes time to station their crafts, but what we saw in Porto Cervo went to the verge of wanton destruction.

A huge motor yacht would approach our stern so closely that it blocked out the sun and then, to our utter amazement and horror, would drop an anchor as large as our dinghy ten feet away from our boat. This process went on from the time we had arrived in the morning until sunset. One boat would leave and two others would take its place.

When we weren't watching and willing the large anchors not to fall on our stern, our attention was riveted on our incredible surroundings. Mooring buoys the size of automobiles lined hundreds of feet of piers, and yachts over two hundred feet long were packed in like sardines. Another set of piers accommodated the more modest yachts—the hundred-foot-and-under knockabouts. There were literally acres of teak decks, shining topsides, and bristling antennas.

Loud honking and pandemonium as a 250-foot four-decker with a helicopter on its stern platform backed into the channel. The yacht was so large and the harbor so congested that it couldn't turn once in and had to make the approach in reverse. By sunset we were surrounded—if the wind had changed, the sound of crunching fiberglass and steel would have filled the air—but it looked stable and what could we do? Why not go ashore and join the beautiful people? The streets were full of see-me's in leather pants, fur lined skirts, gold chains, diamonds—crowding into the cafes and restaurants with the same eagerness their craft had had shown in muscling into the port.

By the time we were back aboard *Skimmer*, the impossible had happened. A 40 footer had somehow squeezed itself between our much too close neighbors and *Skimmer*. Adding cheek to poor judgment, the owner had lined his craft with bumpers before abandoning it for a night of indulgence ashore. Day couldn't come soon enough. At first light *Skimmer* threaded her way among the surrounding boats to retrieve her anchor. Having placed Porto Cervo on the "been there, done that" list, we worked our way out of the harbor and reveled in the luxury of open water and fresh air.

The Canals of France

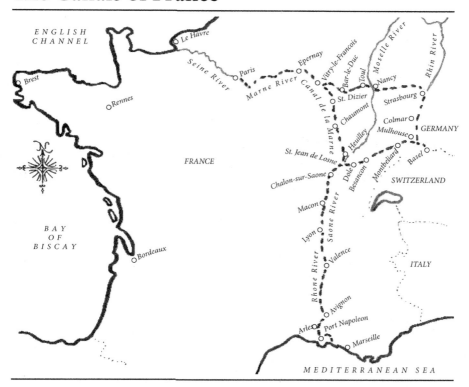

Skimmer had been transformed. Her wings clipped, her decks cleared, the graceful swan had reverted to ugly duckling. The metamorphosis had been a week of frantic activity. Port Napoleon was well equipped and the mast removal went as smoothly as we could have hoped. Postoperative procedures included fabrication of a temporary mast for antennas, extension of the stern platform to accommodate jerry jugs for fuel, and the preparation of a ring of discarded automobile tires to surround and protect Skimmer's topsides. Rube Goldberg would have approved. Discarded material littering the Port Napoleon Shipyard became temporary appendages to Skimmer to meet her needs in her strange new environment. Skimmer had sold her soul. Her primary means of transport, her beauty, all were left behind in a giant warehouse in Port Napoleon. But as compensation, she had received a wonderful reward—the rivers and canals —France had become wide open to us.

But this was the long awaited carrot. If at any point in our previous travels I had so much as suggested that we weren't going to head straight for the French Canals, my first mate, who had so faithfully supported our journeys through gales, sandstorms, and revolutions, would have staged her own revolution and it would have been the end of the travels of *Skimmer*.

Arrival in France

The first canals were built by the Romans, but since that time they have evolved into a system that would have been unimaginable to the founders. Early designers included Charlemagne, Leonardo da Vinci, and Henry IV, but it took the drive of Louis XIV to get in gear the massive program that eventually led to over 5,000 miles of navigable waterways. Louis XIV's Canal du Midi provides the link between the Mediterranean and the Atlantic. Links to the English Channel, the North Sea, Belgium, Germany, and Switzerland have also been added. Now it is possible to go virtually anywhere in France, or anywhere in Europe for that matter, provided that the water draft and air draft (height above water) of the vessel fall within the limits of the chosen route.

Skimmer emerged from her operations in Port Napoleon with an air draft of nine feet and a water draft of five feet. While she couldn't go into all the canals, she could fit quite comfortably in most of the major ones. We chose a route that would take us up the Rhone River to Lyon and then up the Saone River to near Dijon. From there the trip would be through a series of expanded riverbeds and manmade ditches known as the Canal de la Marne.

During the winter, *Skimmer*'s home would be near Place de la Bastille where the wonderful Paris Arsenal Marina sits, just one lock away from the Seine. When the spring thaw receded enough to leave the rivers manageable, she would then quit hibernation in Paris to head back to the Mediterranean and reclaim her former status as sailing vessel.

Skimmer swung wildly. My attention was riveted on the stern so my first indication of the problem was a loud crunch from forward. I didn't have to turn to know that our bow had made the acquaintance of the lock's unyielding side. The Ecluse de Beaucaire was *Skimmer*'s first lock experience and of course we did it all wrong. Sometimes experience is the only teacher. Afterwards we learned that the floating bollards along the sides of the lock are spaced about three *Skimmer* lengths apart to accommodate the long river barges. But on our first try we had put one line way forward and one line way aft—and there had been absolutely no way to keep *Skimmer* still as the hundreds of tons of water began to pour in. As it turned out, the loud crunch was only *Skimmer*'s rub rail filing a minor complaint at our carelessness and no damage was done. As we gathered in our lines, the friendly lockmaster came down the quay to show us how it is done. We learned from the crude diagram he flashed at us that we should have secured both bow and stern lines to the same bollard. But it was only after a second lock experience that we learned the final refinement of having one of us stationed on the bow and one at the stern—each with a long boat hook. We were amazed to find how effective gentle nudges with our sticks were in keeping *Skimmer* perfectly still as the water churned and swirled bringing us up to the level of the next portion of our journey.

At Arles we began to reap the rewards for our efforts. What a feeling to be able to walk off *Skimmer* and right into the center of a city with thousands of years of history. Unlike marinas along the coast that give the tranquillity of isolation, the stops along the rivers are in the heart of civilization. As castles and chateauxs glided by, we read our "Guide Vagnon de Tourisme Fluvial" to decide whether the sight merited a stop, a photo, or just a passing glance. Arles was a jumping off point to one of the most unusual regions of France, the Camargue. Centuries of silt deposits from the Rhone have created two hundred square miles of beautiful, flat marshland—a South Carolinian's idea of paradise.

Mast Removal at Port Napoleon

***

The "halte fluvial" at St. Etienne des Sortes simply didn't exist. All that was left of the pontoon with its welcome for pleasure craft that our Guide Vagnon had recommended so highly were two empty sockets in the sea wall and a sign saying no parking. The powerful Rhone current swept along the unwelcoming sea wall and *Skimmer* faced her first canal dilemma—how to stop and get off. But not to worry. Arnold of *Lhasa* was with us. Undaunted by our forced change of plans, Arnold headed straight for the long river barge (peniche) moored along the line of trees at the end of the sea wall and secured *Lhasa* along side. Within seconds *Skimmer* was comfortably moored outboard *Lhasa*.

Arnold explained that failing a friendly peniche, tying to trees, driving large tent pegs into the shore where there are no trees, or even anchoring outside the channel markers were all valid alternatives. But usually such measures were not necessary. In their efforts to lure pleasure craft into the canals, the French authorities have constructed a large number of "halte fluvials" that provide a pontoon, electricity, water, and sometimes even showers—and all free of charge—free that is if you don't count the $300 that *Skimmer* had to pay for a year's access to the waterways.

Ecluse de Bollene

The following day was one of vertical assault. Seventy-three feet high, the narrow Ecluse de Bollene towered over *Skimmer* as the huge door closed us into a dark and clammy void. This time we were ready with our poles and kept *Skimmer* steady as she rose to the top to give us a totally new perspective from which to admire the chalk-white cliffs, green fields, and scintillating sunshine of Provence. It was a two-lock day, but Charlotte was settling down to the routine. I was not sure how we were going to handle the ten and 20-lock days when they began further north but decided to put that worry aside for the future.

* * *

It wasn't that our guard had been down or that we had become complacent. We simply hadn't perceived the danger. It wasn't the right time of year for flooding, the currents had been gentle, and we had been thoroughly enjoying the good life of easy cruising among the chateaus, vineyards, and beautifully planted farms that comprise the banks of the Rhone Valley. Coming into Lyon was not like anything we'd seen before. Charlotte had spent her junior year of college there and we'd visited it together several times. But never before had we seen France's second largest city in such a light.

Ecluse de Pierre-Benite, the last of the Rhone's giant locks, opened its gates to reveal heavy industrialization and busy shipping as the tip end of

Lyon appeared. We said farewell to the Rhone as we swung to the left and watched it disappear behind Lyon, while *Skimmer* made her way up the east side of the peninsula and into the Saone River. It only took two bridges for the Saone to turn into one of the prettiest rivers we had ever seen. Weeping willows shaded the cobblestone quay while white swans with trails of little brown ducklings circled the opposite bank. And in less than fifteen minutes since leaving the lock we found ourselves moored besides a beautiful park on the Saone side of Lyon with only a short walk separating us from the center of the city.

The spell Lyon was casting over us was broken when we saw a copy of *Le Figaro*. Twenty-six dead. Pictures of cities wholly under water. Heavy rains we had experienced at St. Etienne had apparently gotten worse as we had headed north. The result had been one of the worst flood disasters for the Rhone Valley in modern history.

As we mounted the Saone, the winding river took on an increasingly pastoral

Lyon

appearance. Commercial traffic all but disappeared. The banks were lined with fishermen with long poles and the still water was filled with small boats with patient anglers waiting for a strike. Every bend of the river presented a photo opportunity and we found neither of us wanted to go below when our watch was over.

Heuilley doesn't merit even a small dot on maps of France. But on diagrams of the French Canal system, the town takes on great importance. Along with its seventeen inhabitants, it is the home of the last lock on the Saone before the entrance to the Canal de la Marne. Up to Heuilley we had been traveling mainly on rivers with short stretches of canal interspersed along the route and all the locks had been operated by friendly lockmasters who watched from their giant towers above and controlled the whole operation. After Heuilley, however, it was solid canal with lock after lock looming ahead. We had seen pictures and begun to appreciate the myriad of contraptions that lay ahead. Manual lock gates, automated locks—some triggered by radar and others triggered by turning a cable suspended from another cable that hung over the canal, and locks in a chain controlled by an operator who traveled from lock to lock on his bicycle. The descriptions were conflicting and confusing and we'd wondered how we would cope.

At the Mariner's Museum at Saint Jean de Losne we enjoyed reading the histories of the canals and seeing photographs of them in operation during the heydays of river transportation. My favorite was the photograph of the elderly woman who looked like she should be using a walking cane, but instead had a wide harness across her chest attached to a 50-foot long barge hauling logs. I also liked another that looked like a family outing except that the father was missing and the young children and mother were all harnessed to the family barge. Charlotte wasn't amused when I pointed out to her that of course the father was also busy—he was steering the barge.

Small Canal Locks Begin

Not knowing exactly what to expect, I had climbed up the steep ladder in the middle of our first Canal de la Marne with a long rope in my hand, while Charlotte performed the delicate operation of keeping *Skimmer* in the middle below with only one foot of clearance on either side. And there they were, manual locks with handles that looked like the cranking mechanisms on the old Model T Fords. Perhaps the most important lesson of that first day was that 17 locks in one day is too much, especially when it is raining and freezing cold. The other lesson we learned was that the mandatory two hour wait while the lockmasters ate their lunch was not all bad. French onion soup and a hot baguette with a scenic view from *Skimmer's* cockpit became the best part of our daily routine.

Each lock was different and we never knew exactly what to expect before going in. When the locks were manual, I helped the lock keeper shut the doors and then rushed back to my line on the bollard to pull in the slack as *Skimmer* rose. When the lock was full, I would help open the doors at the other end and then we would be off on another adventure.

The mechanized locks were wonderful when they worked. First, radar would show us coming and the lock would be readied. Then, once in the lock and the boat positioned, I would walk to the control station and lift a long blue pole that went down the side of the lock. This activated the filling cycle and, if all went well, the lower gates closed, the lock filled, the upper gates opened and we would be on our way again.

It was like walking across France. Joggers passed us waving, dogs barked their greetings or their warnings, and children stopped their bicycles to stare and shout bonjour. We were no longer just looking at the countryside, we felt part of it.

The path took *Skimmer* through France's heartland. We crossed fields with broad stripes of brown and green that looked like impressionists masterpieces and admired immaculate farm houses aflame with flowers. An old man cultivating his onions paused to talk with us about our trip and tell us about his experiences in North Africa during the Algerian War. A man driving his giant tractor stopped to give us directions. The days of searching for good stops were over. It no longer mattered. All choices were good. Drive stakes into the ground or find a friendly tree. We'd take our bicycles ashore and pedal into the culture.

***

The canal path that jutted out from the bank under the bridge was long, straight, and had a sturdy steel fence, a perfect substitute for bollards. Feeling a little like hobos camping under a bridge, but not convinced it was illegal, we made our lines fast and rode off on our bicycles to explore the neighboring village.

Mooring by the Bridge at Dommarien

Dommarien's stone houses with tile roofs housed more farm equipment than people. The smell of fresh manure and the sight of tractors carving up the fertile soil dominated the landscape, and we weren't surprised to learn there were no restaurants in the town. Following advice from the young man at the Boulangerie, we crossed a bridge to the Restaurant du Gare in Vaux Sous Aubigny. But just over the bridge we were stopped by an elderly couple in an automobile and asked, "Is that your home under the bridge?" Puzzled, but not alarmed, I replied yes. "How long are you going to stay?" I replied that we would leave the next day. "At what time do you leave?" Alarmed now, I was beginning to formulate my answer when he added, "My wife and I tend the next two locks. If you can tell us what time you will be leaving we will have the locks ready for you when you arrive in the morning."

The seven-kilometer ride through freshly plowed fields and past picturesque churches and villages finally led us to Vaux Sous Aubigny and without much trouble we found our little restaurant. The owner pointed out that dinner was served at 7:00. He was sympathetic to our concern about getting back to our boat before darkness, but some things just couldn't be changed. We chose the charcuterie plate followed by "lapin a la sauce blanche"—a choice made easy by the fact that it was the only plate offered on the menu that evening. At eleven Euros each with wine included, we didn't feel we had much to lose—but when we tasted course after course of delicious food we couldn't believe our good fortune.

In our enjoyment, we had lost complete track of time and when the bill came to our table, it was pitch-black dark outside. Roland, the chef and owner, suddenly remembered our concern about riding our bicycles at night. The next thing we knew we were in Roland's car with our bicycles in the trunk heading back to *Skimmer*.

***

Canal Bridge

The altitude was increasing steadily, sometimes over a hundred feet a day. As we approached the watershed between the Mediterranean and the North Sea, the topography also changed. Steep hills covered with tall pines replaced the fertile farms of Burgundy and our route became more tortuous. Miles of stone-lined embankments held our water road in place, and we were treated to the wonderfully unreal experience of looking down over *Skimmer*'s sides as our man-made river crossed over bridges spanning rapidly flowing mountain streams.

The most awesome sight came as we approached Balesmes Tunnel—a three-mile arrow of water piercing a large hill on the Langres Plateau. Fortunately our Navicarte guide had been wrong and the tunnel was lit, but it took 45 minutes of wracking hand eye coordination.

244

Back in 1879, the actions of a French gentleman named Monsieur Charles de Freycinet had far reaching effects on the canals of France. Minister of Public Works at the time, Freycinet established the standard dimensions for the Peniche Lock: 38.5 meters long, 5.1 meters wide, 1.8 meters deep, and an overhead clearance of 3.4 meters. This standard set the minimum size for most canals and also dictated maximum dimensions for a substantial portion of the barge construction industry. Subtracting *Skimmer*'s width from the Freycinet lock width and dividing by two gives about one and a half feet clearance on each side. But Charlotte had become very good at babying *Skimmer* in and we only occasionally heard the harsh sound of our wooden fenders being ground down by concrete.

The Balesmes Tunnel, however, presented a new challenge. The luxury of a very slow entry speed and a short approach were replaced with the necessity of keeping speed up at four knots and forty five minutes of intense concentration. Not wanting to find out how *Skimmer* would react if it hit the tunnel sides at four knots, we spelled each other at intervals short enough to keep us from being mesmerized by the long string of lights ahead. We found that about

Balesmes Tunnel

ten minutes was all we could take until our eyes began to play tricks on us, making the illumination from the lights look like an opening in the distance. But when the opening finally did come, we were rewarded by one of the most beautiful sections of canal we had yet seen.

After exiting the tunnel, we were so intent on catching our first glimpse of the beautiful walled city of Langres that we hadn't read our Navicarte Guide as carefully as we should have. What was so different about the lock we were approaching? No high walls. My initial survey with the binoculars to determine if the gates were open or shut revealed no gates at all. Then the obvious struck. We had finally reached the watershed of France and our ascent was over. I looked at the altitude on our GPS—1,187 feet. What now lay before us was an open lock, full of water, and ready to receive us for our first descent.

Much to our delight, we found that going down was considerably less stressful than rising. Our new procedure was for me to step off *Skimmer* as we entered with the bow line, secure a stern line around the aft bollard for Charlotte to handle, and then walk over to the lock doors to help the lockmaster crank them closed. The big change came during the actual descent. Going down, the water draining from the locks had practically no effect on *Skimmer*, and our job of keeping lines taught and *Skimmer* in position became almost effortless.

But one thing that didn't change in our then-descending world was the social aspect of locking. Naturally garrulous, the lockmasters opened up even more when they experienced the unusual phenomena of two Americans eager to converse with them in French. The lockmasterss varied from career professionals who lived in the quaint little lock houses to college students making a little money before they resumed their studies. Sometimes we met our lockmaster only once at his assigned lock and other times we had a mobile lockmaster assigned to us for the day who would lead us from lock to lock on his bicycle. One thing they all had in common was their sincere desire to help and their friendly interest in the people on the boats passing through. Probably the biggest danger *Skimmer* faced in her transits through the locks was that the conversations would become so intense that Charlotte would concentrate more on the proper use of the subjunctive than on keeping her line taught enough to keep fiberglass and stone from an unhappy meeting.

Walker and Debby in Chaumont

The visit by my brother Walker and his wife Debby had been in the planning for almost a year and Chaumont turned out to be the ideal meeting place. We quickly discovered that our concerns about Debby's restricted mobility had been ill founded. The ease with which she alighted, descended, and coped with all the claustrophobic curves and passages in *Skimmer*'s compact interior left both Charlotte and me impressed with the versatility of the many hand holds and railings of *Skimmer* and overwhelmed with the amazing recovery Debby had made in her fight against the effects of MS and her quiet determination to enjoy her surroundings as if nothing had happened.

Chaumont to St Dizier—85 kilometers of some of the most beautiful countryside the French canals have to offer—35 locks and their garrulous lock keepers—and a decrease in altitude of 390 feet. All of it with Debby's wheelchair strapped to the stern and Walker's video camera whirring. Bloody Marys, beer and wine—all in heroic quantities while Walker's special collection of oldies but goodies blared away. And at the same time wonderful childhood stories that had gained even more with Walker's eloquent exaggerations in the retelling.

Then came Paris. Our rental car entered along the Avenue de la Grande Army and there they were—the Arch de Triomphe de l'Etoile, the Champs Elysees, and then Place de La Concorde. Charlotte and I began to reel off the list of superlatives that describe one of our favorite cities, but little did we know that a Paris superlative we had never guessed at was about to twist our three-day whirlwind tour in a direction we had never anticipated.

The world's most un-wheel chair friendly city! But how could that be? The country that put subways on inflated wheels, the land of liberty, equality, fraternity, the people who believe they have achieved the highest level of civilization the world has ever known—how could they possibly ignore the plight of those unfortunates who have difficulty coping with stairs, steep curbs, and bumpy roads? But that's the way it was. For those who have dreams of rolling their way around the most beautiful city in the world, the sight of the Eiffel Tower marks the beginning of a wheelchair obstacle course that could hardly be more effective than if it had been planned that way since the early days of the Romans.

Of the 19 metro lines that connect every corner of Paris, only one of them was equipped to receive wheelchairs. But access to this maverick metro was only five short blocks away from our hotel. Line 14 and our metro stop, Bibliotheque Francois Mitterand, were our keys to visiting Paris.

Even with line 14, chairestrian access to Paris wasn't easy. Our descent down Rue Tolbiac ended at the Metro stop Bibliotheque Francois Mitterand. Right where the hotel manager said it would be was the little glass house that encapsulated our elevator. Down into the bowels of the earth and out into a large hall with well-marked access to our metro line fourteen. The special stainless steel structure with its panel of instructions, lights, and buttons inspired confidence and without hesitation Walker had wheeled Debby in. Ticket in the receiving slot, a whirring noise, and then ticket waiting in the out slot. All was going well except for one small detail. The doors failed to open and there were Walker and Debby trapped in the wonderful French invention for automating wheelchair access.

In sharp contrast to the mechanical hostility to wheelchairs was the overwhelming graciousness of the French in their treatment of anyone with a handicap. Just the mention of the word "handicappe" and the attendant would drop everything else and come to the rescue. Those in line for tickets just had to wait while the nice young man with his chain of keys and pocket full of magnetic cards extracted Walker and Debby from the automatic doors. Equally helpful were two firemen we met when we were unable to find a working elevator at our destination station, Chatelet. They laughed and regaled us with stories as they led us through a series of elevators and finally up into the fresh air at an obscure door in the center of what was once the huge market place of Les Halles. There, a the French policeman interrupted his interrogation of drug dealers to lead us to an elevator that would take us back into the security of line fourteen for our return trip home.

Even more touching than the special treatment Debby received from the French was the enthusiasm and courage she and Walker displayed in their positive reactions to the series of setbacks that seemed to continuously plague us. They were primed for their first visit to Paris and seemed to enjoy their subway adventures as much as they enjoyed what Walker coined "the French holy trinity of wine, cheese, and bread." It wasn't an ideal time for Walker's back to start acting up on him, but it didn't slow him down a bit—leaning on the handlebars of Debby's wheel chair and racing towards the next adventure. After Walker and Debby left, Charlotte and I headed back to *Skimmer* to resume our travels.

***

At Vitry le Francois we made the unfortunate choice of mooring at a canal junction right in the heart of the industrial section of the town. We got stuck in the shallow water of a bend and lost propulsion because mud from the bottom clogged the cooling water intake and caused the engine to overheat. I managed to get ashore with a line and then went over to a group of peniches moored along the quay a little further downstream.

Looking at *Skimmer* with her bow pulled tight to the shore and her stern sticking out in the middle of the channel, the weathered man in black turtleneck with two days growth on his cheeks laughed and said not to worry. He opined that there wouldn't be any more traffic that night and we should be okay as long as we left early in the morning. Satisfied that we weren't a hazard to navigation, I returned to the boat to weave a web of lines that would hold us firmly in our awkward position. Before I was far into my task, Turtleneck appeared and began to look at *Skimmer* with a critical eye. At that point, an older man appeared on the scene and began to tell me why *Skimmer* couldn't stay where she was. Turtleneck, who had assumed the role as our sponsor, took exception and I thought a fight was going to break out. I threw a line to each of the two men and suddenly friction turned into cooperation.

The next thing I knew they were pulling *Skimmer* around the bend and parallel to some of the most menacing looking steel plates I have ever seen. Before I had a chance to object, they had *Skimmer* parallel to the steel plates and were drawing her in. My fear of steel cutting into fiberglass was unfounded—the shallow muddy bottom held *Skimmer* a safe three feet away from the steel monster and within minutes we were firmly moored in a bed of mud. Turtleneck then found a long gangplank that he rigged for us and we were set for the night.

What had not been obvious before now became apparent—the steel plates were actually the door to a dry-dock, and on the other side was a huge shallow basin with two maximum sized peniches undergoing overhauls. It was a strange feeling to see a dry-dock that was only about six feet deep and to see for the first time how shallow the drafts of the peniches actually were. Riveted steel, a relic of the past, but also a testimony to the longevity of the old building techniques. River barges that had been built over 60 years ago were still plying the waterways of Europe, and would probably still be around another 60 years down the road.

***

The blue heron stayed with us—waiting on the bank with his long beck proudly pointing skyward until we were almost even, then swooping off down the middle of the canal as if inviting us to follow until he took up a new perch to resume his follow the leader game. Seeming to be one but probably actually many, our beautiful blue mentors had led us from rolling forests

Vineyards of Champagne

ablaze with their autumn leaves into the chalky cliffs of Champagne.

When our last true canal lock at Epernay opened up to the River Marne the sight was breathtaking. Wide stretches of river, flaming trees along the banks, and the beautifully manicured hills of the vineyards of Champagne peeking at us through the gaps. By this time, our herons were replaced by white ribbons of swans leading their young along the riverbanks. The fishing boats were back in force and we once again felt like we were cruising rather than walking through the waterways of France.

***

Bernard had informed us that the lock leading from the Seine into the Paris Arsenal Marina would be closed during our arrival into Paris. But, we could get to the Arsenal Marina by following the Seine north to St. Denis and then coming through the Paris canal system.

For the first time since leaving the Mediterranean, we found ourselves in heavy traffic with giant barges and large wakes reminding us that *Skimmer* could still roll. With cameras clicking and guidebooks spread out, we slid up the Seine and marveled at the beauty of Paris by water. It was getting dark as we approached Paris' Statue of Liberty and we swung to the left to find an empty spot along the quay on the left bank opposite the Allee des Cygnes.

The gray sky, drizzling rain, and biting coldness of the following morning should have tipped us off that it wasn't going to be an easy passage. But we were ready to get to the marina so we headed up the Seine for the 15-mile trip to Isle St. Denis and the beginning of the St. Denis Canal. The St. Denis Canal is part of a system that provides access through the center of Paris. The Paris canals are managed by the city of Paris. The attendant filled out the requisite stack of forms and we were officially logged into the system. He explained that we were to use the narrow locks not the wide ones. He also pointed out what had been disappointingly obvious when we had stopped at the floating dock—*Skimmer*'s easy descent was now over and we would be going back up.

The narrower of the two ugly doors opened, a green light beckoned, and the expanse of a football-field length basin loomed ominously ahead. Was it the height of the concrete walls and length of the basin that made this lock seem so much narrower? The rain, the tension, the cold, and the perception of narrowness all contributed, and despite her experience in guiding us through many locks before, Charlotte began to lose it. I would grab at the tires and boards as the crunch of contact with the lock sides would begin to rip them away and Charlotte would desperately try to compensate with the wheel. The rain wreaked havoc with what was supposed to be a foolproof automated system remotely controlled by the locks at each end, and we experienced interminable delays for doors to open, locks to fill, and doors to close. By the time we reached the seventh and last lock we were worn out.

The world seemed to end in a huge stonewall with two tiny arches coming down to our basin. It would have been tempting to go for the larger of the arches, but we had been told to use the narrower locks so we lined up behind the right door and waited for it to open. Light appeared and we looked in and up. Would *Skimmer* really fit? The gathering crowd on the bridge high above were peering down under umbrellas and we wondered if they were taking bets. As the doors closed and the light dimmed it felt like we were entering into the valley of death. Not only were these walls higher, they were made of uneven bricks with protruding plant growth. As *Skimmer* ground her way up along the rough walls, plants, trash, and dirt wedged their way between our bumper boards and the hull.

That night we warned Bill and Jacqueline that if the St Martin Canal was as bad as St Denis that they wouldn't want to join us for our last leg to the marina. But both were anxious to give it a try so they took a metro from their boat at the Arsenal Marina and joined us for the day. In one of life's interesting coincidences, they had set out from their home on Wadmalaw Island only two docks away from our home a year after *Skimmer* but traveled east instead of west. Once through the St Martin Canal, *Skimmer* and *Sea Swallow* would become near neighbors again.

Saint Martin Canal

The St Martin Canal was every bit as wonderful as the St. Denis Canal had been dreary, and instead of going up, we were going down. It must have been an engineering wonder in its day. The drawbridge that let us into the Bassin de la Villette was a precursor of what was to come. Designed by Gustav Eiffel, its motive force was the water that fell from lock to lock from the canals above. The narrow horrors of St. Denis were replaced with wide

251

locks that descended through tree-lined parks. Finally, the long tunnel under Boulevard Richard Lenoir opened into the Paris Arsenal Marina. After 700 miles and 181 locks *Skimmer* had made it. Our new home was a floating dock in the shadows of where the French Republic had had its origins. From *Skimmer*'s bow we could see the glittering gold winged figure of Liberty at the top of the giant column that marks the spot where the Bastille once stood. Right in the center of the Marais district with the metro only three minutes away, and all Paris was within an easy bike ride.

***

The doors had just closed and the crowded jostling was settling down when Charlotte's loud voice produced an attentive silence. "Qui m'a volé mon portefeuille?" Suddenly all eyes in our half of the metro car were riveted on Charlotte as she pleaded to whomever had taken her wallet that they give it back. She even offered a reward. But the three girls and two boys who were her prime suspects pleaded ignorance. The next stop was Chatelet, and two of the girls were getting off. A quick decision—I had felt the two girls push up against me as we boarded and suspected them of having made an attempt on my wallet—we both got out with the two girls. We weren't the only two to get off at Chatelet. A tall Frenchman who had seen it all followed us off and pulled out his mobile phone. As he dialed he called to me "Suivez les. Ne les laissez pas partir!"

We were beginning to make quite a scene—Charlotte's loud and persistent questioning in her strong American accent, the girls' loud and persistent denial in equally strong Balkan accents, and the tall Frenchman delivering his message to the police as he shouted into his mobile phone. Although I sensed that the gathering crowd was sympathetic to our case, I was hesitant to follow the Frenchman's advice. What right did I have to prevent the girls from boarding the approaching metro car? I hadn't seen them take Charlotte's wallet and only suspected them of having made an attempt on my wallet. But the presence of two new members to our group—another man with a mobile phone who made another call to the police and a woman who worked for the metro who rattled instructions into her hand held radio—lent legitimacy to our cause and I firmly guided the two girls away from the opening metro car doors as the rest of our group encircled.

It was the persistence of our tall Frenchman that saved the day. His loud insistence that he had seen it all and his announcement that the police were on the way was beginning to have an effect on the girls. Righteous denial gave way to admission that there had been a third person who had actually taken Charlotte's wallet, and if we followed them to the next metro stop, they could recover it for her. Our rapidly increasing entourage was unanimous in their opinion that such a search should wait for the presence of the police—so with the girls loudly complaining and the crowd metering out advice, we waited … and waited.

From the tall Frenchman, angrily: "I have seen them operate before. Romanians. Its always the same. No one notices that the wallet is gone until it is too late. And France gets the blame. I am glad to help—I want to see this stopped." From the metro lady, helpfully: "The Romanians are everywhere and always there is trouble." From the two girls, indignantly: "We are not Romanians, we are from Yugoslavia!" From the second man with a mobile, vindictively: "Yugoslavians, Romanians, what's the difference. You are all giving France a bad name! I have also called the police and they will be here soon!"

Fourty five minutes later four policemen arrived, huge in leather jackets and cutter hats. With hands cuffed behind their backs, suddenly our Yugoslavian friends became more cooperative and agreed to finger their accomplice to retrieve the wallet. Back on the metro, but this time with the four policemen and two girls. Noses to the wall and arms held firmly by two of the policemen, the two girls continued to attract attention as we sped from Chatelet to Palais Royal. One of the four policemen was noticeably different from the others. Dark complexion, Arab by birth, Ahmed had a special ax to grind. His theory was that the systematic robbery by Romanians and Yugoslavians on Paris metros was increasingly being blamed on Paris' Arab population, and he was determined to do his best to root out this evil.

Once at Palais Royal Ahmed was swift and efficient. Taking the steps two at a time, he ran ahead of the others and grabbed the third girl before she knew what was happening. As Ahmed got louder, the three handcuffed girls became quieter and above the din we would hear expressions such as "casser la gueule" and then suddenly it was decided. Ahmed and his prisoner marched off at a brisk pace while Charlotte, the two original girls, the three policemen, and I waited.

Pascal, the least aggressive of the policemen, speculated that we would never see the wallet again and in a whisper he was sure the girls couldn't hear, he explained that there was actually nothing they could do about the robbery. Because the girls were minors they would be free before the day was out—even if it could be proved that they had stolen. But after a ten-minute wait the impossible happened. Ahmed returned with his charge in one hand and Charlotte's wallet in the other. Exactly how he got the information we will never know, but in the bathroom in a Greek restaurant around the corner he'd found Charlotte's wallet wedged behind the toilet. Amazingly, nothing had been removed.

***

Before entering France's canal system there would have been only one answer to the question, "What is the most important piece of equipment on board?" Either one of us would have given it immediately and without hesitation—"The autopilot." But settled down for the winter in Paris our needs had changed radically and the most important item on *Skimmer* had become the ratty electric blanket that, as an afterthought, we had brought back from our recent trip to Charleston.

Winter at Paris Arsenal Marina

Skimmer was designed for warm weather, and winter in Paris presented challenges we'd never dreamed of. First was the rain. Only a few drops at a time—but they had been falling inside the boat. What devilry of design guided the slow trickle of condensation so precisely that the freezing cold droplets would collect just above my head and then drop at intervals long enough that I wouldn't get up with a towel but short enough to keep me annoyed throughout the night? The rain was heavier in the bow compartment, but the worst was inside the cabinets and closets where drops would form on all the top surfaces and fall all over the well-packed contents. We learned a new French word—deshumidificateur—and 200 Euros later we had a partial solution to the moisture problem. By lugging the 50-pounder from bow to stern on alternate days we kept the skies in *Skimmer* clear.

Keeping them warm was an entirely different matter. We found that if we stayed within two feet of one of our three portable electric heaters, and managed not to trip over the tangle of wires as we dashed from one heater to the next, we could almost succeed in cutting the early morning chill in our bones. Without the discipline of our 10:45 AM class at the Alliance Francaise, we would probably not have had the fortitude to poke our heads out of our electric blanket cocoon to face the biting chill that would seep into *Skimmer* during the long cold nights. Turtleneck sweaters with necks fully extended, long scarves spiraled up to our ears, gloves and hats, and then the mad dash to the warmth of the Paris metro. By the third stop we were almost thawed and by the time we arrived at St. Sulpice, warmth had set in, so we were reluctant to make the final dash from the metro station to Boulevard Raspail.

The Alliance Francaise was a melting pot and we were amazed to find that over half our class was oriental. We chose our level-three course with the hope of improving our accents, broadening our vocabularies, and (at least in my case) reducing the inordinate number of grammatical mistakes that seem to flow as smoothly as my words.

Jeanne was a wonderful teacher. Each day she would covers the board with chalk and fill the air with musical subtleties of her language, sharing her love of her country's culture. Understanding her was no problem for us, but when she divided students into groups to work on exercises and create dialogues, trouble began. It was not that the Chinese don't work hard. What Shifeng had learned in less than a year was almost unbelievable. But without his writing out what he was saying, I was utterly lost. The unintelligible words torturously came out one at a time and with a pronunciation so strange that I could only guess at the meaning. But nodding approval from Jeanne confirmed that aside from his diction, his phrases were almost always grammatically correct and were surprisingly rich in vocabulary. Shifeng's opposite sat to my right. Glib, confident, and aggressively talkative, Juan's sentences flowed with the smoothness of mountain streams in his native Ecuador, but with almost half his words in Spanish he was actually harder to understand than Shifeng. As the speakers bounced from Iranian to Japanese to Hungarian, to Egyptian to Charlestonian we all struggled to follow.

The cultural exchanges were priceless. In discussing whether or not we believed in a certain miracle, Zhuzing enlightened us by stating that she didn't need to have an opinion because religion was illegal in China. My group was to prepare a paper on how to solve the growing environmental problems of the world, and I made the mistake of disagreeing with the young Chilean beauty whose solution was that future generations would migrate to other planets. With a tolerant smile and patient understanding of the impaired imaginative ability of the aged, she pointed out to me that she had seen American movies in which these emigrations had taken place. In the face of this irrefutable proof, I conceded.

Jeanne's explanation that in French the article is always used before the names of countries, with the exception of a few islands that are independent countries themselves, was greeted by stony looks from the Chinese contingent when she had cited "Taiwan and not La Taiwan" as an example. Xing quickly set us straight by pointing out, while her countrymen nodded vigorously, that Taiwan was a part of China and not an independent country.

Bernard, the manager of the Paris-Arsenal Port de Plaisance, had cautioned me not to fly our American flag while we were in the marina. It hadn't seemed to be a big issue at first, but as the road to war accelerated, maintaining a low profile became important. Cheers, jeers, singing, chanting, and loud horns filled the air as a sea of humanity rolled down Avenue Henry IV and flooded around the monument in Place de la Bastille on Saturday February 15. Paris was showing its support for the French position on Iraq. It was an orderly crowd and there were police everywhere in case things got out of hand, but I was glad *Skimmer* was not sporting her large American flag that day.

A hundred and fifty miles from Paris and a world away from the hotly divisive politics, we   visited the beaches of Normandy where so many Americans had lost their lives during World War II. It was hard to believe we were in the same country. There—still hanging in his parachute straps— suspended high above the town square—was nostalgic evidence that the residents of Saint Mere-Eglise hadn't forgotten. The first thing that had greeted us as we entered Saint Mere-Eglise was the Joe Steele Restaurant and Hotel. But around the corner and in the town square was the main attraction—the cathedral. Towering above the tiny square below, its high gothic windows and imposing steeple dominated the city. And hanging just as it hung many years before was the listless body of Joe Steele—only now it was just a dummy dressed in fatigues and dangling from a parachute entangled in the steeple.

Almost as if by magic, the bells started ringing just as we arrived, giving us proof of how loud they could be and demonstrating how Joe Steele had been permanently deafened before he had finally been cut down and saved at the end of his night long ordeal. Two of the church's huge stained glass windows told the story of the air drop into Saint Mere-Eglise the night of June 5, 1944 and how their city was the first to be liberated during the Normandy landing. Our day ended with the lowering of the American Flags at the cemetery at Omaha Beach and the caretaker presenting us with small American and French flags, the same ones that each memorial day he places before each of the 9,387 graves.

***

Harmonious sounds wafted over the sides of *Skimmer*, across the long floating dock, and into the manicured flowers and shrubbery of the Jardin de l' Arsenal. Families eating their picnic dinners, young lovers demonstrating their affections to all who cared to watch, and tired workers quaffing a quick wine before the onset of boules all riveted attention on *Skimmer*—where Jean-Michele arranged his tripod and musical score, before taking a deep breath and leaning forward into his flute. Boat watching was always a favorite for passersby in the Jardin de l' Arsenal—but a concert—and on a boat—it was a crowd stopper.

When Charlotte explained her invitation to me several weeks earlier, I made a quick calculation. She mistakenly had thought I was deciding if there was enough seating space for her Alpha Group on *Skimmer*. Actually it had been to see if *Skimmer* could still float if all thirty of her new closest friends accepted and showed up for hors d'oeuvres and cocktails.

It began with Charlotte's search for a church we could attend in Paris. Notre Dame was too touristy, the American Cathedral was too far away and too American, but the third try had been a wonderful success. St. Paul, exquisite, rich with history but still unspoiled by tourism, was situated on the Rue St. Antoine, in the heart of the Marais, and became the center of gravity of our life in Paris. When Charlotte perused the bulletin boards at the end of our first service, she exclaimed, "Look, Heyward, they have an Alpha Course. I didn't know there was such a thing in the Catholic Church. And look, it starts this Tuesday evening!" I knew there was no point arguing. The fact that she had already taken an Alpha Course at St. Michael's Church in Charleston, the fact that she was Episcopalian and this course was for Catholics—these considerations didn't dampen her enthusiasm at all, and when we reached the end of the line leaving the church, she used her best French to persuade Pere Marc to invite her to attend.

The slow start of polite refusals for wine and an inordinate numbers of requests for orange juice abruptly changed when the Alpha Group chef, Guitte, and retired policewoman Ginet both showed up with chilled bottles of champagne. My concerns that the mountains of food Charlotte had been preparing for three days would go to waste evaporated as champagne bubbles loosened appetites for more serious pursuits.

Jean-Michele

Jean-Michele, resplendent in red, was the only participant in a coat and tie. His deep Auvergne accent made him difficult to understand, but apparently he had no problem in understanding Charlotte's request for him to bring his flute. The spectators on shore hadn't been disappointed with Jean-Michele's concert, but when the evening turned to Gaulic Gospel, the crowds had begun to disperse. Soothing or boring—I couldn't possibly hold myself out to be the judge—but the fact that our flutist collapsed into a deep slumber after the sixth hymn suggested perhaps a combination of the two and gentle snores accentuated the Alleluias and Amens that continued to swirl through *Skimmer's* cockpit

***

Charlette of *Phoque* emerged early each morning with sacs of bread crumbs and a flock of grateful pigeons would surround her on the quay. *Skimmer's* Charlotte instinctively knew better than to infringe on Charlette's domain, and she restricted her stale bread feedings to hungry ducks in the water. Kindred spirits, similar names, and boats pointed bow to bow—the friendship that ensued was inevitable.

It had been too subtle for us to understand when we had first arrived, but after the spring thaw and when hibernating yachties began to reappear on the quay, we finally began to understand the bifurcation of the Paris Arsenal community. Bow to bow, *Skimmer* and *Phoque* represented the two extremes—cruisers who live in a boat that happens to be a home and residents who live in a home that happens to be a boat. Our neighbor Charlette was the Commodore Emeritus of Paris Arsenal Yacht Club, and of course we had accepted her invitation to attend its annual meeting, shelling out the 23 Euro annual dues to become members in good standing. Jean-Claude, who lived on a barge, gave a presentation on Yacht Club finances and preliminary information on the upcoming yacht club annual cruise. Thinking of all the wonderful routes for a cruise out of Paris I had asked Jean-Claude where they planned to go that year. To my surprise, my question elicited more embarrassment than enthusiasm. Had I heard wrong? "But Jean Claude, with all the wonderful places on the Marne, on the Seine, and on the Oise, why would boats just go across the Seine to the left bank and then tie up?"

The incredible fact was that the majority of the Paris Arsenal Yacht Club were not yachties, and most of them had never before owned a boat. Phillippe was typical. He had come to Paris three years earlier with his wife and young daughter to work as an accountant. He had fallen in love with the area near the Place de la Bastille and had spent almost six months searching for an apartment when suddenly a whole new opportunity had opened up when he stumbled on a sign. Peniche for Sale. The fact that he had never been on a boat in his life didn't deter him, and less than five weeks later he was the proud owner of a 60-foot-long steel motor barge. "The price" he explained "you simply could not beat the price! And right in the heart of Paris."

Probably more important to Phillip than the barge itself had been the contract with the Paris Arsenal Marina that came with the purchase and guaranteed his barge a place in the Marina. But there was a catch. Every year, each boat was required to leave the Marina for twenty-one days. And for someone with no boat experience—well, this presented quite a problem. It's a rare person who can learn to handle a 60-foot barge by taking a crash six-week classroom course. The result was that the annual Yacht Club Cruise generally consisted in dashing across to the other side of the Seine from the Arsenal Marina and hanging on for dear life as wakes from giant barges taught the new homeowners there was something else to living on a boat than tightening shore lines in a protected basin.

Cruisers or not, there was a common thread that tied us tightly to our neighbors in the marina. It was our common respect for our neighborhood. Spared the ravages of Hausseman's renovations in the eighteenth century, the Marais is one of the only parts of the city that retains the charm of meandering streets and private mansions that date back to pre-revolutionary Paris. From our boat we could see the statue that now stands in the center of what was the Bastille and commemorates patriots who died in the uprisings of 1830 and 1848. And for food and supplies, there was the bustling charm of Rue St. Antoine with its butchers, bakers, cheese shops, and wine shops.

After six months, the ties to Paris had become strong and it was hard to even think about leaving. The decision came down to "should we stay for two more weeks or for two more years?" The call of adventure won out and on the seventh of May we passed through the locks separating Paris Arsenal Marina from the Seine to begin our long journey south. Our route back to the Mediterranean would take us through Nancy and Strasbourg and then along the Rhine, Saone and Rhone back to Port Napoleon where we would once again become a sailboat.

* * *

The Rhine River. Victor Hugo described it as "swift as the Rhone, broad as the Loire, cliff-covered like the Meuse, serpentine as the Seine, limpid and green as the Somme, historic as the Tiber, as royal as the Danube, mysterious as the Nile, spangled with gold like a river of America, laden with fables and phantoms like a river of Asia…"

My "Fluvial Carte Guide for the Rhine" was less poetic and warned of heavy shipping and fierce currents that range from eight to twelve kilometers per hour. Tension was high as we approached the Ecluse de Raccordement de Rhinau and the steel jaws that separated us from the fury of the Rhine. The Guide had warned us of the strong cross current just after exiting the lock and I instructed Charlotte to increase speed and divert to the left to compensate.

The doors closed behind us and our spirits soared as we viewed the wide expanse before us. But high enthusiasm changed to high adrenaline as *Skimmer* surged upwards and turned violently to the left. I could almost picture the mound of soft mud below us that picked us up and spun us around almost 180 degrees before the swirling current pulled us onward. Fortunately the steel Dutch boat that had been behind us in the lock had seen our difficulties in time to give us a wide berth and watched us struggle as we backed our way into the river.

Once the scare was over, we began to appreciate the majesty of the river. Mountains in the background, giant locks that came in pairs and spouted out mammoth seagoing barges, and a relentless current against us that cut our speed in half and kept us on alert. It didn't take long for a screw-up to occur.

Engine temperature was climbing as the second of the giant locks approached. A quick calculation convinced me we would get a high temperature alarm either just before or while entering the lock. Not ideal. The reason was as obvious as the solution. The giant mound of mud we'd hit had clogged the seawater intake to our cooling system, and the only remedy was to stop and back flush the lines. But how to stop in eight knots of current in a section of canal with sloping cement sides and a cement bottom?

We nudged our way over to the German side of the canal—far enough from the center to keep us away from shipping but not close enough to shore to risk our hull rubbing to shreds against the concrete sides. Then a cautious lowering of the anchor. The initial results were as I feared. Jerk, slack, jerk, slack—I could actually hear the anchor sliding along the concrete bottom. More chain. Same results. Again more chain and again jerk, slack, jerk slack. But was the interval lengthening? More chain and then silence. We were holding.

Twenty minutes later *Skimmer* was back in gear and we began to enjoy our surroundings. The next morning we diverted onto a lateral canal that took us through calm waters to Colmar. Right at the epicenter of Alsace's famous wine industry and chock full of some of the finest restaurants in France, Colmar gave us a brief respite before continuing to Basel.

Our final adventure on the Rhine was taking *Skimmer* into Switzerland where the beauty of Basel by water dazzled us, but our visit had to be brief. It was time to begin the trek back to the Mediterranean via the Canal du Rhin au Rhone.

***

Snaggle-toothed smiles and freckled faces—maybe two dozen of them—intently watched as *Skimmer* inched her way into the waiting lock. A grammar school field trip was greeting our arrival into Montbeliard. Their questions were fun and we were thoroughly enjoying ourselves when a query from the lockmaster started a dialogue that went from delight to fright.

Grammar School Field Trip at Montbeliard

"Our draft is five feet," I replied with confidence, knowing the Canal du Rhone au Rhine was designed to handle boats up to six feet for its entire length. But his reply—"Ah, monsieur, I think you have a big problem." The heat wave that had been with us for almost a month was doing more than allowing French vacationers to fry their bared parts. It was depriving the Doubs River of water and slowly eroding its level through evaporation. Our guaranteed six feet was suddenly gone and, in the opinion of at least one lock keeper, the limit was now dangerously close to *Skimmer*'s five feet—and getting closer every day!

What happened if we couldn't continue forward? Only one real alternative and that was unthinkable. Back to the Rhine, back to Strasbourg, back to Nancy and then down the Canal de L'Est—a 400-mile, 220-lock detour!

Actually *Palyka* was more concerned than *Skimmer*. Our new cruising companions since Mulhouse, Claude and Lise were bringing their 38-foot

Hallberg-Rassy from their home in Switzerland to the Mediterranean, and *Palyka* had a draft that was three inches greater than *Skimmer's*.

Wait for rain? It could be weeks or even months. And with the rain would come the problem for which the Doubs is famous. Flooding! There is a reason why the doors of the locks of the Doubs are three feet higher than normal water level. From the Rhine up to Montbeliard it had been all canal, deep, and safe. But after leaving Montbeliard, lock number 27 was lurking ahead to deposit us onto the mighty Doubs.

Cautiously, we inched our way out of lock 27 and hoped the low water level would negate strong currents threatening to push us across the channel as the Doubs entered the dredged section of canal. Good news—no current. Bad news—CRUNCH! *Skimmer* had found her first gravel bank and we were hard aground. The cacophonous whirring that startled us in the locks when *Palyka* revved her bow thrusters to get positioned behind *Skimmer* now came as a welcome sound. I swam over to her with a long line. A lot of bow thruster whirring and *Skimmer* was free. *Palyka* had been ready to turn back, but we decided that with the security of two boats, it was worth a try. A hundred miles and 50 locks before we were out of the Doubs and back in sure water, but we took it slowly and despite an average of three groundings a day, we enjoyed the strange new land we had just entered.

Efforts to tame the Doubs started in 1776 when Louis XV commissioned a study of the river, and the subsequent report recommended the construction of a canal to link the Rhine with the Rhone. Subsequent canal champions included Napoleon and Louis XVIII and finally, by 1834, the canal was open to traffic. But even after the many enlargements and improvements, the Doubs still has a mind of its own.

After three weeks of wild swings from fascination with our surroundings to fear of groundings, *Skimmer* and *Palyka* made it through the last lock in the Canal de Rhone-Au-Rhin at Saint Symphorien and basked in the security and beauty of the Saone. From there we retraced our route of the previous fall but this time with the warmth and beauty of summer.

The Atlantic

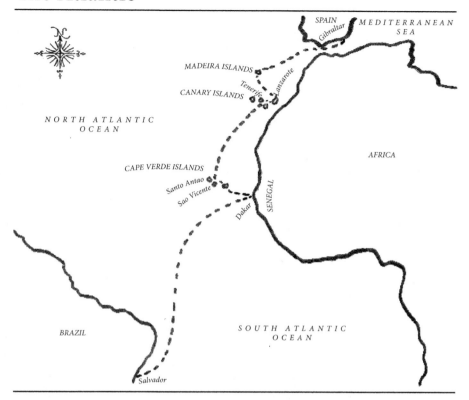

The shortest distance between two points is a straight line. Or is it? Navigation necessitates some familiarization with spherical geometry, and here the rule changes. Instead of a straight line the shortest distance between the same two points becomes a great circle known as a rhumb line. Cruising navigation also involves circular logic, and destinations are often decided more on the basis of rum logic rather than rhumb lines. And so it was that we decided on a route from the Canary Islands to the West Indies that included stops in the Cape Verde Islands, Senegal, and Brazil and a 1,000 detour up the Amazon.

The rum logic had actually begun with a very good bottle of Cote du Rhone at Le Potin Gourmand in Cluny the previous October, when the owner and chef of the restaurant produced a map and explained to us the dream vacation he was planning to take the following winter. A close friend of his was one of the 30 like-minded French sailboat owners who had decided to participate in the annual "Rallye des Iles du Soleil," and our host was going to join him for a portion of the leg up the coast of Brazil. His map intrigued me even more than his wild enthusiasm and, as I began to digest the route, the seed germinated and began to take root.

Charlotte's logic that the rum route was 7,000 miles instead of the rhumb line's 3,000 miles, was irrefutable. But after almost six months of debate we reasoned: "What difference did it make anyway?" We hadn't made the final decision until we attended the organization meeting for the tenth annual rally that was held in May. Leaving our boat in Toul, we had gone to Paris by train to meet the other prospective participants before deciding whether to make the six months commitment. New friendships, lots of enthusiasm, and lots of wine—the decision had been easy.

So, the final plan had been to join the group in the Canary Islands in late October. Sail to the Cape Verde Islands and then to Senegal where we would visit Dakar and take a trip up the Sine Saloum River. From Senegal cross the Atlantic and head to Salvador, Brazil, where we would spend Christmas. After Salvador cruise up the coast of Brazil to Belem to begin our trip up the Amazon. After the Amazon, sail to French Guyana and then to Trinidad where we would finally enter the Caribbean.

* * *

Heyward Dressed for Bottom Painting

Three weeks in the black hole of the Port Napoleon shipyard. Re-masting. A simple concept but in actuality an emotionally packed event where success and disaster are separated by a hair's breadth. And then out of the water to apply bottom paint and repair damage inflicted by the mighty Doubs River. And finally a massive restocking.

Skimmer was back in her element, and I gloated as we sailed past the glassy waters around the dreaded Cape Creus where sudden winds descending the steep Pyrenees can unpredictably vent their fury. We had been spared the violent seas so often generated by the Mistral and then the Tramontana in this shallow and dangerous area of the Mediterranean, and *Skimmer* had passed her initial post-French Canal sea trials with flying colors.

At anchor in a lovely cove surrounded by golden brown mountains. Swim call—the first since entering the French Canal system a year earlier, a salad nicoise lunch, and finally launching the dinghy for exploration ashore—we were back to the easy living of gunk hole cruising. But not so fast—the gremlins struck before we were half way to shore.

"Why is the engine smoking?" from my ever-cautious first mate. "Oh, it's only the extra oil I added to the gas," I replied confidently ... just before the engine quit. Hot to the touch. The smoke had been steam and the sure sign of overheating. It was a sad paddle back to the boat and it was my turn to steam at my stupidity at not realizing that the water-cooling had not been working. Was this the end of life for my prized Yamaha eight-horsepower outboard?

Our neighbor in Barcelona had been a mechanic before chucking his career in the Supermarket Industry to sail, and no, he did not think I had destroyed my outboard motor. In his opinion it was probably just a bad impeller and, yes, he would be happy to guide me through the intricate process of removing the foot from my Yamaha to install a new one. Several hours later, my Yamaha was purring—and we were again ready to explore the wonders of the many anchorages during our descent along the Spanish coast.

An overnight sail from Barcelona took us to Moraira, a beautiful cove just north of Alicante and there we learned an important lesson about cruising the Mediterranean coast of Spain. Upon arrival we had had to circle twice to find an appropriate vacant space to drop our anchor. But as the afternoon progressed, our cove became less and less crowded. Did it have to do with the steadily increasing roll? As our last neighbor picked up and left it occurred to us that a steady wind shift had left us completely exposed to waves rolling in from open sea and suddenly the sunset didn't seem so pretty. The rolls were so large we couldn't hold our plates, so Charlotte shelved our three-course dinner and we followed our neighbor into the nearby marina where we were successful in begging a place to stay for the evening. For once the high marina prices in Spain didn't seem so high.

And that's the problem with cruising the Spanish coast—finding sheltered anchorages. When the wind is blowing from the right direction the enchanting coves are magic, but a shift to the wrong direction leaves no choice but to pull anchor and leave. This is why marinas along the Spanish coast are able to get away with their exorbitant prices.

During our pre-departure conference from Cartagena there were heated discussions concerning the weather forecast posted on the marina bulletin board. It was our first in Spanish and Charlotte's initial reading caused consternation. The incomprehensible array of numbers and directions had us both baffled, but Charlotte's keen eyes picked out the appearance of several 7's scattered about the maze of numbers. "I don't care what you say, I am not going out in a force 7!"

I began to understand the matrix and pointed out that it looked like the wind speeds were actually in meters per second and that seven meters per second wasn't so strong. A table translating meters per second into the Beaufort Scale showed that in fact the prediction facing us for the next day was for a force three to four—well within our comfort zone. But it was disturbing to both of us how much worse the prediction had been for the day before our departure. I brushed that concern off by explaining that the worst we could expect was some large swells in the morning that would be carried over from the heavy seas.

There had been no wind in the marina since midnight—the forecast seemed correct, the weather had turned. Once outside the breakwater heavy swells turned into very heavy swells, but still no wind. Little white caps by noon turned into solid white caps by mid afternoon and the wind was solidly on our nose. Waves and wind against us. A bad combination, especially in the relatively shallow waters of the Mediterranean. Slam, crash, shudder—and *Skimmer*'s speed would drop to almost nothing. A lull and then our engine would take over. But progress was slow and it became obvious that we could not make our planned destination of Puerto de Carboneras—a friendly fishing port that welcomed transient yachts. It wasn't exactly a "I told you so" look on Charlotte's face, but there was anger in her voice as she began to explain why she wasn't going to cross the Atlantic with me.

I decided to thrust *Skimmer* on the mercy of Port Garrucha that I was sure we could make comfortably before darkness. The entrance between a long beach and a breakwater was tricky, and our approach would be into the glare of the afternoon sun. But just before our entry a tanker assisted by a tug made the necessary hairpin turn in heavy wind and foaming surf, and all I had to do was follow her in.

Domingo had a frown on his face as he waited for us at the fuel dock and it looked like rejection was imminent. Our request to take on fuel bought us some time and the cold beer Charlotte thrust into his hands cinched the deal. We could stay at the fuel dock for the evening and if the weather was still bad in the morning we could remain in the port at anchor. When I went to the marina office to pay, I looked at the bill from Domingo with amazement. "Friday? I thought today was Saturday!"

"No, Senior, es Viernes." It was almost funny, but not quite. We had left Cartagena confident of our excellent weather forecast for Saturday, but what we had faced was the terrible weather that had clearly been posted for Friday.

Day hops in settled weather bought us to Almerimar, Spain's answer to the deterioration in service and accommodations that have steadily made Gibraltar less and less attractive to visiting yachts. Acres of boats, chandlers, and shops—an ideal place to stock for an Atlantic crossing and an ideal place to leave a boat for the winter.

It should have been an easy overnight trip from Almerimar to Gibraltar. Flat seas, only a slight wind on our nose, and an excellent lunch before preparing *Skimmer* for the night. But shortly after I drifted into sleep during Charlotte's first night watch, I heard her shouts for me to come help. "The autopilot keeps failing. I can't control the boat."

Half-dressed, half-asleep I climbed up the companionway and looked at the instruments: "It's only blowing fifteen knots, why are you having trouble?" But as I emerged from my stupor and looked out over churning white foam it certainly didn't look like fifteen knots. Sudden realization. The anemometer was no longer working properly and the wind had been steadily building without us realizing it. With typical *Skimmer* caution we were on the third reef and motoring into what we had thought was very moderate wind, a task that should have been well within *Skimmer*'s capabilities.

Into 30 to 40 knots and three-meter Mediterranean waves, however, was an entirely different matter and I reluctantly had to admit that *Skimmer* was out of control. There were two alternatives and we tried them one after the other. Change course 90 degrees to the left or right and roll out a small amount of Genoa. Magic. *Skimmer* responded and the autopilot purred. But now we were heading away from Gibraltar and would have to spend more time in the bad weather.

Alternative two took some convincing before Charlotte would agree to my leaving the cockpit to lower the mainsail. But it worked and we were able to maintain control as *Skimmer* attacked successive walls of water ahead. We could make Gibraltar during the next day—but at the price of 12 bone-jarring hours. A final compromise took us on a course inshore where we planned to stop at a small port and wait out the weather, but as land drew into sight the seas calmed as if by magic and we were able to continue on to Gibraltar that day.

The rock. Point Europa was a breathtaking experience, and I took a dozen pictures while *Skimmer* smoothly rounded the point and headed for the security of Marina Bay. While our boat had passed her sea trials in the Gulf of Lyon and the trip down the coast of Spain, it was not until that black and windy night that her crew had finally passed theirs.

Everything about Marina Bay was great except our greeting from Alice, who we kept meeting at every Spanish port. With a gleeful smile she listened to Charlotte's description of the weather we had encountered and eagerly explained how nice their trip from Almerimar to Gibraltar had been. "We just hugged the coast. You know, it always stays calm there—it's only when you go way off shore that you catch the strong winds." Charlotte had the restraint not to ask why she hadn't shared this important bit of information when we had told her that our plan was to take the offshore route because it was shorter and avoided most of the shipping lanes.

Approaching Point Europa

The best thing about Gibraltar wasn't British and wasn't Gibraltar. We waited almost an hour at the airport for the jet fighter and passenger airline traffic to slow down enough for us to walk across the runway to the Spanish boarder. La Linea is a quaint Spanish town and our taxi driver took us through a maze of streets and deposited us at an inconspicuous door to a small whitewashed house as he explained: "Es Jiiimy's, Senior!"

How twenty people could fit into the crowded room we didn't know, but there was space for two more. Happily there was a Brit at a neighboring table who explained how it worked and I squeezed my way up to the bar at the far end of the room where Jimmy was conducting his one-man show.

All I had to do was say "cervesa" and then point at some of the delicacies I saw others eating and I was then on my way back to our table with two large glasses of very cold San Miguel. Periodically, Jimmy would signal me and I would make my way back to the bar to pick up course after course of the best food we had tasted since arriving in Europe the previous year. How Jimmy had calculated the price we couldn't figure out, but at 15 euros for the two of us it was also our most inexpensive meal in Europe.

✳✳✳

Cruising life is fraught with emotional barriers. Some were small, some were huge, but they were always there. And they defined our lives. They loomed in the foggy distance—problems to be faced in the future, but problems whose presence dominated our preparations and sapped our emotional energy.

The dramatic beauty and exciting bustle of our entry into Gibraltar masked the anxiety of this important crossroads for cruising sailors. From the Mediterranean it's an easy passage—just around the corner—a large bay snuggled up to the giant rock that not only protects it from the elements but also has protected it from invasion since the British seized it from the Spanish in 1704. But for sailors and their tiny craft there is much more to it than beauty and history, and it had been nagging at the back of our minds ever since we had entered the Mediterranean the previous June.

Because the Mediterranean is almost completely landlocked, it doesn't act like the oceans and most of the other seas of the world. For most of the Mediterranean this topography means an almost complete lack of tides. This is not the case for Gibraltar. The thirty miles of narrow straits that separate the Mediterranean from the Atlantic is the only source of water to make up for evaporation from the entire Mediterranean, and the result is a constant inflowing current that is quite powerful, particularly during high tide in the Atlantic. Three knots is not a problem for ships that cruise at 20 to 30 knots, but for a sailboat it can make the passage all but impossible. Leaving during a Poniente with its powerful blast from the west is out of the question. Leaving during a Levanter as it roars in from the east can be terrifying.

There was a solution and Adrian, the harbormaster at Marina Bay, had explained it to me: "Wait for the wind to change. It will blow from the west for five to ten days and then switch and blow from the east for another five to ten days. The trick is to leave just when it is switching from west to east and before it picks up strength. If it's blowing a force five in Gibraltar Bay, it

Leaving Gibraltar Bay

will be force seven at Tarifa! And leave three hours after high tide—if you stay close to the coast of Spain, there are counter currents that will carry you all the way through."

For anyone leaving from the security of Gibraltar Bay for the Atlantic, Tarifa is a household word. It's the physical choke point of the straits where Europe comes the closest to Africa and it's the emotional choke point where violent winds appear out of nowhere and vent their fury on passing sailors. *Star Cruiser, Ballou, Hiva Oha,* and *Skimmer*—we had all done our homework and the conditions were right. After waiting out seven days of powerful west winds, it was finally changing. Seven a.m., still dark, and not a breath of wind. Trusting in our forecast from Weatheronline that we all examined in such detail the night before, we set out across the breathless bay. Heavy shipping in the bay gave way to an almost complete absence of traffic as we worked our way close enough to the Spanish coastline to feel the effects of the counter currents.

Slowly, slowly, the wind picked up from the east, but as we sailed past the dreaded Tarifa we were astounded to find flat seas and almost no wind. I was so impressed that I took a series of photos to be able to prove to others that such conditions could actually exist. We were still congratulating ourselves on our good fortune when the strong winds finally did hit us. For two days we had 30 knots and confused seas as we sailed out of the Gulf of Cadiz, but the wind was on our stern and *Skimmer* handled it very well.

Not all of us were so lucky. *Hiva Oha*, ten feet shorter than the rest of us, drifted behind almost immediately. Unfortunately, Patrick did not follow Adrian's advice and had wandered too far from the shore. Instead of getting the lift the rest of had been enjoying, he fought a strong current. By the time he got to Tarifa, it had become an entirely different place. Forty knots and churning waves were more than his autopilot could handle and for two days he had to hand-steer *Hiva Oha*. Mary-Helene was so seasick that she lay incapacitated below while Patrick fought seas and fatigue. His only rest came when he would periodically heave to and catch half an hour of sleep. But finally the wind calmed and the last three days of his passage went smoothly as his mate came back to life.

Arriving at Porto Santo

We learned later that other boats that had been planning on leaving the next day had to wait an additional two weeks for the weather to turn to allow their departure.

***

Rising from the depths of the Atlantic, a brown mountain topped by a white-washed lighthouse with an orange tile roof appeared through the morning mist. It was beautiful, security after four days at sea. It was Porto Santo, the easternmost of the Madeira Islands. *Skimmer* was back in an honest ocean where winds blow strong but steady and waves are rolls rather than walls. Our long voyage home had finally begun.

Porto Santo was the first of the Madeira Islands to be discovered. I thought about how the Portuguese explorer Zarco must have felt when he stumbled on its shore in 1418. Rising from the depths of the Atlantic Ocean, Porto Santo and her larger neighbor Madeira are gems in an azure blue setting. In the 1400's they represented the outer fringes of the known world.

An early visitor to Porto Santo not only found a local woman who captured his heart but also found himself wondering how seeds and wood washed up onto the beaches of this remote island. Christopher Columbus had followed his heart and married Filipa, the governor's daughter, and followed his dream and discovered America.

Driving over modern highways that consisted more of tunnel than open road, we were recipients of the enormous benefits Common Market expenditures have showered upon Madeira over the previous few years. Viewed from one of the world's most expensive stretches of highway, the contrast of what we saw, compared with the traditional vineyards of France, was astounding. In Madeira the meaning of vertical farming took on an entirely new dimension as vineyards laddered their way up steep hills. At first we hadn't even recognized them as vineyards. No long neat stripes of green and brown. Instead there were unending canopies of green that could have been anything from Kudzu to tropical rain forest vegetation.

Noting a few dozen buckets full of ripe black grapes and a young boy sitting on a log, we pulled off the road to take a look. I approached the canopy next to the boy and bent down to look beneath. A withered smiling face looked up at me. If she hadn't been holding firmly onto the massive roots, she would almost certainly have slid down the almost vertical slope. With curved knife, bucket, and an incredible sense of balance, she was

Grape Harvest in Madeira

cutting, filling, and passing up to the boy above. She stopped what she was doing to greet me and then to cut three bunches of grapes that she passed up to me as a gift. As I looked around and further down the hill, I could see dozens of others just like her and suddenly realized that the green canopies we had been driving around for the past two hours were productive Madeira vineyards in the process of being harvested.

***

Then for a three-day trip southeast to one of the Canary Islands' most exotic locations. Just 80 miles off the coast of Africa, Lanzarote, "The Island of Volcanos," charmed us with its stark, eerie beauty.

Pollo de Arrecife. Three hundred pounds of slow shuffle with more gold than white showing in his ever-present grin. How we met him was as unlikely as who he turned out to be.

At the end of our first day in Arrecife, Lanzarote's largest city, our inevitable task had turned to finding a good restaurant. Where better to inquire than the lady in the sidewalk lotto stand. Her bored look turned to interest and she actually came out of her cubicle to talk with us, but almost collided with the hulk making its way up the street. A sharp interchange in rapid fire Spanish ensued and to our surprise it turned out to be a friendly exchange with us as the primary subject matter. We had been turned over to Pollo for the important mission.

On the subject of eating, Pollo was a self-proclaimed expert and even though we only understood one word in four, his magnetic smile drew us on as he made his way down the street with painful slowness. We had seen it earlier that afternoon and if there had been only two restaurants on the entire island, undoubtedly the Los Angeles would have been our last choice. But this was exactly where Pollo decided to lower himself into a chair—right in front of the picture of a hamburger that seemed to say it all about the restaurant.

Trapped, but not willing to be rude, we also pulled up chairs to the rickety sidewalk table. As Pollo pulled the large sandwich out of the paper bag he had been carrying with him our confidence sank even lower. The waiter bought Pollo a bottle of carbonated water without even asking him what he wanted and dumped a greasy menu on the table in front of Charlotte and me.

Hamburgers, cheeseburgers, sandwiches—not exactly the typical Canaries meal we had been craving, but before we had lost all hope, Pollo signaled us to turn the menu over. Tapas. And a pretty good variety. Maybe there was some hope.

Pollo became more animated as he began to fill his cheeks with the huge ham sandwich and we were somehow able to understand that he was recommending the Paella Tapas. At three Euros it hadn't seemed promising, but Pollo insisted and told us to order only one as we could share it. His recommendations also included an order of garlic shrimp and an order of roasted peppers. Our San Miguel was very cold and as we watched Pollio down his sandwich and soda water we decided that if the food was terrible, we could always fix something else back on *Skimmer*.

To our utter amazement, the Paella was the best we had had in Spain and the other dishes were equally delicious. But even more amazing was Pollo. Once he was done with the sandwich and we could finally look at his face without feeling ill, he began to enthrall us with the story of his life.

Former chief of police, wrestling champion of the island, and some story we couldn't quite follow about his role in a famous international

Pollo de Arrecife

film. Fact of fiction? Our interest was fading as the hot rodder in the shiny red Peugeot made his third pass to impress the Spanish beauties at the table next to ours. Pollo had been irritated by the squeal of his tires and smell of burning rubber, and his steely look at the boy put an abrupt end to his automotive antics. A smile of appreciation from two elderly ladies at another table acknowledged Pollo's continued authority, and a steady stream of well-wishers stopping to chat confirmed his popularity in the community.

Meal ended, Pollo pulled out half a Euro to pay for his water and the waiter bought us our bill. A single figure, no itemization—fifteen Euros. Exactly the same price we had paid at Jimmy's during our stay in Gibraltar.

The next day we learned in the tourist office that Pollo had indeed been the chief of police of Arrecife and was one of its most respected citizens. And the name Pollo? Well, it seemed that during his colorful career as wrestling champion of Lanzarote, the nickname had been born and all three hundred pounds had been known and loved as the "Chicken of Arrecife."

***

Although the island of Tenerife covers only 5,300 square miles, it is blessed with a geographical and cultural diversity that would do credit to a continent. El Teide at 12,000 feet is taller than any mountain in continental Spain, and we marveled at the bleak beauty of volcanic stone and lava as we stepped out of the cable car and tried not to slip on the ice covered paths. The town of La Orotava charmed us with its exquisitely carved wooden balconies, and La Laguna intrigued us with its world-class university, exotic botanical gardens, and exciting history and architecture.

But despite all this rich civilization, I found that the repair of starter motors for diesels was not Tenerife's forte and this was too bad because *Skimmer*'s starter had developed a gremlin. Redundancy is almost a religion aboard *Skimmer*. Ever since I had set out to rebuild and refit her eight years earlier, I have tried to have back ups for all vital systems. But where does redundancy end and folly begin? With two of everything, *Skimmer* would sink to the bottom. In all but a British Man of War, a spare mast would be ridiculous. But to set out to cross an ocean without a full set of spare parts for the motor and other critical equipment would be madness. I had drawn the line with the 35-pound hulk of ugly metal that converts electrical energy into rotational torque and makes our engine come alive.

Sweating but optimistic, I peddled my bicycle up the steep streets leading to the smoggy district of Buenos Aires, with the starter digging into my back through the thin lining of my tote bag, in search of the establishment that all sources had pointed me towards. At the huge loft belonging to Domingo Garcia Y Vidal, SL, the fact that everything I saw looked like it would never come back to life didn't inspire confidence. And then I met Parilla. Two days stubble on his chin, a cigarette hanging out his mouth, wearing coveralls that looked like they might once have been blue beneath the layers of grease, he had the air of one who knew about electric motors.

During my whole trip up the hill I had thought about how I would explain the gremlin in my motor. Armed with a Xeroxed copy of the internals of the motor from my manuals and full of new vocabulary I had learned from fellow cruisers, I was ready to discuss the problem and potential solutions. I had been constantly amazed with the detailed knowledge about all aspects of mechanical equipment that flowed through conversations with other cruisers with such easy fluidity and had recently learned a new word with which to impress others and to help me fix my starter. The Bendix. Surprisingly, each time I tried to show off my new knowledge to other cruisers they had already known all about it. Each had then provided his own unique solution on how to free a frozen Bendix so that the solenoid could move the ingenious wishbone lever that would then thrust an all-important gear into place between the starter motor and the engine at the critical moment.

But Parilla didn't speak English, was unimpressed with my diagrams of the motor, and couldn't understand a word of my Spanish. Juan, the firm's young accountant, spoke passable English but unfortunately knew even less than I did about electric motors and was absolutely baffled about the concept of a Bendix. He attempted to translate. I felt like a patient just diagnosed with cancer as Parillia examined my starter motor with critical eyes and began a long dissertation to Juan with hand gestures and tones that left me convinced the situation was hopeless. Juan translated the dissertation as: "No have Lucas Starter Motors in Canaries and Parillia not want to take motor apart because he not able to find spare parts here. Better we should see if can buy replacement motor here." I couldn't have been more in agreement.

My mistake was to follow Juan back to his office while Parillia proceeded back to the loft with my starter motor propped up on his shoulder. On my way out I went by the loft to say good-by to Parillia and that was when I discovered that my small potential problem had just been transformed into a major disaster. As I approached, Parillia was pulling the shaft out of the body. I tried to convince myself that I had not heard the sound of a piece dropping on the cement floor, but then Parillia bent down to search among the rubble beneath his workbench in a unsuccessful attempt to find the object that had fallen. And to my utter horror, there on Parillia's crowded work bench lay a confused heap of parts that had only a few moments before been my only slightly malfunctioning starter motor. Parillia then proudly shoved a gear under my nose and pronounced it to be the problem.

In a state of near panic I peddled back to the boat wondering how I was going to convince Parillia that his "villain gear" couldn't possibly be the problem and how to redirect his efforts away from finding a part I didn't need into concentrating on finding a replacement motor.

It didn't take long to decide that the situation at Domingo Garcia Y Vidal, SL was hopeless, and that afternoon I was on the phone with the firm in the US who had provided all the spare parts I had needed when rebuilding my diesel engine eight years earlier.

In seconds my depression went to elation on the promise of a brand new Lucas starter motor that could be put on an airplane that afternoon. I then went to Juan and Parillia to stop their search and reclaim my "rebuilt" starter motor.

Back on the boat I decided to see if by any miracle the old starter motor could possibly work. Second only to my surprise in finding that the bill for two hours of Parillia's labor was only nineteen Euros, I was utterly astonished to find that the rebuilt motor worked perfectly and despite repeated attempts, I was unable to get it to repeat its earlier failures. Maybe the grease on Parillia's hands had been just the medicine my ailing motor had needed. *Skimmer* wound up with the air freighted brand new Lucas installed, promising undying reliability, and Parillia's rebuilt masterpiece sitting in a spare parts bin that was beginning to resemble *Noah's Arc*.

***

Our arrival in Tenerife marked the beginning of the "rum route." This was the starting point of the 7,000-mile diversion to Africa and South America, and our new French sailing companions who were to make up the 22-boat Rallye des Iles du Soleil were arriving daily. Our group would depart south for the Cape Verde islands in late October. Almost all other sailboats planning to cross the Atlantic would wait until the end of the season for tropical storm formation in late November and then head west.

It took a lot of explaining to convince Charlotte that the tropical storms keeping all our previous sailing companions safely moored in Tenerife until the end of November would not pose a hazard to us in our passage to Mindelo on the Cape Verde Island of St Vincent. At 850 miles, it was almost as long as the trip from Panama to the Galapagos Islands and all of it through potentially rough seas.

Another worry was how to avoid a collision in the forthcoming parade of boats through Santa Cruz's harbor. French over-organization, questionable boat-handling experience on the part of some of the participants in our rally, and insistence from Philippe, our organizer and leader, that all boats be under sail had both of us concerned about how a parade of 22 boats through Santa Cruz's crowded harbor would manage. Our real concern was the mad scramble bound to occur just outside the harbor when Philippe dipped various flags as a countdown for the firing of the cannon and signal for all vessels to rush to the narrow start line for the tenth annual Rallye des Iles du Soleil.

The German couple aboard *To Life* and we aboard *Skimmer* were the only non-native French crews in the rally. While we could normally get along pretty well in French, the specialized vocabulary of sailing and meteorology, combined with the complications of radio communications, presented a challenge. Philippe's third weather forecast provided ammunition for an argument that was to pervade *Skimmer* for the entire six day trip. What I had understood to be a long-term prediction for a normal low forming off the coast of Cape Verde in West Africa before its long journey west, Charlotte had interpreted as the sure presence of a tropical depression over the Cape Verde Islands that would exactly coincide with our arrival.

When, during the fourth day of our voyage, beautiful weather and steady light following winds gave way to cloudy skies, rough seas, and gusts up to 40 knots, Charlotte became convinced that we were heading for the black hole.

Alpha Alpha Three Gulf Zulu and Eight Papa Six Quebec Mike, sometimes also known as Jack and Trudy, were devoted mother hens tending their chicks as we crossed the wide expanses of the Atlantic Ocean. We had met them in the Madeira Islands as we had heard Jack's voice booming through our SSB radio as if he were sitting on *Skimmer*'s stern. But Jack's friendly voice had originated at his powerful ham radio in his Doylestown, Pennsylvania home, traveled up through the wire antenna he had shot into the tall maple tree in his back yard with a bow and arrow, and reached us half a world away. Trudy's voice, equally as cheerful and friendly, came in so clearly from her base in the Barbados Islands that we could almost smell the Mont Gay Rum.

Their daily weather forecasts for our area and assurance that there were no tropical depressions on the horizon did much to allay Charlotte's concerns, but their most astounding communication concerned an event they were monitoring—a rowboat race between the Madeira Islands and the Barbados. Trudy and Jack were monitoring the progress of the fifty small rowboats via a ham operator on a powerboat that was following the regatta and alerted us that they might cross our path. Bobbing around in tiny boats, unlit, crossing the Atlantic during a period where tropical storms were still menacing—we could hardly believe such a race existed. But our neighbor *Maggie* had sighted one of the boats a day after we had been alerted of their presence. *Maggie* had approached the lonely spect on the horizon, showered them with encouragement, and tossed down cold beer and paté. Hopefully this was not the same crew that Jack and Trudy later told us about that had had to be transported back home because of seasickness.

***

How many times will it take before we finally learn how different a country can be from our preconceived notions? We had read the guides and talked with people who claimed to know. Why had they all damned the Cape Verde Islands with their faint praises? Situated just 300 miles from where the African Continent bulges furthest west, the Cape Verde Islands stand alone.

After barreling through the powerful wind that froths up the narrow channel between Sao Vicente and Santo Antao Islands, we ended our seven-day trip from the Canary Islands in the wonderful security of Mindelo Harbor. When coal was king, Mindelo had been one of the most important crossroads in the world, with low rainfall, barren soil, but a superb harbor in a strategic link between West Africa and the rest of the world. Ships' transition from coal to oil left Mindelo an overdeveloped city with no means of support.

Our books talked of poverty, of crime, and rundown facilities. What they failed to emphasize was the warmth, the industriousness, and the beauty of the amalgam of cultures and races that populated Sao Vicente and its neighboring islands.

We first met Touga when he sped his white Boston Whaler water taxi towards a salt encrusted *Skimmer* as she rounded the jetty at the harbor entrance. About in the middle of the twenty-one shades of social status between Portuguese White and African Black, Touga displayed the typical handsome features of the Cape Verde population. Poverty has bred an aggressive generation of youths more set on extracting money from tourists than on actually providing services they claim to be offering, but Touga was the honest link that enabled us to do business in the confusion that greeted us each time we went ashore.

Champagne corks had popped, we had finished celebrating Martine's birthday aboard *Skimmer*, and we were ready to head for shore for our initial exploration of Mindelo. Our incongruous group arrived at Nella's, and with motion still in our limbs from seven days of rolling, we settled down to enjoy the freshly (and illegally) caught Cape Verde lobsters. Relations forged from close proximity sailing and radio communications, we had become good friends with Martine and Jean of *Magie*, Regine and Pierre of *Blaireau*, and the still proliferating family of Olivier and Patricia of *Zenovent*. As we crowded around the small table Charlotte and I again marveled at how easily Olivier and Patricia coped with all the necessary paraphernalia to transport their four-month-old son and his two-year-old and four-year-old brothers through seas, dinghies, and shore, but in a way they had been typical of our newfound friends.

Club Nautico of Mindelo

For the most part, the participants in the rally were new to long-distance cruising, and the obstacles they had had to overcome to prepare themselves and their crafts for our 7,000-mile journey were impressive. When we met Olivier and Patricia at the rally organization meeting in Paris five months earlier, Romain had not yet been born and we couldn't believe they would really go through with the trip. But there they were—stroller, portable baby seat, two toddlers, and Patricia with full breasts to keep Romain happy as we all enjoyed our lobster dinners.

Our sanctuary ashore looked like a warehouse, but actually it was the Club Nautico of Mindelo. Touga would escort us from the dinghy dock through the crowd of hawkers to the open doors and room full of people. The beer was always cold and from there we could get reliable advice about the amenities of Mindelo in relative security.

It was across the windswept Sao Vicente Channel on the island of Santo Antao that we fell in love with Cape Verde. Our group arrived by ferry from Mindelo into Porto Novo, a dirty harbor surrounded by parched hills. Somehow all 12 of us were able to squeeze into the iron frame and wooden benches that enabled our driver to call his pickup truck an aluguer. Our two hour journey ended as the road abruptly terminated at the northernmost tip of the island at the small fishing village of Ponta do Sol.

Waves crashing between a crude jetty on one side and huge boulders jutting from the sea on the other formed what the citizens of Ponta do Sol called their harbor. In disbelief I watched their skill in maneuvering brightly colored fishing boats into just the right position to catch the ride on just the right wave as it broke into the narrow pass between boulders and jetty. A waiting line of fishermen and fisherwomen were on shore to catch a line and then form a human chain to rapidly draw the boats up the ramp and out of the churning sea. Tuna was unloaded, butchered, and sold on the spot.

Fishermen Bringing Boats Ashore

If Ponta do Sol seemed isolated from the civilized world, our hike into the mountains the next day showed what remote can really mean. Jeanadon's aluguer took us up the dried riverbed of Riberia do Paul to where footpaths began. The brush was thick, the path narrow and sometimes almost vertical and just when I thought we were heading into real isolation, a group of gaily clad women with baskets full of fruit balanced on their heads passed us by as if we were standing still. Their effortless gait and merry laughter made me ashamed, and I tried not to think about how sore my muscles were becoming.

All around the mountainsides there was intensive cultivation of sugar cane, coffee, squash, corn. But, in contrast to other countries, the terracing was being expanded rather than being abandoned. On practically every slope I could see workers carving flat out of vertical and walling it with stone. Santo Antao was blessed with plentiful rain on the northern portion of the island. Miles of dams, aqueducts and trenches captured what nature would have wasted, and through an intricate maze of channels water gently found its way to the meticulously planted terraces.

At the summit we peered down into a giant volcanic crater that was home for dozens of villages. There we were overtaken by groups of children skipping over the same paths we had labored so hard to climb. For us the hike required a day of preparation making sure of water, shoes, sunscreen, and mosquito repellant, while for the children it was their daily routine to wake up early, hike ten kilometers up and down mountains to go to school, and then hike ten kilometers back home in the afternoon.

Cape Verde Grog

The Cape Verde islands had one thing in common. Grog. Each village on each island boasted its own special methods. On Sao Nicolau our aluguer driver merely laughed when we told him about the wonderful rum we had purchased in Sao Vicente and led us to an ancient sugar cane crusher in the center of a courtyard with several tired oxen scattered about.

Mohammed, the owner, claimed he produced the finest grog in Cape Verde. As he waived a dusty bottle under my nose, Mohammed boasted that Napoleon Brand was the best to be found anywhere. The picture of Napoleon on the bottle looked familiar, and I realized it was the largest of the oxen lazing next to the crusher.

Whether Mohammed's Napoleon Brand was the finest in the islands was debatable, but it did have the distinction of being the only labeled grog I was to sample. Generally, at small stores that could be mistaken for residences, the proprietor would dip a pitcher into a container that looked suspiciously like a plastic garbage can, funnel the contents into an empty plastic water bottle, and then hand over the bottle explaining it was near the last of his very special aged grog. The price he extracted served as proof of the scarcity of the vintage specimen he was offering for sale.

Fabian, a retired engineer turned bookstore owner who was visiting *Blaireau* during our stay in Cape Verde, was our rum connoisseur and categorically stated that what we were amassing in quantity in various shapes of plastic bottles was among the best rum he had ever tasted. After a night of celebration aboard *Skimmer* where I supplied endless glasses of rum punch made from Fabian's finest, Fabian and the rest of us became less enthusiastic about the virtues of Cap Verde Grog and subsequently many of the boats in our fleet were trying to decide which was more valuable—the containers or the content.

With two weeks of exploration and rum under our belts and with strong winds howling through our final anchorage, our fleet set out for the 430-mile trip to Dakar, Senegal, where we would "discover West Africa" and make final preparations for the big crossing to Brazil.

***

Just around Cap Manuel and well before the busy harbor of Dakar is a small horseshoe cove with white sandy beaches. It was not in my pilot books that advised which was the least dirty and least unattractive of the mooring alternatives in and around Dakar. I began to wonder if I had misplotted. But, no, there they were—boats bobbing at anchor with Isles du Soleil flags fluttering. Within thirty minutes of our arrival Charlotte and I were swimming in the beautifully manicured swimming pool of the Hotel Teranga with our dinghy tied up to the hotel pier.

The hotel and the reception around the pool given by the Governor, the Mayor, and the French Ambassador contrasted starkly with what awaited us just across the street—modern buildings among decaying colonial structures, beggars, aggressive hawkers, and relentless traffic that was menacing even to pedestrians on sidewalks. Once outside the confines of the Hotel Teranga it was a constant fight with crowds that cajoled, begged, followed, touched, and absolutely refused to be put off. The women with the stuffed dolls were the worst. "Hello mister, you want buy my dolls. I sell you, pas chere?"

I had tried everything from no thank you to an accelerated pace, no eye contact, and pretended ignorance of her presence. To no avail. The faster I walked, the more aggressively she engaged in the art of one-party bargaining: "Mister, how much you pay?" No answer. "Five thousand francs, is no expensive, here take, how many you like, you buy five I give you very special price." Still no answer and not even a nod of my head. "How much you pay?" Then I made the big mistake—recognition. "I don't want your dolls and would not accept one if you gave it to me. Please leave me alone!" This was just the in she had been searching for and with renewed vigor followed me three blocks trying to wear me down.

Finally I found refuge on a park bench in Independence Square and took advantage of my tranquility to make a call to the US on my portable phone. Right in the middle of my conversation I looked up to see two dolls thrusts in my face as the same woman renewed her attack. It was the only time I really lost my temper and I'm sure most of my vocabulary was totally incomprehensible—but it did have the desired effect and I was finally left alone.

Despite these hassles, Dakar is an intriguing city. It was formerly the capital of France's West African Empire, and behind the aggression of the hawkers it's a cosmopolitan city with good restaurants, shops and museums. It was from the small island near Dakar that many of the unfortunates sold as slaves in the US had their origins. Here we began to make the connection with our heritage. The dialect had sounds that were similar to Gullah that is still spoken by some blacks of the Carolina Coast, the grass baskets were identical to those sold on the streets of Charleston, and there were stands selling Okra and boiled peanuts everywhere.

***

Exploring the Sine Saloum

There were other connections to our heritage and they were waiting 70 miles to the south at the Sine-Saloum, a salt water river that pierces Senegal, where we toured the delta in a pirogue. Birds, salt marsh, endless sand, and hot sun shimmering over soft lapping waves—it was like coastal South Carolina except for a slightly different variety of Palms, endless knolls of Baobobs and Mangroves instead of pine and live oak, and grass huts shouting Africa instead of blue-roofed condominiums.

Our guide took us ashore on a small island and explained a phenomenon he thought was unique to his region—massive oyster shell banks constructed thousands of years ago and thought to commemorate huge feasts and consecrate burials. Pottery interspersed with the shells helped date and document the sites. Charlotte and I smiled at each other and marveled at the similarity with Wadmalaw Island back home and our Indian mounds.

Up the river—more like a trip up Carolina's North Edisto than a journey into Africa—we motor-sailed in close formation behind a native pirogue that shepherded us between the banks and fish traps, until we arrived at Foundiougne. That evening the moon was judged to be just right by the village elders and the town declared an end to Ramadan. Drums beat, fires burned, and people laughed and danced into the morning hours, celebrating the end of a month of abstaining from fleshly pleasures and from food and water by day.

The heartland was very different from Dakar. The begging and hawking, if not completely gone, was at least tuned down. The inevitable crowd of urchins surrounded us everywhere we went to stare at our whiteness. Nowhere was the greeting warmer than Akuna Matata, where we attended the Sunday service at the local Catholic Church. Charlotte's gift of notebooks, pens, and crayons for students was so appreciated by Sisters Clodia and Francoise that we had a hard time prying ourselves away to catch the donkey cart reserved to take us through the scorching heat back to our anchorage.

There was another cultural event. Turning 60 can be sad, but not for the skipper of *Skimmer,* as *L'Emmanuel* and *Zenovent* rafted up to form a tri boat party platform. The Sine-Saloum reverberated with French chansons, toasts over champagne, beer, and the dwindling remnants of Cape Verde Grog as our intimate party of 60 people celebrated well into the night.

Heyward's 60th

We returned to Dakar to complete final preparations for departure for Brazil. Fuel, water, beer, wine, supplies, more beer, more wine, and finally the big day arrived. Horns sounded, cheers rang out, anchor chains rattled, and we were away.

***

The loud clicking took us by surprise. The reel was literally hot to the touch and screaming so loud I could hardly hear what Charlotte was saying.

With my body bent against the force on the rod and my attention focused on the rapidly diminishing spool of line, I almost missed it. But suddenly in the corner of my eye I saw it far to the left and almost even with *Skimmer*'s stern— twisting, turning, straining—dancing on its tail with the sun reflecting off its glistening body—the largest marlin I had ever seen.

If he hadn't put on his show, the 400 yards of 50-pound test line on my reel would have run out without my ever gaining an inch. But his antics delayed the inevitable and for ten wonderful minutes we admired the display of energy and determination as he struggled for his freedom. Charlotte had rolled in the Genoa and was just getting ready to jibe towards the fish when the last yard of monofilament played out with a twang and a snap.

This was on the fourth day of our transatlantic voyage. Over 2,000 miles of open ocean—the longest stretch yet for just the two of us. Studying the winds and currents, I understood why Captain Jack Aubrey's route from England to Cape Town had him zigzagging to Rio de Janeiro. The classic logistical problem for mariners of old—where to cross the equator in heading south had become a problem that faced *Skimmer* and the 22 other boats of the rally.

Wind was a consideration because of our limited fuel capacity. The ITCZ, or Doldrums, is that area where the northeasterly trade winds from the northern hemisphere meet the southeasterly trade winds of the southern hemisphere—and go still. Bad weather and bad humors are sucked in alike. Sailboats roll endlessly to opposing swells as empty sails flap. Hot sultry air feeds violent thunder showers.

The technical name for this phenomenon is the Intertropical Convergence Zone, and while its presence is a sure thing, its exact location varies constantly and wildly. In this part of the world it forms a triangle with the longest side extending north to south along the African coast and the point somewhere out there in the Atlantic far to the west. But how far out— that was the question. Weather predictions give estimated daily locations, but they move much more rapidly than our little sailboats could possibly travel, and yesterday's predictions are almost certain to be different from tomorrow's reality.

Leaving Dakar, the northeasterly trades provided easy propulsion. The difficult decision was when to turn south to slog through confused seas and long monotonous calms interspersed with violent squalls. Statistically, the further west we rode the northeasterly trades, the narrower the slice of the unpleasant triangle would be. Once south of the troubled zone, southeasterly trades prevailed, and if one crossed too far west the last thousand miles along the South American coast to Salvador could be a very unpleasant beat into wind and seas.

Conventional wisdom was to cross somewhere between 26 and 28 degrees west. But with various weather predictions coming in daily and our boats strung out, giving each other positions and wind reports, the question made for heated conversations over the radio waves—as important as the never-ending topic of who was having what for lunch and which wine was best with it.

Skimmer chose 25 degrees west to take the plunge and settled on a very nice Hermitage Cote du Rhone to accompany Charlotte's Hampton House Plantation Shrimp, as we celebrated crossing the equator after two days of motoring. The day sparkled, we landed a pan-size dolphin just before sitting down to our three-hour lunch, and best of all we had finally found the gentle winds of the southeast trades with fuel still left in the jerricans.

Day after day on the port tack with steady wind of 15 knots. Charlotte became so confident of continuing good conditions and so excited about seeing our children that she finally consented to removing the conservative fetters that were normally such a hamper to *Skimmer's* forward progress. Smiling, happy, and hoping Charlotte wouldn't change her mind, *Skimmer* skipped through the waves at nearer seven knots than six and seemed to beg, with flowing, gurgling sounds: "more sail, more sail."

Brazil

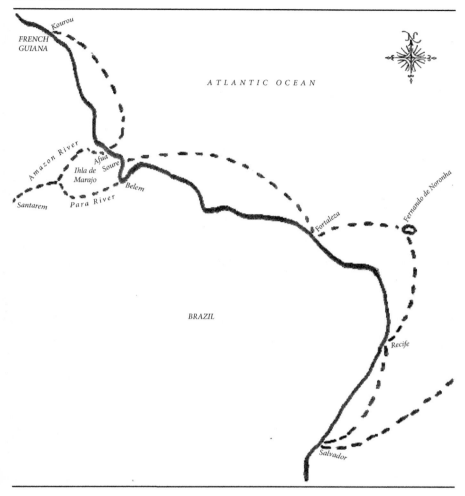

A city of contradictions, mystical beliefs and overwhelming energy. Yemanja is God of the Sea whose powers flow to selected "Orixa" who have been ordained to share these powers with less fortunates during elaborate Candomble services. Women clad in white twirl, sing, and pray to Samba rhythms of drums in the strange mixture of Christianity and African pagan rites that constitute Salvador's primary religion.

Salvador boasts of having more churches than days in the year, but there are three times as many "Terreiros" as churches. And it is in these special houses where animal sacrifices, drums, and frantic dancing induce Orixas to enter the bodies of the initiates.

Hands clapping, hips swaying, feet shuffling to unheard tunes of Samba, Daisy's warm smile greeted us as fellow cruisers took our lines. A short leap from *Skimmer's* stern, two frosted glasses of Caipirinha, a kiss from Daisy, our welcoming hostess, as she tied the traditional fita bracelets to our wrists, wild cheering from our earlier arrived companions, and our voyage from Africa to Salvador was complete.

Arrival at Salvador

Salvador was the logical conclusion to our travels. The Madeira Islands, the Cape Verde Islands, and Senegal. We followed the route of the Portuguese explorers and the route of the African slaves. Salvador was the melting pot. Unlike North America where British morality prevailed, racial mixing was the norm here. What greeted us as we stepped into this new world was an apparent lack of racism as we know it in the United States. Beautiful women oozed sex and friendly people went about their daily lives with carefree enthusiasm. And who better to describe it all than Salvador's favorite son, Jorge Amado. Thanks to advice from a friend who had lived in Salvador for several years, we came well armed with Amado novels and before even arriving in Salvador we were beginning to understand the unique mixture of Candomble and Christianity. But our guided tour of Salvador with Pierre allowed us to live Amado's experiences first hand.

Pierre was a Catholic worker priest from France who had spent his career helping Salvador's underprivileged while entangling himself in efforts to free Brazil of its suppressive leaders. His life had been a hard one, and his political meddling had ultimately resulted in his dismissal from the church. But his social work continued and he took us through parts of Salvador we would never have seen otherwise.

At the Church of Bomfim, high on a hill overlooking Salvador's harbor, is the site where a mariner, saved from a shipwreck, built a church to honor a promise made when he thought death was imminent. It also is where the Catholic Church and Candomble Paganism parted ways, and the bishop had forbidden further Candomble rites in the church. But in the strange way of Salvador, the Candomble community took this rebuff in stride and redoubled their efforts to cleanse the church and its surroundings in what has become one of the city's biggest celebrations. Born from a tradition where slaves cleaned the church, on the second Thursday of January crowds clad in white sing and dance their way to the top of the hill where they overflow into the park and church, scrubbing everything in their path. Jorge Amado had described it all in his wonderful novel, *War Of The Saints*, but Pierre made it come alive for us and even filled in the missing pieces on the clandestine role of the church in selling religious relics to fund revolutionary activities.

Pierre was one of the many great things that came to us through our French sailing companions. As time went on we became more and more attached to our new French friends. Their love for adventure and travel and their insatiable curiosity to delve into the culture of our destinations was infectious. Charlotte's French went from very good to outstanding, and although my grammatical handicaps remained, my conversational prowess increased to the point I could be an almost full participant in dirty joke telling. Our group consisted of the crews of the other 21 boats and their never ending stream of guests from home.

Church of Bomfim

But the propensity of the French to do it their own way led to situations that had us scratching our heads, wondering if it was us or them who were the crazy ones. Sailing experience varied wildly—from Bretons as salty as any we'd ever met to novices who'd never anchored a boat before and knew more about how to use a corkscrew than a wrench. During our Atlantic crossing snatches of conversations had raised warning flags: "The ocean is so big that a collision is statistically impossible," "I would have never made this trip if I didn't have all the other boats around me for security," "La Solidarite! Isn't it wonderful to know that help is always there."

All of that ran opposite to what we and most of those we had cruised with before had come to know as reality—"Once in the ocean, you are alone and it's up to you, your boat, your crew, and your wits to keep out of trouble— outside help would be a nice luxury, but don't count on it." Close neighbors and close shores can be more of a danger than a help.

On our third night out from Senegal, I had noticed a dim white light and called on the radio to see if it was one of our group far ahead with its stern light showing. In answer to my call I suddenly saw a bright flash of light and found myself looking almost straight up into the green running light on top of the mast of a neighbor who had been far too close. I dropped the microphone in my haste to get to the helm to separate us, but when calm returned I started thinking again about the strange comment from another cruising companion that Charlotte had passed on to me: "We are getting ready for the evening and turning off the lights." Charlotte and I had discussed the meaning and had both concluded that it couldn't possibly mean … but now with this new piece of evidence I began to wonder.

Radio in hand again I asked the obvious question and had received the astounding reply: "There wasn't much sun today and our solar panels didn't work, so we are conserving electricity and our running lights use two amperes." A brief flash and there they were—uncomfortably close and in an area I had previously thought was empty. The reply to my subsequent request had been a reluctant agreement for a brief flash every hour. The third shoe dropped at dawn when coming out of the darkness I watched the white sails and shiny aluminum hull of another close neighbor materialize. To my radio call expressing my amazement, a good-natured reply came back "Oh, not to worry, we could see YOUR running lights fine." It had not even occurred to Charlotte and me that all the boats wouldn't be using their running lights, but there they were, three unlit boats around us in the middle of the Atlantic where we had thought we had been completely alone.

I came to think of it as the wet dog syndrome. Whereas we wanted to get as far away as possible from the others, our cruising companions drew together like magnets firmly believing that safety lay in numbers. To our amazement we subsequently found that some of the wet dogs didn't keep continuous watches and depended on quick visual sweeps at set intervals if they happened to awaken when their alarm clock rang. When we brought up our concerns about these loose practices at a subsequent skippers meeting, our fearless leader, with tongue in cheek, admonished the group to clean up their act and explained that keeping running lights on at night was an Anglo Saxon idiosyncrasy.

Heyward Jr.'s arrival in Salvador after a strenuous two-day flight from Japan was the beginning of a great family reunion. Margot came in from Los Angeles and Alex from Charleston and we all spent the Christmas vacation together. Salvador bulged as bands, parades, and endless crowds of people filled the squares and narrow winding streets. When we had finally had all we could take, we departed in *Skimmer* to explore the wonders of the Baia de

Todos Santos. New Year's Eve saw us at the fireworks display in the Barra district of Salvador, where beer-drinking spectators watched white-clad believers samba their way into the cleansing waves of Yemanja's ocean.

Our six week's stay in Salvador gave time for some overland travel and we were narrowing the choices when Charlotte noticed an attractive family standing on the dock staring at *Skimmer* with longing in their eyes. They were from Rio de Janeiro, spoke a little English, and it so happened that they had just spent two weeks vacationing on Ilha Grande. Their description clinched our decision.

The Coleman Family in Salvador

A hundred and two beaches, no automobiles, mountainous tropical rainforest in the interior surrounded with snowy white sand on the exterior, Ilha Grande is a paradise that attracts mainly families from Rio. Unpretentious pousadas provide simple but clean accommodations and quaint restaurants are scattered throughout the island. In the little community of Vila do Abraao, footpaths and wooden bridges meander from beach to pousada to small grocery stores. Trails lead to isolated beaches, blue grottos, and small coves with charming restaurants. Nothing is more than a two-hour hike or an hour boat ride away and the island bustles with the low-key energy of vacationers thoroughly enjoying themselves and their beautiful surroundings. We found that our efforts to learn a little Portuguese were finally paying off, and we could carry on simple conversations as we hiked along with families from beach to beach.

Salvador to Recife can be four hundred miles straight into wind and current, but nature blessed us with a southeasterly wind that allowed us to sail much of the way. More rain than we have ever had before, frequent and sometimes violent squalls, and pounding waves, but four days after our departure we moored in Recife's Cabanga Yacht Club for a week of exploration of one of Brazil's most historic cities.

After Recife, we left on our last trip to windward to visit Brazil's answer to the Galapagos Islands—Fernando de Noronha. Three days later we arrived at the semi-protected anchorage of Baia de Santo Antonio. Twenty-degree rolls as swells surged through our anchorage weren't pleasing, and our radio was abuzz with complaints and stories of seasickness. Boat to boat visiting came to an abrupt halt. Ashore the same swells crashed down on snow-white beaches where frigate birds dove into the foam.

Like the Galapagos, the wildlife on Ilha Fernando de Noronha was almost tame, with birds and huge populations of turtles that have become almost extinct in other parts of the world. Water with visibility down to 100 feet, dolphins frolicking on the shores, caves and reefs teeming with activity, who wanted to stay on board anyway?

***

Dozens of dim white lights cluttered the horizon, demanding attention. My mind was still dull with sleep as I tried to grasp the situation from a very tired Charlotte who was already making her way to the bed in eager anticipation. Suddenly the magic of the sky exploded into jagged rays of red, orange, and yellow, removing the frustration of having to worry about 20 other boats as we approached way point one. The strengthening morning light revealed more dramatic changes. Muddy brown turbulence had replaced clear blue and I smiled as realization dawned—*Skimmer* was now enveloped in the waters of the Amazon.

Though still over 30 miles from land we were beginning to experience the power of the world's mightiest river system that provides nearly a quarter of the planet's fresh water supply. Rain from Peru, mud from Amazonia, drainage from an area the size of Europe was now speeding along *Skimmer*'s sides.

The trip from Fortaleza was one of our most rapid to date. Favorable winds and currents that sometimes averaged as much as two knots made 180-mile days the norm. I might have been able to convince Charlotte that she actually loved being at sea, if it hadn't been for the violent squalls that always seemed to strike in the middle of her watches. But the "I hate sailing" harangues had become less frequent, and both of us spent our free time on the five-day trip reading about the Amazon and deciding what we wanted to see.

What awaited us in the tiny community of Soure was beyond anticipation. Dressed in fatigues, riding on massive water buffaloes, the mounted police of Soure escorted us to the Hotel Ilha do Marajo, where huge banners and a crowd of dignitaries welcomed us into the state of Para. They had gone all out, assigning us a military escort boat with a crew of twenty policemen and firemen.

The name of the state comes from the Tupi Indian name meaning "vast ocean" and it literally was a vast ocean that had grasped us with muddy waters as we entered the giant Para River to begin our exploration of the Amazon. Ilha do Marajo—an island the size of Switzerland—is situated like a giant cork pushed loose from the bottle of the Amazon basin by the massive forces of the Para River flowing along its south side and the Amazon

Mounted Police of Soure

River along its north. Dense compact soil, rich in minerals, low in nutrients, miserable for drainage, flooded half the year, parched the other half, what use could this land possibly have?

The ingenuity and persistence of the Jesuits in the 17th Century provided the answer. Importation of cattle failed miserably, but their next attempt worked so well that the industry is still alive and thriving today—water buffalo. The first came from Italy and were soon followed by vast herds from India. In Soure they wander the streets, in the countryside they graze up to their necks and are half hidden in endless flooded fields.

***

Water was almost up to my waist and my greatest fear was that the digital camera in my pocket would get submerged. But, Jose, our swarthy vaquero leader was intent on rounding up the buffalo. Fortunately my steed, like Charlotte's and the other six in our group, was thoroughly tame and was content to follow the others, so I just held on tight and hoped. Clutching the saddle, I leaned forward as instructed, as my horse clawed its way up the muddy slope to regain the grass deep water. It was wonderful—riding along with the vaqueros—herding the giant water buffalo into the coral—sharing the beauty and joys of ranch life with our charming hosts.

Fazenda Sanjo was typical of the huge ranches that covered the island. Fields flooding in the rainy season give the appearance of vast lakes dotted with trees and carpeted with thin green stalks of grass. For six months of the year roads are completely covered, isolating the ranches from all but river access. Our entry had been by pirogue.

One and a half hours up tributaries of the Rio Paracauari—mangrove trees with their spider-like roots towered along the shores, howler monkeys swung in trees, toucans flew from branch to branch, and flaming red ibises soared in formations overhead.

I would have characterized it as a cross between Texas and South East Asia if it had not been for the photo in a newspaper of a long, coiled tube, grossly inflated in the middle. The second page of the newspaper had a photo of what was left of the hapless six-foot vaquero once he had been removed from the belly of the Anaconda.

Round Up at Fazenda Sanjo

Sanjo, like its neighboring ranches, was self-sufficient. It produced its own electricity, husbanded its water from rainy season to dry, and maintained its links with civilization by river. Barges brought in supplies and carried water buffalo out to market.

***

Our leader, Philippe, had given the wake-up call at five a.m. for 21 sleepy crews. His coordination had been superb, anchors up at six o'clock would put us at just the beginning of the flood tide so that instead of bucking five knots of current we would have it pushing us along. Charlotte had grumbled something about a funny angle when she put the coffee pot on and shook me again to get me out of bed. Immediately on deck, my worst fears were confirmed. A quirk of wind and current had left *Skimmer* in just the wrong position and Charlotte's funny angle was the result of our stern sitting firmly on a mud bank. Despite their charitable silence, we knew the other 20 boats were not happy about the delay, the only saving grace was the sight of our neighbor also stranded on the mud.

Two hours later, finally afloat again, the odyssey started. What took more concentration, dodging the uprooted trees or avoiding collisions with our neighbors? Apparently "Indian File" has a different meaning in French than in English and no matter who we tried to steer behind, another boat would come looming out of nowhere and pass close enough to terrorize.

But finally we worked ourselves into a semblance of a formation, and before tempers had a chance to reach kindling point Belem took us in.

Gateway to the Amazon, a city of one and a quarter million inhabitants, the capital of Para, and our jumping off point. Poverty and dirt cover Belem with decay that almost conceals the beauty beneath. Real wealth had come here with the rubber boom, and by the end of the 18ᵗʰ century Belem was by far the largest city in South America and by an even wider margin the most cosmopolitan. Wealthy British, French, Italian, and Portuguese rubber magnates

Baby Ben in Belem

vied for garish enhancements of their city, trying to outdo each other in transplanting examples of their culture into this unlikely equatorial metropolis. An exact replica of Milan's La Scalla Opera House, a scaled down version of Rome's Saint Peter's Basilica, beautiful wrought iron works from Glasgow making the central market look more like Scotland than Amazon, a scaled down Big Ben, and even a faithful reproduction of Paris' Gallerie Lafayette. It was depressing to witness what 30 years of corrupt dictatorships had all but destroyed. We could see signs of efforts to clean and restore, but they had a long way to go.

Another surprise awaited. The *Alvaro Furtado*, gleaming white wood and graceful lines, Amazon charm exuded from the three decks of the 90-foot vessel provided by the state of Para to escort us up river. We would also be protected by *Capitania Dos*, a gray steel monster with its compliment of 20 policemen and firemen.

***

A loud crunch followed by a grinding noise. Already on deck, thinking that the diesel thumps I had heard approaching signaled the arrival of our water taxi, I spun around and watched with horror as the fifty-foot wooden ferry boat disengaged itself from *Zenovent* and then headed off into the night. Patricia, Olivier, and their three small children—were they all right?

It hadn't taken long to realize the power of the enormous river system we were about to tackle. Even at anchor I could see a huge wake behind *Skimmer* and get a five-knot reading on my speed log. Even when I wasn't looking, the sound of rushing water along *Skimmer*'s sides told me it was true, and I would check again the bearings I had chosen on land to make sure our anchor wasn't dragging.

Alvaro Furtado

Police Escort

This was a power we had never experienced. Impossible to row against, often too deep to anchor—suddenly dinghy travel had taken on a new dimension and we were happy our Rally leader, Philippe, had arranged a water taxi to ferry us to and from our boats.

Having an anchor drag is always dangerous, but in Belem it could spell disaster. As anchoring techniques were still in the development stage for some of our cruising mates, I worried about the near proximity—often far too near—of the other twenty boats of our rally. But this night, a new danger appeared. In trying to weave its way through the field of anchor lights, a ferry cut its turn too close and the racing current had brought it smack into *Zenovent*. Immediately VHF's became alive and the night was pierced by the sirens of our police escort speeding downriver in pursuit of the ferry.

Fortunately the five-inch hole in *Zenovent* was above the waterline, and no one aboard was hurt, but a bureaucratic nightmare followed for Olivier. Fiberglass patch, police reports, and delicate negotiations with both insurance companies. Would he be able to finish in three days?

Our Amazon schedule was fixed. *Alvaro Furtado* and *Capitania Dos* would leave on March 17, and all who wished to make the trip would have to leave with the escorts. For six weeks, it would be convoy travel with no possibility of leaving the group. Boats with problems would be towed by *Furtado* until repaired, but the group would follow the strict requirement that all travel at a minimum speed of six knots. Once in, it was over 600 miles against strong currents up the Para river, a meandering trail from river to river through the Straits of Breves, and then on up the Amazon river.

Against odds, *Zenovent* was ready when the 21 boats headed out to the small island of Cotejuba for our first night's anchorage. Whether the tides dictated or it was Philippe's way of whipping us into shape for what lay ahead, the next day began with anchors up at four o'clock a.m. Pouring rain, pitch-black dark, and 21 boats circling around, trying to figure out where to go while *Furtado* took up position in the lead. Spot lights blinded us as panicky voices boomed over the VHF, trying to establish which boat was which and reminding each other to turn on their running lights. It was pandemonium.

The voices were coming so fast we couldn't understand most of it, and what difference did it make anyway which boat was ahead of which boat? We were all a danger to each other, and the important thing was to get into line and follow *Furtado*, keeping safe distances between our boats. Why anyone would need a reminder to turn his running lights on was as baffling to us as the necessity of shining 10,000 candlepower search lights into each others eyes. From 4 a.m. to 6 a.m. were the longest two hours we ever spent on *Skimmer*, and our heated discussions centered on whether to make a 180-degree turn back to Belem and quit the Rally.

But daylight and the sight of hundreds of parrots setting out in pairs for their day's foray revived our spirits. Crude houses built with thatched roofs dotted the riverbanks, and children and mothers came to the open windows and doorways to stare at our strange procession. We passed fishermen filling their dugout canoes with bamboo shrimp traps and school boat ferries loading for their morning runs. Occasionally we would pass a whitewashed hut marked Hospital or a long airy shed marked Escola.

The Para River bulged to giant proportions as we transited the bays of Marajo and Marapata and it was almost like being at sea. But as the Para narrowed to the point where we could see both shores at the same time the magic intensified. Leaving Ilha Paqueta, and swinging in close to shore, we were greeted by an enormous snow white Jesus Cristo on his cross, dominating Boa Vista, a town on stilts.

Hardware stores, fruit and vegetable stands, grocery stores, and small sheds covering boat construction—all was accessible only by the continuous system of docks that tied the maze together.

Fifty miles after Boa Vista, we left the mighty Para River to enter the Straits of Breves and then the intricate, winding, fingers of water that divide The Island of Marajo from mainland Brazil. Hundreds of islands, a watery maze going in every direction, river life was closing in and it was wonderful.

How the word spread, I never figured out, but they knew we were coming. They swarmed us in dugout canoes so low in the water that a mother holding a baby with one arm was constantly bailing with the other. Small girls, barely old enough to be able to walk, wielded paddles.

Family on the Amazon

Philippe announced that our stream was about to deliver us into the Amazon, and there it was, turbulent, brown power extending as far as we could see. Suddenly, instead of varying and sometimes weak currents we were right in the middle of a relentless flow that we would fight for the rest of our journey to Santarem.

Dodging massive tree trunks and scattered limbs became the norm, and the *Furtado* took two wounded boats in tow. Floating islands of water hyacinths would

appear out of nowhere and speed past us.

At our first anchorage, the current racing through was so strong that during my evening swim I had to struggle to keep even with *Skimmer's* stern. Swimming laps in place was a sinister reminder of the power of the Amazon.

Early that morning I had watched with interest as a random floating island of vegetation approached, and went forward with a boat hook to try to divert its path from *Skimmer.* But my efforts were only partially successful and a clump of green the size of my dinghy tangled on our anchor chain. I had a machete but found that strenuous chopping for fifteen minutes accomplished almost nothing. Fortunately *Buffalo*, the dinghy towed by our escort ship *Furtado* came to our rescue, and with four policemen swinging machetes managed to remove the tangle of vines.

I thought no more about it until a cry in the night from *Peppy II.* A floating island ten times the size of his boat had attached and begun dragging them with irresistible force through the group of sleeping boats. A voice from *Zenovent* came next as the island and *Peppy II* swept down upon them. While *Buffalo* was speeding to the rescue, cries from two other boats joined the chaos of a night that never seemed to end. Daylight, anchors up, back in formation on the river, we tried hard to believe Philippe's assurance that floating islands shouldn't pose a problem at our future anchorages.

***

The boats ahead called our attention to the object floating in the water off our starboard bow. A rope like tangle came into focus in my binoculars as we approached. Coiling and uncoiling and obviously very large. And then, as the object drew closer, I saw the head—perhaps the size of a small dog—and I wondered how wide those jaws could stretch open. Twenty feet long, who knows? But I was happier viewing our first Anaconda from *Skimmer's* deck, rather than in our new dinghy.

In Belem when I had discovered that our inflatable dinghy was no longer functional, the word went out that there was an American looking for a dinghy. It was impossible to find an inflatable, but why not one of the aluminum boats that appeared everywhere on the rivers? After much searching, it finally arrived—three meters long and brand new. With pointed bow, no oar locks, no flotation, and rated for a motor half the size of my eight horsepower Yamaha. But it was that or nothing so I jury-rigged oar locks, stuffed sheets of styrofoam under the seats, and lowered my motor onto the stern for a trial run. We were careful to stay low and distribute our weight to counterbalance the motor, but what speed and what a pleasure to be mobile once again!

If we could manage to avoid sinking it, our new dinghy was ideally suited for the Amazon, and we were the envy of the fleet as we sped ahead. The real advantage manifested itself when we tried penetrating our first small stream. Thorns, vines, branches—the rubber inflatables dared not enter. But the briar patch was no obstacle to us and what a fascinating world lay behind those seemingly impenetrable jungles along the river banks. Even small openings were possible, and suddenly the tiny fingers of water would expand and twist, enticing us to penetrate further and further.

Exploring in Our New Dinghy

Fortunately our first dinghy expedition into the interior came before our sighting the anaconda, and Charlotte was so busy collecting exotic red, yellow, and blue flowers and craning her neck to catch sight of brightly colored birds that she hardly thought about snakes and insects. Our guide Oswaldo, with a huge spider in his hand, had previously explained to us that tarantulas were not really a problem and would only bite if angry. But his English had not been good enough to convey the secret of how to keep a tarantula happy, and Charlotte had not been convinced at all that she should emulate Oswaldo in gently pushing in loose bark on a Samauma tree to try to find a tarantula of her own. In fact, Charlotte's anti-snake and anti-spider sentiments periodically expressed themselves in a loud shriek as an unseen vine slid past her neck. On the whole, though, she was so happy gathering flowers that she was always the one to urge us on further and further.

***

The family was standing on a log, wedged in place with wooden stakes that served as the dock to their little hut on stilts. With waves and smiles they urged us in. It was our first visit to an isolated river dwelling and I was fascinated to see how well constructed and laid out their little home was. There was a wood burning stove in the kitchen along the back, three dugout canoes tied up on the right, one of them filled to the brim with stalks of heart of palm. What riveted our attention was the furry little bundle that was so ugly it was cute.

Sloth

Hanging by long claws from its foot and oh-so-slowly turning its round face to focus on us—it was the first Parasseuse, or Sloth, we'd seen up close. We took pictures and watched in fascination—Tarzan in slow motion, swinging from kitchen rack to rail, smiling at us with its ugly little face all the while. Then we saw the pot with boiling water. The pot. The Parasseuse. With horror the possibility began to dawn and knowing smiles from the family seemed to confirm. But surely this cuddly little animal was a pet.

The children took us through the woods behind their house, showing how they gathered oil nuts for making soap that they would sell and pointing

300

out the grove of trees where they harvested heart of palms. They explained how they deployed the bamboo fish traps to catch shrimp and promised that if we came back the next day they would have some to sell. When we returned to the hut our smiling furry friend was no longer there and the pot was full of simmering meat and vegetables. As much as we liked our little family, we decided not to stay for lunch.

Charlotte was on the bow shouting "Come quick—it's just in front of us—as pink as bubble gum!" Her simile was perfect. The same brightness that had greeted me as a youth when the soft cylinder of double bubble emerged from its wrapper was there in the water. We had found Boto, the largest freshwater dolphin in the world, born gray but then turns pink. Six feet of sleek power with a long narrow mouth protruding from a small head. Boto was following and frolicking with *Skimmer*, so close we could hear the breathing.

The legend came to life! Villagers would always be suspicious when the handsome stranger wore a cowboy hat, but the pregnant beauty left behind when the stranger quit town was the final proof. The hat had been to hide the hole in his head and the poor maiden could be forgiven for her weakness in succumbing to the irresistible charm of Boto. We had seen the drama enacted in a folklore dance during our village receptions, but to our utter delight we had finally met Boto in person.

***

Clear green water, the first we had seen in a month and a half, the Tapajos River was opening to us. At the confluence of the Amazon and Tapajos Rivers is Santarem, and as if by some magic force, its shores are protected from the murky brown Amazon by a wide swath of Tapajos green that refused to mix until well past the city.

Ten miles up the Tapajos—the "Caribbean of the Amazon" actually

Island off Alter do Chao

did exist. Clear green water, a long narrow island of snow-white sand dotted with palms, and a string of busy little pirogues ferrying their cargoes of sun

301

worshipers between the quaint little village and the island. Our armada passed in single file between the island and the village of Alter do Chao, swung to the left into the crystal clear waters of Largo Verde, and then nosed up to the lake side of the island where we remained detached from reality for five days before returning to Santarem.

The second largest city in the state of Para, Santarem was the nearest we had been to civilization since leaving Belem, and we restocked our boats for the trip back down the Amazon. With the current behind us our trip out would take only four days.

***

Potted Tree at Afua

Most of the city had turned out—loud, cacophonous music from the brass band, cheering from the shore, cheering from the dozens of circling boats—our arrival was the event of the year. Afua was our final destination in Brazil and the site where we would celebrate the end of the Rally. Afua is a city on stilts with no access except by water. Concrete slab streets, houses, stores, schools, and parks—all perched above water and marshland and sitting on pilings. Trees in giant clay containers, gardens in tubs, shady squares off the main roads with their potted forests—and all of it bustling with bicycle traffic with not a motor vehicle anywhere in sight.

Exhausted from the strain of our marathon trip out of the Amazon, we settled down for a good night's sleep. Then came a beeping that was unmistakable. Half asleep, I felt my way to the navigation table to silence the anchor drag alarm, knowing that it was just the shift in tide. We always set the alarm so the movement caused by changes in direction of the current was sufficient to set it off. That way I could verify that the anchor was still holding in the new direction. Caution had made me look outside anyway.

My slow climb up the ladder turned into a dash to the helm as I saw the shoreline whizzing by. Cough, cough, motor on—whirr whirr as I shifted to full rpm—and bang bang as Charlotte almost broke her neck in her vertical ascent up the aft companionway. Over the motor roar I shouted, "Damn it Charlotte, the engine IS in gear and I have it at full throttle! I don't know why we are still going backwards!" Then she cried: "We are going to hit, we are going to hit!" Hard right rudder and then just as our stern was approaching the fifty-two foot Super Maramu anchored behind us, a loud grinding noise from our bow. Suddenly we began to move to the right and with just feet to spare, *Skimmer* slowly clawed her way out into the center of the river.

Once in the center, the combined force of our anchor and motor finally halted our backwards motion and I turned the wheel over to Charlotte as I went forward to investigate. There was a log longer than *Skimmer,* and firmly wedged on our anchor chain. With the log's full length broadside to the powerful outgoing current, the force was irresistible. Despite *Skimmer's* 82-horsepower diesel, and her 60-pound anchor with two hundred feet of chain, we had dragged as if there had been neither motor nor anchor.

But what to do now? While Charlotte stayed at the helm with motor racing and called for help over the VHF radio, I climbed into our dinghy and pulled myself against the current up to the bow, on the side with the short end of the log. Water swirling madly past the log created eddies that almost capsized the tipsy aluminum dinghy. Abandoning my attempt to push at the short end, I pulled the dinghy along the other side of *Skimmer* with the idea of tying a line around the long end and trying to pull the log off with the dinghy motor.

After a futile attempt to pass a line around the log I realized the magnitude of our problem. With my chest on the log and my arms fully extended, I found to my horror that I couldn't reach even half way around. This wasn't a normal log. It was a tree with a diameter of over four feet and there wasn't anything I could do by myself to dislodge it. It seemed like forever, but actually was only about twenty minutes when we saw the spot light approaching. Jean of *Maggie* with Jean-Jaques of *Brigantine* were coming to the rescue in *Maggie's* dinghy, but their attempts to push the log with their dinghy were futile.

I was pondering solutions when *Buffalo* finally arrived. *Furtado* had been much further away but Philippe immediately responded to Charlotte's call for help, and now their long sleek dinghy with three husky policemen aboard was speeding towards us. Lieutenant Mahashad was wider than he was tall and without hesitation he jumped from *Buffalo* onto the long end of the tree. Holding onto *Skimmer's* bow with one hand and onto the anchor chain with the other, he began to jump up and down in an effort to twist the log free. But, despite his size and strength, the log refused to budge.

I was more concerned for Mahashad's safety than about getting the log free, but Jean and Jean-Jaques made one more assault with their dinghy on the short end. They were able to push the log around so that it was almost parallel with *Skimmer*. The current's pressure was so reduced that Mahashad was finally able to succeed in rocking the trunk. And then, like an arrow released from a taught bow, the tree shot down the side of *Skimmer*, almost impaling *Buffalo*, and leaving Mahashad hanging for life from our bow. I leaned over and pulled with all my might, but it was Mahashad's strength that finally had him safely aboard.

***

Charlotte's 59th Birthday

April 26, the day before the official end of the rally, was the 59th birthday of *Skimmer*'s first mate. What better way to celebrate than by commandeering the Marajo Restaurant and trying to drink Afua dry of caipirinha and beer and feasting on Langostino and feijoada. With pledges of undying friendship came the sad realization that we were about to part from our friends of six months.

Five-thirty came early and, with *Furtado* escorting us to the mouth of the South Channel, we began our trip out. The Amazon didn't let go easily. Shallow muddy water extended for over a hundred miles. I could imagine what a squall with 30-knot winds would do to the 20-foot-deep water and kept the motor racing as we clawed for sea room. It wasn't until late the following afternoon that Amazon brown finally gave way to Atlantic blue.

***

The Iles du Salut, home of the infamous Devil's Island where Captain Dreyfus had been interred, stand guard over the entrance to a narrow channel that is the only safe passage through shallow waters along this lonely stretch of French Guyana. Now a space center where Ariane missiles are launched, Kourou is home to a large detachment of French Foreign Legion and a major tourist attraction.

We found wildly inflated prices that French dependencies are so adept at producing and a population spoiled by privileges showered upon them as a reward for being a French state. Prices were ten times what we had seen in Brazil and even more preposterous when compared to neighboring Surinam. I had to walk two miles to purchase diesel fuel because what few taxis there were refused to haul jerry jugs. With relief we prepared for our departure to Trinidad.

Drinking late into the night is not a good way to prepare for an early departure, but this was the last time with many of our friends, and we found it hard to let go. As we were passing Devil's Island the squalls began, and the wind clocked around to make our ride to deep water bumpy. For the first time since the beginning of our trip, Charlotte was seasick. Fortunately she had not given away all of our seasick pills, and after two uncomfortable days with 35-knot squalls, both she and the weather settled down. The remainder of our 700-mile trip to Trinidad went more smoothly.

Journey's End

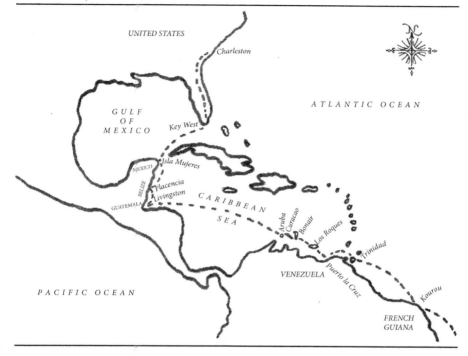

Vertical walls of water surrounded us in the troughs. Foamy horizontal streaks of water shot out as the powerful wind decapitated wave crests. It was a classic force eight, one notch down from Strong Gale on the Beaufort Scale and one notch past panic on the Charlotte "I hate wind scale." Our new passenger, Noddy, was the only one aboard that took it with equanimity and, as 45-knot gusts doused the cockpit with salty spray, he simply flapped his wings and adjusted his perch on the mounting pile of roller furling line. There was no real possibility of turning back

Before departure we had studied the weather more intensely than ever before. George, the weather guru on the 7:00 a.m. Ham Caribbean Weather Net, predicted safe sailing for our 1,100-mile trip from Aruba to Guatemala. Everything had been a go and I was congratulating myself on all the homework done on the weather predictions we had been studying for the past week. But when I returned to the boat from paying the marina bill the expression on Charlotte's face immediately alerted me that everything had changed.

In an attempt to be super-cautious, I had engaged the services of a second weather guru, and I had compounded the error by leaving Charlotte alone to get one final forecast. She hadn't understood all of his answer regarding high winds and thunder storms associated with an approaching tropical wave, but the part she did hear clearly was his recommendation to wait until Monday to depart.

I argued: "It always blows twenty or thirty knots around Aruba. Once we are out the wind will go down. We have already been told by one 'expert' that conditions are good for going." But my logic didn't work, the tears were real and we both decided that waiting one more day in Aruba was the right thing to do.

Ever since receiving an email from our friends on *Voyager* about their knockdown wave one day out of Aruba, Charlotte's anxiety level had been building. I tried to explain that the feared "wave triangle" off the coast of Colombia was more of a problem for vessels such as *Voyager* that were heading from Aruba to Panama, than for vessels heading for Guatemala. I promised to go out of our way to the north from Aruba to avoid the dreaded area of wind funnels and giant breaking waves.

Now at sea, our argument built as the waves mounted. It came to a head when our second forecaster explained that the squalls he had originally warned us against had failed to materialize, and his recommendation to head south after leaving Aruba had not really been necessary.

"Not necessary, not necessary!" I mimicked, complaining that the giant waves and high wind we were experiencing was because, against my better judgment, we had followed Chris's advice to divert south. For the tenth time I griped "The problem with these gurus is that they always have to give advice. Otherwise they think you will feel that you wasted the 75 dollars you paid for their trip consultancy. Then you wind up doing something you were against in the first place and find yourself fighting wind and waves while the guru smugly munches donuts and sips hot coffee from his warm dry office."

When the weather began to pass the discussion turned to whether it was just the bad luck associated with Friday departures that had been the genesis of our problems. It was during the height of the strong winds that Charlotte had spied a bird's bill jutting from behind our mast. Sharp, sinister, and backed up with two piercing evil eyes. Another bad omen presaging evil to come or a good omen signifying an approaching change in conditions? Actually it was only a very tired Brown Noddy looking for a free perch.

At first Noddy was a good shipmate, but after the first day he became bossy. We hadn't minded when he decided to shift his quarters from the bow to *Skimmer*'s cockpit, but it was a little tiresome shooing him away from our favorite perching places and disconcerting to feel his cold black eyes examining our every move. Good luck or bad, neither one of us had any interest in receiving a puncture wound from his beak. But at the same time we found him good company. My theory that he was very sick fell apart when he snatched the proffered flying fish out of Charlotte's hand and then sucked down the bowl of water we had kept trying to make him notice. After two days of rest and two more fish, Noddy turned our cockpit back over to us and flew off to join his own.

* * *

Our whirlwind trip across the Caribbean started in Trinidad, where we learned that if you want to visit Venezuela, this was not the place to start your travels. Trinidad is a place where anchors take root, where rebellious wives and faint-hearted skippers forsake wanderlust for dominoes, bridge, and potluck dinners. It's a community that has become entrenched, and what better reason for

Noddy

entrenchment than piracy. The stories abound and reinforce themselves in the retelling as would-be adventurers make the inevitable decision to remain for one more season of social activities.

There were some who believed even a daylight exit through Boca de Monos without the company of a fleet of Trinidadian fishing vessels was fraught with the risks of bandits lurking to pounce on lone cruisers. We became convinced we should give mainland Venezuela a bye. While our firm intention was to steer clear of the pirate-infested mainland, a cataclysmic event occurred aboard *Skimmer* after our departure from Los Testigos Islands, 100 miles north of Trinidad, that resulted in a 90 degree turn to the left.

Although we tried to stay self-sufficient aboard *Skimmer*, there are certain malfunctions so serious that for the safety and well being of the crew we felt that immediate remedial action was imperative. Our refrigeration was no longer working. My efforts to resuscitate had been unsuccessful. Faced with a choice of the prospect of no more cold beer for our 1,500-mile trek to Guatemala, or to chance the pirates we'd heard so much about, the decision had been simple. After an overnight sail around Isla Margarita and then through tranquil waters to the continent, we entered Puerto la Cruz on

Venezuela's coast. Shortly after our arrival, we made the happy discovery that the refrigeration problem had solved itself.

If you are not bothered by the potential of an occasional mugging or put off by dealing in the black market to obtain funds, Venezuela is a wonderful country to visit. The people are friendly, the food is delicious, but most important of all are the prices. Naturally low prices are now made ridiculously low by rampant inflation. With supermarkets and shops chock full of wonders we had not seen since the states, it was a buyer's paradise.

There were, however, drawbacks. Credit cards were not to be used under any circumstances because of the almost certainty of fraudulent aftermaths. ATM's were out of the question for the same reason. Changing money at banks or other establishments using the official exchange rate resulted in a 30-percent reduction in value. We were assured, however, that using the black market presented little or no risks, so we joined the crowd.

Los Roques Islands

Pushing two grocery carts filled to overflowing with items that included seven cases of Polar Beer at the equivalent of $3.00 US a case and six liters of Venezuelan Anjeo Rum at a third that price per bottle, I worried that maybe I didn't have enough Venezuelan currency. Juan had been so helpful in finding various items that I decided to chance it. Leading him to a quiet corner and speaking just above a whisper, I made it known that I needed to change some dollars. In response Juan boomed in a loud voice "Si, Senior, is possible change dollars here—come with me." Trying to look as inconspicuous as possible I followed him over to the customer service counter where a boisterous conversation in Spanish ensued with fingers pointing to me, to Juan, and then back to me. Juan then loudly translated: "How many dollars do you want to change?" Once Charlotte had pushed the two heaping carts through the checkout line, the young lady at the register stopped the line while I took my ticket with the exact amount to the customer service desk. With waiting shoppers watching my every move, I then counted out my illegal US dollars.

A surprise came when I dinghied over to Marina Americo Vespucio to get my permit to purchase duty free diesel fuel. Again the clandestine exchange of dollars, but to my amazement I realized that the price of the fuel was six cents US per gallon. As we left Puerto la Cruz, Charlotte and I both decided that we were happy our refrigerator had decided to hick up when it did.

It was late in our voyage to claim we had found the prettiest place in the world—but to describe the Venezuelan Archipelago of Los Roques Islands as anything else would be an injustice. Pancake flat waters, and an unlimited number of shades of transparency—how can some beaches be so much more beautiful than all the others? Visit Los Roques to find the answer.

Ever since leaving Puerto La Cruz, the wind had continued to build as we came more squarely into the trades. Bonair to Curacao was a rocket ride, but the strong wind was behind so we barely felt the effects. At Curacao our daughter Margot joined us and we marveled at the beauty of colonial Dutch architecture combined with the emerald waters and white sands of the Caribbean. The rocket

Charlotte and Margot at Curacao

picked up speed on the trip from Curacao to Aruba and we were proud of Margot for not falling victim to her customary bouts of seasickness.

June 6, 2004, three days after leaving Aruba, at precisely 23:40, *Skimmer* sailed through the same point where she had been at 19:35 on December 11, 1999 en route from Jamaica to Panama. We had completed our circumnavigation. During almost five years *Skimmer* had traveled over 40,000 miles and entered into 43 different countries. For the next two days we raised glasses to *Skimmer*, our voyage, Alex who had been aboard with us up until Tahiti, those who had visited aboard for shorter passages, and all those at home who had made our trip possible.

The celebrations were short lived. We were learning the hard way that Friday departures were not to be trifled with. Things were just settling down after our second series of high winds and squalls came to an end, and Charlotte was taking a well-deserved nap. Alone in the cockpit, I was admiring the colors of the late afternoon sky when suddenly my attention was diverted forward by a loud zipping noise.

Without even turning around I shouted to Charlotte to come immediately, dressed or not, and then headed to the bow with its loudly flailing canopy of white. Our giant Genoa was down, half in the water and half madly flapping around on deck. One look at the six inches of frayed line still attached to the head of the sail told the story, but what was the solution? Nightgown billowing in the twenty-knot wind, Charlotte took the wheel while I pondered what to do next.

The force of rushing water on the sail was enormous and eight-foot waves made work on the bow tricky at best. Charlotte turned us into the wind while I lowered the mainsail and suddenly the world seemed to slow down. With no sails up *Skimmer* naturally assumed the heave to position and violent motion was replaced by slow rocking as we slid backwards with wind and seas gently pushing. But heave as I might, the Genoa wouldn't budge—the force of the water was simply too great. Reverse under motor seemed like a logical solution so after making sure no lines were trailing Charlotte started backing. I pulled with renewed effort. At first nothing, but then slowly, slowly I started to gain. It was exhausting work, but after a half an hour our 180-percent Genoa was safely lying on top of the starboard side of *Skimmer's* bow.

Fortunately, I had a spare halyard, and with Charlotte cranking at the mast and me feeding sail into the track at the bow, we had her halfway back up when the other shoe dropped. Again the loud zipping noise and suddenly I found myself covered with sail. Was it the Friday departure? Was it Noddy's evil eye? The second halyard had also failed, but this time the problem had been the loss of a cotter pin.

Over five hundred miles to go and no possibility of flying a jib. The next day I tried climbing the mast to mount a new halyard, but only a third of the way up I began to feel like a human catapult and finally accepted the wisdom of Charlotte's urging that I return to deck. But, as always, there had been a solution—our tiny cutter sail and a deck littered with jerry cans full of six-cent Venezuelan diesel—we had enough to make it with plenty to spare. So up went the cutter and on went the iron spinnaker.

With both of us on deck, soaked to the bone, and not just a little tired, Charlotte treated me to her usual "I hate sailing" sermon, but this time with a new twist: "Never again—I'm never going to sea again in anything other than a luxury liner!" I couldn't help smiling, as I said to myself, with all the renovations I am going to make over the next five years, *Skimmer* will be like a luxury liner. Out loud in reply, it was "Don't worry Charlotte—never again, I promise. We will never again leave on a Friday."

About the Author

Heyward Coleman served as a submarine officer in the US Nuclear Navy before entering a business career. His education includes a master's degree in nuclear physics and an MBA from the Harvard Business School. Initially in the oil and gas industry, he became a senior officer and part owner of a large oil shipping company. After selling his interest in the company, he founded an environmental laboratory that specialized in radiochemistry analysis. During his career he cultivated a love for travel and adventure. Now retired, he and his wife have three children and live in Charleston, South Carolina.

Request for Review

Thank you for reading my book. This was my first book and it was inspired by a series of emails that I wrote during our trip and the encouraging return emails from many readers who urged me to write a book. My objective in writing this book was to share Charlotte's and my experiences with both potential world cruisers and armchair adventurers who like to travel vicariously.

If you have enjoyed the reading, I would be grateful if you would write a review so that others might be encouraged to also share our experiences. I love getting reviews and read all of them.

To submit a review to Amazon go to:
http://www.amazon.com/review/create-review?&asin= B0035RPGT0

Printed in Great Britain
by Amazon

45241594R00189